THE *ADVANCE* TEAM

THE *ADVANCE* TEAM

WRITTEN BY **WILL PFEIFER**

PENCILED AND INKED BY **GERMÁN TORRES**

LETTERED BY **TOM ORZECHOWSKI**

A TOM DOHERTY ASSOCIATES BOOK  NEW YORK

This is a work of fiction. All of the characters, organizations, and events portrayed in this graphic novel are either products of the authors' imaginations or are used fictitiously.

ADVANCE TEAM

A Tor Book
Published by Tom Doherty Associates, LLC
175 Fifth Avenue
New York, NY 10010

www.tor-forge.com

Tor® is a registered trademark of Tom Doherty Associates, LLC.

ISBN 978-0-7653-2712-3

First Edition: March 2012

Printed in the United States of America

0 9 8 7 6 5 4 3 2 1

THE *ADVANCE* TEAM

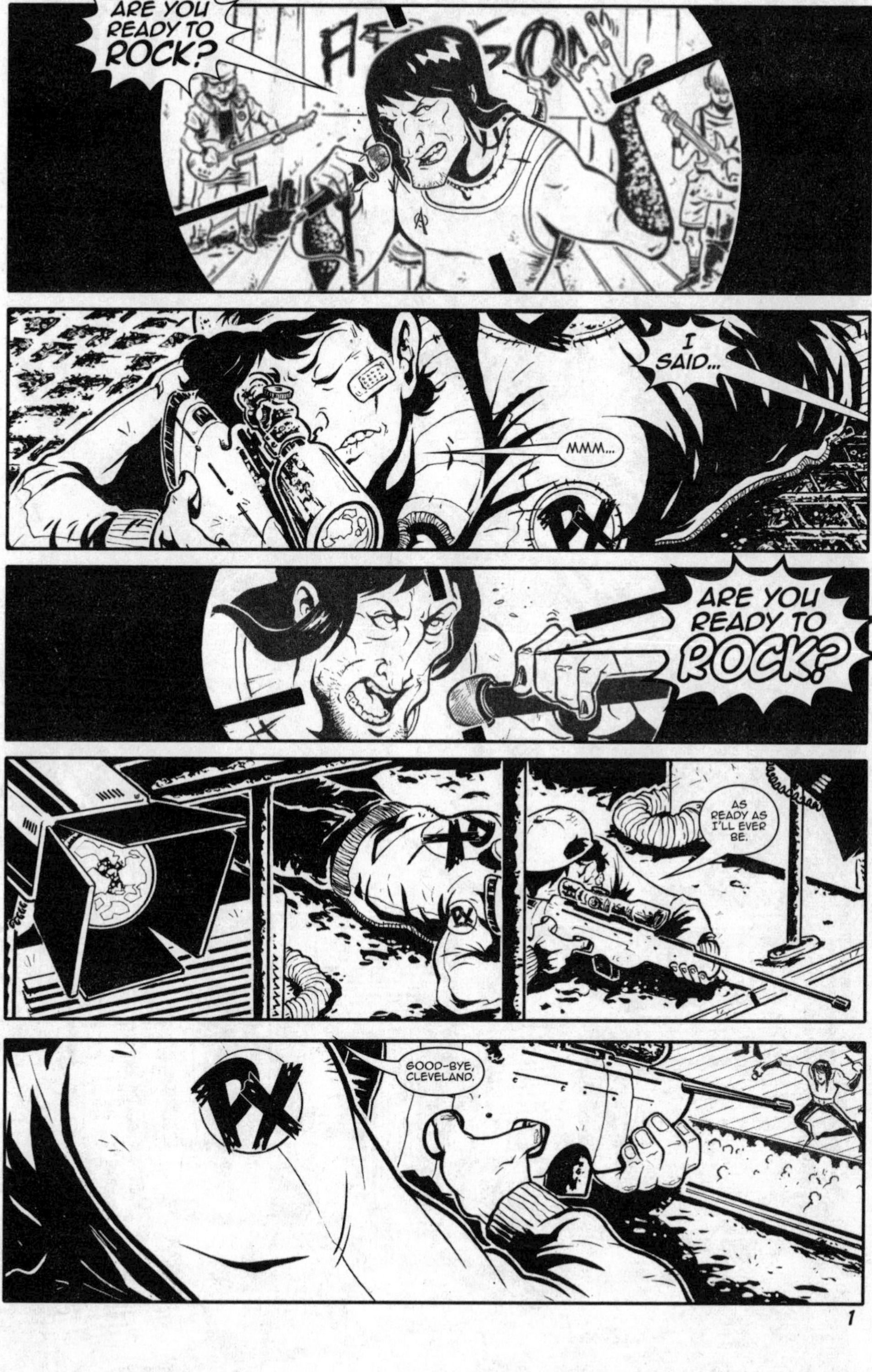
ARE YOU READY TO ROCK?
I SAID...
MMM...
ARE YOU READY TO ROCK?
AS READY AS I'LL EVER BE.
GOOD-BYE, CLEVELAND.

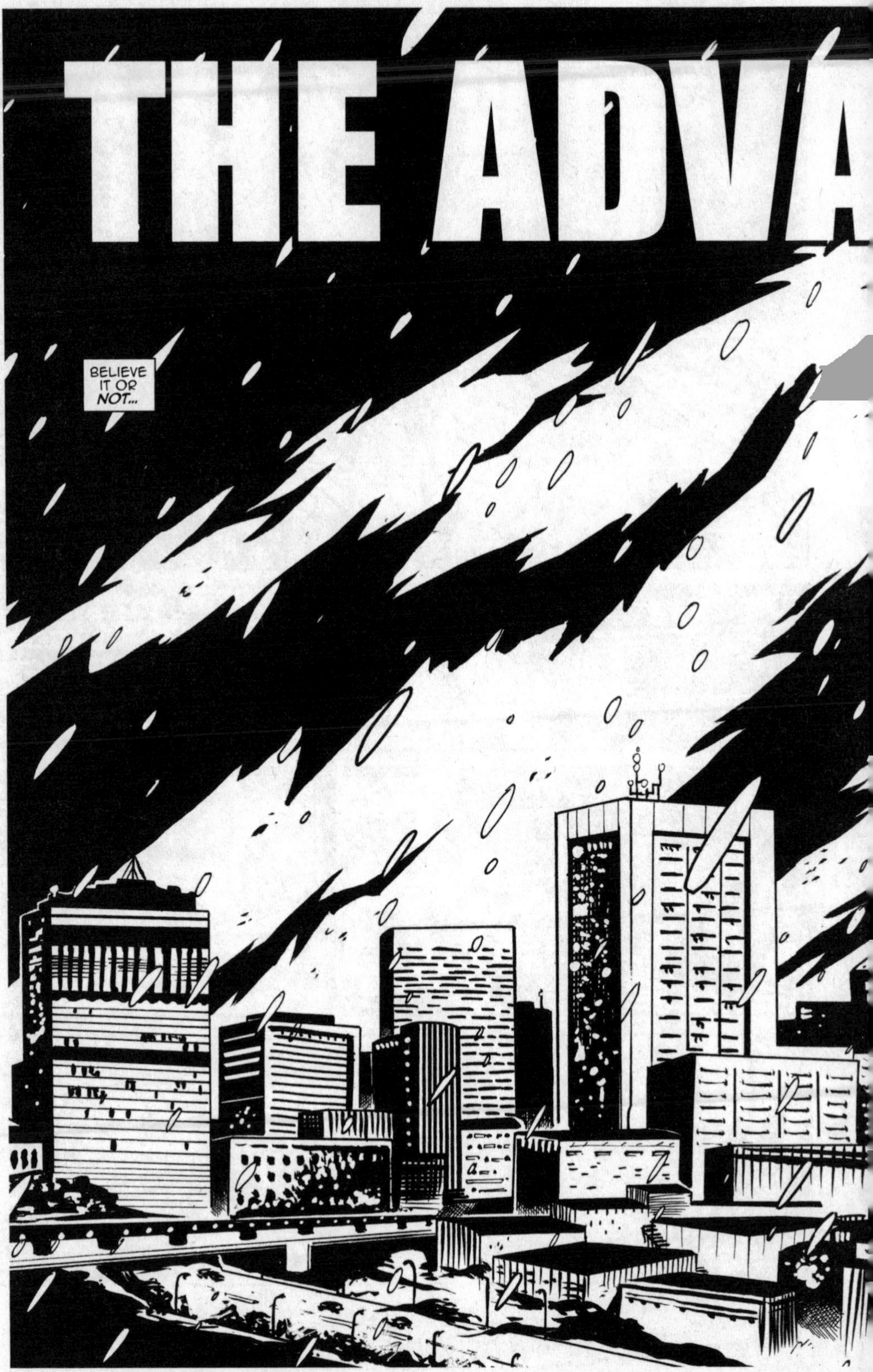
THE ADVA
BELIEVE IT OR NOT...

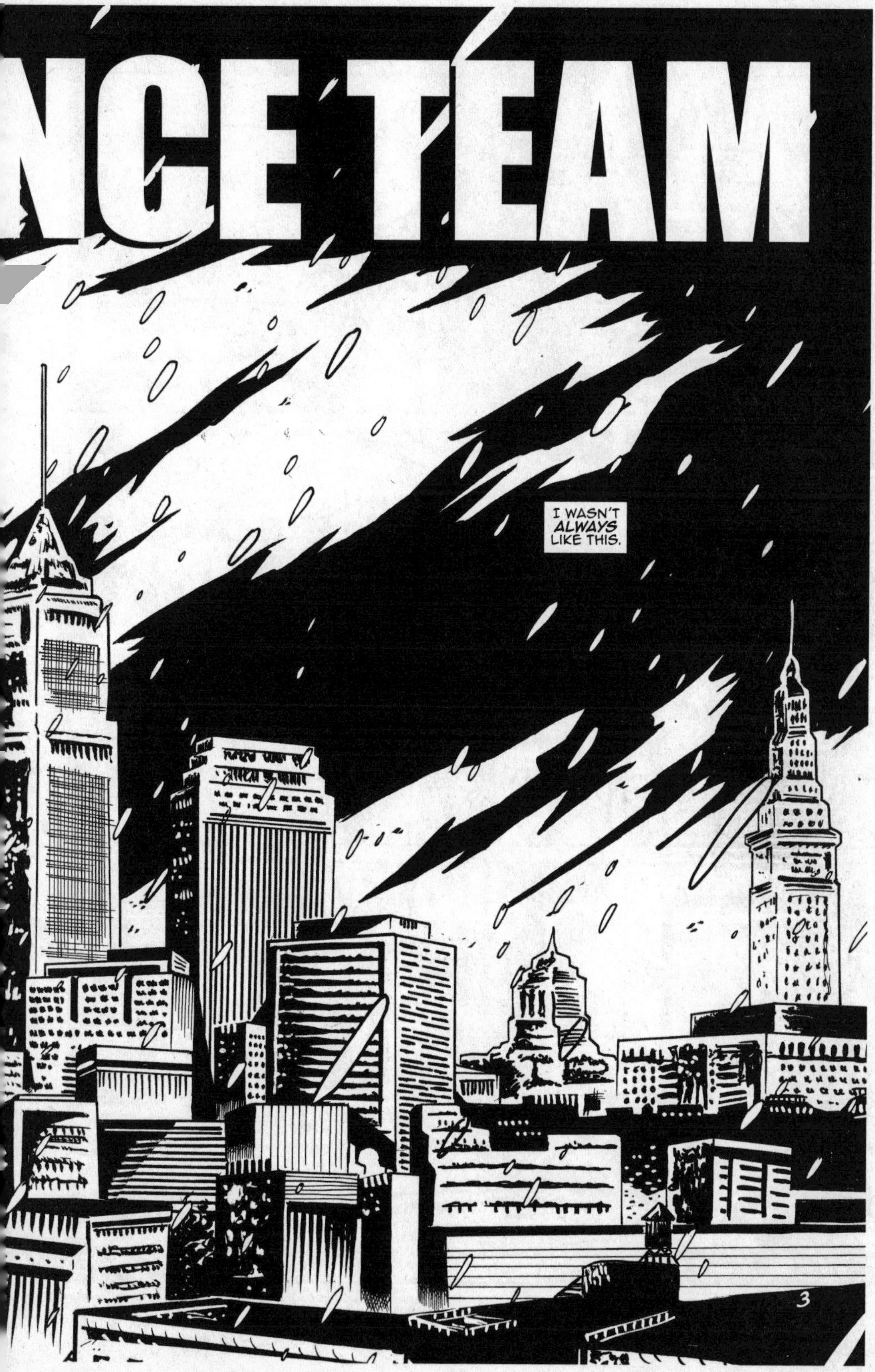
NCE TEAM
I WASN'T *ALWAYS* LIKE THIS.

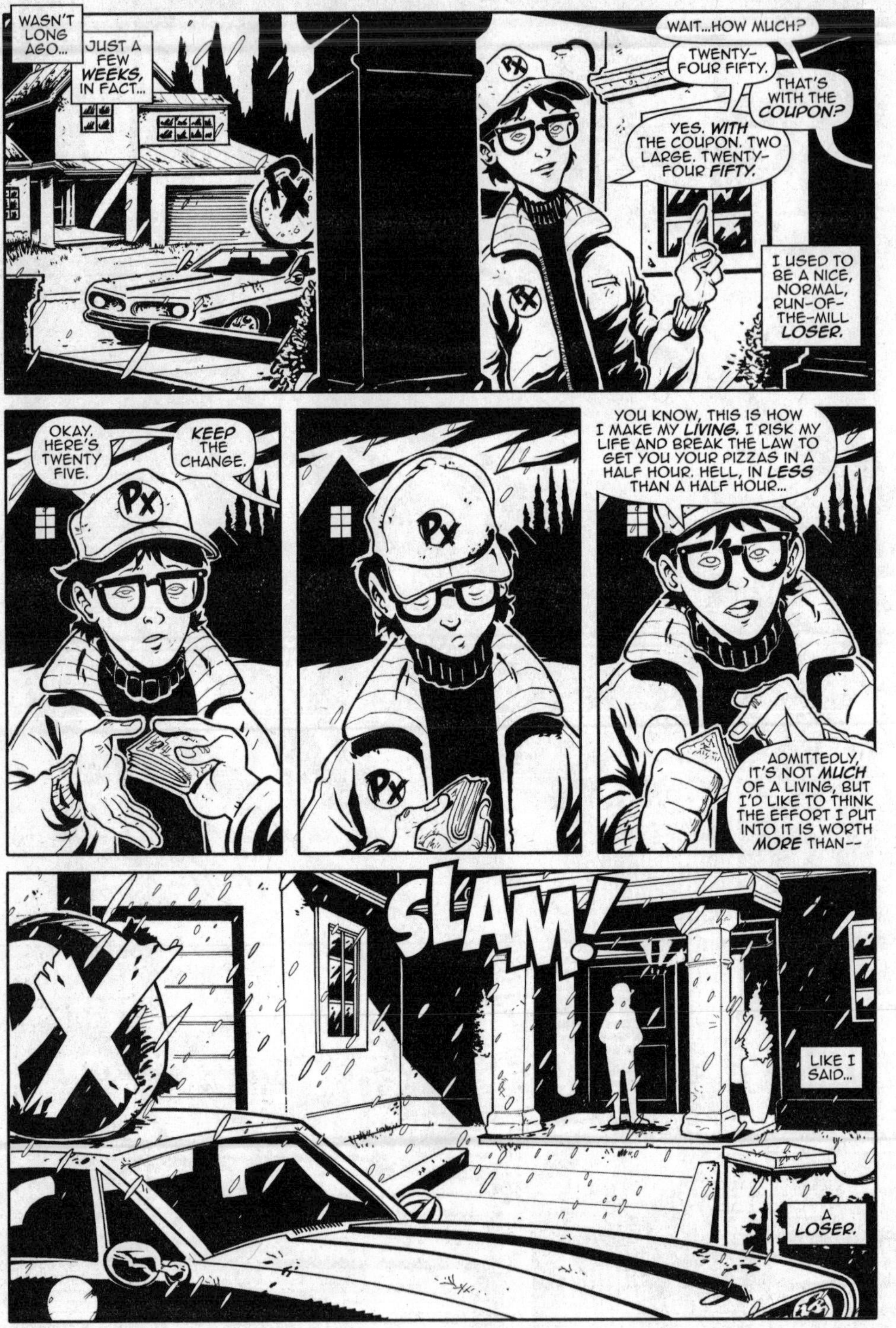
WAIT...HOW MUCH?
WASN'T LONG AGO...
JUST A FEW WEEKS, IN FACT...
TWENTY-FOUR FIFTY.
THAT'S WITH THE COUPON?
YES. WITH THE COUPON. TWO LARGE. TWENTY-FOUR FIFTY.
I USED TO BE A NICE, NORMAL, RUN-OF-THE-MILL LOSER.
OKAY. HERE'S TWENTY FIVE.
KEEP THE CHANGE.
YOU KNOW, THIS IS HOW I MAKE MY LIVING. I RISK MY LIFE AND BREAK THE LAW TO GET YOU YOUR PIZZAS IN A HALF HOUR. HELL, IN LESS THAN A HALF HOUR...
ADMITTEDLY, IT'S NOT MUCH OF A LIVING, BUT I'D LIKE TO THINK THE EFFORT I PUT INTO IT IS WORTH MORE THAN--
SLAM!
LIKE I SAID...
A LOSER.

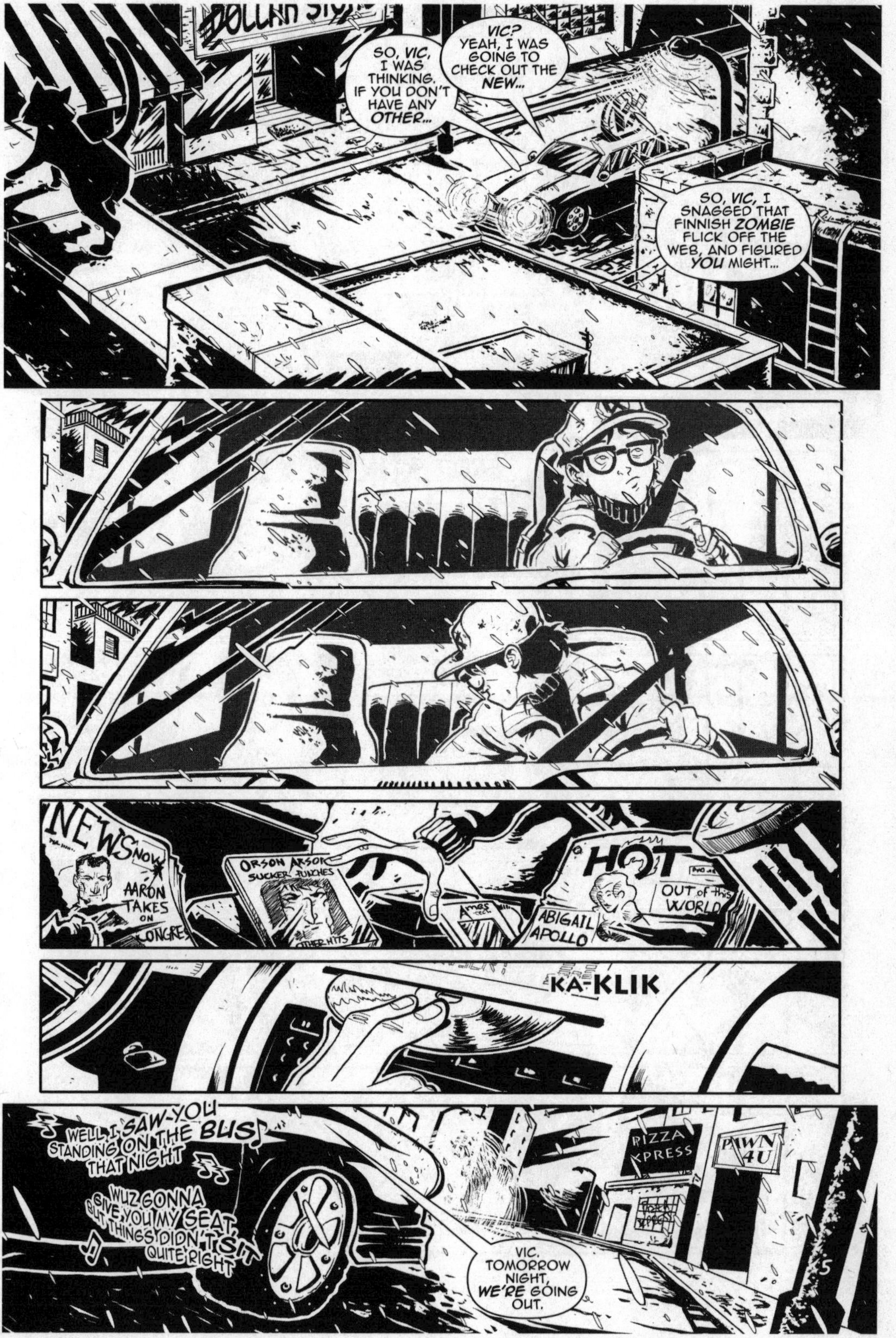
DOLLAR STORE
SO, VIC, I WAS THINKING. IF YOU DON'T HAVE ANY OTHER...
VIC? YEAH, I WAS GOING TO CHECK OUT THE NEW...
SO, VIC, I SNAGGED THAT FINNISH ZOMBIE FLICK OFF THE WEB, AND FIGURED YOU MIGHT...
NEWS NOW
AARON TAKES ON CONGRES
ORSON ARSON SUCKER PUNCHES
OTHER HITS
HOT
OUT of this WORLD
ABIGAIL APOLLO
KA-KLIK
WELL I SAW-YOU STANDING ON THE BUS THAT NIGHT
WUZ GONNA GIVE YOU MY SEAT, BUT THINGS DIDN'T SIT QUITE RIGHT
PIZZA XPRESS
PAWN 4U
VIC. TOMORROW NIGHT, WE'RE GOING OUT.

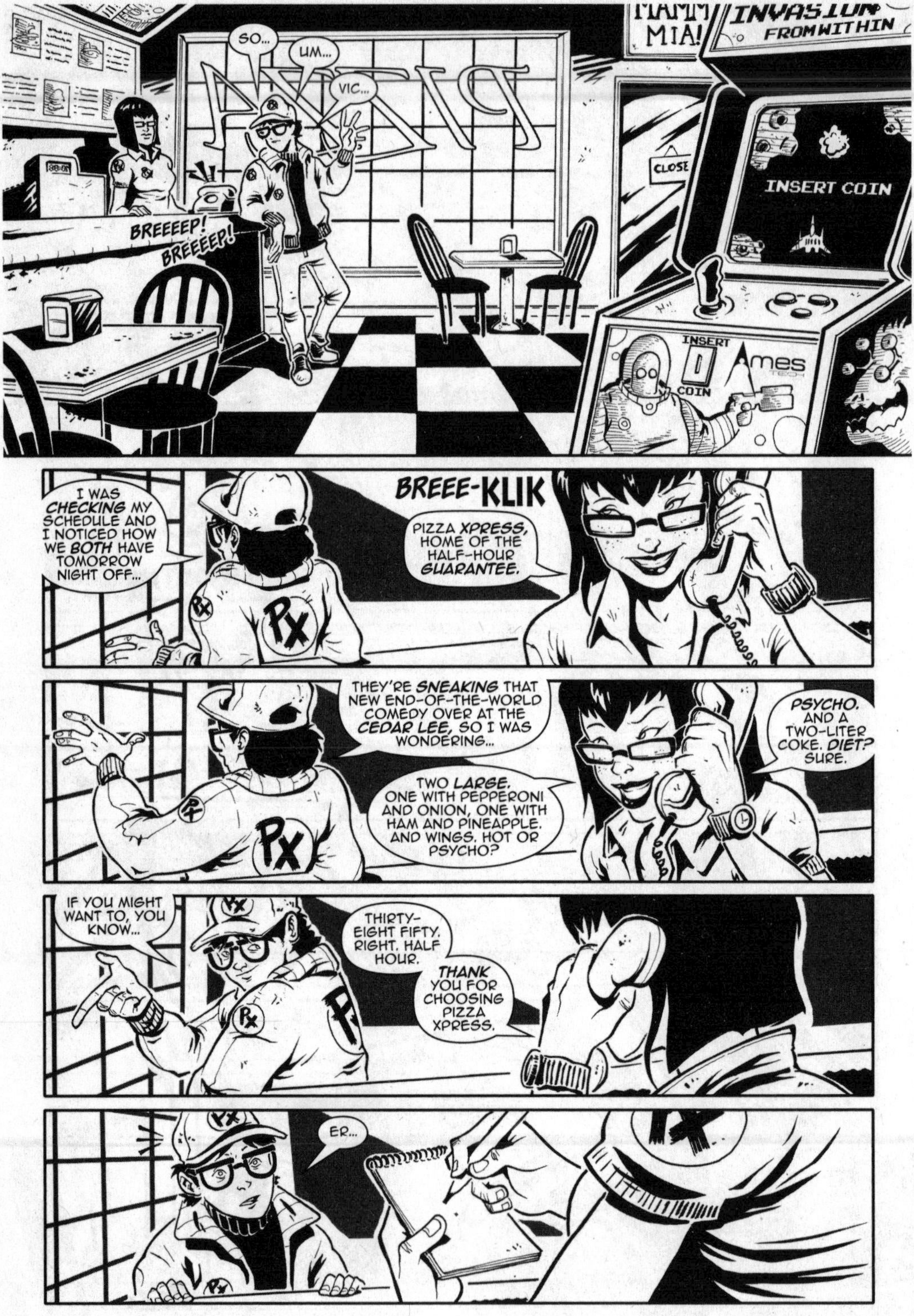

MAMMA MIA!
INVASION FROM WITHIN
SO...
UM...
VIC...
CLOSE
INSERT COIN
BREEEEP!
BREEEEP!
INSERT COIN
Ames
BREEE-KLIK
I WAS CHECKING MY SCHEDULE AND I NOTICED HOW WE BOTH HAVE TOMORROW NIGHT OFF...
PIZZA XPRESS, HOME OF THE HALF-HOUR GUARANTEE.
THEY'RE SNEAKING THAT NEW END-OF-THE-WORLD COMEDY OVER AT THE CEDAR LEE, SO I WAS WONDERING...
TWO LARGE. ONE WITH PEPPERONI AND ONION, ONE WITH HAM AND PINEAPPLE. AND WINGS. HOT OR PSYCHO?
PSYCHO. AND A TWO-LITER COKE. DIET? SURE.
IF YOU MIGHT WANT TO, YOU KNOW...
THIRTY-EIGHT FIFTY. RIGHT. HALF HOUR.
THANK YOU FOR CHOOSING PIZZA XPRESS.
ER...

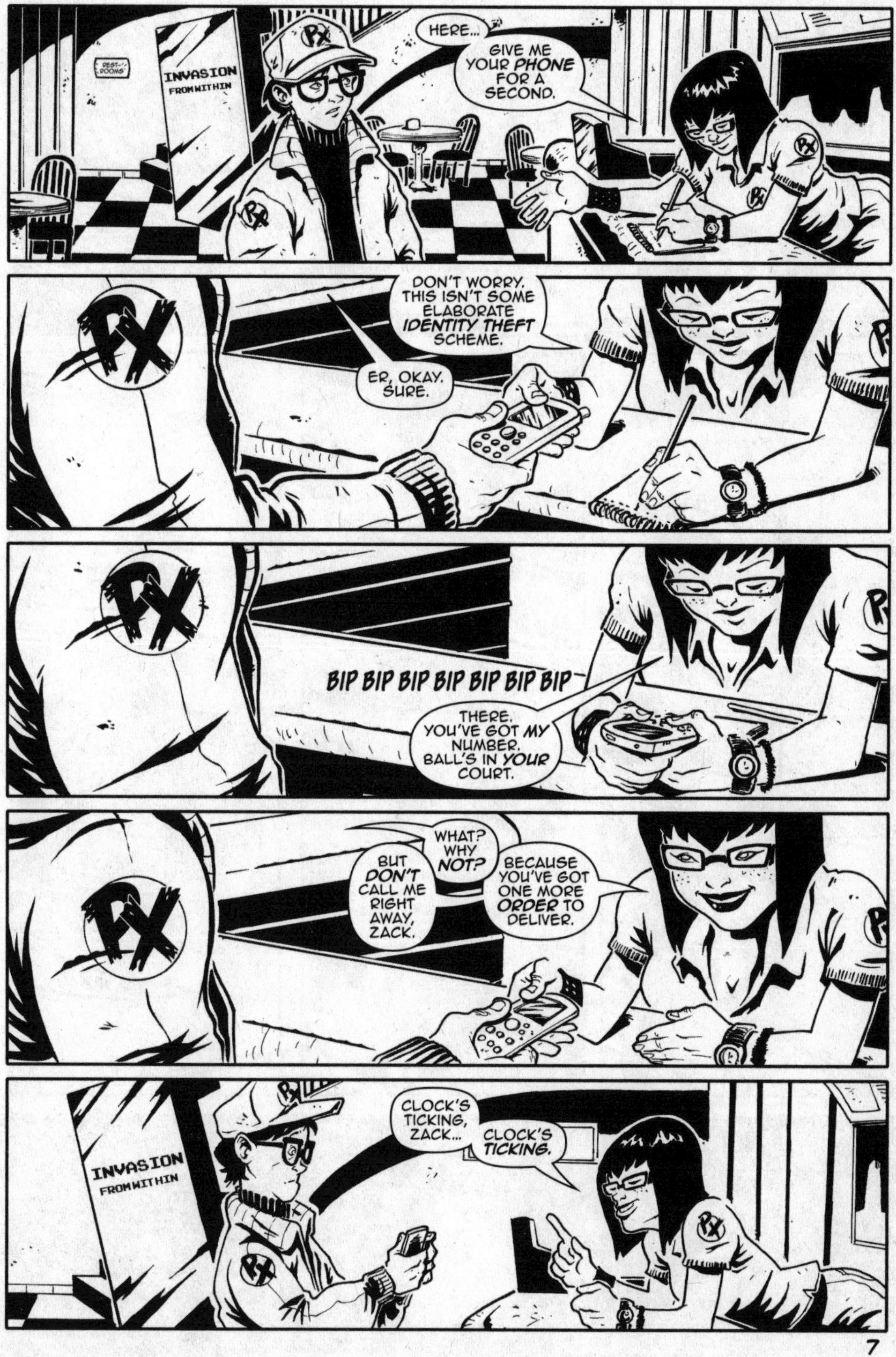
REST-ROOMS
INVASION FROM WITHIN
HERE...
GIVE ME YOUR PHONE FOR A SECOND.
DON'T WORRY. THIS ISN'T SOME ELABORATE IDENTITY THEFT SCHEME.
ER, OKAY. SURE.
BIP BIP BIP BIP BIP BIP BIP
THERE. YOU'VE GOT MY NUMBER. BALL'S IN YOUR COURT.
BUT DON'T CALL ME RIGHT AWAY, ZACK.
WHAT? WHY NOT?
BECAUSE YOU'VE GOT ONE MORE ORDER TO DELIVER.
INVASION FROM WITHIN
CLOCK'S TICKING, ZACK...
CLOCK'S TICKING.

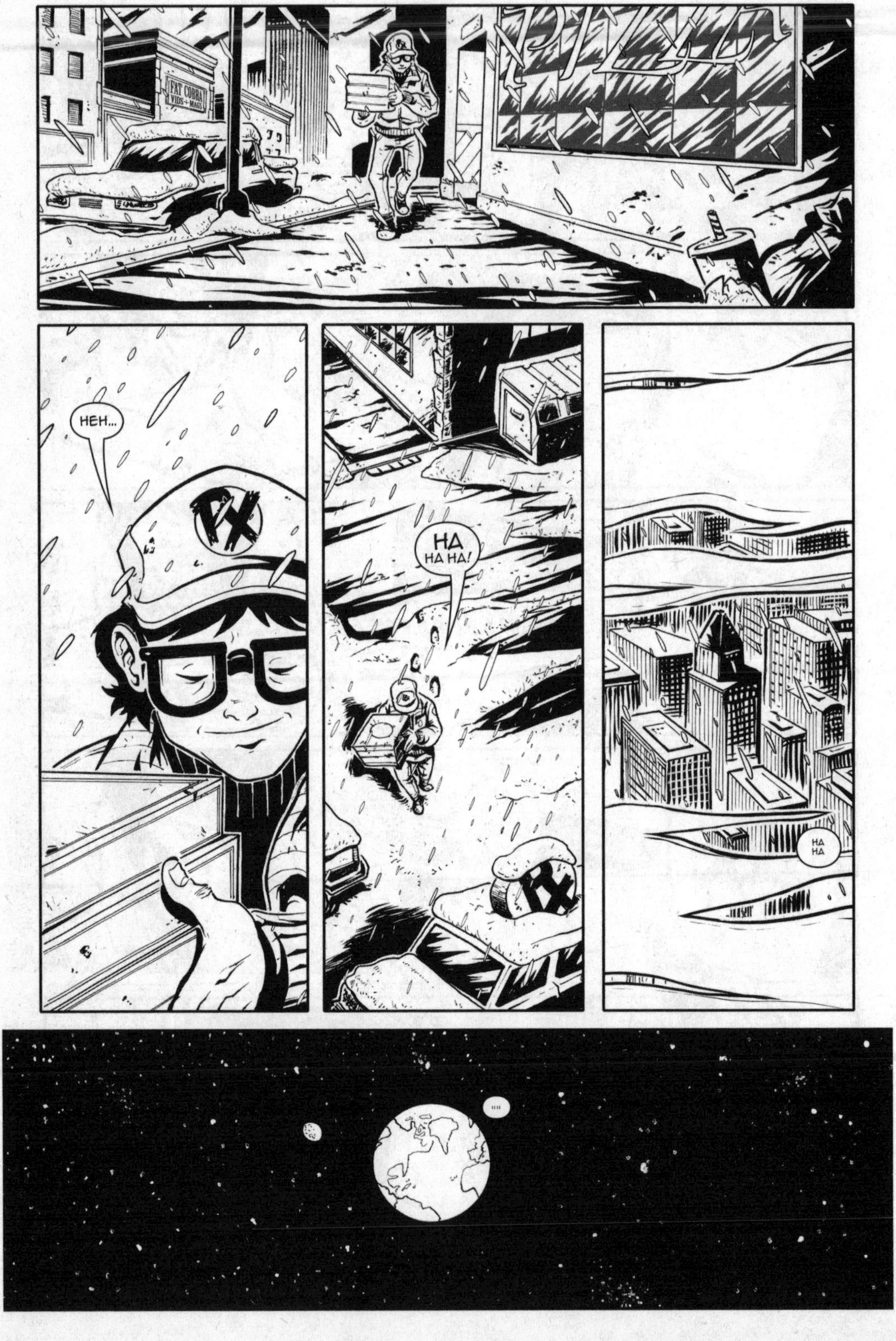
FAT COBRA
VIDS + MAGS
PIZZA
HEH...
HA HA HA!
HA HA

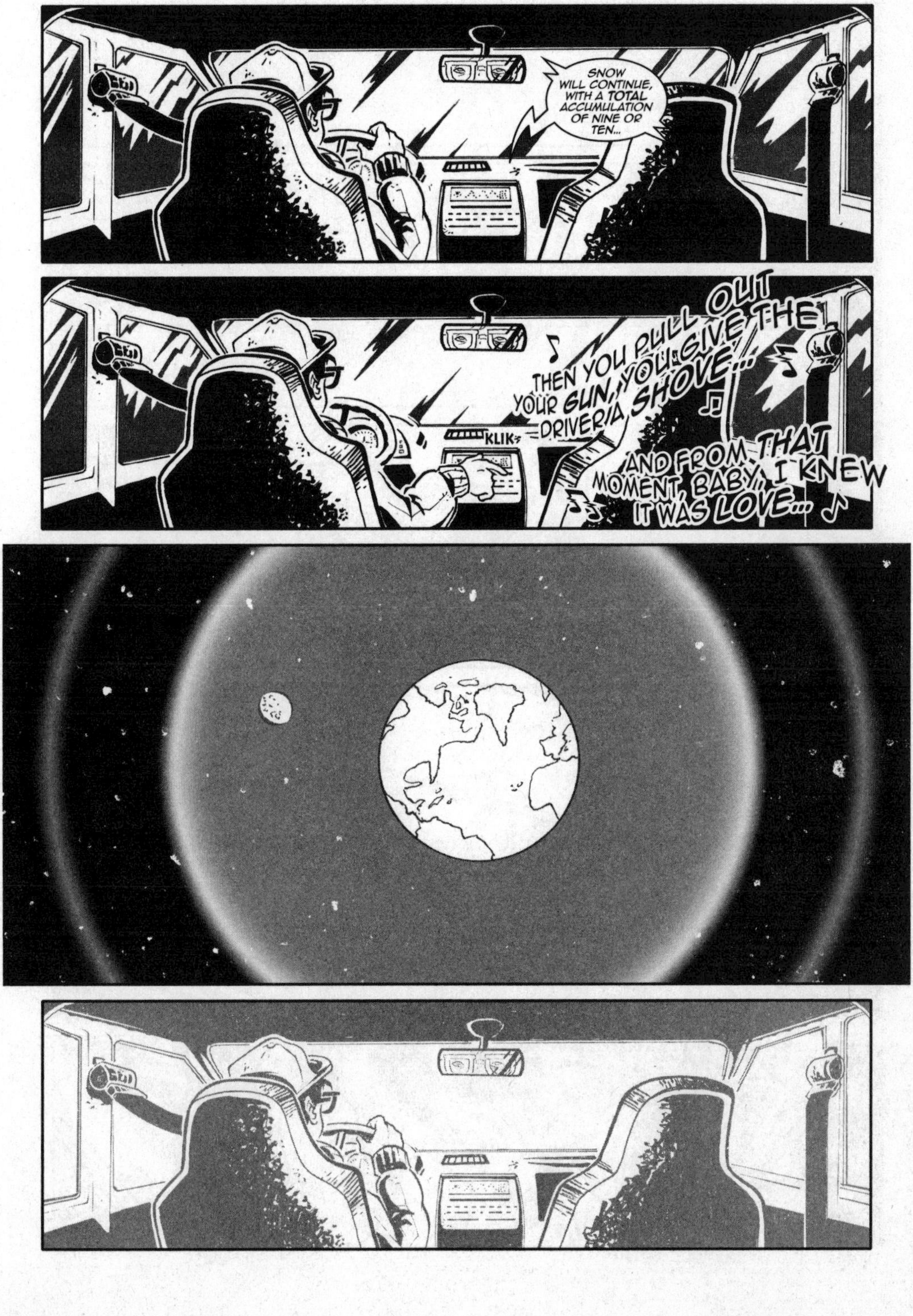
SNOW WILL CONTINUE, WITH A TOTAL ACCUMULATION OF NINE OR TEN...
KLIK
THEN YOU PULL OUT YOUR GUN, YOU GIVE THE DRIVER A SHOVE...
AND FROM THAT MOMENT, BABY, I KNEW IT WAS LOVE...

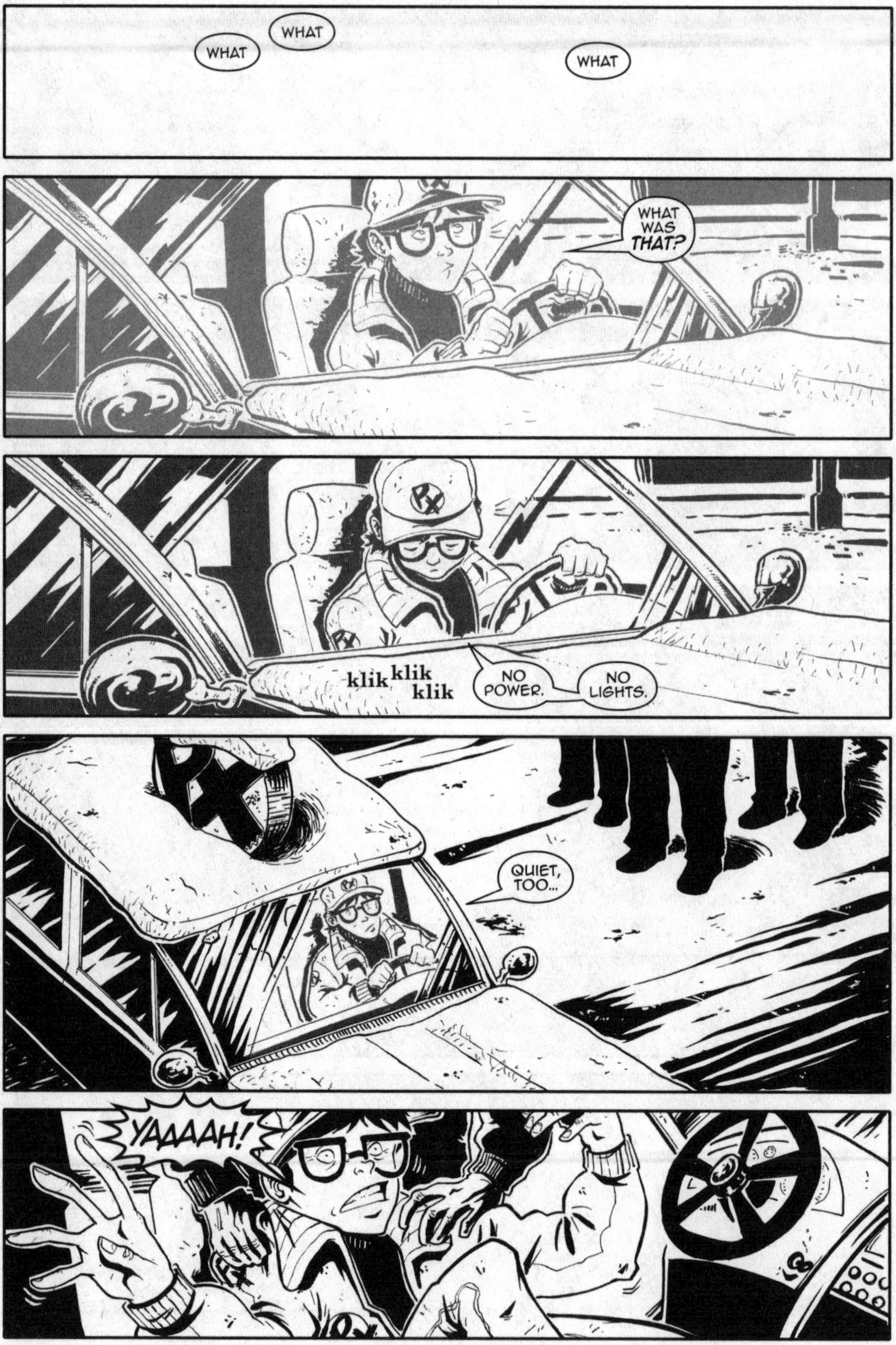
WHAT
WHAT
WHAT
WHAT WAS THAT?
klik klik klik
NO POWER.
NO LIGHTS.
QUIET, TOO...
YAAAAH!

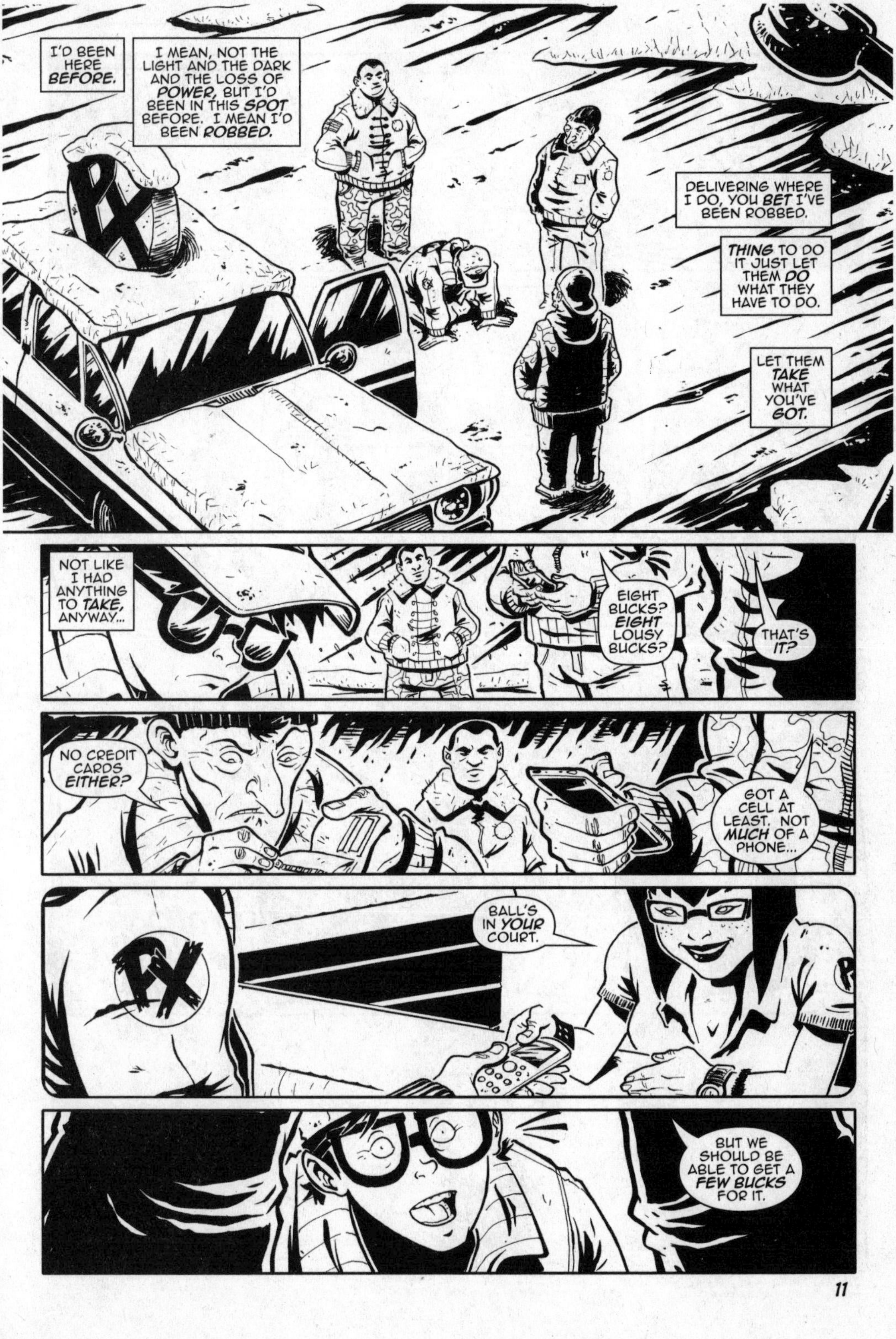
I'D BEEN HERE BEFORE.
I MEAN, NOT THE LIGHT AND THE DARK AND THE LOSS OF POWER, BUT I'D BEEN IN THIS SPOT BEFORE. I MEAN I'D BEEN ROBBED.
DELIVERING WHERE I DO, YOU BET I'VE BEEN ROBBED.
THING TO DO IT JUST LET THEM DO WHAT THEY HAVE TO DO.
LET THEM TAKE WHAT YOU'VE GOT.
NOT LIKE I HAD ANYTHING TO TAKE, ANYWAY...
EIGHT BUCKS? EIGHT LOUSY BUCKS?
THAT'S IT?
NO CREDIT CARDS EITHER?
GOT A CELL AT LEAST. NOT MUCH OF A PHONE...
BALL'S IN YOUR COURT.
BUT WE SHOULD BE ABLE TO GET A FEW BUCKS FOR IT.

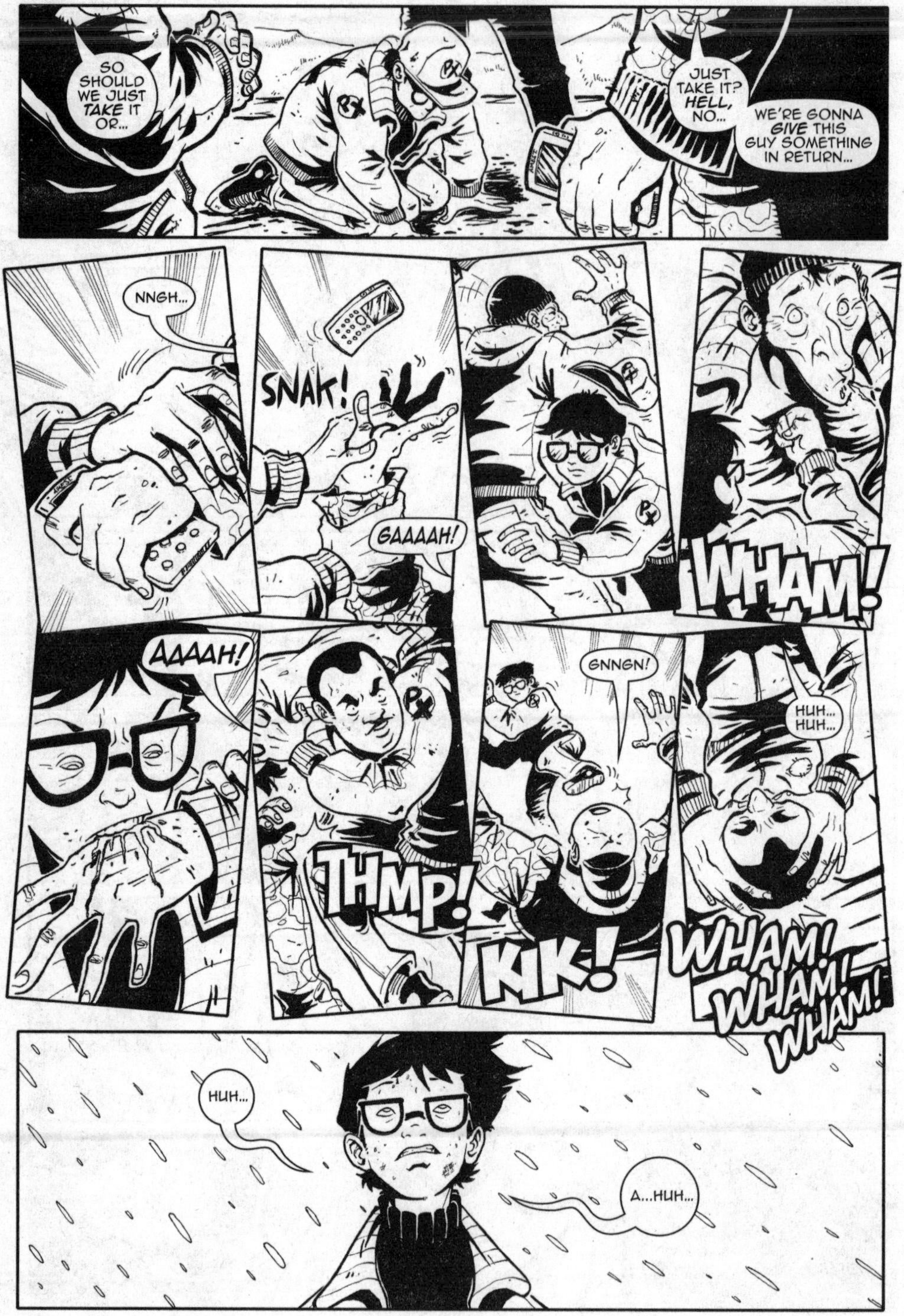
SO SHOULD WE JUST TAKE IT OR...
JUST TAKE IT? HELL, NO...
WE'RE GONNA GIVE THIS GUY SOMETHING IN RETURN...
NNGH...
SNAK!
GAAAAH!
WHAM!
AAAAH!
THMP!
GNNGN!
KIK!
HUH... HUH...
WHAM! WHAM! WHAM!
HUH...
A...HUH...

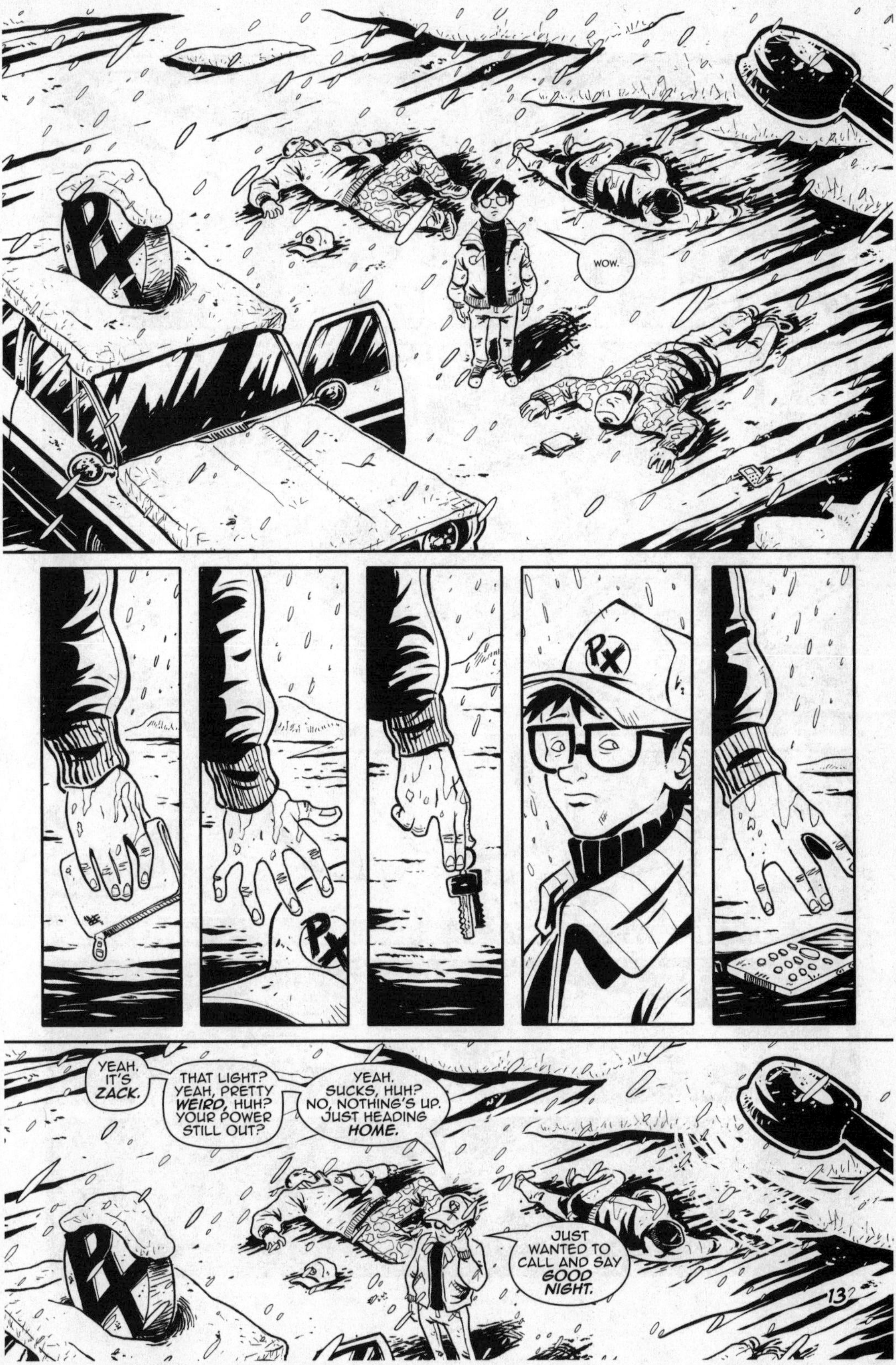
WOW.
YEAH. IT'S ZACK.
THAT LIGHT? YEAH, PRETTY WEIRD, HUH? YOUR POWER STILL OUT?
YEAH. SUCKS, HUH? NO, NOTHING'S UP. JUST HEADING HOME.
JUST WANTED TO CALL AND SAY GOOD NIGHT.

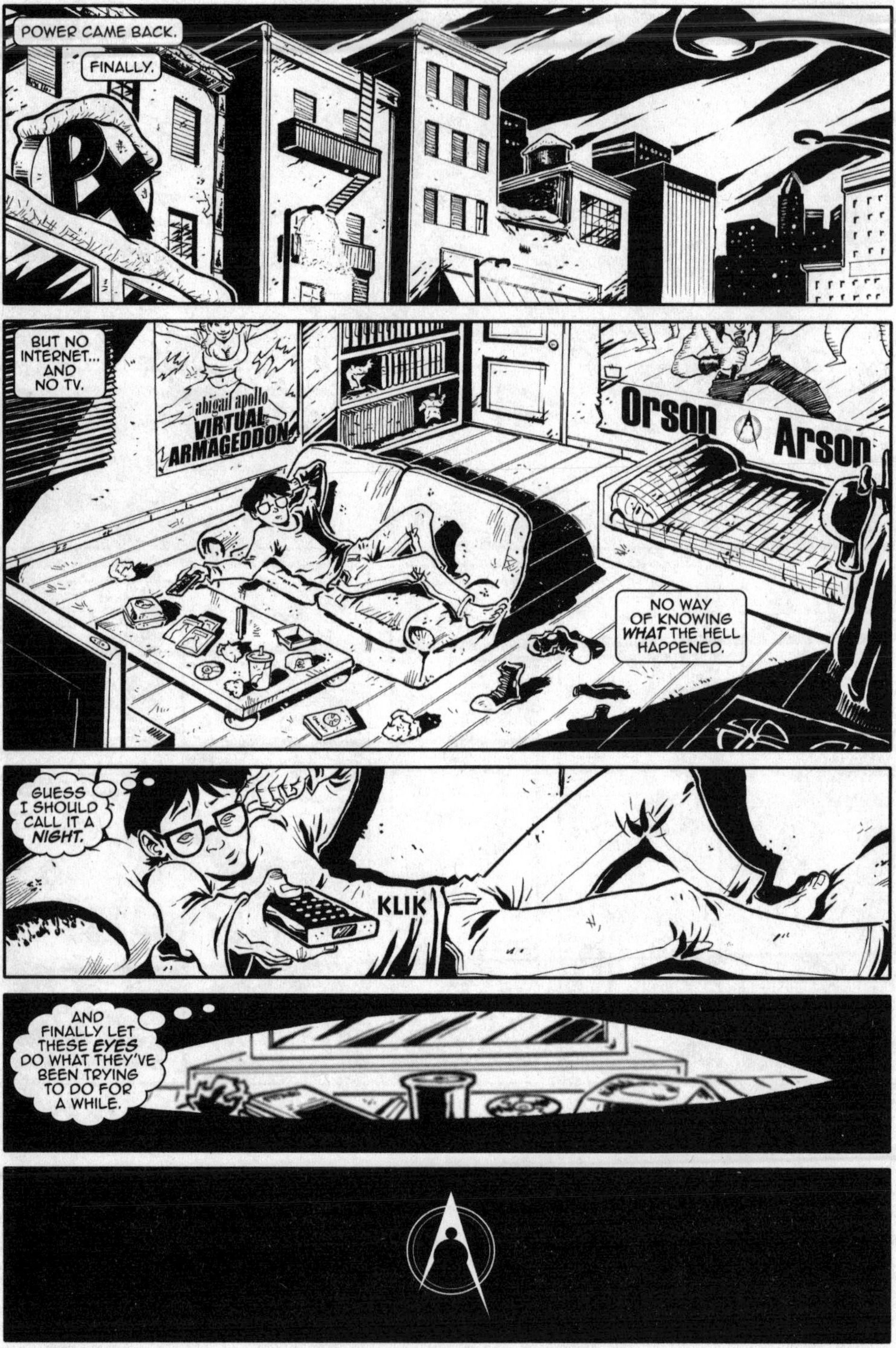

POWER CAME BACK.
FINALLY.
BUT NO INTERNET... AND NO TV.
abigail apollo VIRTUAL ARMAGEDDON
Orson Arson
NO WAY OF KNOWING *WHAT* THE HELL HAPPENED.
GUESS I SHOULD CALL IT A *NIGHT.*
KLIK
AND FINALLY LET THESE *EYES* DO WHAT THEY'VE BEEN TRYING TO DO FOR A WHILE.

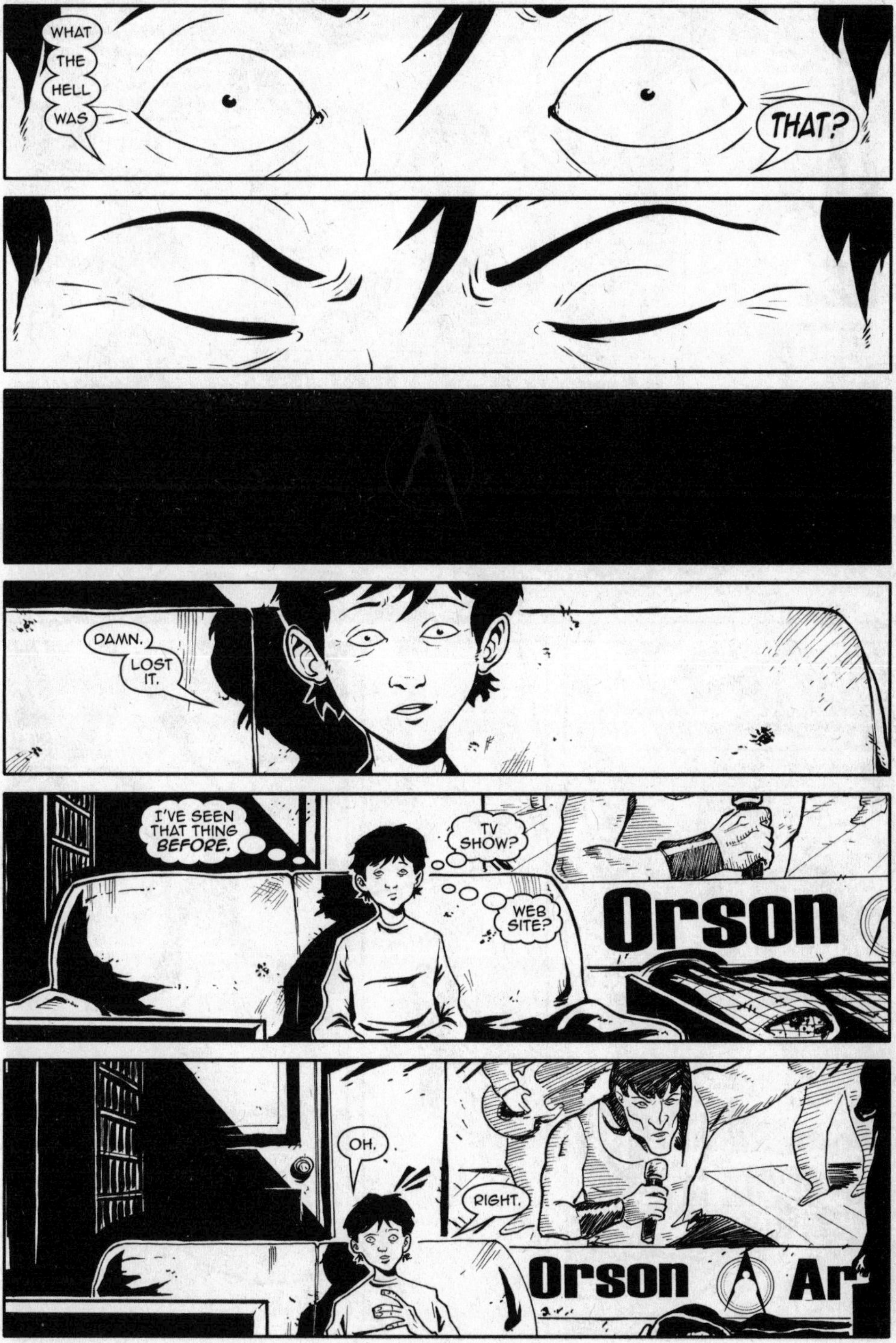
WHAT THE HELL WAS
THAT?
DAMN. LOST IT.
I'VE SEEN THAT THING *BEFORE.*
TV SHOW?
WEB SITE?
Orson
OH.
RIGHT.
Orson Ar

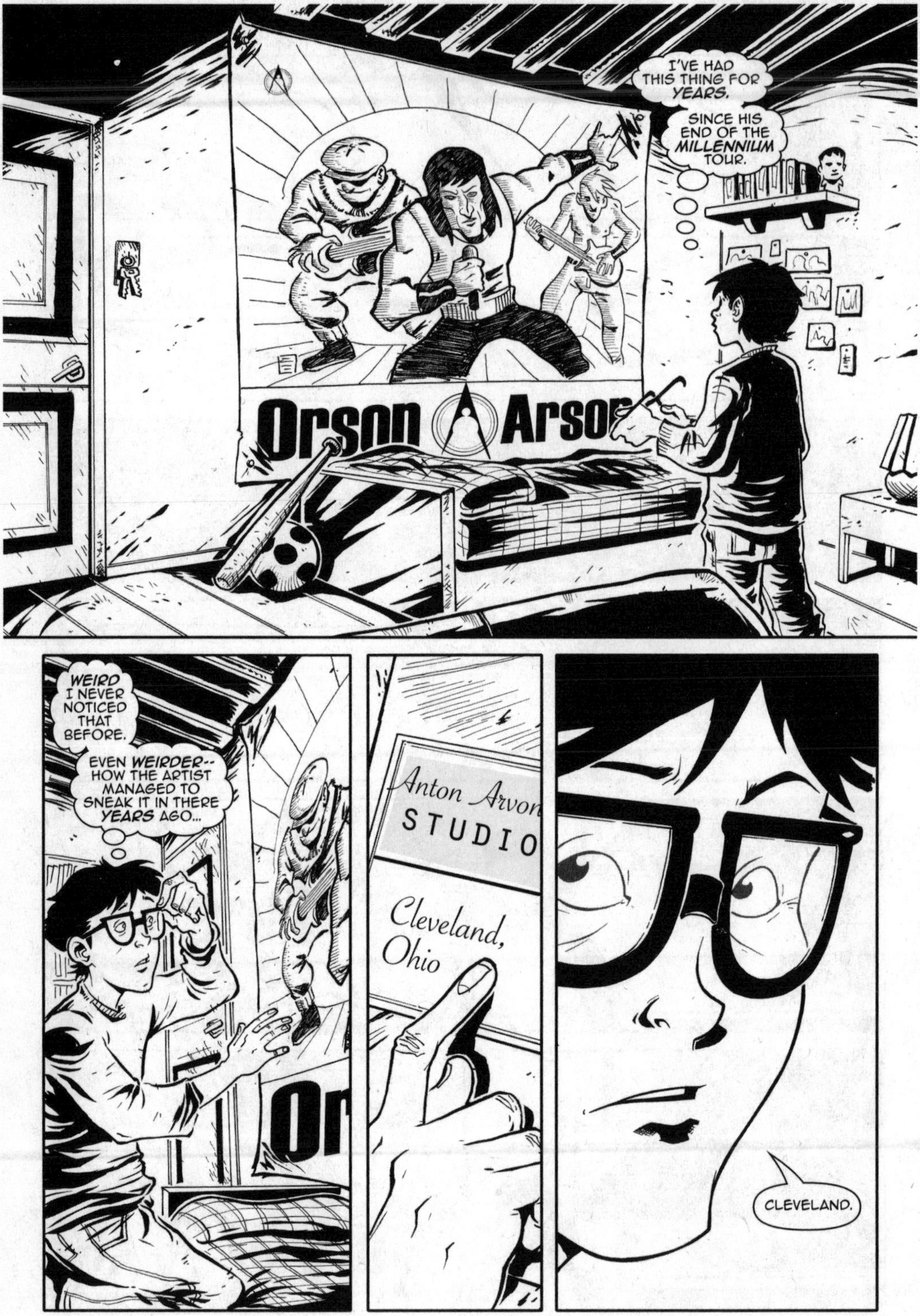
I'VE HAD THIS THING FOR YEARS.
SINCE HIS END OF THE MILLENNIUM TOUR.
Orson Arson
WEIRD I NEVER NOTICED THAT BEFORE.
EVEN WEIRDER-- HOW THE ARTIST MANAGED TO SNEAK IT IN THERE YEARS AGO...
Anton Arvon STUDIO
Cleveland, Ohio
CLEVELAND.

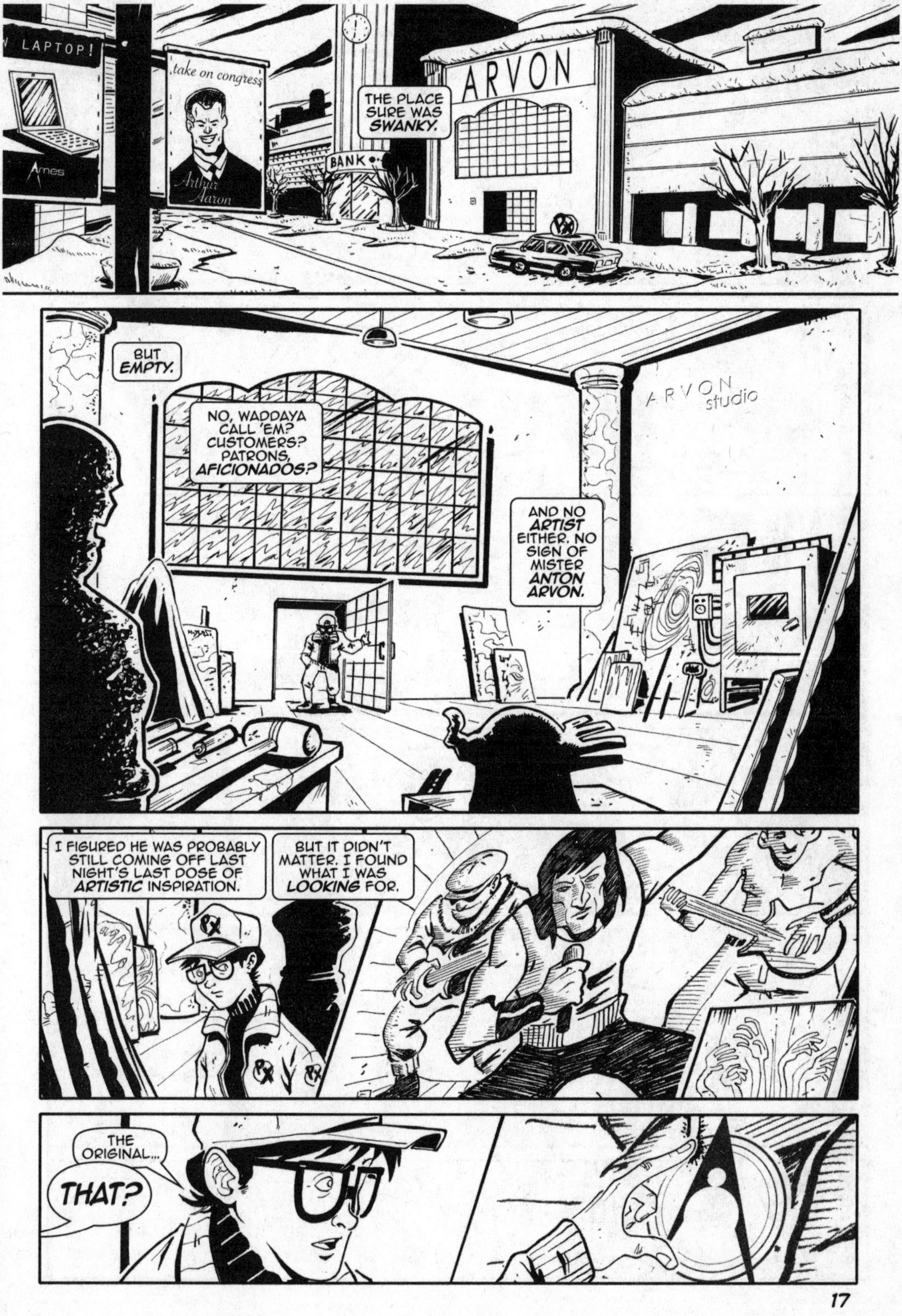
LAPTOP!
take on congress
Arthur Aaron
Ames
BANK
ARVON
THE PLACE SURE WAS SWANKY.
BUT EMPTY.
NO, WADDAYA CALL 'EM? CUSTOMERS? PATRONS, AFICIONADOS?
ARVON studio
AND NO ARTIST EITHER. NO SIGN OF MISTER ANTON ARVON.
I FIGURED HE WAS PROBABLY STILL COMING OFF LAST NIGHT'S LAST DOSE OF ARTISTIC INSPIRATION.
BUT IT DIDN'T MATTER. I FOUND WHAT I WAS LOOKING FOR.
THE ORIGINAL...
THAT?

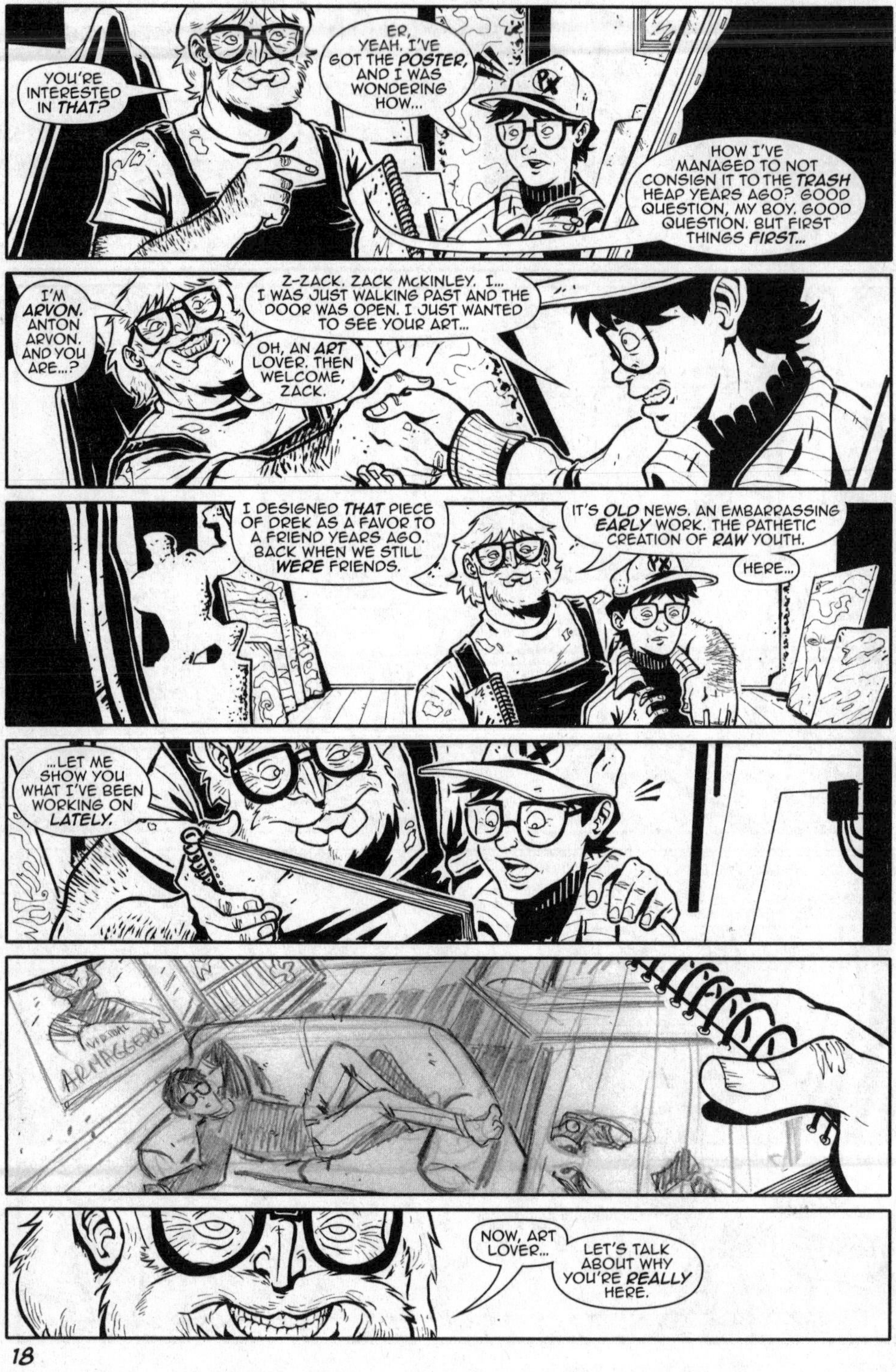

YOU'RE INTERESTED IN *THAT?*
ER, YEAH. I'VE GOT THE *POSTER,* AND I WAS WONDERING HOW...
HOW I'VE MANAGED TO NOT CONSIGN IT TO THE *TRASH* HEAP YEARS AGO? GOOD QUESTION, MY BOY. GOOD QUESTION. BUT FIRST THINGS *FIRST...*
I'M *ARVON.* ANTON ARVON. AND YOU ARE...?
Z-ZACK. ZACK McKINLEY. I... I WAS JUST WALKING PAST AND THE DOOR WAS OPEN. I JUST WANTED TO SEE YOUR ART...
OH, AN *ART* LOVER. THEN WELCOME, ZACK.
I DESIGNED *THAT* PIECE OF DREK AS A FAVOR TO A FRIEND YEARS AGO. BACK WHEN WE STILL *WERE* FRIENDS.
IT'S *OLD* NEWS. AN EMBARRASSING *EARLY* WORK. THE PATHETIC CREATION OF *RAW* YOUTH.
HERE...
...LET ME SHOW YOU WHAT I'VE BEEN WORKING ON *LATELY.*
VIRTUAL ARMAGEDDON
NOW, ART LOVER...
LET'S TALK ABOUT WHY YOU'RE *REALLY* HERE.

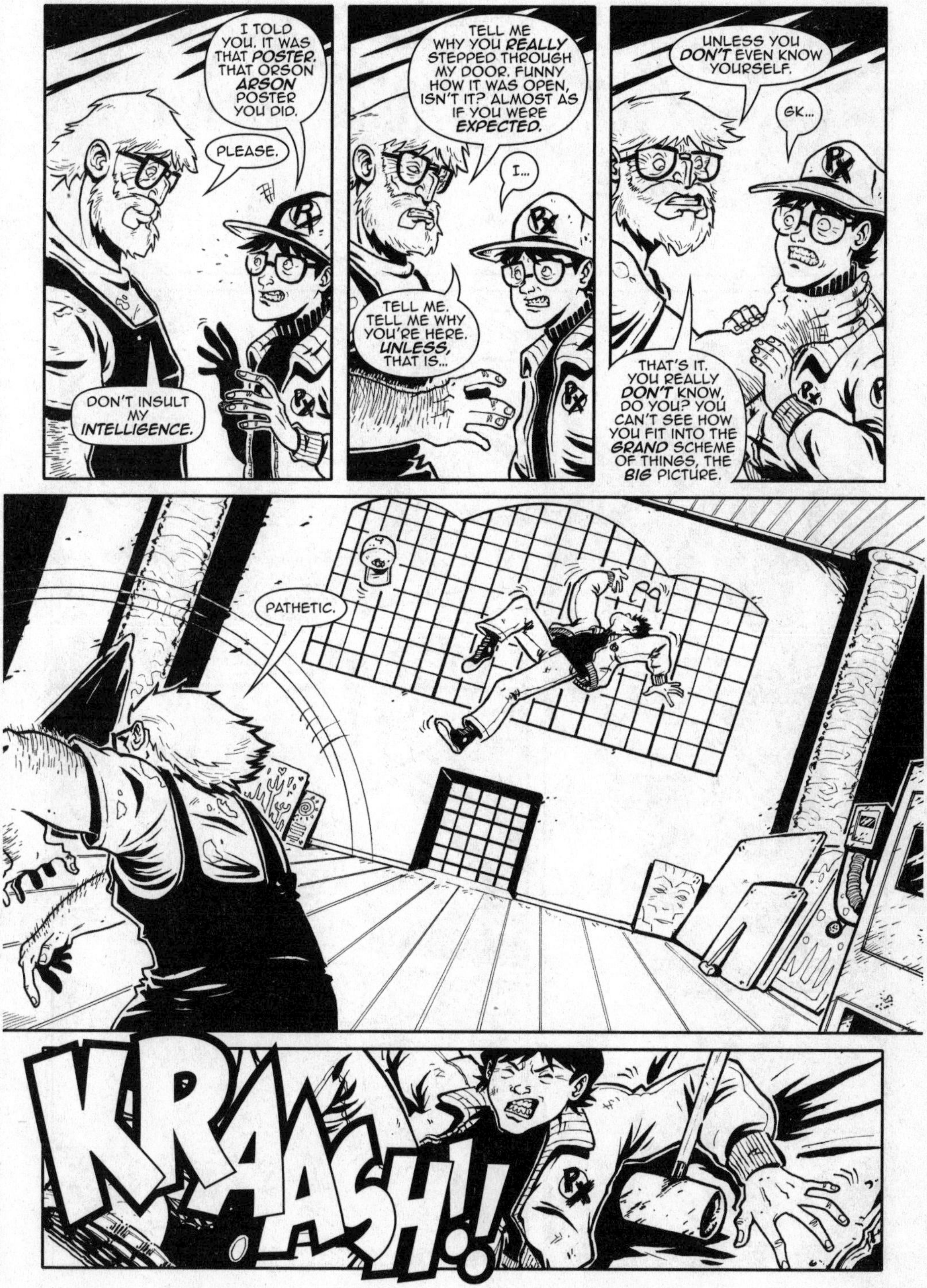
I TOLD YOU. IT WAS THAT POSTER. THAT ORSON ARSON POSTER YOU DID.
PLEASE.
DON'T INSULT MY INTELLIGENCE.
TELL ME WHY YOU REALLY STEPPED THROUGH MY DOOR. FUNNY HOW IT WAS OPEN, ISN'T IT? ALMOST AS IF YOU WERE EXPECTED.
I...
TELL ME. TELL ME WHY YOU'RE HERE. UNLESS, THAT IS...
UNLESS YOU DON'T EVEN KNOW YOURSELF.
GK...
THAT'S IT. YOU REALLY DON'T KNOW, DO YOU? YOU CAN'T SEE HOW YOU FIT INTO THE GRAND SCHEME OF THINGS, THE BIG PICTURE.
PATHETIC.
KRAASH!!

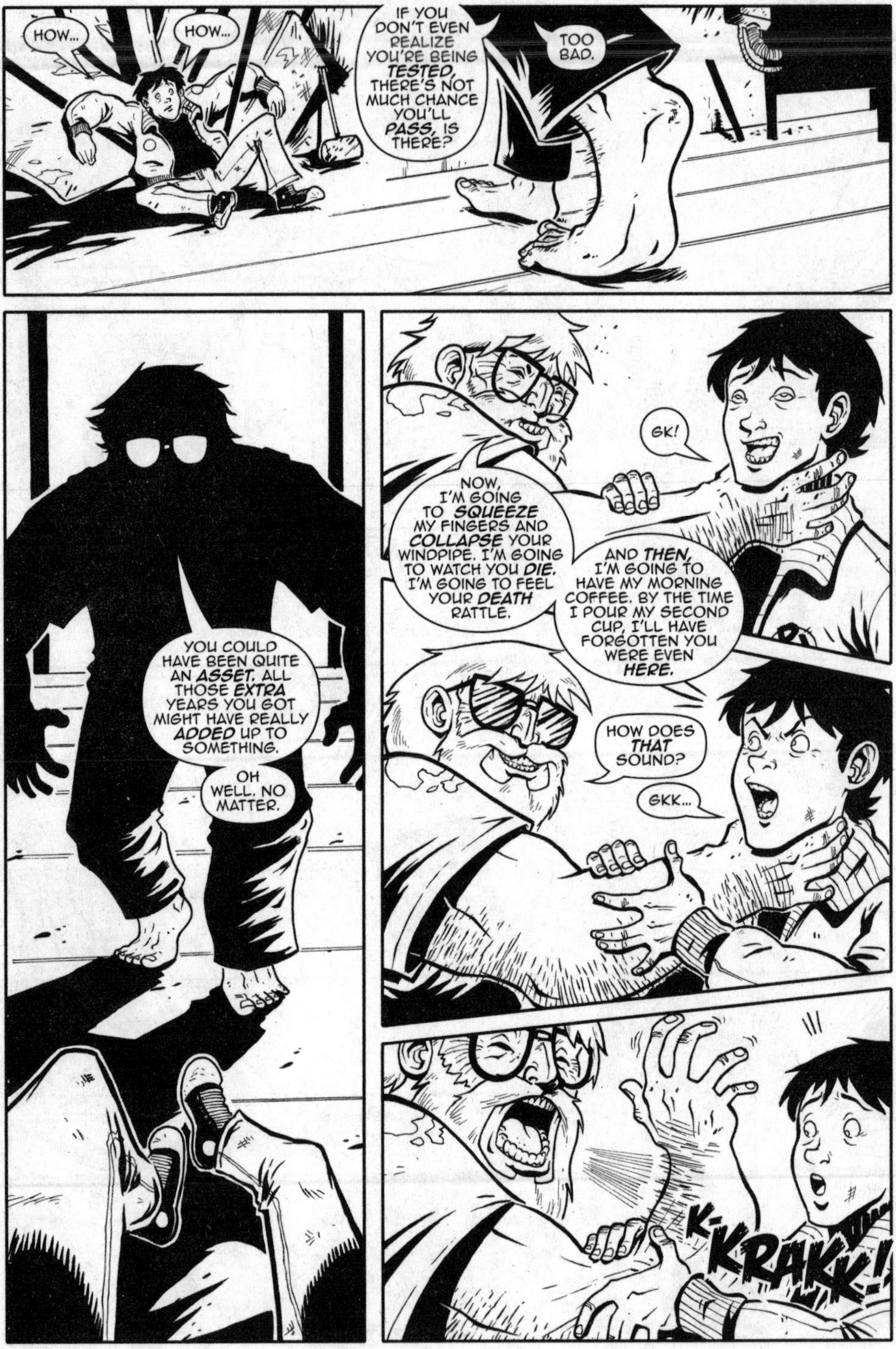
HOW...
HOW...
IF YOU DON'T EVEN REALIZE YOU'RE BEING TESTED, THERE'S NOT MUCH CHANCE YOU'LL PASS, IS THERE?
TOO BAD.
YOU COULD HAVE BEEN QUITE AN ASSET. ALL THOSE EXTRA YEARS YOU GOT MIGHT HAVE REALLY ADDED UP TO SOMETHING.
OH WELL. NO MATTER.
GK!
NOW, I'M GOING TO SQUEEZE MY FINGERS AND COLLAPSE YOUR WINDPIPE. I'M GOING TO WATCH YOU DIE. I'M GOING TO FEEL YOUR DEATH RATTLE.
AND THEN, I'M GOING TO HAVE MY MORNING COFFEE. BY THE TIME I POUR MY SECOND CUP, I'LL HAVE FORGOTTEN YOU WERE EVEN HERE.
HOW DOES THAT SOUND?
GKK...
K-KRAKK!

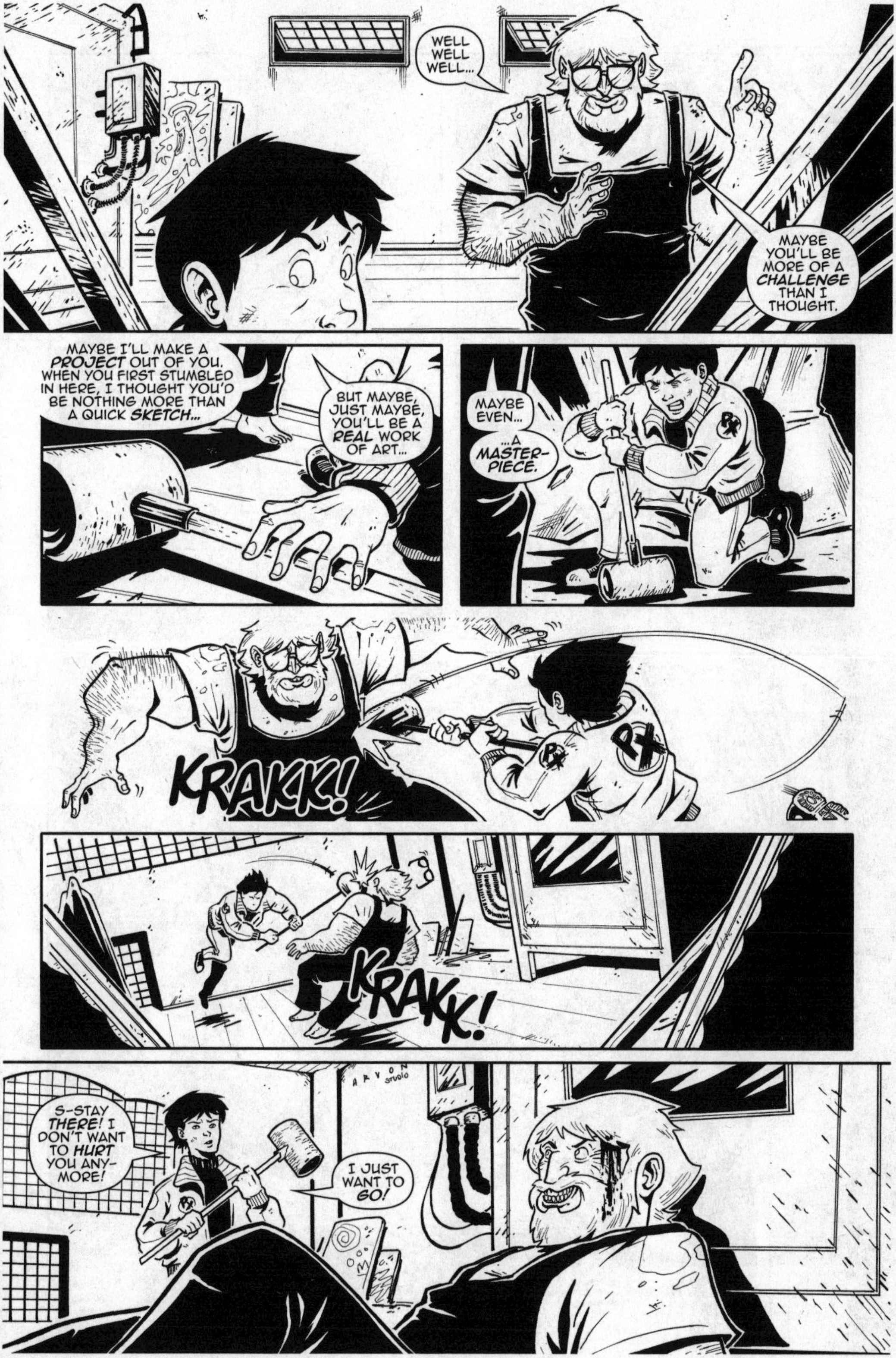
WELL WELL WELL...
MAYBE YOU'LL BE MORE OF A CHALLENGE THAN I THOUGHT.
MAYBE I'LL MAKE A PROJECT OUT OF YOU. WHEN YOU FIRST STUMBLED IN HERE, I THOUGHT YOU'D BE NOTHING MORE THAN A QUICK SKETCH...
BUT MAYBE, JUST MAYBE, YOU'LL BE A REAL WORK OF ART...
MAYBE EVEN...
...A MASTER-PIECE.
KRAKK!
KRAKK!
S-STAY THERE! I DON'T WANT TO HURT YOU ANY-MORE!
I JUST WANT TO GO!

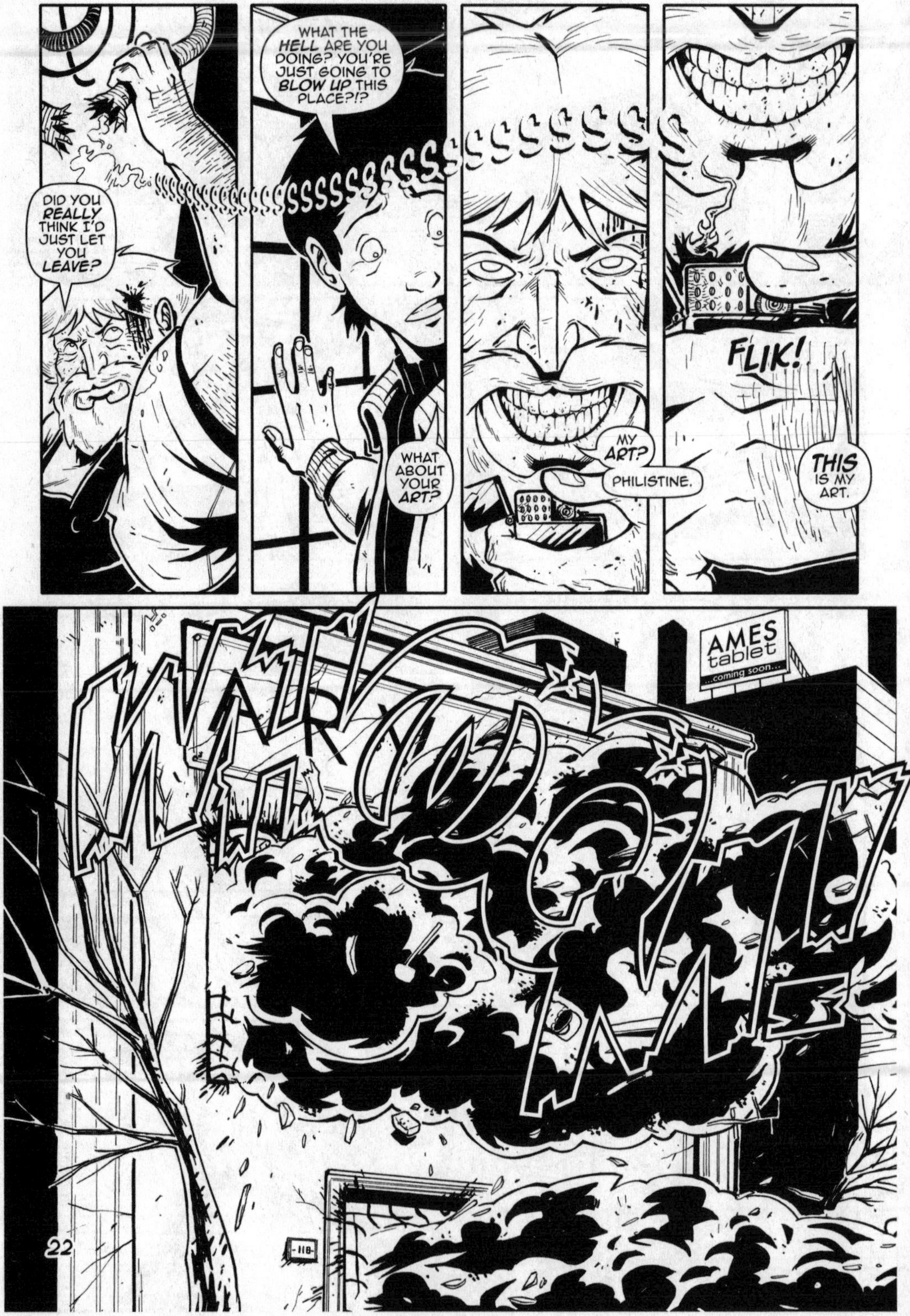
DID YOU REALLY THINK I'D JUST LET YOU LEAVE?
WHAT THE HELL ARE YOU DOING? YOU'RE JUST GOING TO BLOW UP THIS PLACE?!?
WHAT ABOUT YOUR ART?
MY ART?
PHILISTINE.
FLIK!
THIS IS MY ART.
AMES
tablet
...coming soon...
-118-

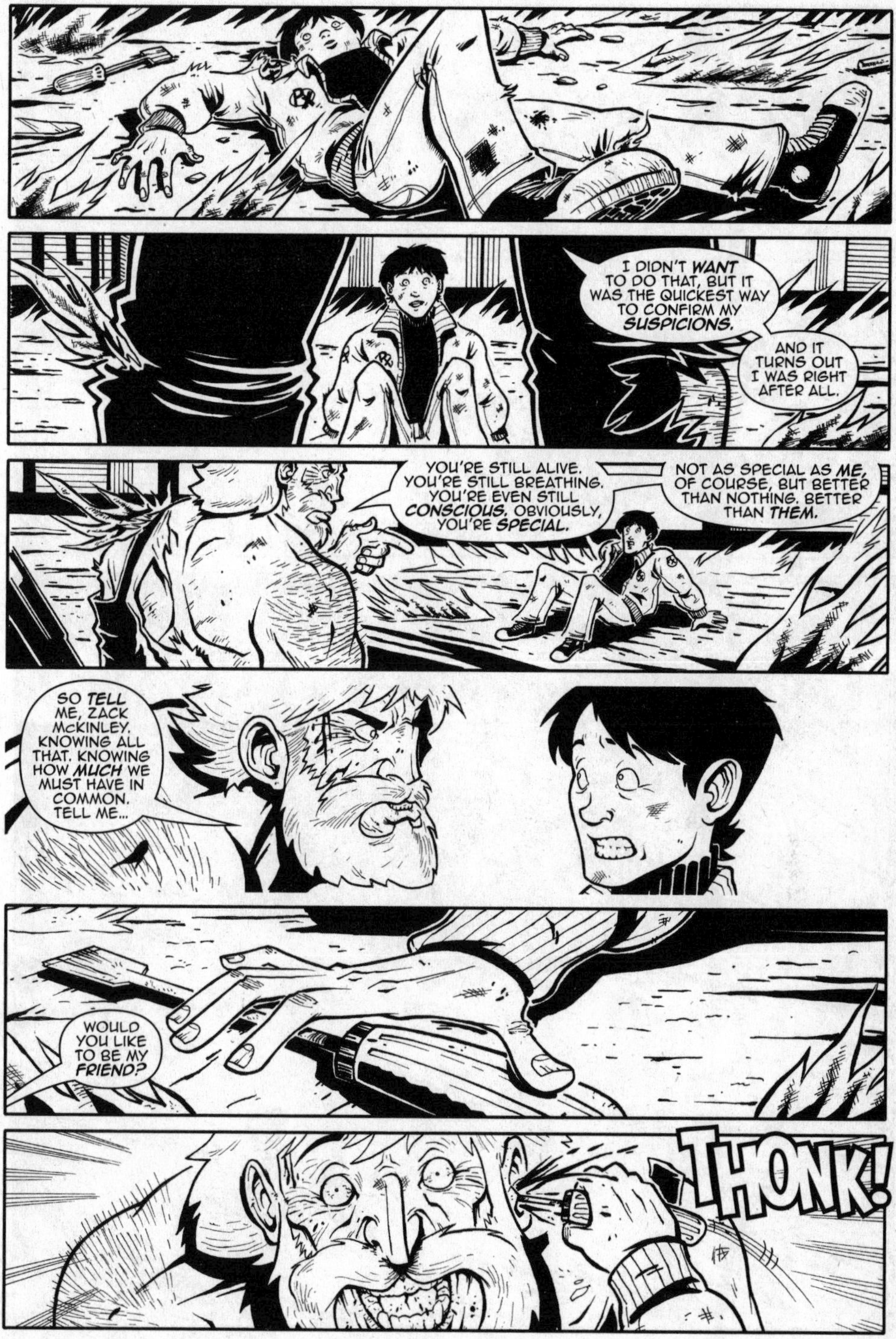
I DIDN'T WANT TO DO THAT, BUT IT WAS THE QUICKEST WAY TO CONFIRM MY SUSPICIONS.
AND IT TURNS OUT I WAS RIGHT AFTER ALL.
YOU'RE STILL ALIVE. YOU'RE STILL BREATHING. YOU'RE EVEN STILL CONSCIOUS. OBVIOUSLY, YOU'RE SPECIAL.
NOT AS SPECIAL AS ME, OF COURSE, BUT BETTER THAN NOTHING. BETTER THAN THEM.
SO TELL ME, ZACK McKINLEY. KNOWING ALL THAT. KNOWING HOW MUCH WE MUST HAVE IN COMMON. TELL ME...
WOULD YOU LIKE TO BE MY FRIEND?
THONK!

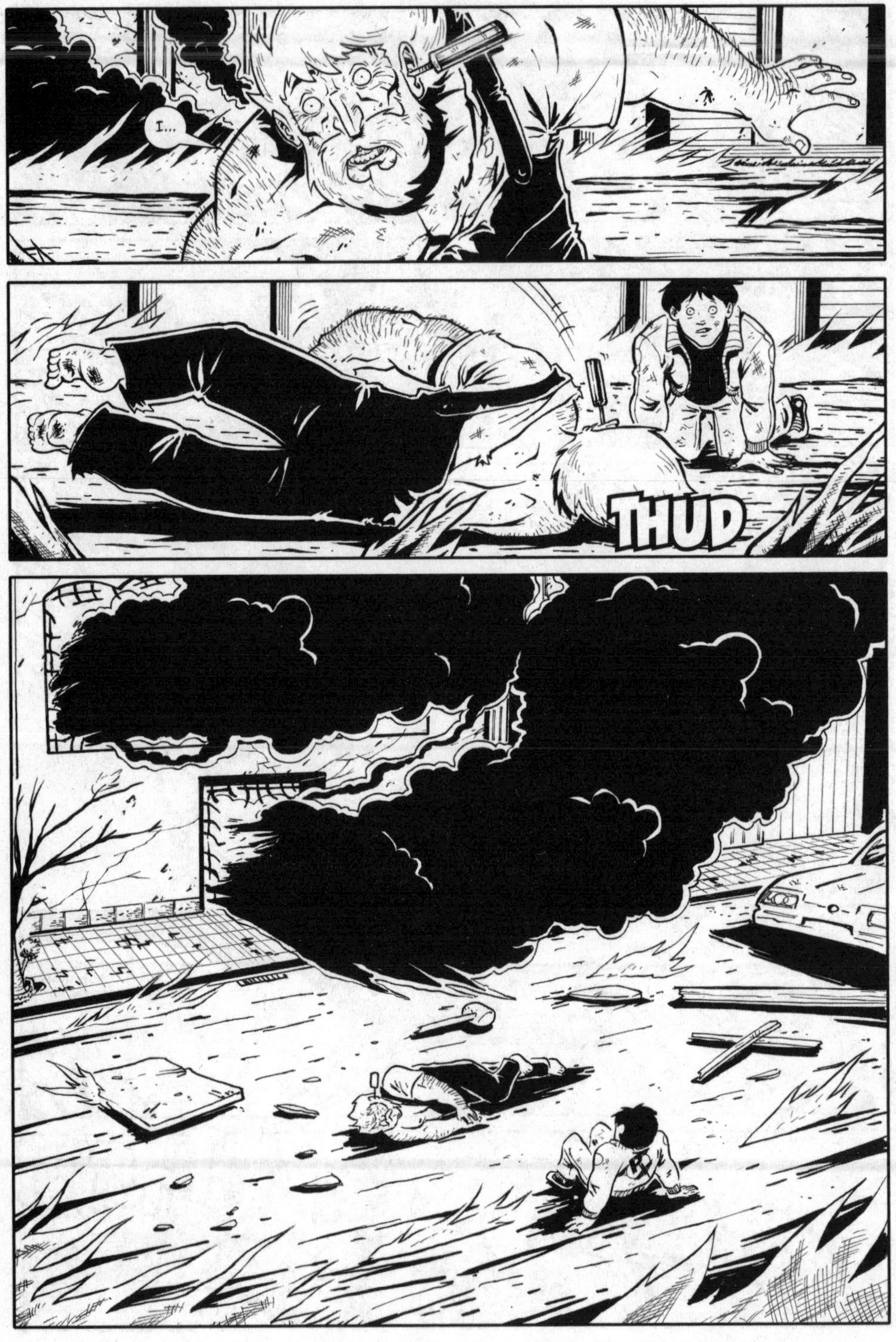
I...
THUD

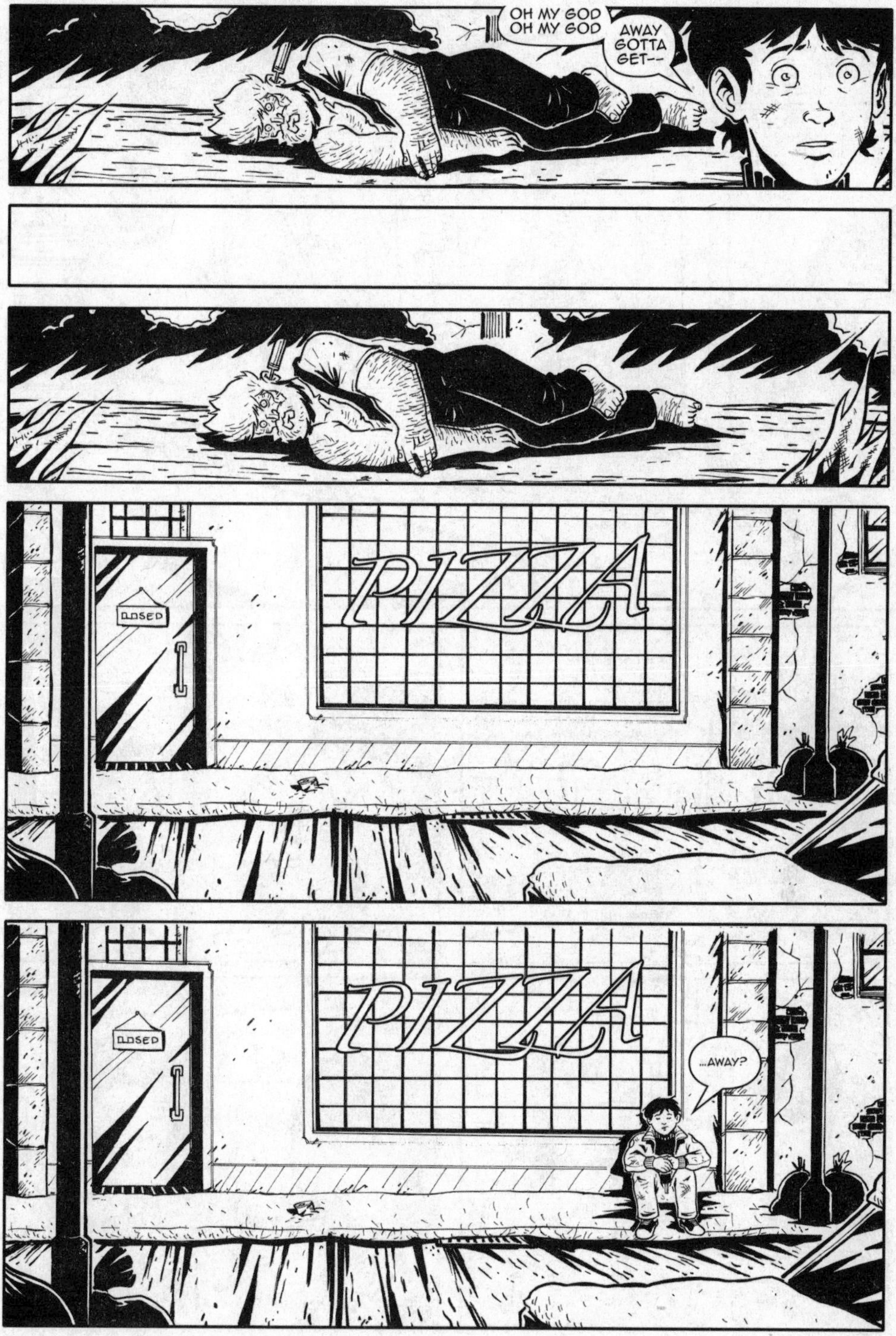
OH MY GOD
OH MY GOD
AWAY
GOTTA
GET--
PIZZA
CLOSED
PIZZA
CLOSED
...AWAY?

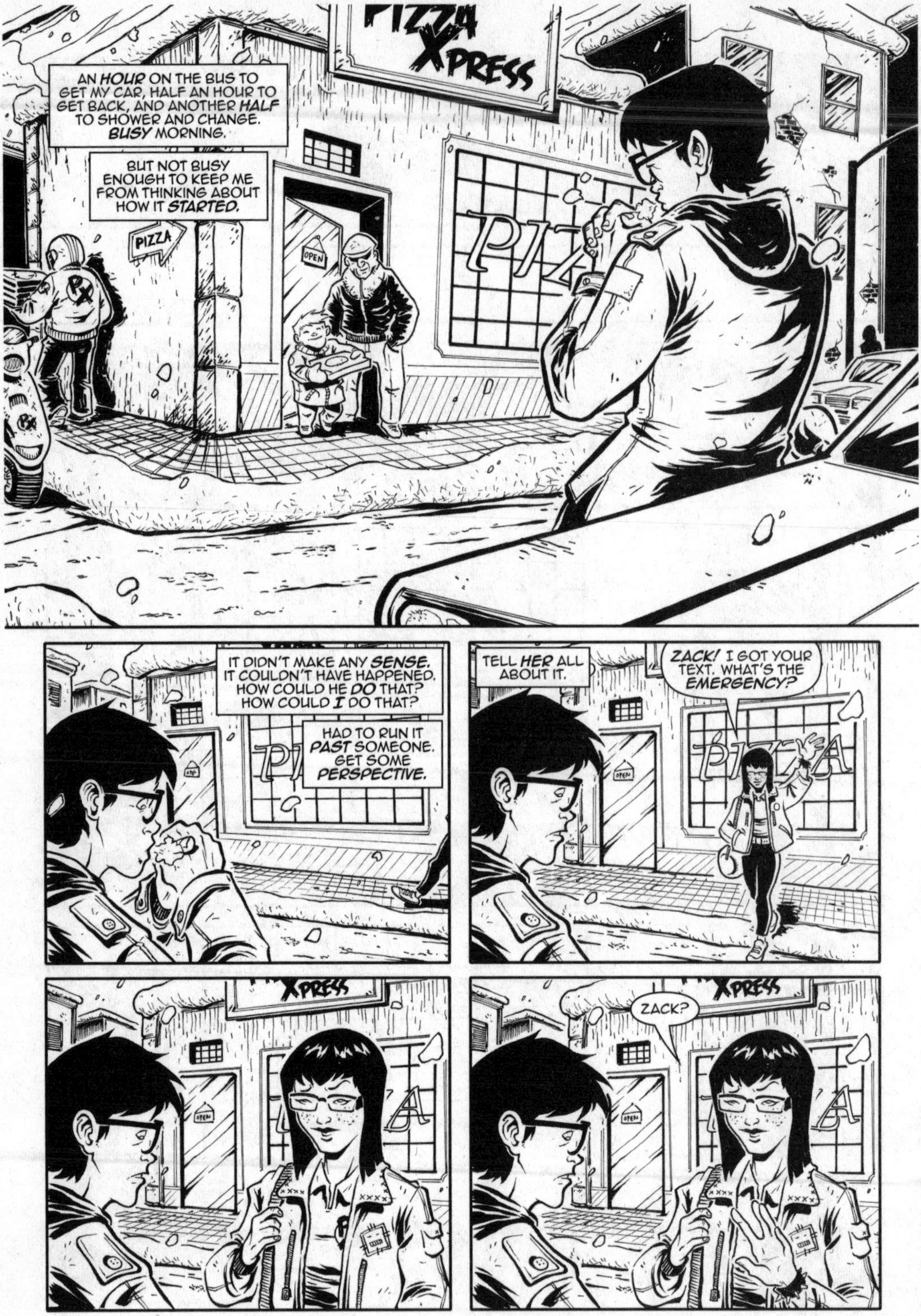
PIZZA XPRESS
AN HOUR ON THE BUS TO GET MY CAR, HALF AN HOUR TO GET BACK, AND ANOTHER HALF TO SHOWER AND CHANGE. BUSY MORNING.
BUT NOT BUSY ENOUGH TO KEEP ME FROM THINKING ABOUT HOW IT STARTED.
PIZZA
OPEN
IT DIDN'T MAKE ANY SENSE. IT COULDN'T HAVE HAPPENED. HOW COULD HE DO THAT? HOW COULD I DO THAT?
HAD TO RUN IT PAST SOMEONE. GET SOME PERSPECTIVE.
TELL HER ALL ABOUT IT.
ZACK! I GOT YOUR TEXT. WHAT'S THE EMERGENCY?
XPRESS
XPRESS
ZACK?

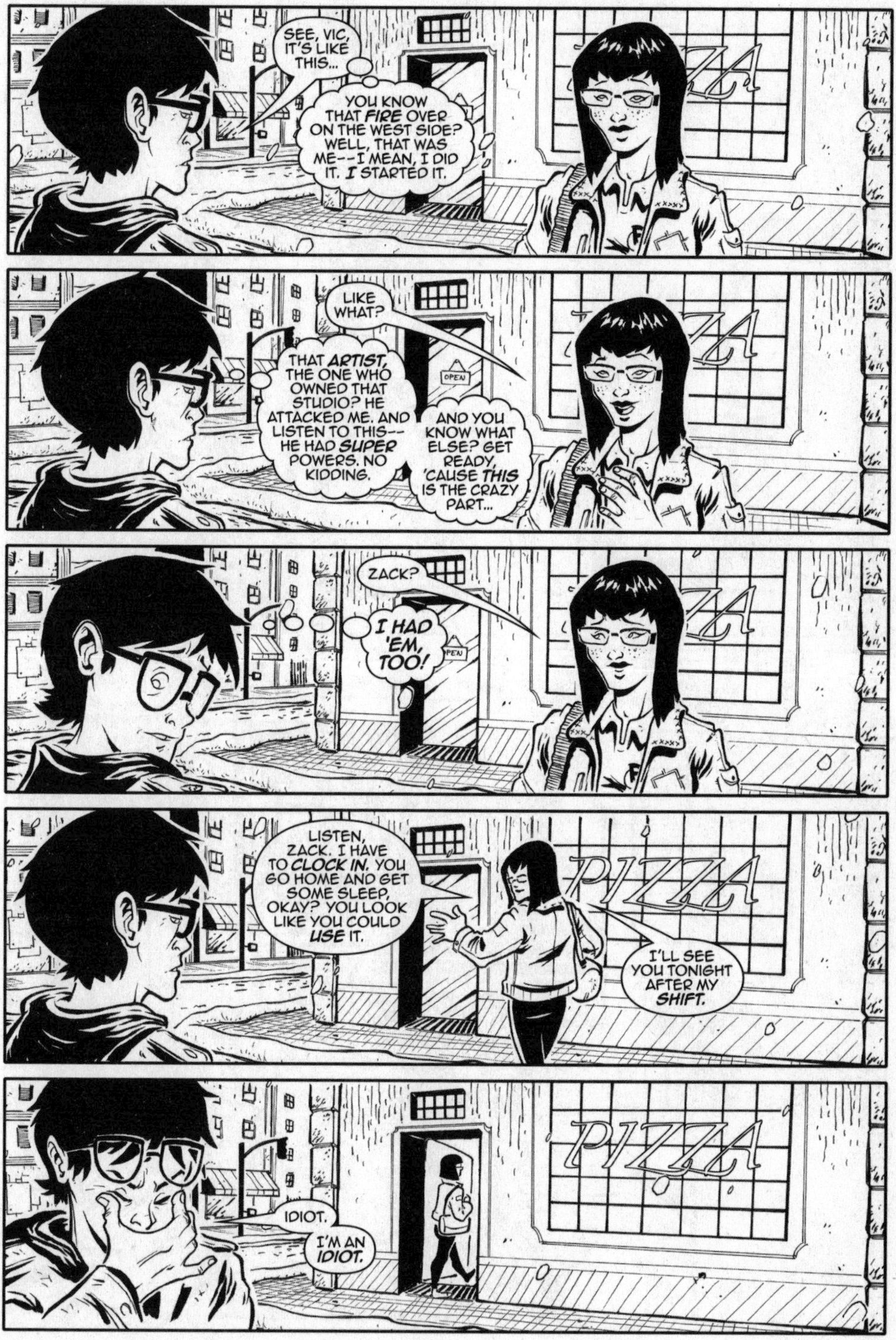
SEE, VIC, IT'S LIKE THIS...
YOU KNOW THAT FIRE OVER ON THE WEST SIDE? WELL, THAT WAS ME--I MEAN, I DID IT. I STARTED IT.
PIZZA
LIKE WHAT?
THAT ARTIST, THE ONE WHO OWNED THAT STUDIO? HE ATTACKED ME. AND LISTEN TO THIS--HE HAD SUPER POWERS. NO KIDDING.
AND YOU KNOW WHAT ELSE? GET READY, 'CAUSE THIS IS THE CRAZY PART...
OPEN
ZACK?
I HAD 'EM, TOO!
LISTEN, ZACK. I HAVE TO CLOCK IN. YOU GO HOME AND GET SOME SLEEP, OKAY? YOU LOOK LIKE YOU COULD USE IT.
PIZZA
I'LL SEE YOU TONIGHT AFTER MY SHIFT.
PIZZA
IDIOT.
I'M AN IDIOT.

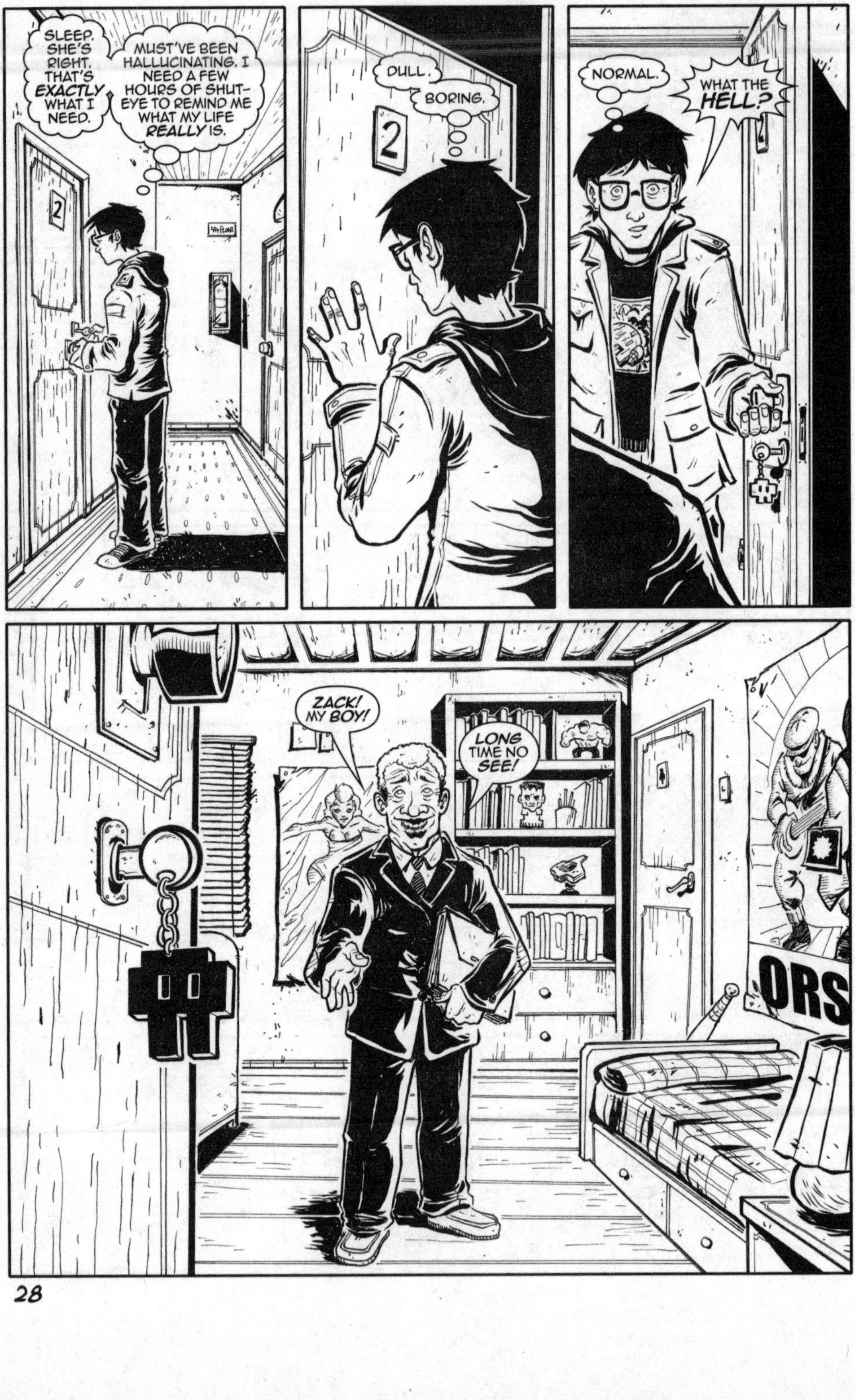
SLEEP. SHE'S RIGHT. THAT'S EXACTLY WHAT I NEED.
MUST'VE BEEN HALLUCINATING. I NEED A FEW HOURS OF SHUT-EYE TO REMIND ME WHAT MY LIFE REALLY IS.
DULL.
BORING.
NORMAL.
WHAT THE HELL?
ZACK! MY BOY!
LONG TIME NO SEE!
ORS

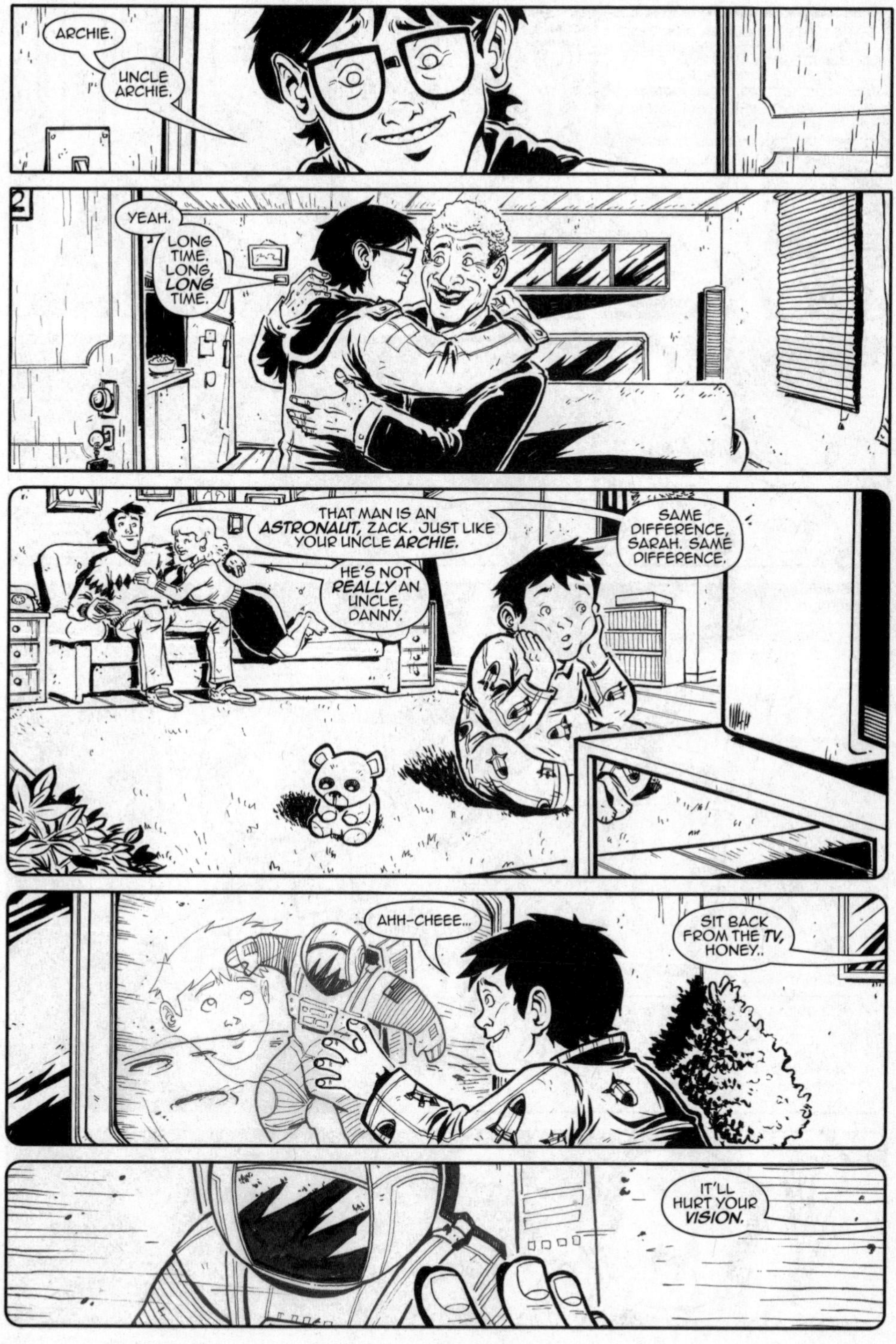
ARCHIE.
UNCLE ARCHIE.
YEAH.
LONG TIME. LONG, LONG TIME.
THAT MAN IS AN ASTRONAUT, ZACK. JUST LIKE YOUR UNCLE ARCHIE.
HE'S NOT REALLY AN UNCLE, DANNY.
SAME DIFFERENCE, SARAH. SAME DIFFERENCE.
AHH-CHEEE...
SIT BACK FROM THE TV, HONEY..
IT'LL HURT YOUR VISION.

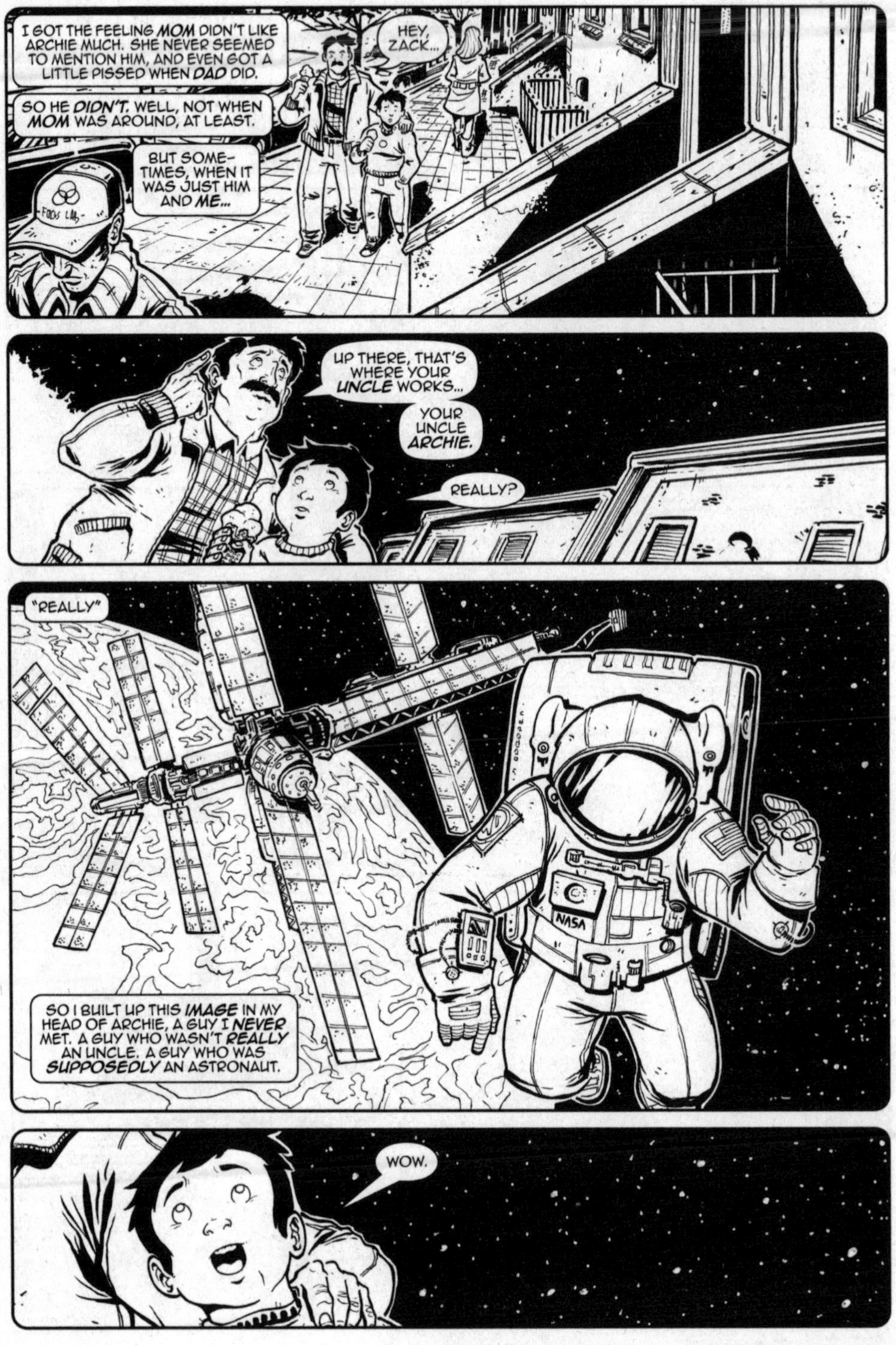

I GOT THE FEELING MOM DIDN'T LIKE ARCHIE MUCH. SHE NEVER SEEMED TO MENTION HIM, AND EVEN GOT A LITTLE PISSED WHEN DAD DID.
HEY, ZACK...
SO HE DIDN'T. WELL, NOT WHEN MOM WAS AROUND, AT LEAST.
BUT SOMETIMES, WHEN IT WAS JUST HIM AND ME...
UP THERE, THAT'S WHERE YOUR UNCLE WORKS...
YOUR UNCLE ARCHIE.
REALLY?
"REALLY"
NASA
SO I BUILT UP THIS IMAGE IN MY HEAD OF ARCHIE, A GUY I NEVER MET. A GUY WHO WASN'T REALLY AN UNCLE. A GUY WHO WAS SUPPOSEDLY AN ASTRONAUT.
WOW.

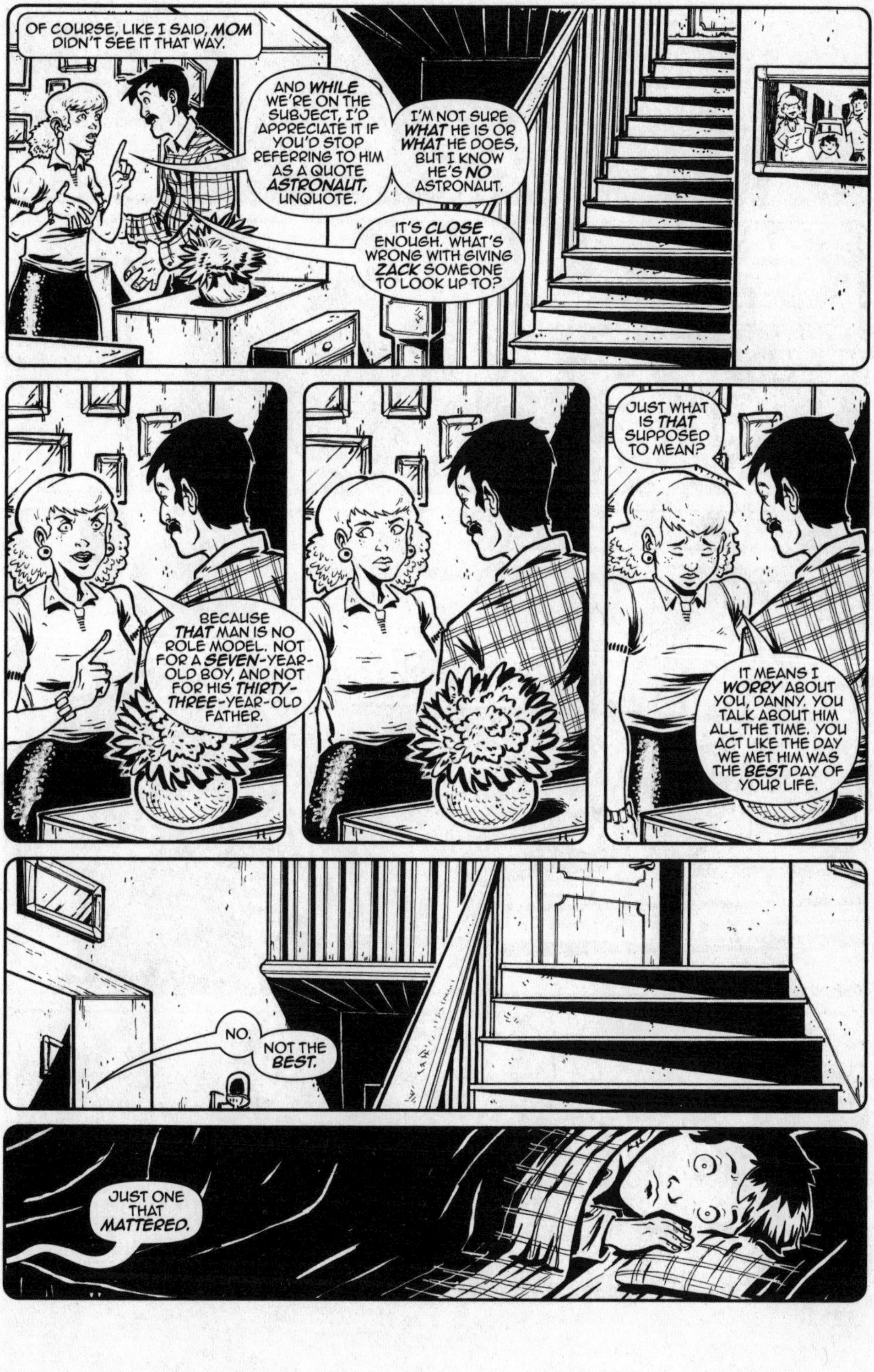
OF COURSE, LIKE I SAID, MOM DIDN'T SEE IT THAT WAY.
AND WHILE WE'RE ON THE SUBJECT, I'D APPRECIATE IT IF YOU'D STOP REFERRING TO HIM AS A QUOTE ASTRONAUT, UNQUOTE.
I'M NOT SURE WHAT HE IS OR WHAT HE DOES, BUT I KNOW HE'S NO ASTRONAUT.
IT'S CLOSE ENOUGH. WHAT'S WRONG WITH GIVING ZACK SOMEONE TO LOOK UP TO?
BECAUSE THAT MAN IS NO ROLE MODEL. NOT FOR A SEVEN-YEAR-OLD BOY, AND NOT FOR HIS THIRTY-THREE-YEAR-OLD FATHER.
JUST WHAT IS THAT SUPPOSED TO MEAN?
IT MEANS I WORRY ABOUT YOU, DANNY. YOU TALK ABOUT HIM ALL THE TIME. YOU ACT LIKE THE DAY WE MET HIM WAS THE BEST DAY OF YOUR LIFE.
NO.
NOT THE BEST.
JUST ONE THAT MATTERED.

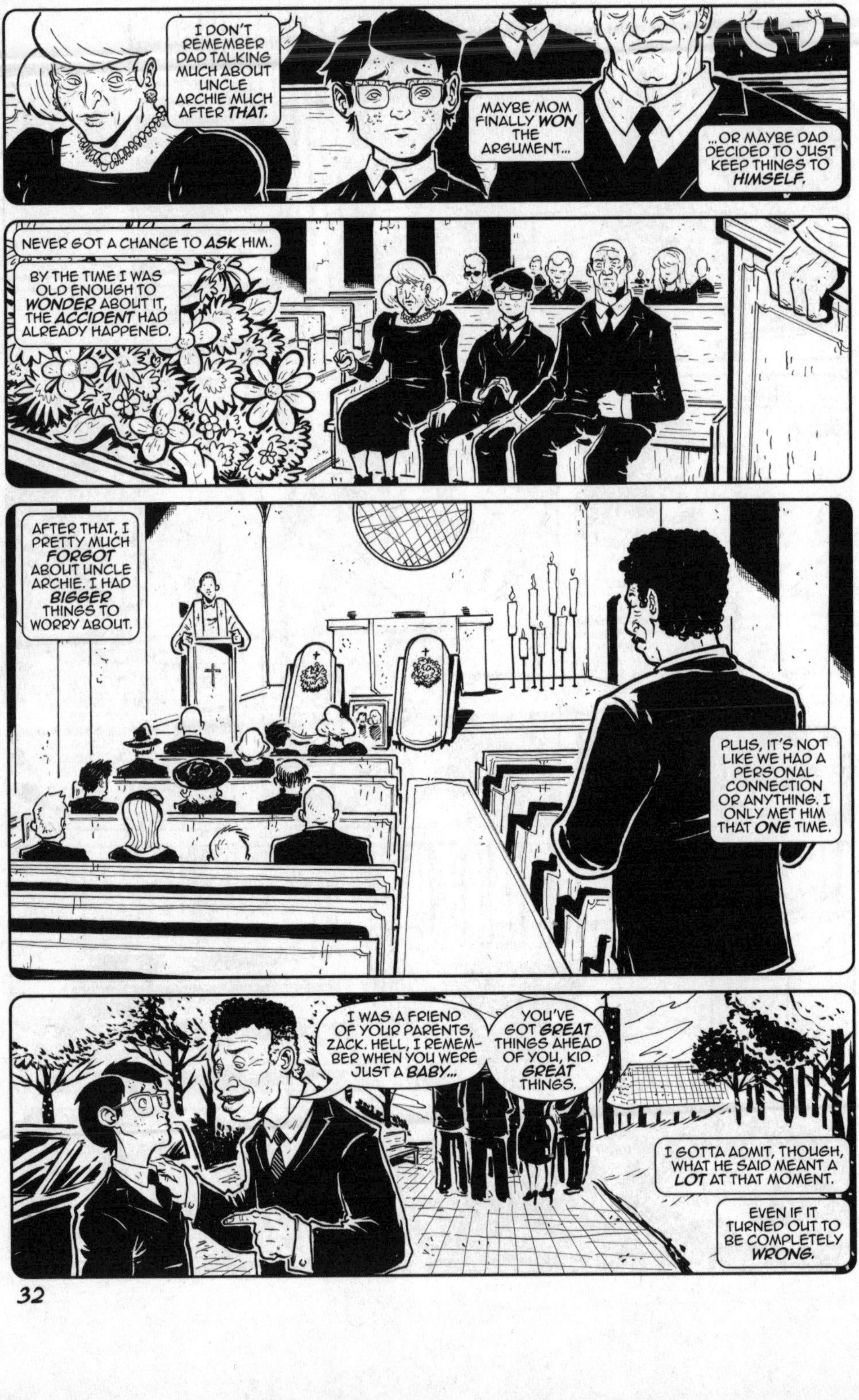
I DON'T REMEMBER DAD TALKING MUCH ABOUT UNCLE ARCHIE MUCH AFTER THAT.
MAYBE MOM FINALLY WON THE ARGUMENT...
...OR MAYBE DAD DECIDED TO JUST KEEP THINGS TO HIMSELF.
NEVER GOT A CHANCE TO ASK HIM.
BY THE TIME I WAS OLD ENOUGH TO WONDER ABOUT IT, THE ACCIDENT HAD ALREADY HAPPENED.
AFTER THAT, I PRETTY MUCH FORGOT ABOUT UNCLE ARCHIE. I HAD BIGGER THINGS TO WORRY ABOUT.
PLUS, IT'S NOT LIKE WE HAD A PERSONAL CONNECTION OR ANYTHING. I ONLY MET HIM THAT ONE TIME.
I WAS A FRIEND OF YOUR PARENTS, ZACK. HELL, I REMEMBER WHEN YOU WERE JUST A BABY...
YOU'VE GOT GREAT THINGS AHEAD OF YOU, KID. GREAT THINGS.
I GOTTA ADMIT, THOUGH, WHAT HE SAID MEANT A LOT AT THAT MOMENT.
EVEN IF IT TURNED OUT TO BE COMPLETELY WRONG.

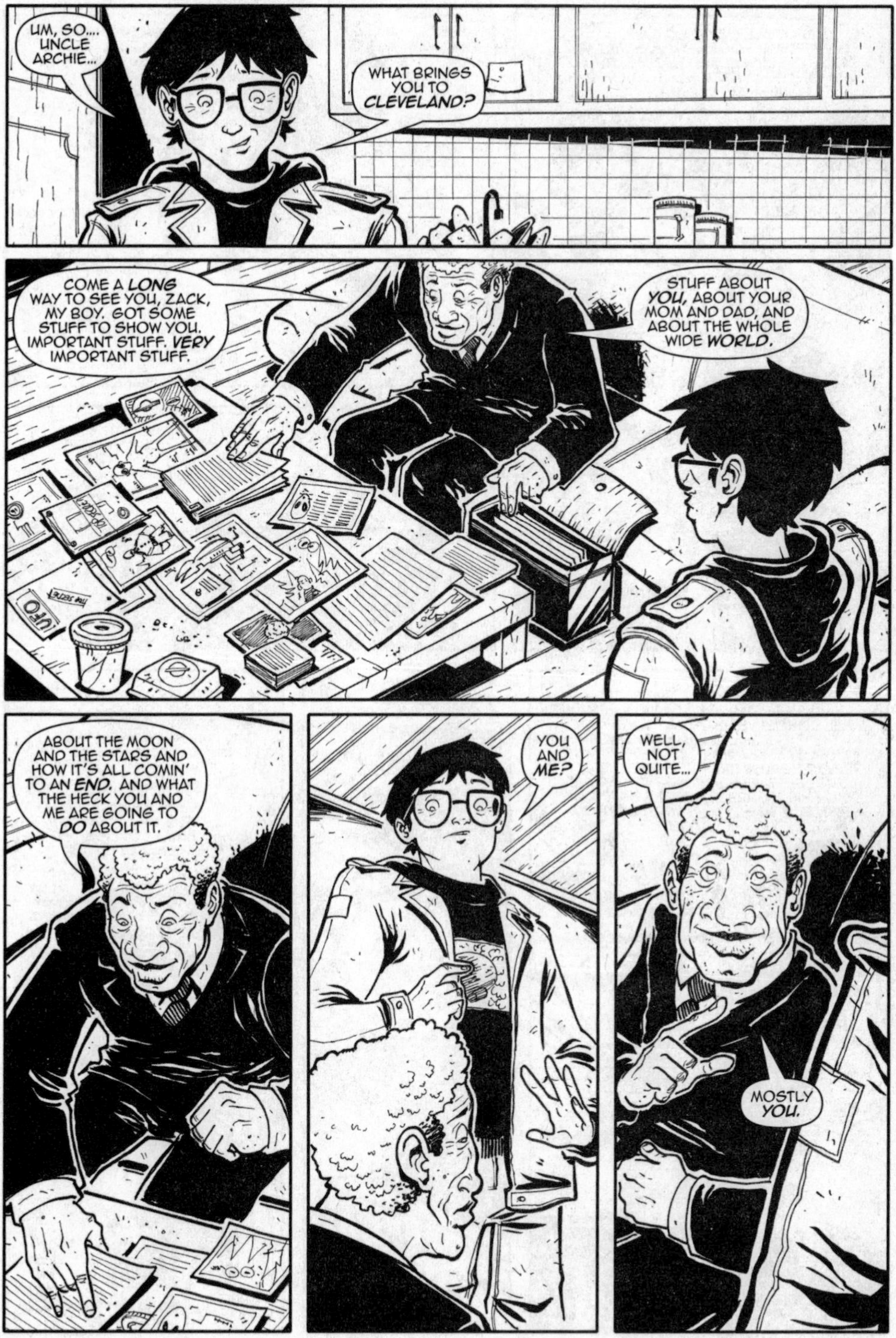
UM, SO.... UNCLE ARCHIE...
WHAT BRINGS YOU TO CLEVELAND?
COME A LONG WAY TO SEE YOU, ZACK, MY BOY. GOT SOME STUFF TO SHOW YOU. IMPORTANT STUFF. VERY IMPORTANT STUFF.
STUFF ABOUT YOU, ABOUT YOUR MOM AND DAD, AND ABOUT THE WHOLE WIDE WORLD.
UFO
ABOUT THE MOON AND THE STARS AND HOW IT'S ALL COMIN' TO AN END. AND WHAT THE HECK YOU AND ME ARE GOING TO DO ABOUT IT.
YOU AND ME?
WELL, NOT QUITE...
MOSTLY YOU.

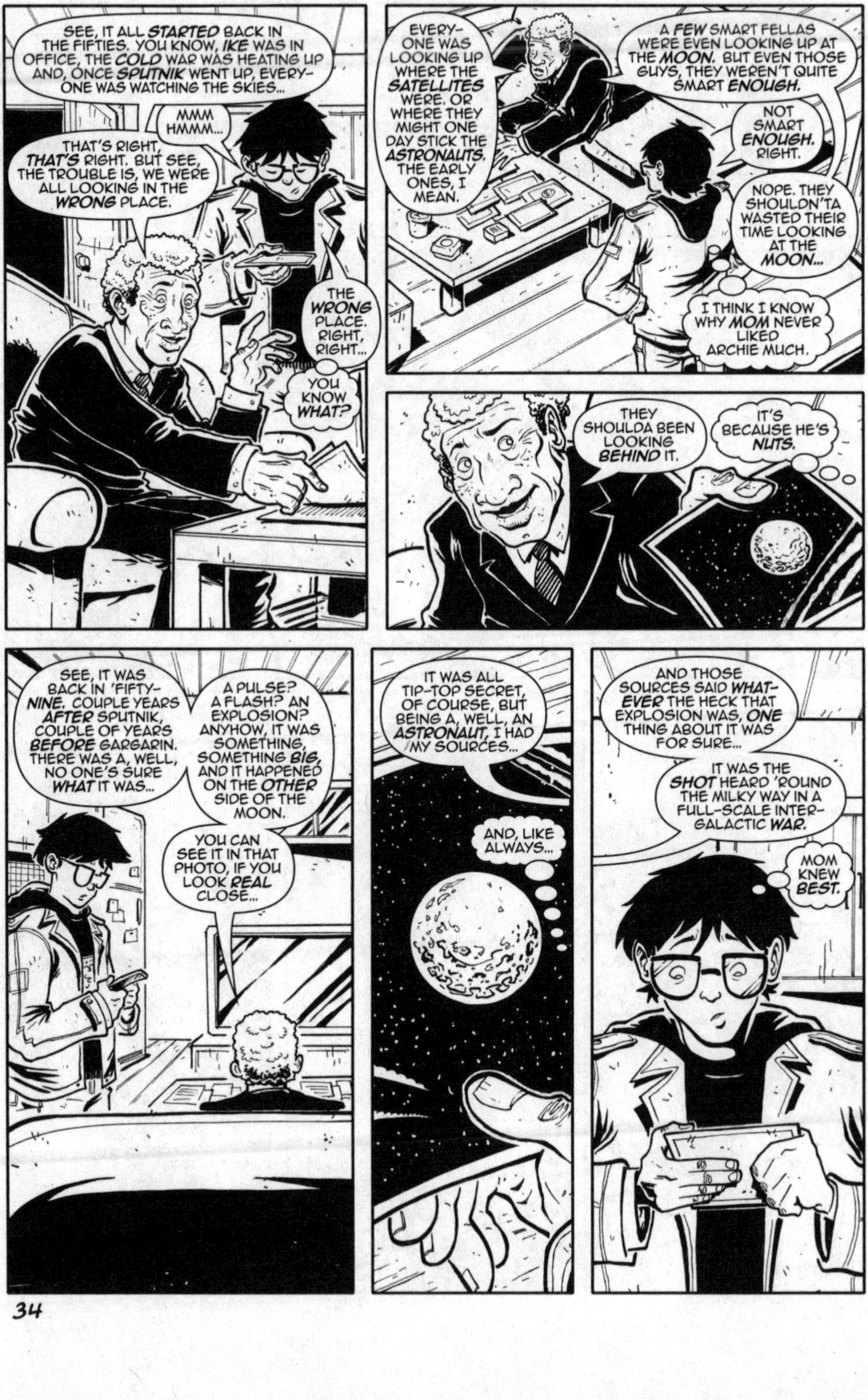
SEE, IT ALL STARTED BACK IN THE FIFTIES. YOU KNOW, IKE WAS IN OFFICE, THE COLD WAR WAS HEATING UP AND, ONCE SPUTNIK WENT UP, EVERY-ONE WAS WATCHING THE SKIES...
MMM HMMM...
THAT'S RIGHT, THAT'S RIGHT. BUT SEE, THE TROUBLE IS, WE WERE ALL LOOKING IN THE WRONG PLACE.
THE WRONG PLACE. RIGHT, RIGHT...
YOU KNOW WHAT?
EVERY-ONE WAS LOOKING UP WHERE THE SATELLITES WERE. OR WHERE THEY MIGHT ONE DAY STICK THE ASTRONAUTS. THE EARLY ONES, I MEAN.
A FEW SMART FELLAS WERE EVEN LOOKING UP AT THE MOON. BUT EVEN THOSE GUYS, THEY WEREN'T QUITE SMART ENOUGH.
NOT SMART ENOUGH. RIGHT.
NOPE. THEY SHOULDN'TA WASTED THEIR TIME LOOKING AT THE MOON...
I THINK I KNOW WHY MOM NEVER LIKED ARCHIE MUCH.
THEY SHOULDA BEEN LOOKING BEHIND IT.
IT'S BECAUSE HE'S NUTS.
SEE, IT WAS BACK IN 'FIFTY-NINE. COUPLE YEARS AFTER SPUTNIK, COUPLE OF YEARS BEFORE GARGARIN. THERE WAS A, WELL, NO ONE'S SURE WHAT IT WAS...
A PULSE? A FLASH? AN EXPLOSION? ANYHOW, IT WAS SOMETHING, SOMETHING BIG, AND IT HAPPENED ON THE OTHER SIDE OF THE MOON.
YOU CAN SEE IT IN THAT PHOTO, IF YOU LOOK REAL CLOSE...
IT WAS ALL TIP-TOP SECRET, OF COURSE, BUT BEING A, WELL, AN ASTRONAUT, I HAD MY SOURCES...
AND, LIKE ALWAYS...
AND THOSE SOURCES SAID WHAT-EVER THE HECK THAT EXPLOSION WAS, ONE THING ABOUT IT WAS FOR SURE...
IT WAS THE SHOT HEARD 'ROUND THE MILKY WAY IN A FULL-SCALE INTER-GALACTIC WAR.
MOM KNEW BEST.

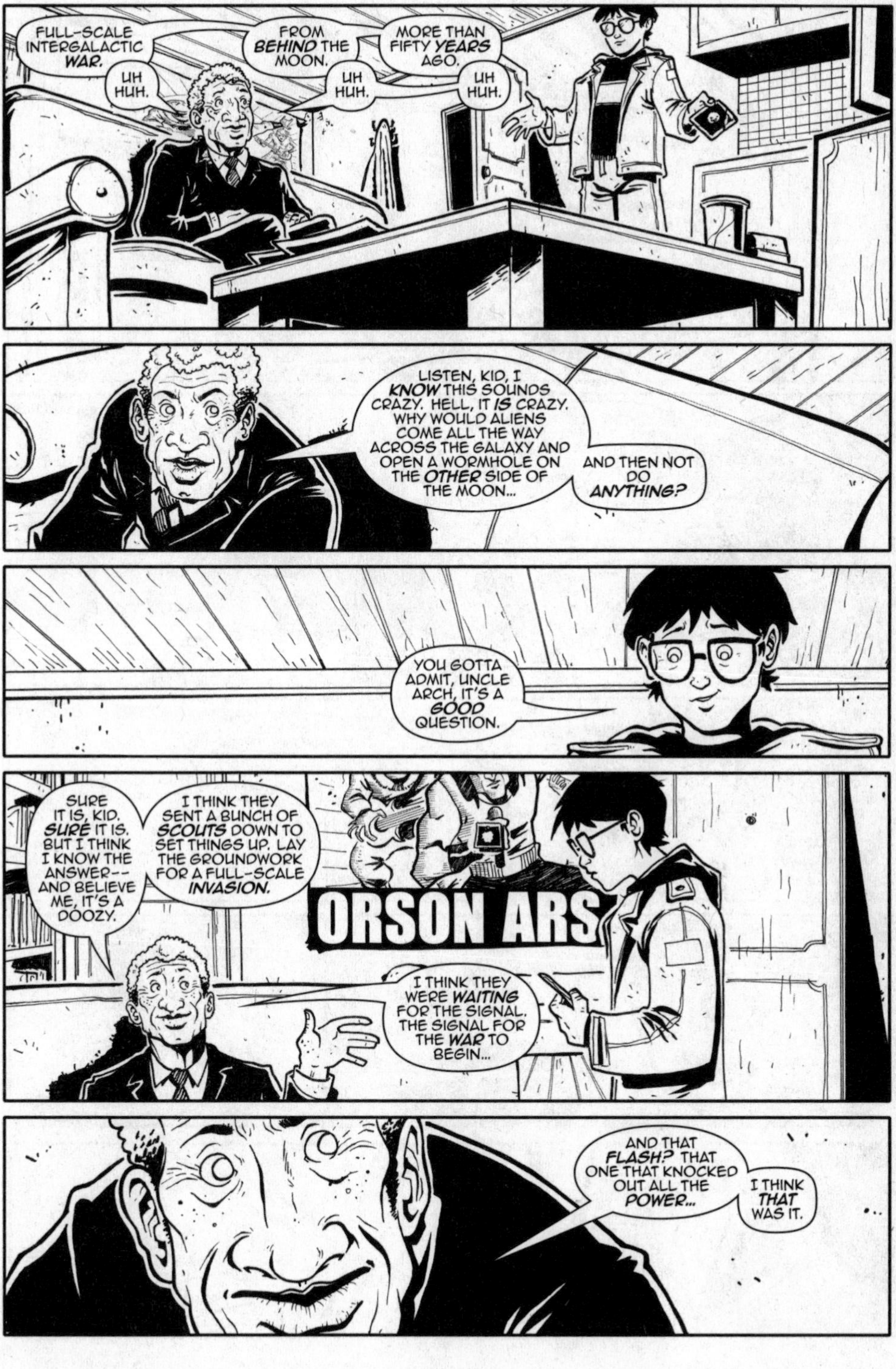
FULL-SCALE INTERGALACTIC WAR.
UH HUH.
FROM BEHIND THE MOON.
UH HUH.
MORE THAN FIFTY YEARS AGO.
UH HUH.
LISTEN, KID, I KNOW THIS SOUNDS CRAZY. HELL, IT IS CRAZY. WHY WOULD ALIENS COME ALL THE WAY ACROSS THE GALAXY AND OPEN A WORMHOLE ON THE OTHER SIDE OF THE MOON...
AND THEN NOT DO ANYTHING?
YOU GOTTA ADMIT, UNCLE ARCH, IT'S A GOOD QUESTION.
SURE IT IS, KID. SURE IT IS. BUT I THINK I KNOW THE ANSWER-- AND BELIEVE ME, IT'S A DOOZY.
I THINK THEY SENT A BUNCH OF SCOUTS DOWN TO SET THINGS UP. LAY THE GROUNDWORK FOR A FULL-SCALE INVASION.
ORSON ARS
I THINK THEY WERE WAITING FOR THE SIGNAL. THE SIGNAL FOR THE WAR TO BEGIN...
AND THAT FLASH? THAT ONE THAT KNOCKED OUT ALL THE POWER...
I THINK THAT WAS IT.

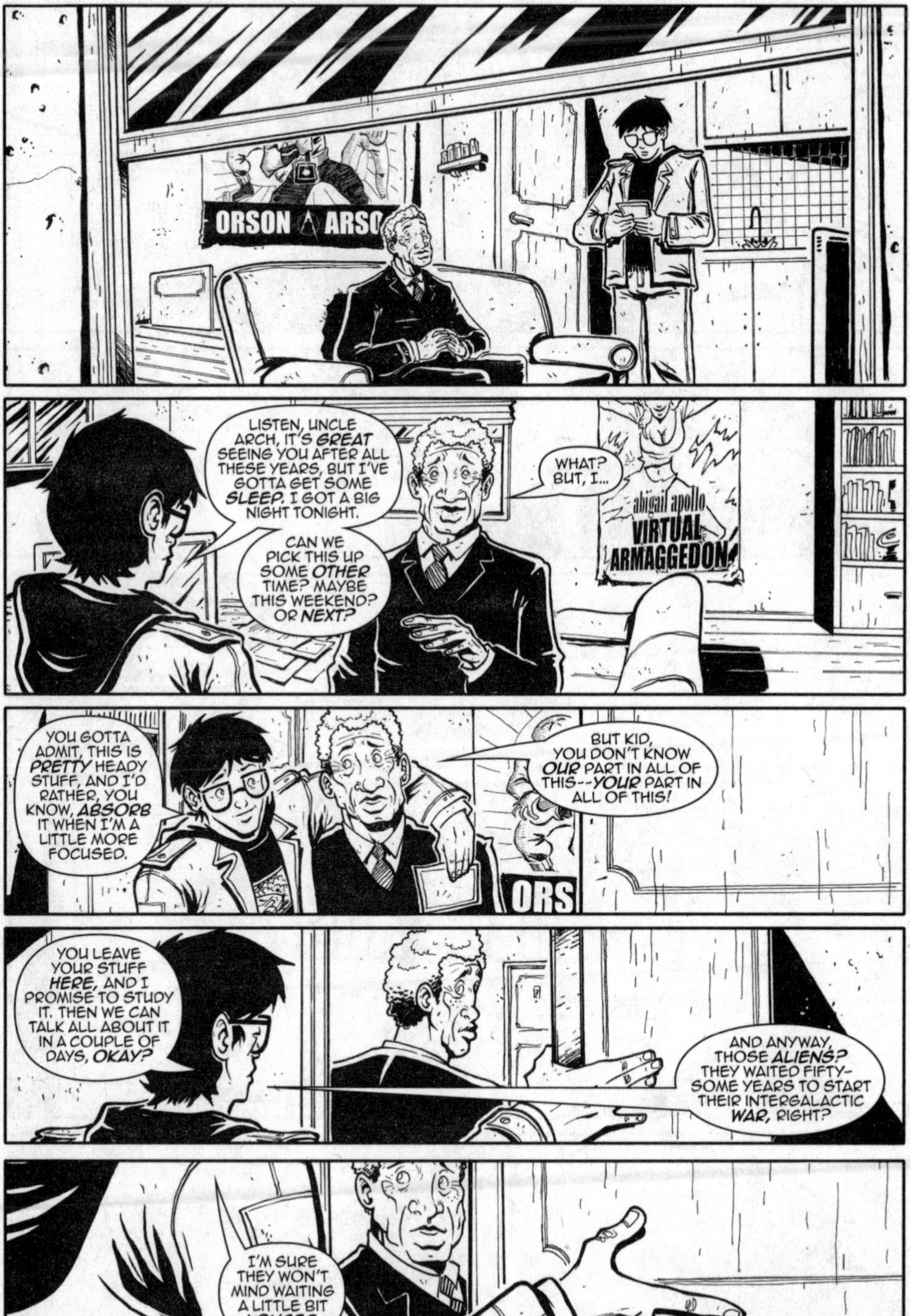
ORSON ARSO
LISTEN, UNCLE ARCH, IT'S GREAT SEEING YOU AFTER ALL THESE YEARS, BUT I'VE GOTTA GET SOME SLEEP. I GOT A BIG NIGHT TONIGHT.
CAN WE PICK THIS UP SOME OTHER TIME? MAYBE THIS WEEKEND? OR NEXT?
WHAT? BUT, I...
abigail apollo
VIRTUAL ARMAGGEDON
YOU GOTTA ADMIT, THIS IS PRETTY HEADY STUFF, AND I'D RATHER, YOU KNOW, ABSORB IT WHEN I'M A LITTLE MORE FOCUSED.
BUT KID, YOU DON'T KNOW OUR PART IN ALL OF THIS--YOUR PART IN ALL OF THIS!
ORS
YOU LEAVE YOUR STUFF HERE, AND I PROMISE TO STUDY IT. THEN WE CAN TALK ALL ABOUT IT IN A COUPLE OF DAYS, OKAY?
AND ANYWAY, THOSE ALIENS? THEY WAITED FIFTY-SOME YEARS TO START THEIR INTERGALACTIC WAR, RIGHT?
I'M SURE THEY WON'T MIND WAITING A LITTLE BIT LONGER.

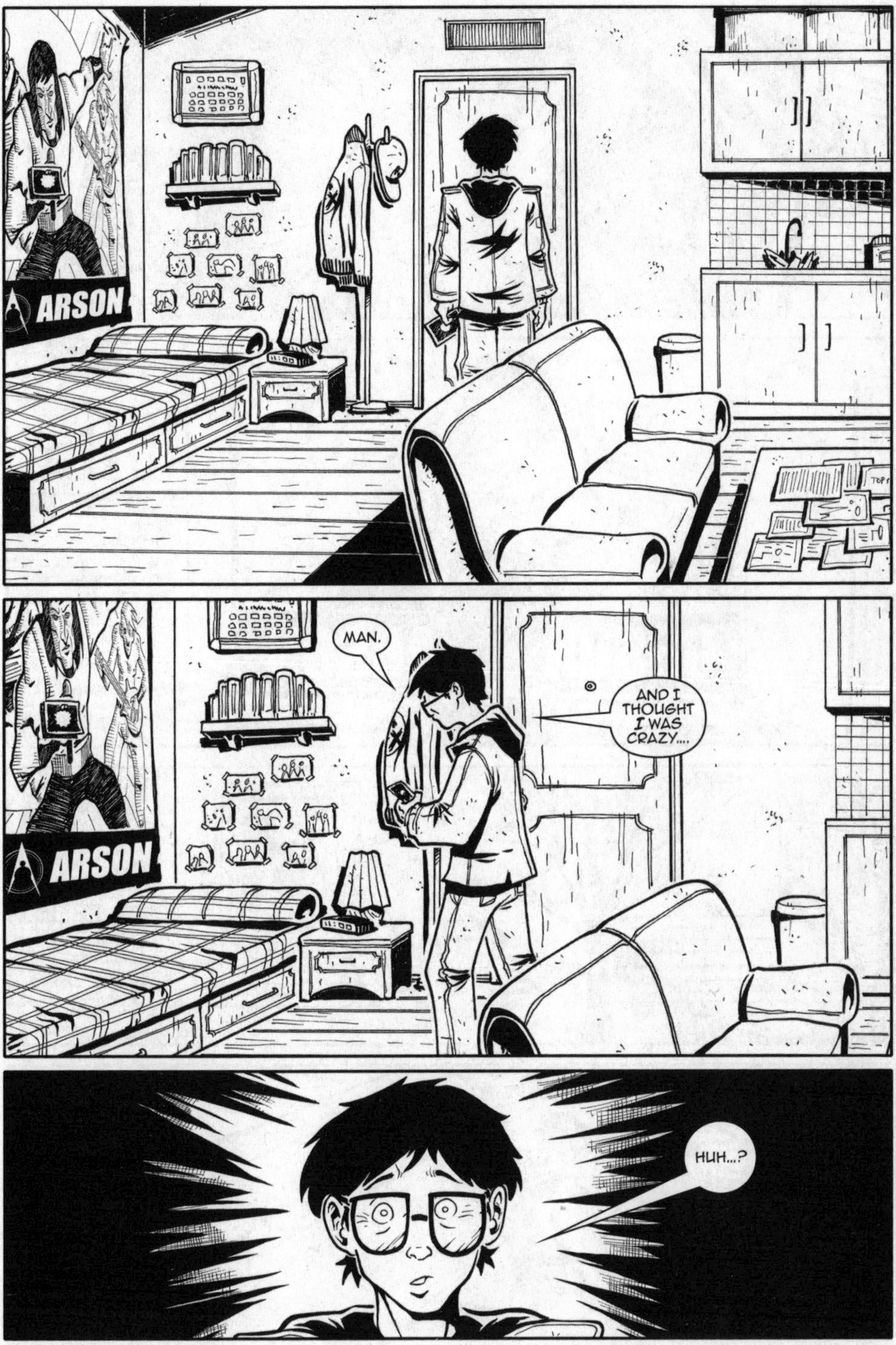
ARSON
ARSON
MAN.
AND I THOUGHT I WAS CRAZY....
HUH...?

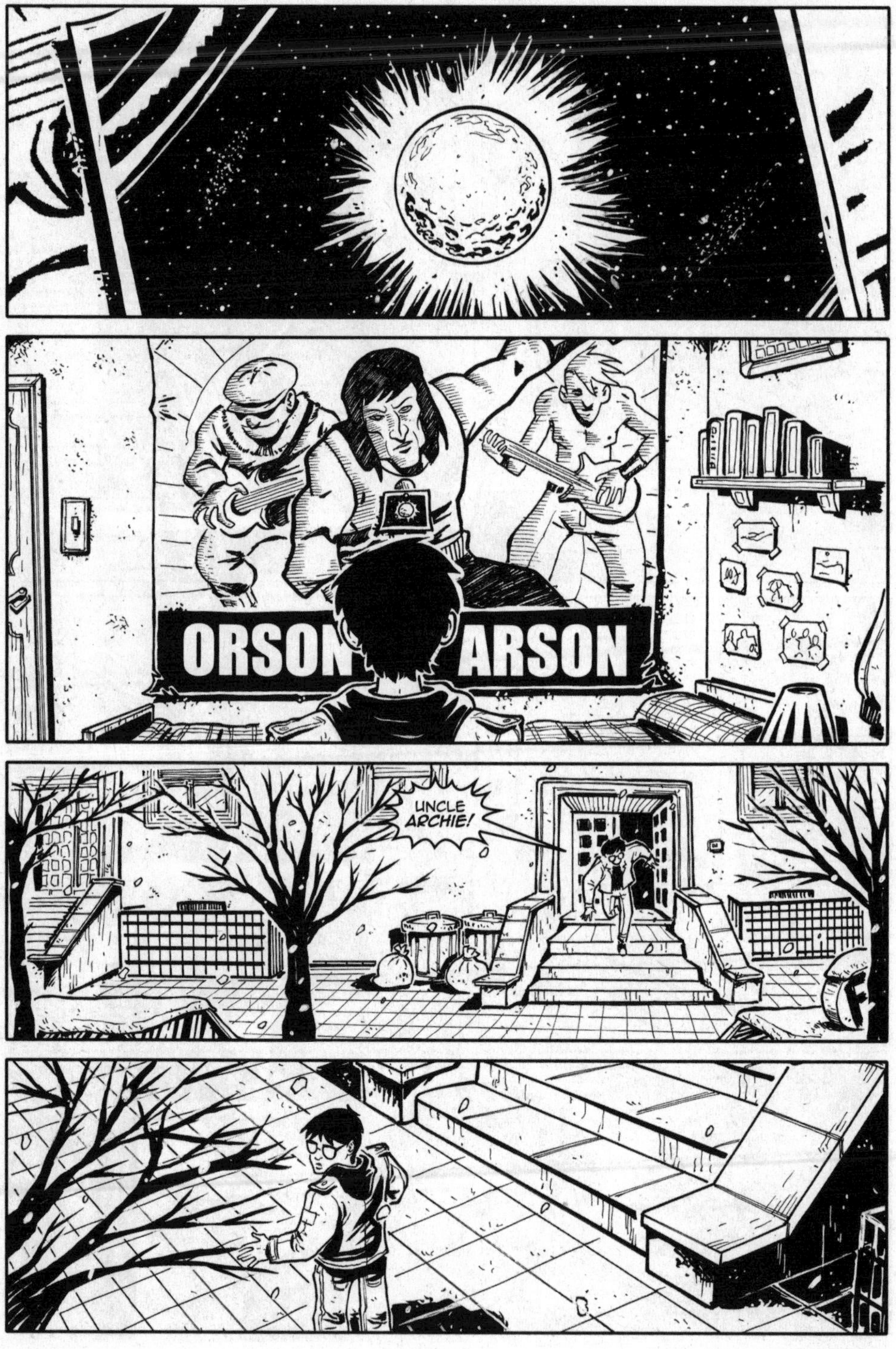
ORSON ARSON
UNCLE ARCHIE!

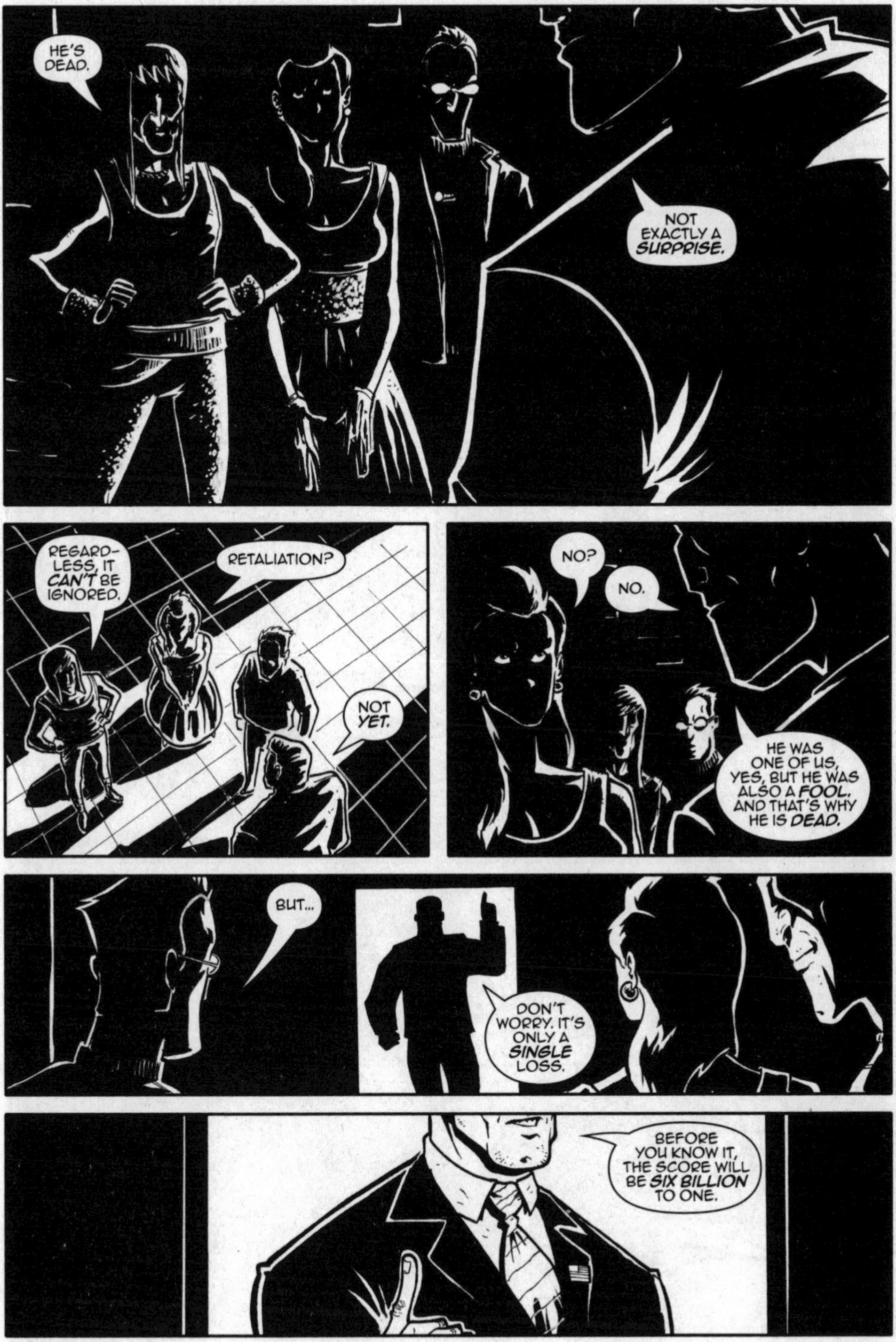
HE'S DEAD.
NOT EXACTLY A SURPRISE.
REGARDLESS, IT CAN'T BE IGNORED.
RETALIATION?
NOT YET.
NO?
NO.
HE WAS ONE OF US, YES, BUT HE WAS ALSO A FOOL. AND THAT'S WHY HE IS DEAD.
BUT...
DON'T WORRY. IT'S ONLY A SINGLE LOSS.
BEFORE YOU KNOW IT, THE SCORE WILL BE SIX BILLION TO ONE.

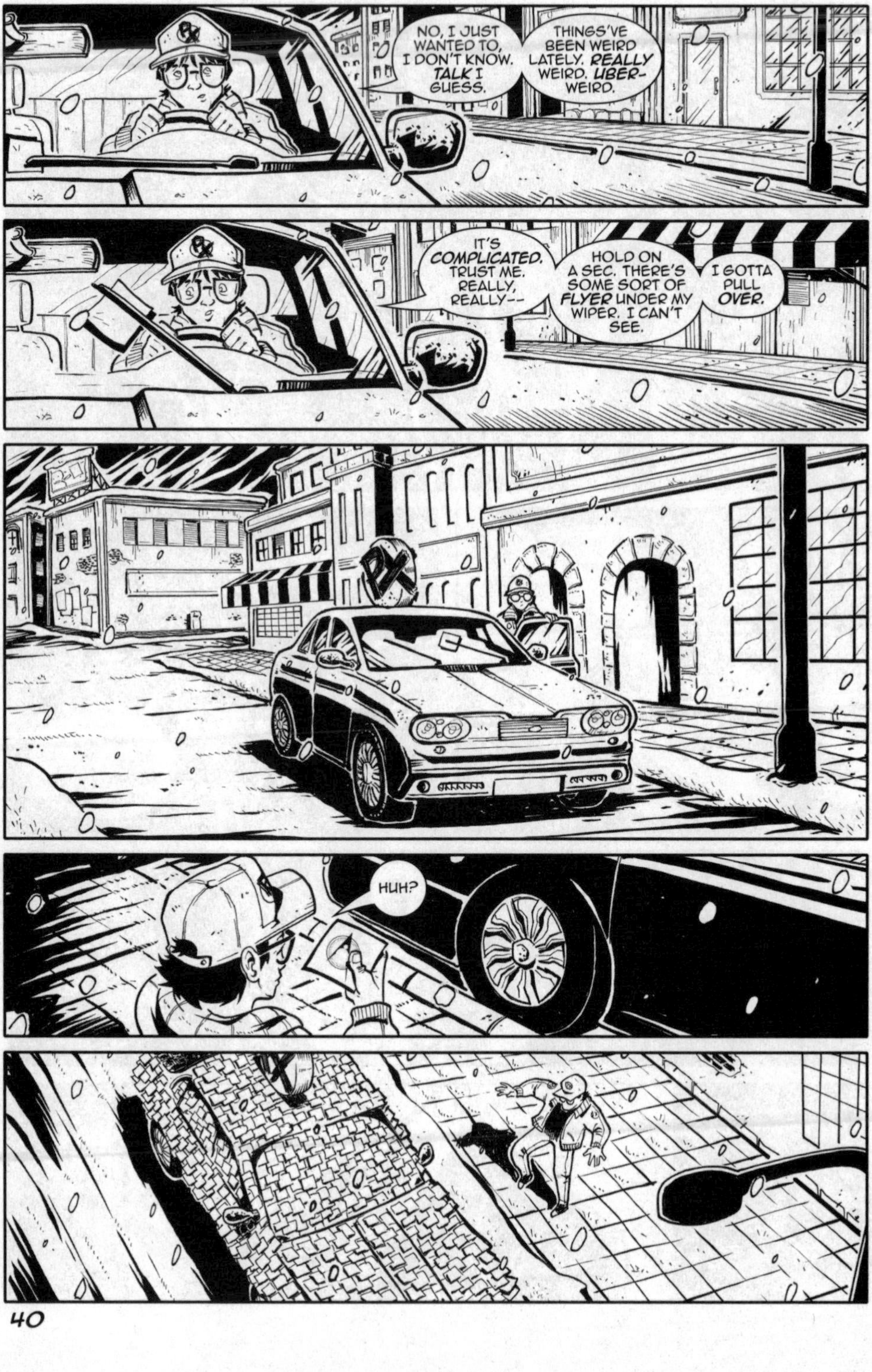
NO, I JUST WANTED TO, I DON'T KNOW. TALK I GUESS.
THINGS'VE BEEN WEIRD LATELY. REALLY WEIRD. UBER-WEIRD.
IT'S COMPLICATED. TRUST ME. REALLY, REALLY--
HOLD ON A SEC. THERE'S SOME SORT OF FLYER UNDER MY WIPER. I CAN'T SEE.
I GOTTA PULL OVER.
HUH?

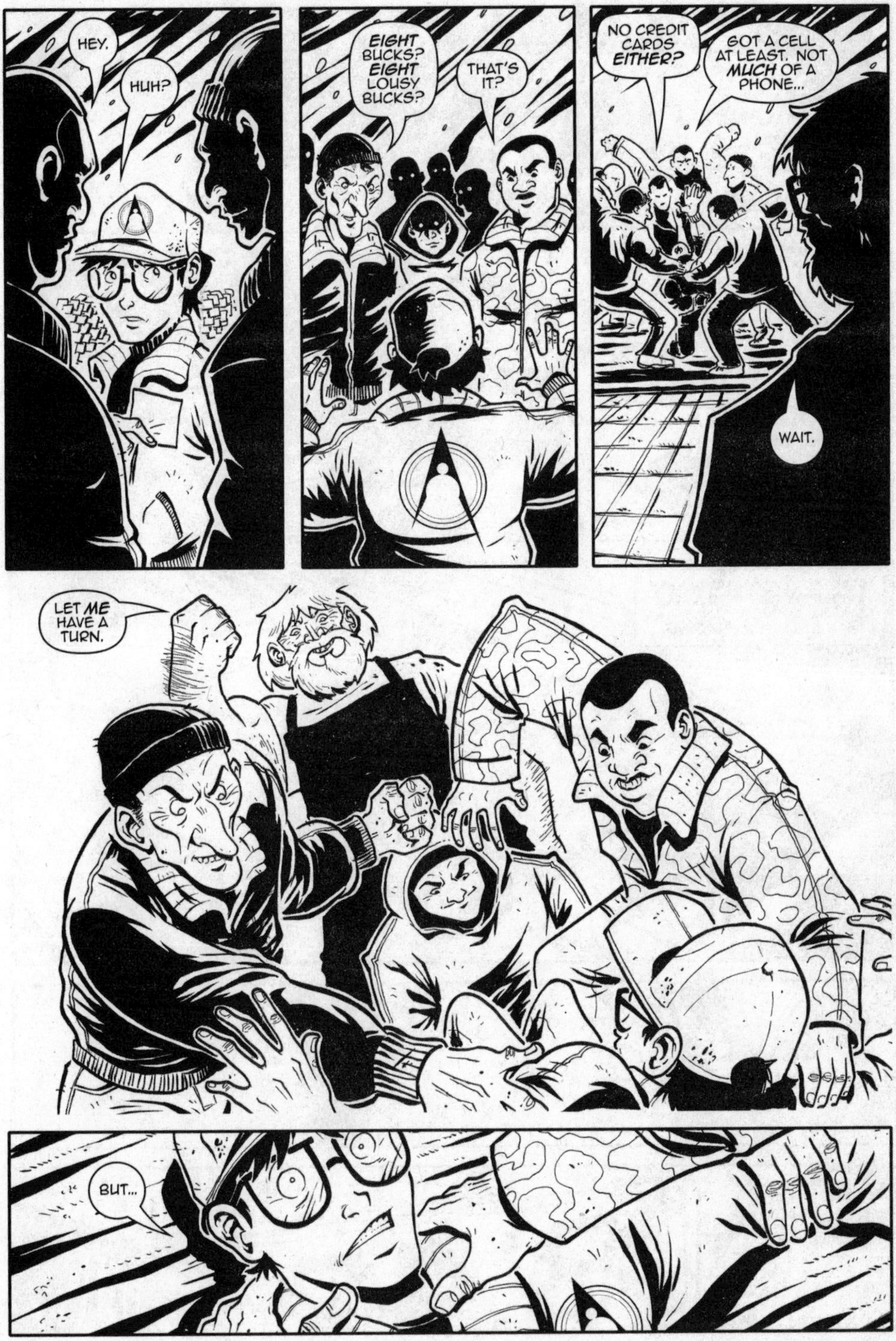
HEY.
HUH?
EIGHT BUCKS? EIGHT LOUSY BUCKS?
THAT'S IT?
NO CREDIT CARDS EITHER?
GOT A CELL AT LEAST. NOT MUCH OF A PHONE...
WAIT.
LET ME HAVE A TURN.
BUT...

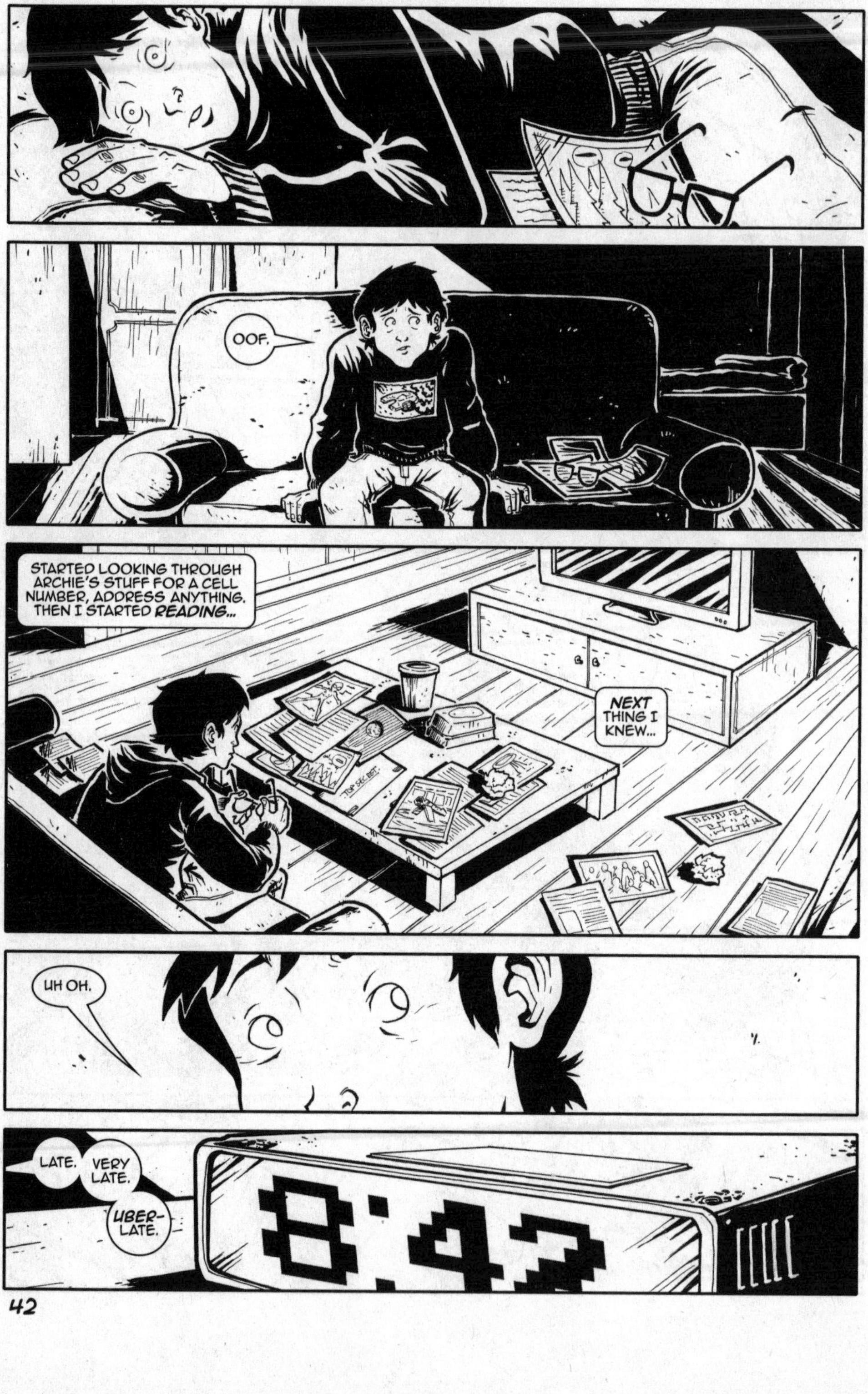
OOF.
STARTED LOOKING THROUGH ARCHIE'S STUFF FOR A CELL NUMBER, ADDRESS ANYTHING. THEN I STARTED *READING*...
NEXT THING I KNEW...
TOP SECRET
UH OH.
LATE.
VERY LATE.
UBER-LATE.
8:42

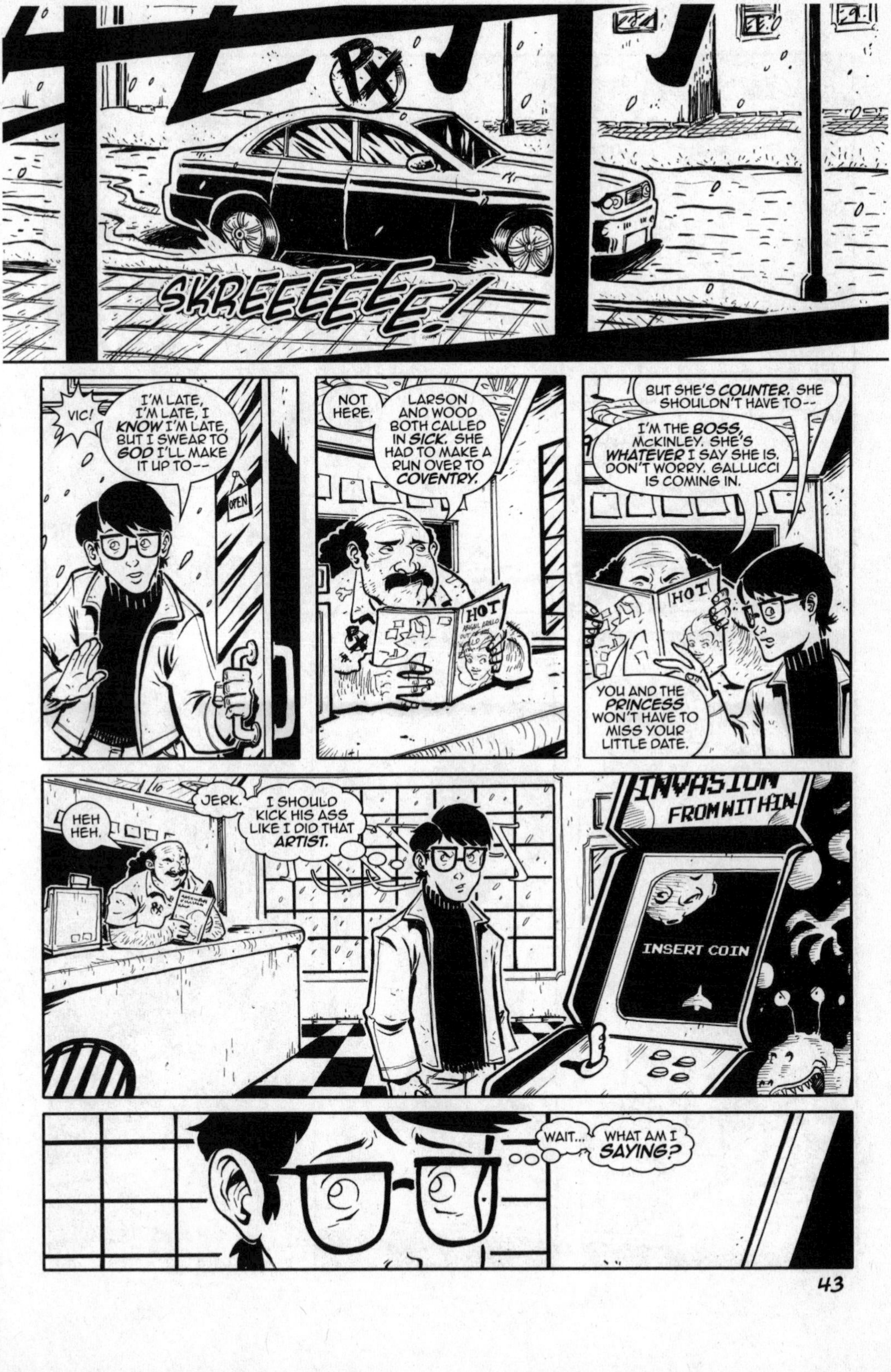
SKREEEEEEEE!
VIC!
I'M LATE, I'M LATE, I KNOW I'M LATE, BUT I SWEAR TO GOD I'LL MAKE IT UP TO--
OPEN
NOT HERE.
LARSON AND WOOD BOTH CALLED IN SICK. SHE HAD TO MAKE A RUN OVER TO COVENTRY.
HOT
BUT SHE'S COUNTER. SHE SHOULDN'T HAVE TO--
I'M THE BOSS, McKINLEY. SHE'S WHATEVER I SAY SHE IS. DON'T WORRY. GALLUCCI IS COMING IN.
HOT
YOU AND THE PRINCESS WON'T HAVE TO MISS YOUR LITTLE DATE.
HEH HEH.
JERK.
I SHOULD KICK HIS ASS LIKE I DID THAT ARTIST.
INVASION FROM WITHIN
INSERT COIN
WAIT...
WHAT AM I SAYING?

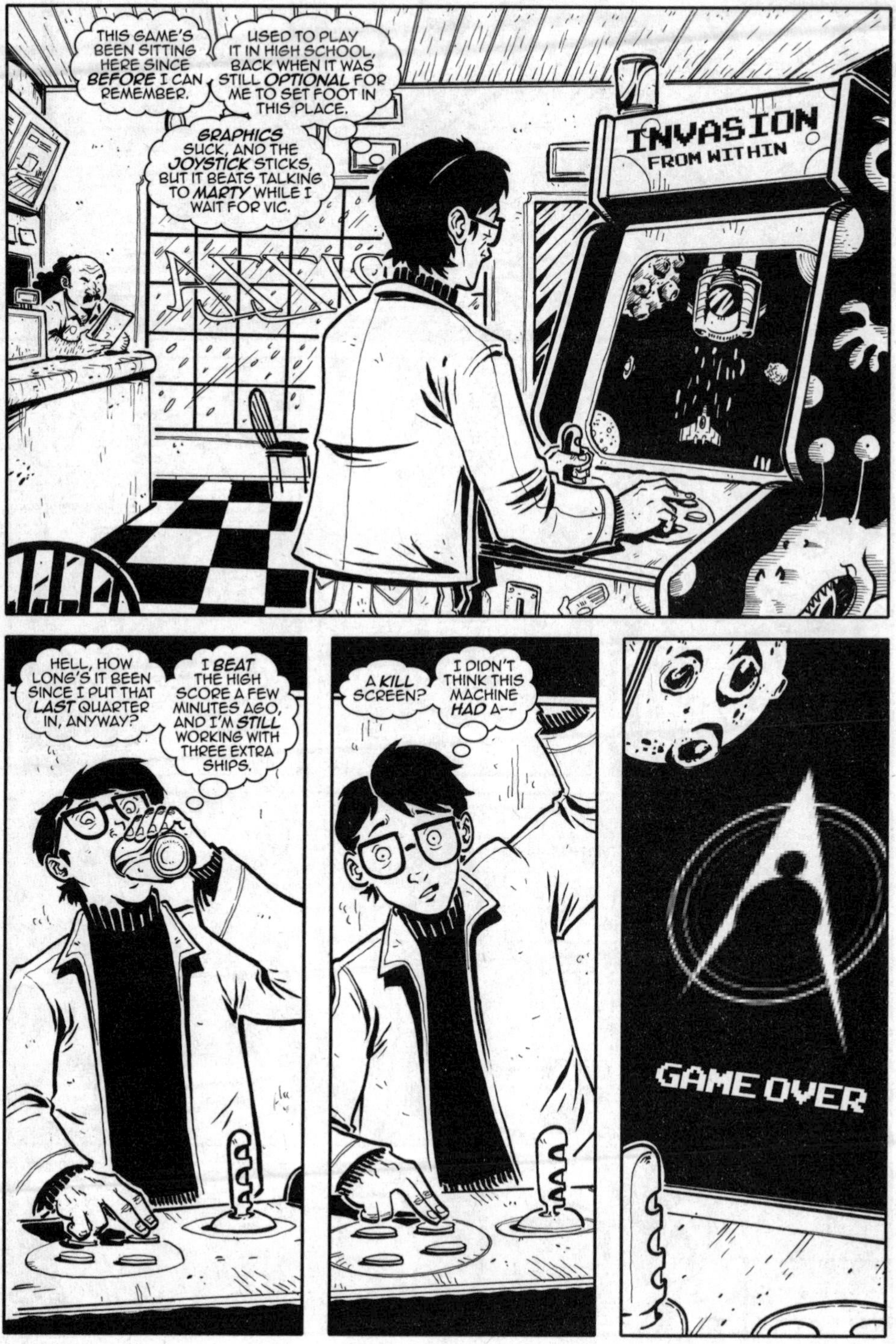
THIS GAME'S BEEN SITTING HERE SINCE BEFORE I CAN REMEMBER.
USED TO PLAY IT IN HIGH SCHOOL, BACK WHEN IT WAS STILL OPTIONAL FOR ME TO SET FOOT IN THIS PLACE.
GRAPHICS SUCK, AND THE JOYSTICK STICKS, BUT IT BEATS TALKING TO MARTY WHILE I WAIT FOR VIC.
INVASION FROM WITHIN
HELL, HOW LONG'S IT BEEN SINCE I PUT THAT LAST QUARTER IN, ANYWAY?
I BEAT THE HIGH SCORE A FEW MINUTES AGO, AND I'M STILL WORKING WITH THREE EXTRA SHIPS.
A KILL SCREEN?
I DIDN'T THINK THIS MACHINE HAD A--
GAME OVER

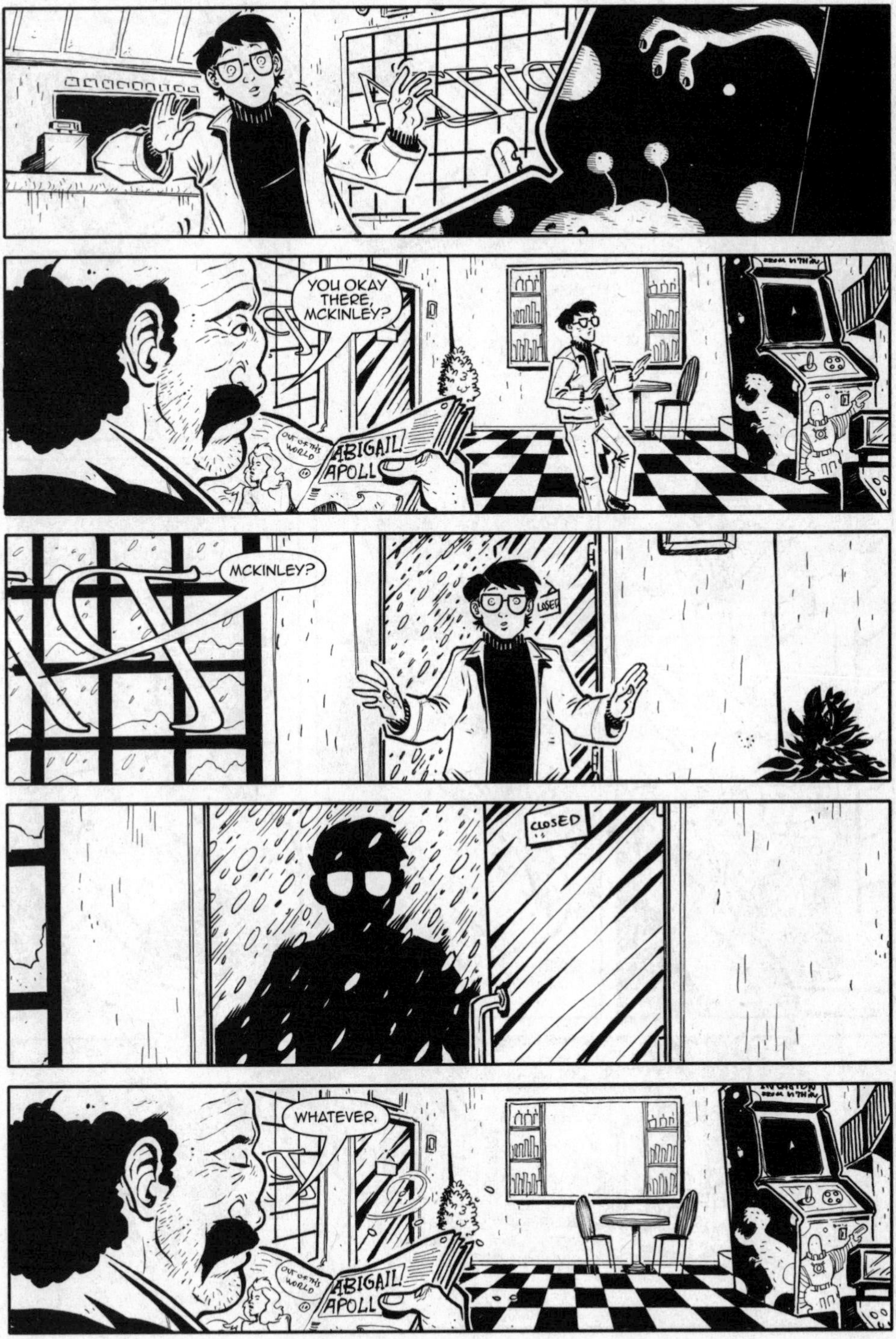
YOU OKAY THERE, MCKINLEY?
ABIGAIL APOLL
MCKINLEY?
CLOSED
WHATEVER.
ABIGAIL APOLL

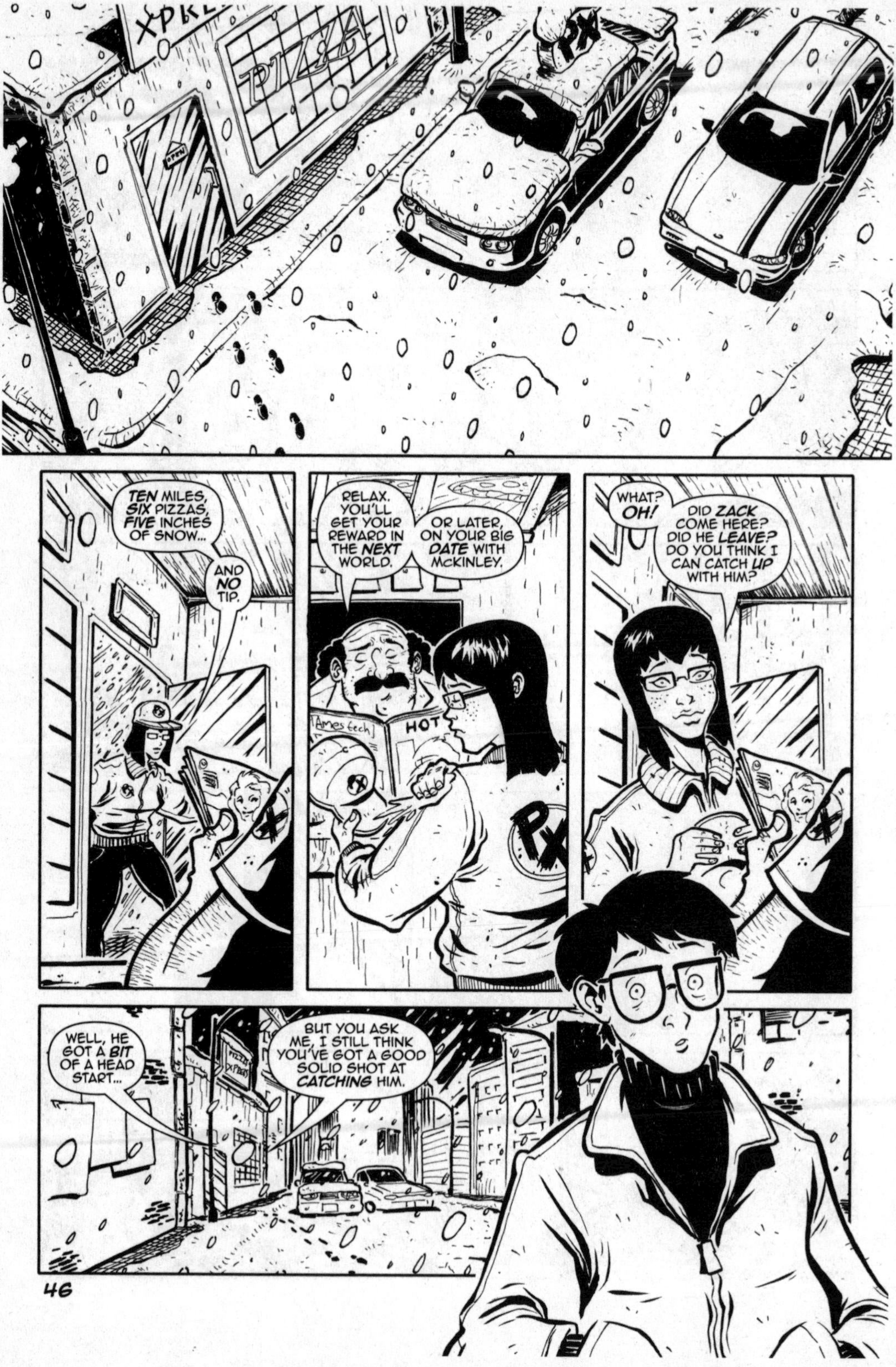

PIZZA
TEN MILES, SIX PIZZAS, FIVE INCHES OF SNOW...
AND NO TIP.
RELAX. YOU'LL GET YOUR REWARD IN THE NEXT WORLD.
OR LATER, ON YOUR BIG DATE WITH McKINLEY.
HOT
WHAT? OH!
DID ZACK COME HERE? DID HE LEAVE? DO YOU THINK I CAN CATCH UP WITH HIM?
WELL, HE GOT A BIT OF A HEAD START...
BUT YOU ASK ME, I STILL THINK YOU'VE GOT A GOOD SOLID SHOT AT CATCHING HIM.

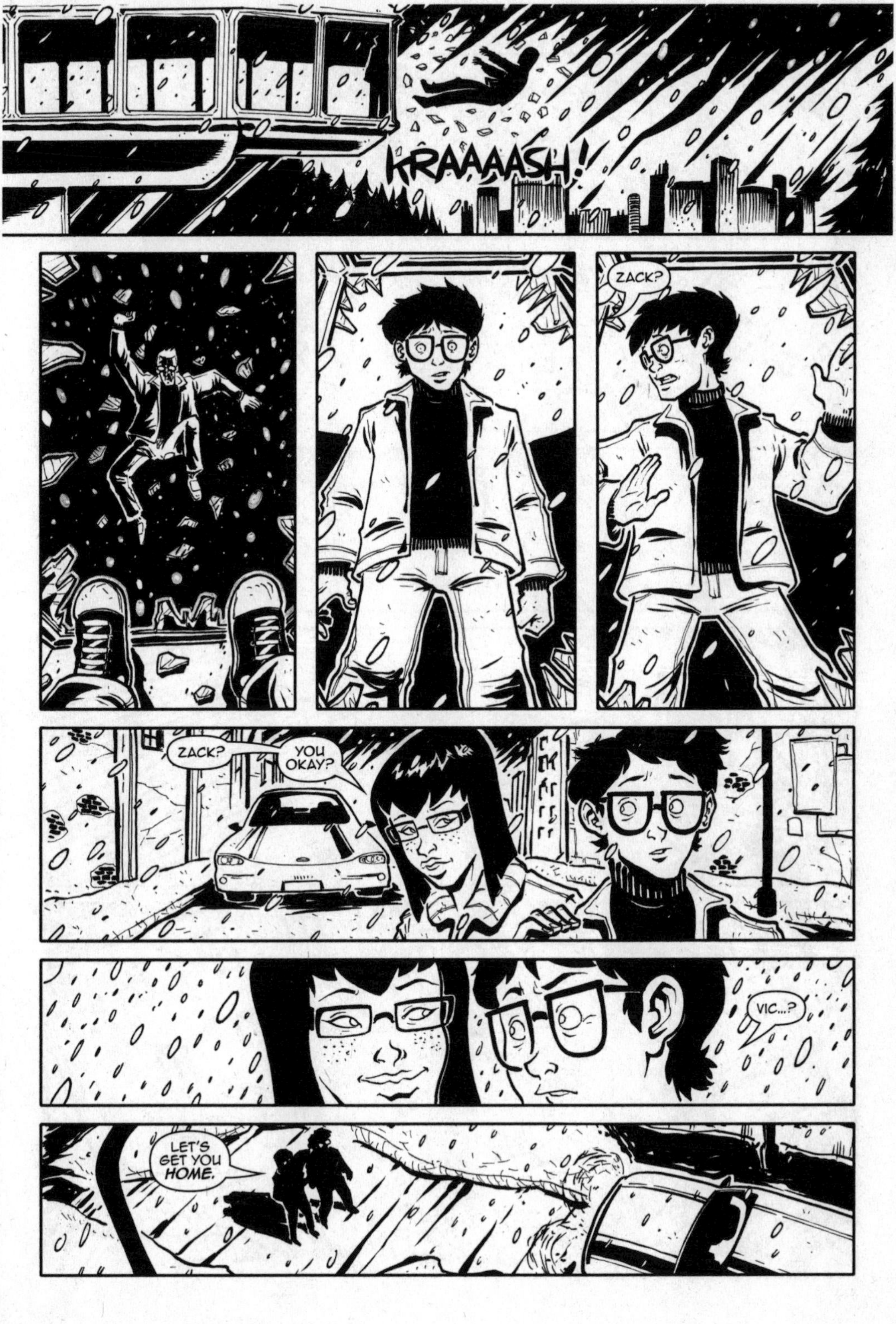
KRAAAASH!
ZACK?
ZACK?
YOU OKAY?
VIC...?
LET'S GET YOU *HOME*.

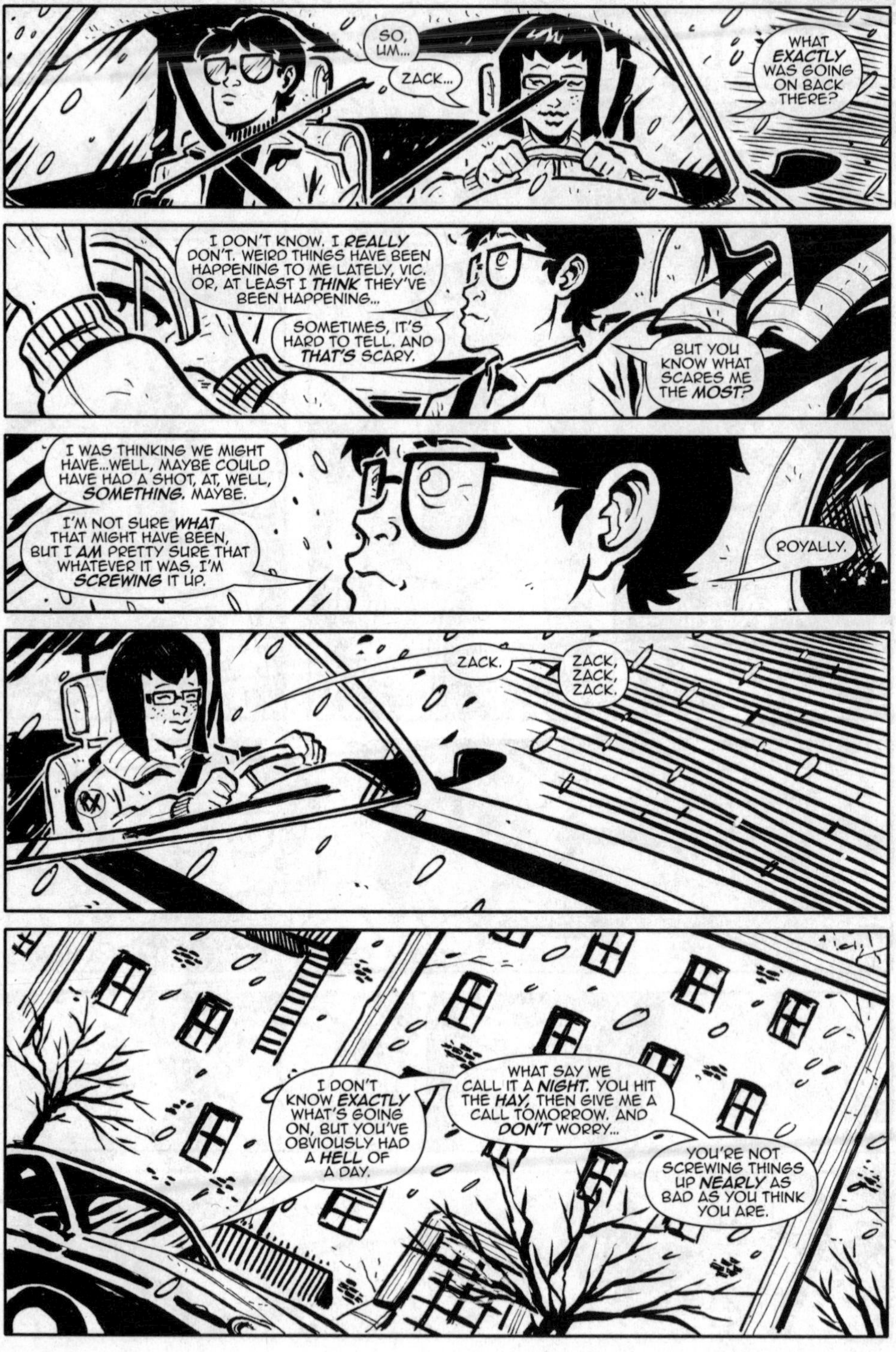
SO, UM...
ZACK...
WHAT EXACTLY WAS GOING ON BACK THERE?
I DON'T KNOW. I REALLY DON'T. WEIRD THINGS HAVE BEEN HAPPENING TO ME LATELY, VIC. OR, AT LEAST I THINK THEY'VE BEEN HAPPENING...
SOMETIMES, IT'S HARD TO TELL. AND THAT'S SCARY.
BUT YOU KNOW WHAT SCARES ME THE MOST?
I WAS THINKING WE MIGHT HAVE...WELL, MAYBE COULD HAVE HAD A SHOT, AT, WELL, SOMETHING. MAYBE.
I'M NOT SURE WHAT THAT MIGHT HAVE BEEN, BUT I AM PRETTY SURE THAT WHATEVER IT WAS, I'M SCREWING IT UP.
ROYALLY.
ZACK.
ZACK, ZACK, ZACK.
I DON'T KNOW EXACTLY WHAT'S GOING ON, BUT YOU'VE OBVIOUSLY HAD A HELL OF A DAY.
WHAT SAY WE CALL IT A NIGHT. YOU HIT THE HAY, THEN GIVE ME A CALL TOMORROW. AND DON'T WORRY...
YOU'RE NOT SCREWING THINGS UP NEARLY AS BAD AS YOU THINK YOU ARE.

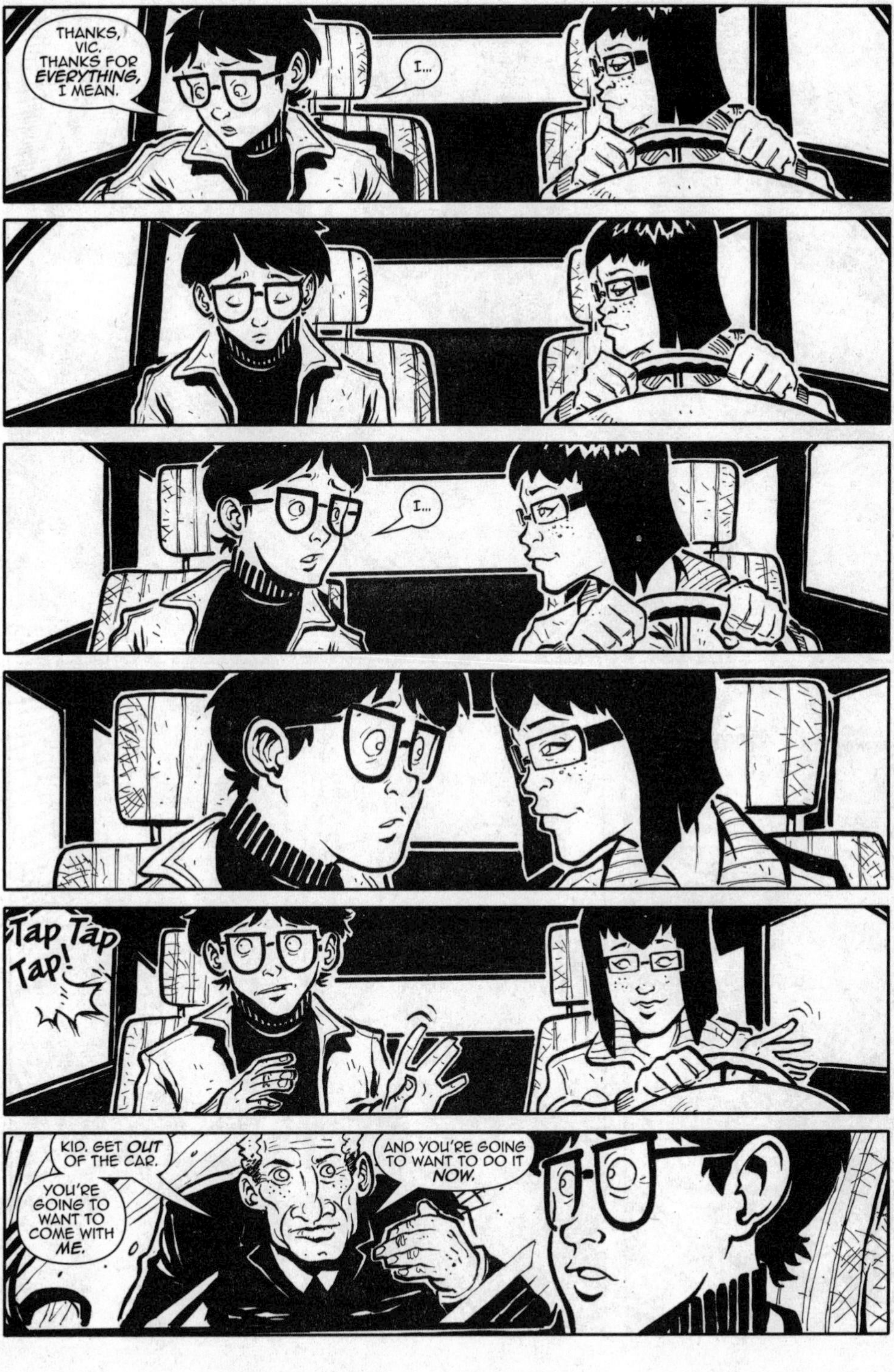
THANKS, VIC. THANKS FOR EVERYTHING, I MEAN.
I...
I...
Tap Tap Tap!
KID. GET OUT OF THE CAR.
YOU'RE GOING TO WANT TO COME WITH ME.
AND YOU'RE GOING TO WANT TO DO IT NOW.

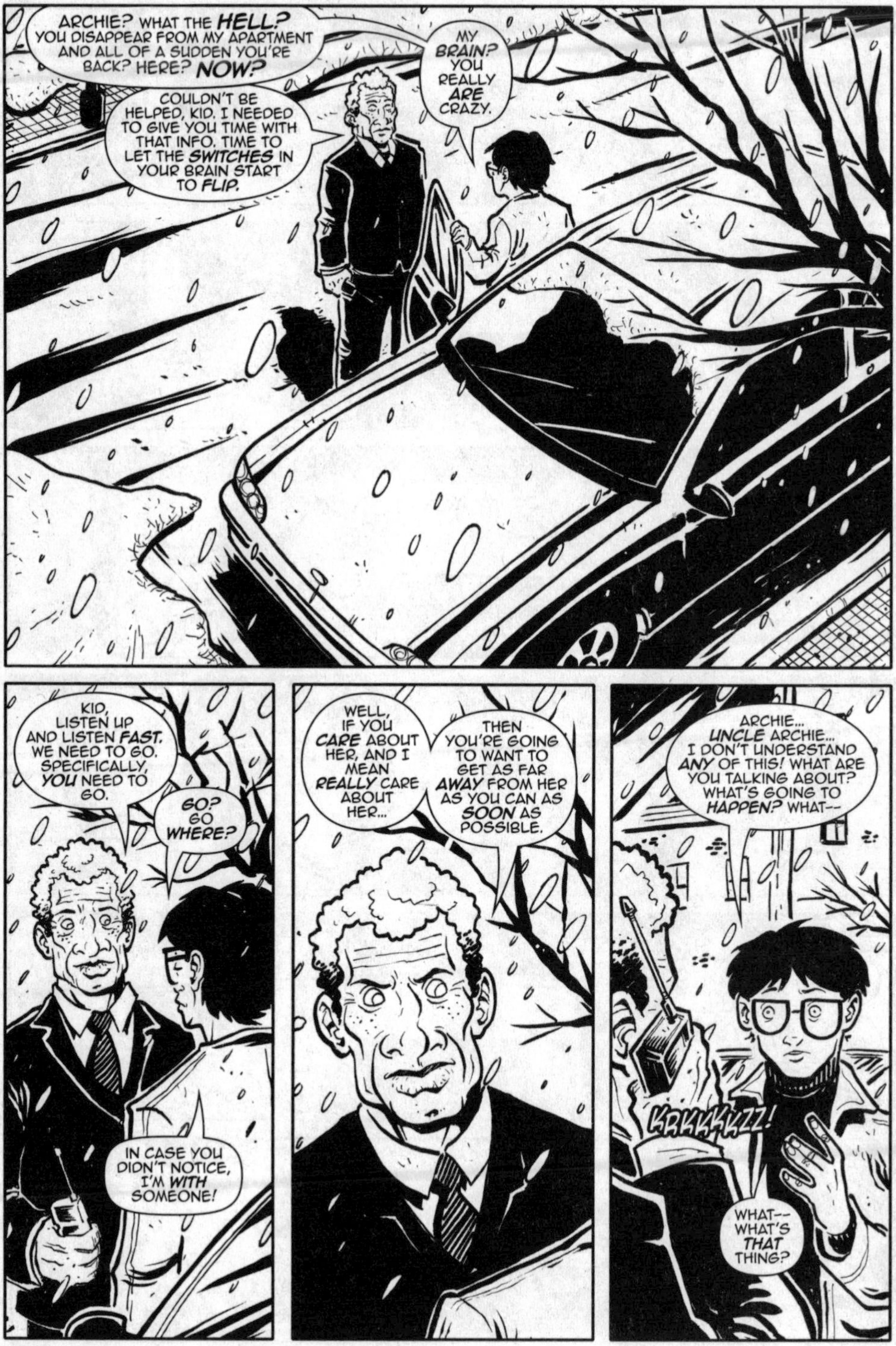
ARCHIE? WHAT THE HELL? YOU DISAPPEAR FROM MY APARTMENT AND ALL OF A SUDDEN YOU'RE BACK? HERE? NOW?
COULDN'T BE HELPED, KID. I NEEDED TO GIVE YOU TIME WITH THAT INFO. TIME TO LET THE SWITCHES IN YOUR BRAIN START TO FLIP.
MY BRAIN? YOU REALLY ARE CRAZY.
KID, LISTEN UP AND LISTEN FAST. WE NEED TO GO. SPECIFICALLY, YOU NEED TO GO.
GO? GO WHERE?
IN CASE YOU DIDN'T NOTICE, I'M WITH SOMEONE!
WELL, IF YOU CARE ABOUT HER, AND I MEAN REALLY CARE ABOUT HER...
THEN YOU'RE GOING TO WANT TO GET AS FAR AWAY FROM HER AS YOU CAN AS SOON AS POSSIBLE.
ARCHIE... UNCLE ARCHIE... I DON'T UNDERSTAND ANY OF THIS! WHAT ARE YOU TALKING ABOUT? WHAT'S GOING TO HAPPEN? WHAT--
KRKKKKZZ!
WHAT-- WHAT'S THAT THING?

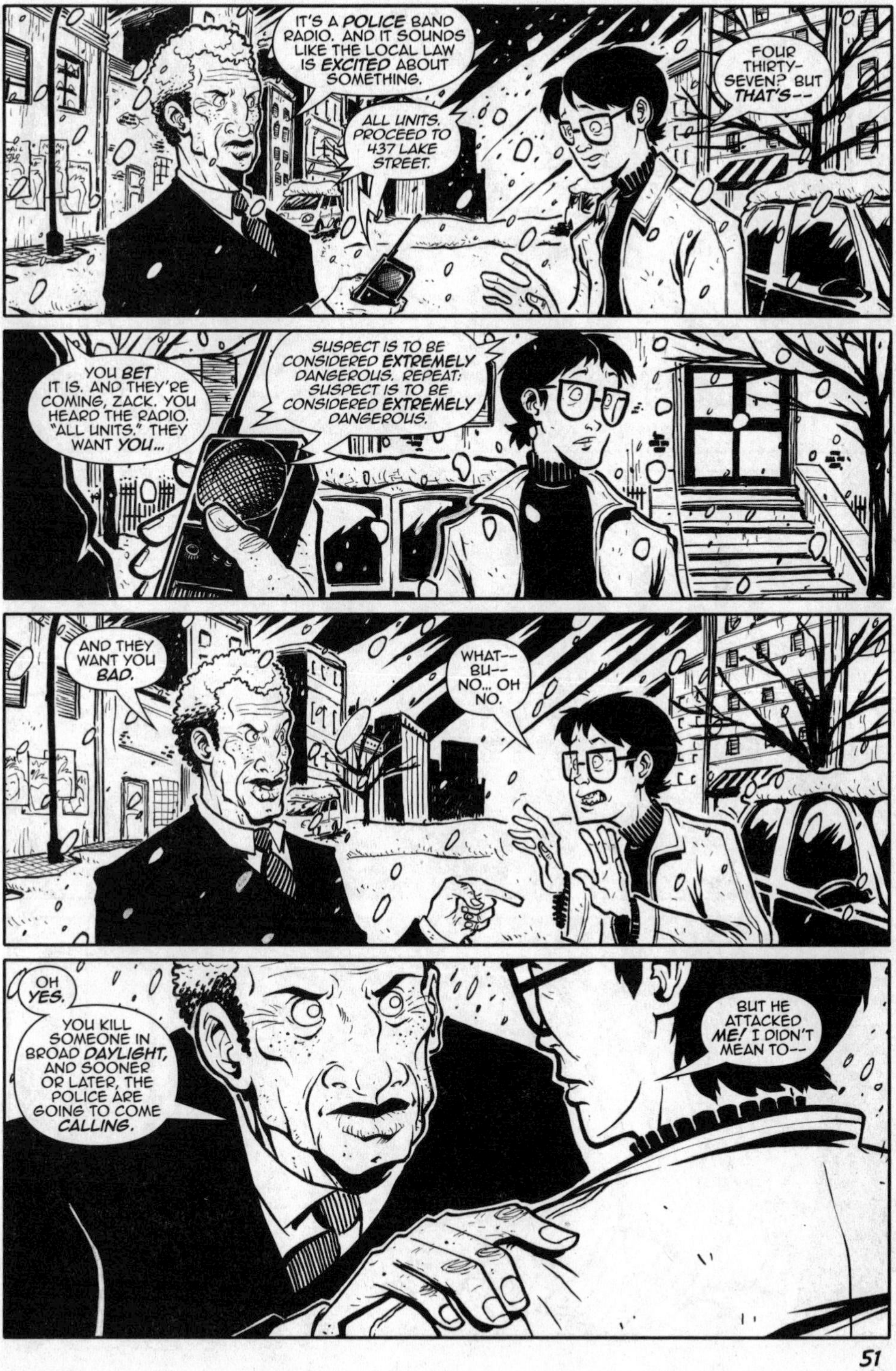
IT'S A POLICE BAND RADIO. AND IT SOUNDS LIKE THE LOCAL LAW IS EXCITED ABOUT SOMETHING.
ALL UNITS. PROCEED TO 437 LAKE STREET.
FOUR THIRTY-SEVEN? BUT THAT'S--
SUSPECT IS TO BE CONSIDERED EXTREMELY DANGEROUS. REPEAT: SUSPECT IS TO BE CONSIDERED EXTREMELY DANGEROUS.
YOU BET IT IS. AND THEY'RE COMING, ZACK. YOU HEARD THE RADIO. "ALL UNITS." THEY WANT YOU...
AND THEY WANT YOU BAD.
WHAT--BU--NO... OH NO.
OH YES.
YOU KILL SOMEONE IN BROAD DAYLIGHT, AND SOONER OR LATER, THE POLICE ARE GOING TO COME CALLING.
BUT HE ATTACKED ME! I DIDN'T MEAN TO--

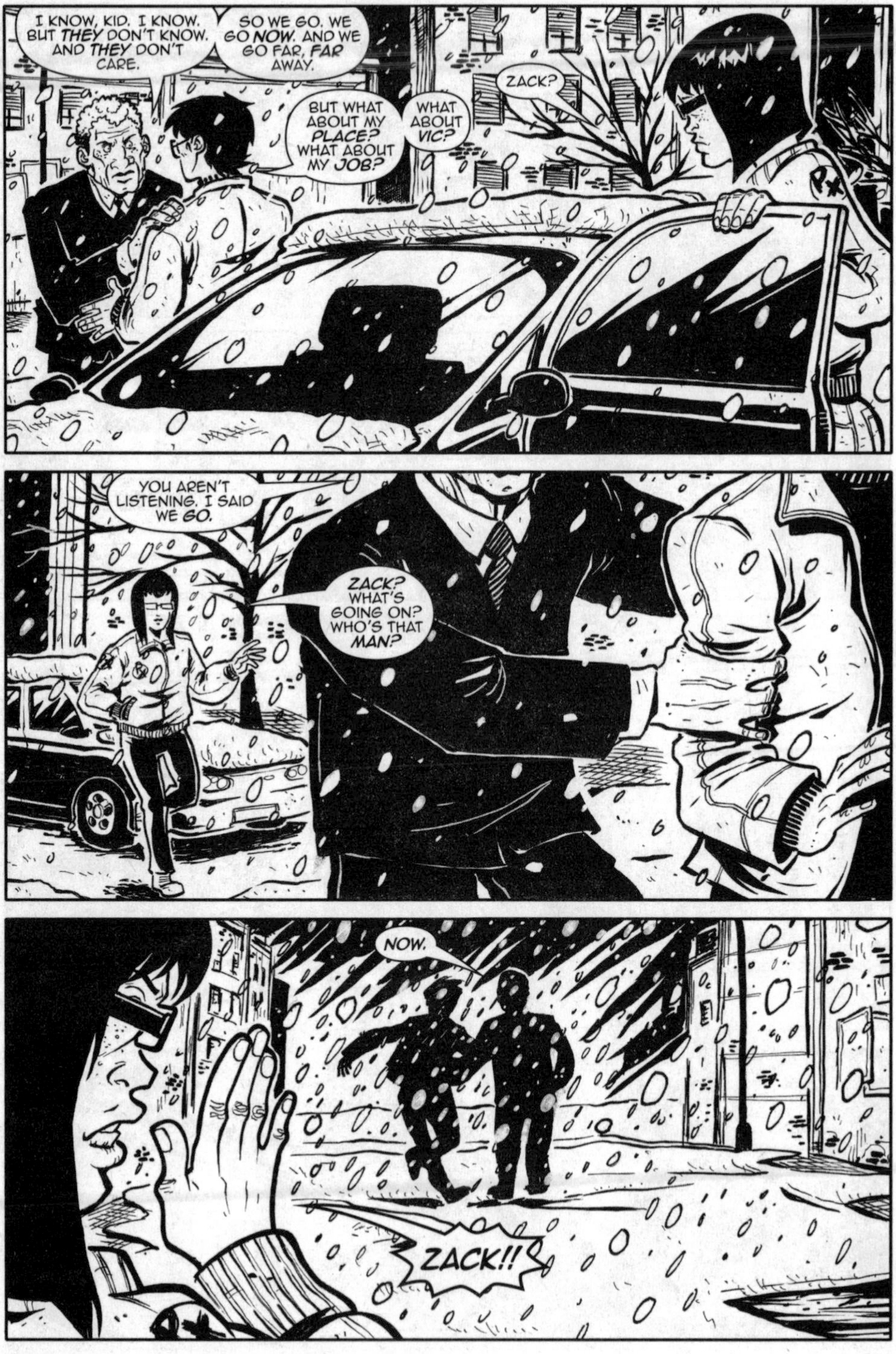
I KNOW, KID. I KNOW. BUT THEY DON'T KNOW. AND THEY DON'T CARE.
SO WE GO. WE GO NOW. AND WE GO FAR, FAR AWAY.
BUT WHAT ABOUT MY PLACE? WHAT ABOUT MY JOB?
WHAT ABOUT VIC?
ZACK?
YOU AREN'T LISTENING. I SAID WE GO.
ZACK? WHAT'S GOING ON? WHO'S THAT MAN?
NOW.
ZACK!!

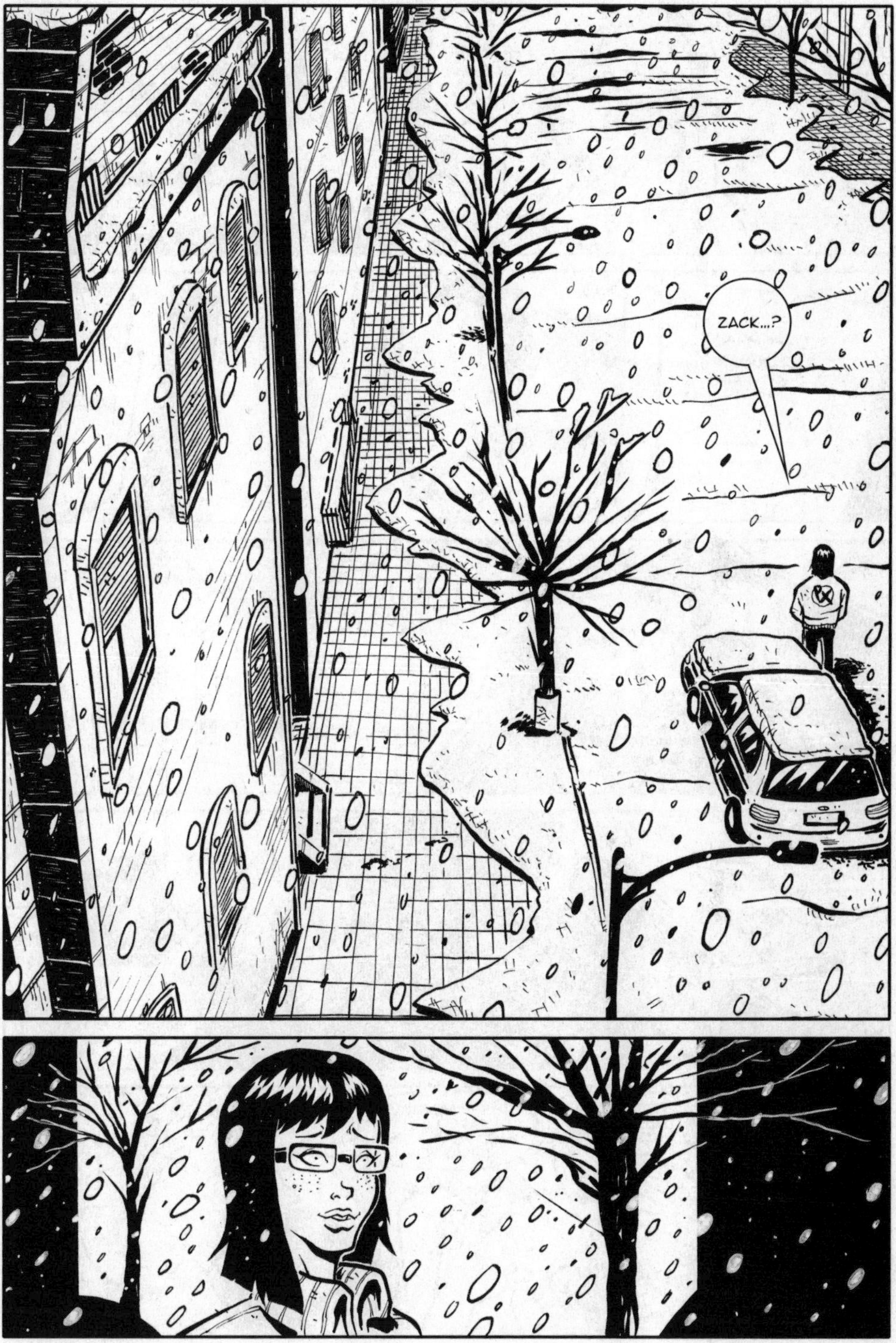
ZACK...?

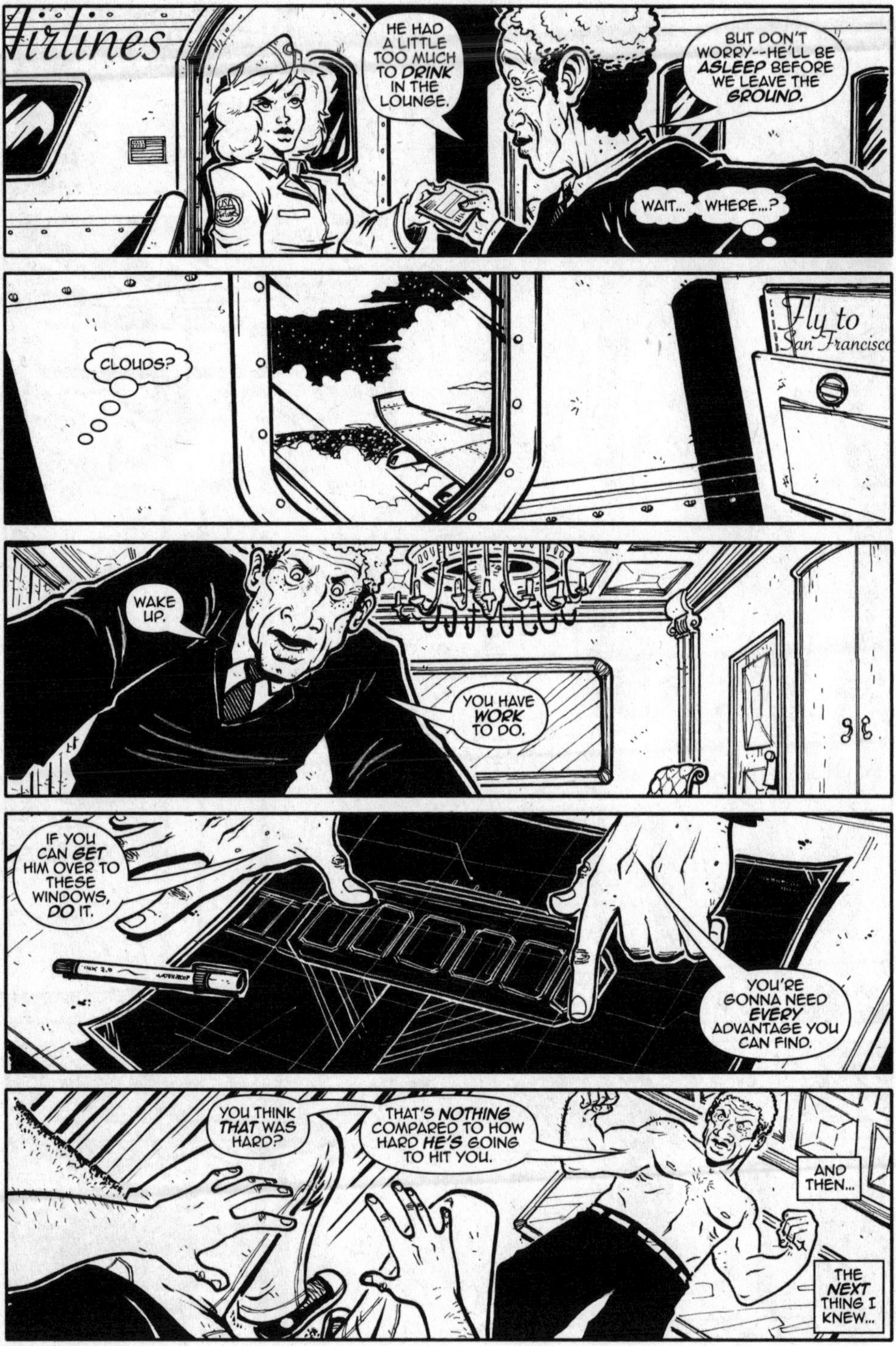

Airlines
HE HAD A LITTLE TOO MUCH TO DRINK IN THE LOUNGE.
BUT DON'T WORRY--HE'LL BE ASLEEP BEFORE WE LEAVE THE GROUND.
WAIT...
WHERE...?
CLOUDS?
Fly to San Francisco
WAKE UP.
YOU HAVE WORK TO DO.
IF YOU CAN GET HIM OVER TO THESE WINDOWS, DO IT.
YOU'RE GONNA NEED EVERY ADVANTAGE YOU CAN FIND.
YOU THINK THAT WAS HARD?
THAT'S NOTHING COMPARED TO HOW HARD HE'S GOING TO HIT YOU.
AND THEN...
THE NEXT THING I KNEW...

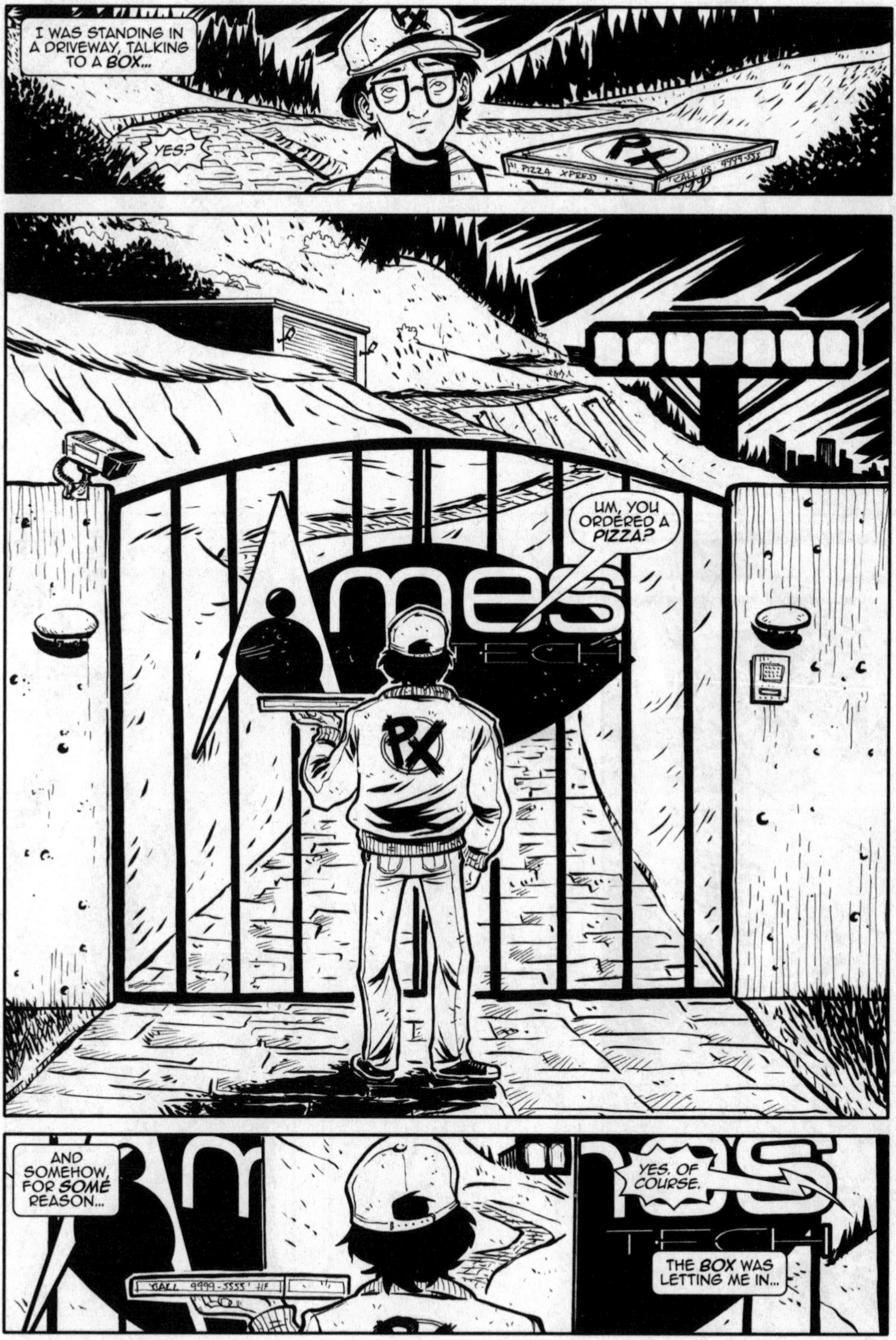
I WAS STANDING IN A DRIVEWAY, TALKING TO A BOX...
YES?
PIZZA XPRESS
UM, YOU ORDERED A PIZZA?
AND SOMEHOW, FOR SOME REASON...
YES. OF COURSE.
THE BOX WAS LETTING ME IN...

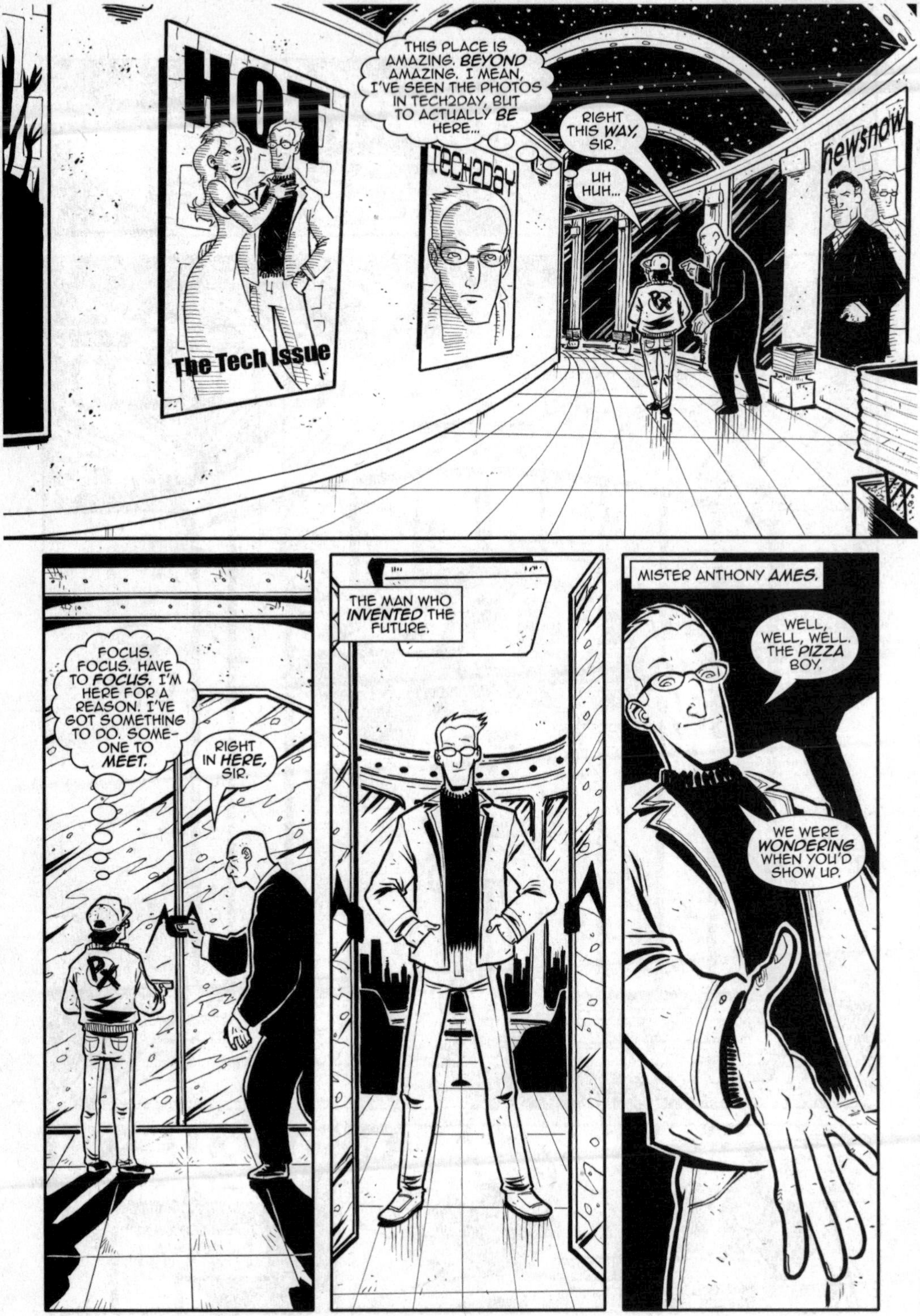
THIS PLACE IS AMAZING. BEYOND AMAZING. I MEAN, I'VE SEEN THE PHOTOS IN TECH2DAY, BUT TO ACTUALLY BE HERE...
RIGHT THIS WAY, SIR.
UH HUH...
HOT
The Tech Issue
TECH2DAY
newsnow
FOCUS. FOCUS. HAVE TO FOCUS. I'M HERE FOR A REASON. I'VE GOT SOMETHING TO DO. SOME-ONE TO MEET.
RIGHT IN HERE, SIR.
THE MAN WHO INVENTED THE FUTURE.
MISTER ANTHONY AMES.
WELL, WELL, WELL. THE PIZZA BOY.
WE WERE WONDERING WHEN YOU'D SHOW UP.

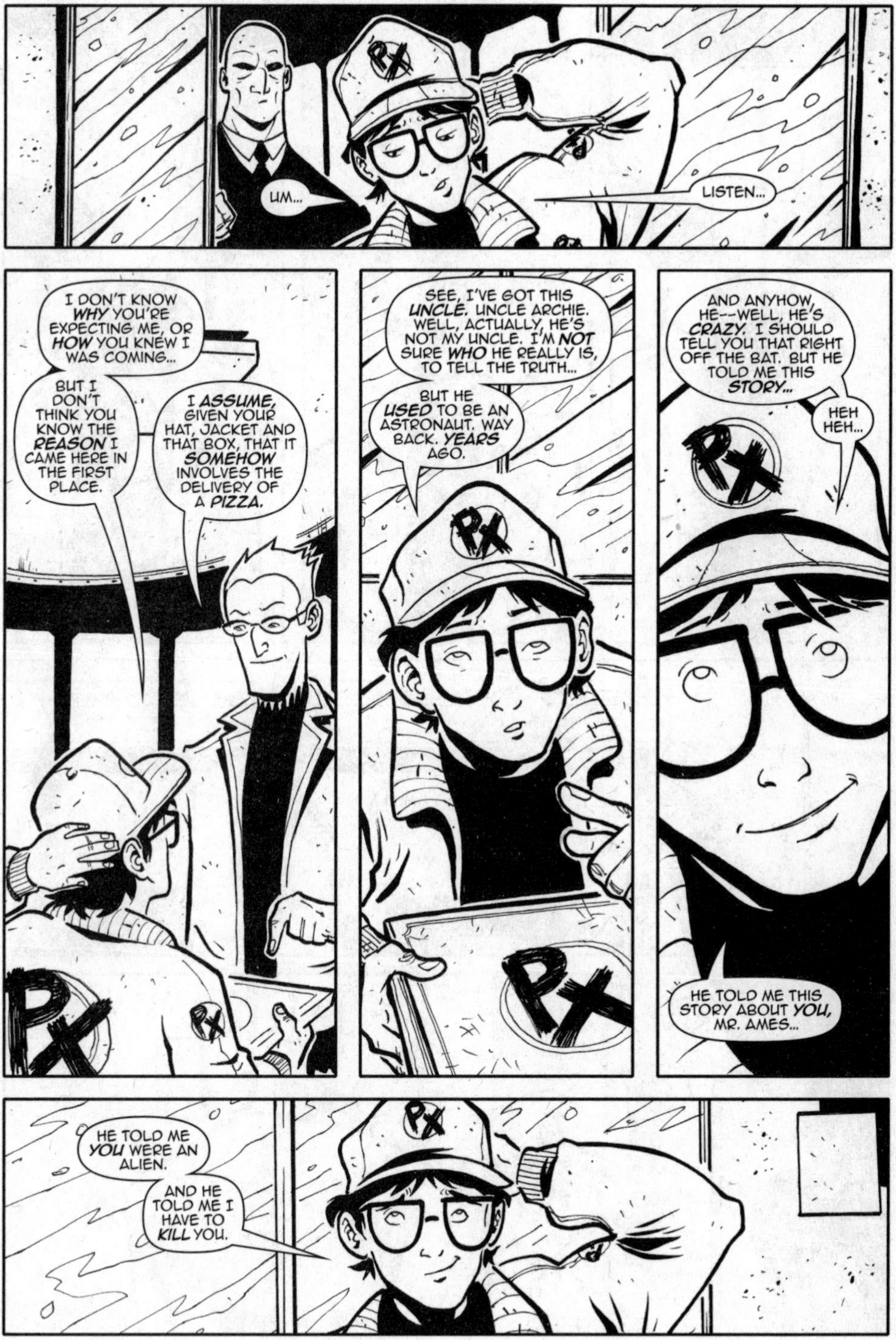
UM...
LISTEN...
I DON'T KNOW WHY YOU'RE EXPECTING ME, OR HOW YOU KNEW I WAS COMING...
BUT I DON'T THINK YOU KNOW THE REASON I CAME HERE IN THE FIRST PLACE.
I ASSUME, GIVEN YOUR HAT, JACKET AND THAT BOX, THAT IT SOMEHOW INVOLVES THE DELIVERY OF A PIZZA.
SEE, I'VE GOT THIS UNCLE. UNCLE ARCHIE. WELL, ACTUALLY, HE'S NOT MY UNCLE. I'M NOT SURE WHO HE REALLY IS, TO TELL THE TRUTH...
BUT HE USED TO BE AN ASTRONAUT. WAY BACK. YEARS AGO.
AND ANYHOW, HE--WELL, HE'S CRAZY. I SHOULD TELL YOU THAT RIGHT OFF THE BAT. BUT HE TOLD ME THIS STORY...
HEH HEH...
HE TOLD ME THIS STORY ABOUT YOU, MR. AMES...
HE TOLD ME YOU WERE AN ALIEN.
AND HE TOLD ME I HAVE TO KILL YOU.

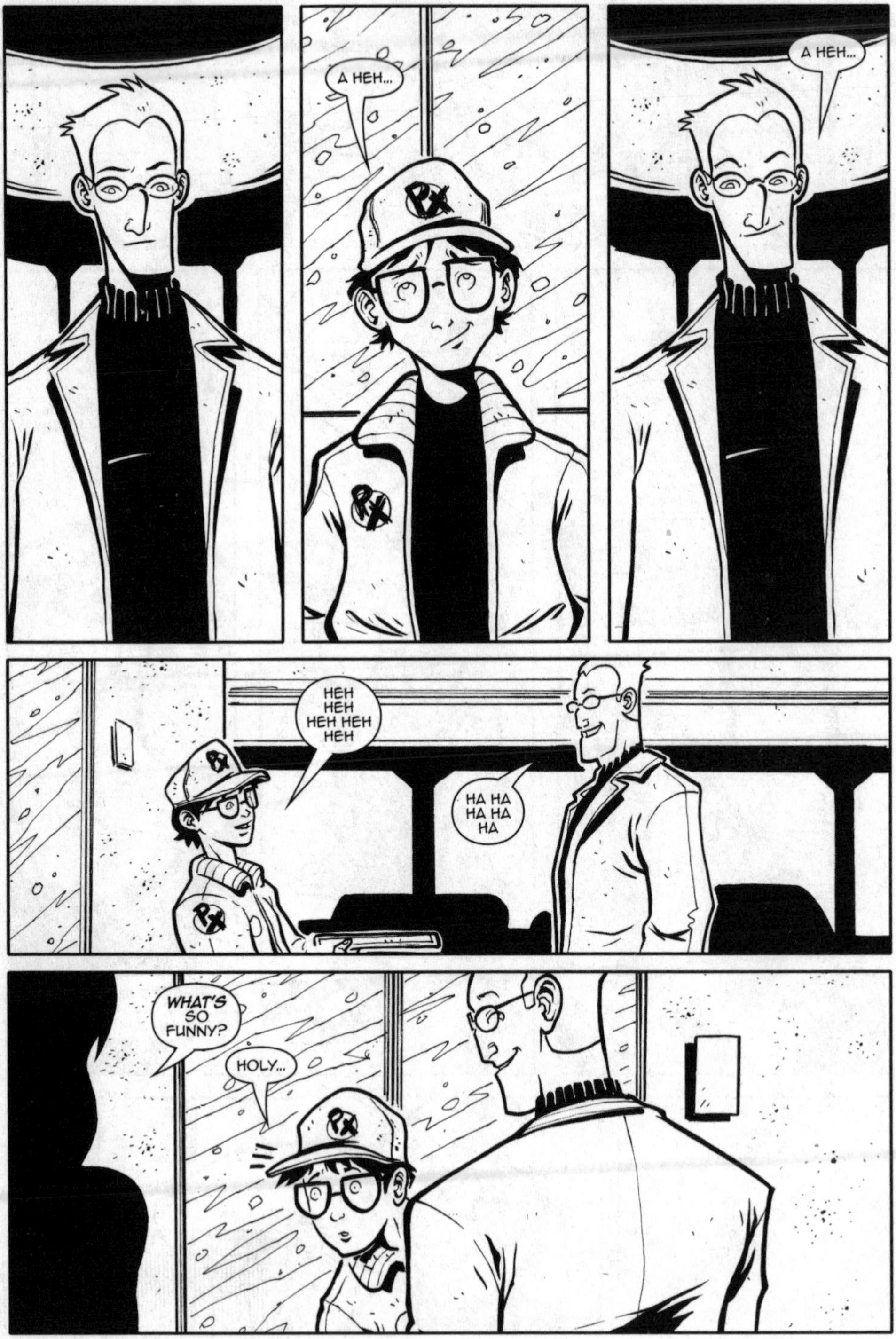
A HEH...
A HEH...
HEH HEH HEH HEH HEH
HA HA HA HA HA
WHAT'S SO FUNNY?
HOLY...

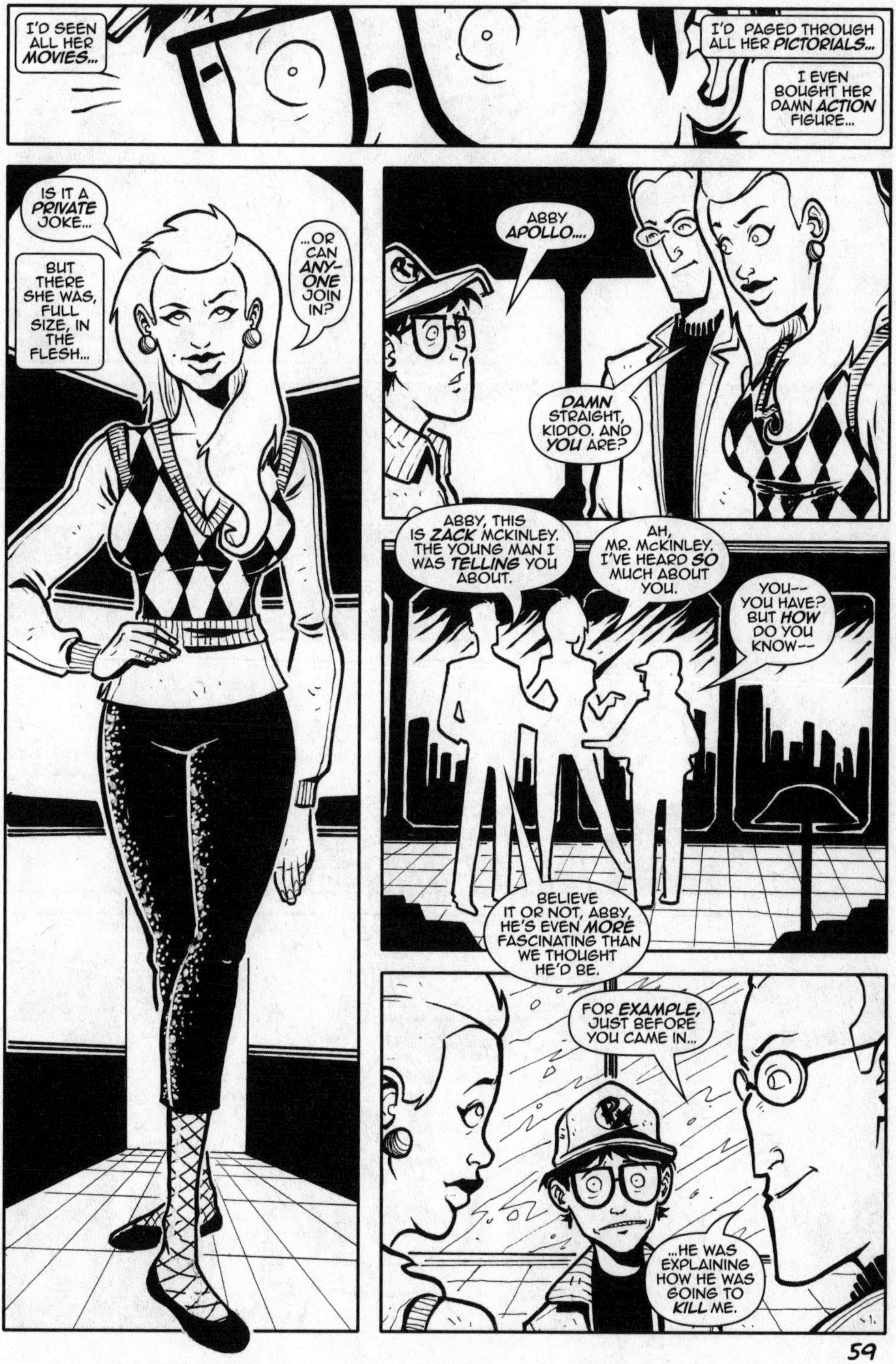

I'D SEEN ALL HER MOVIES...
I'D PAGED THROUGH ALL HER PICTORIALS...
I EVEN BOUGHT HER DAMN ACTION FIGURE...
IS IT A PRIVATE JOKE...
BUT THERE SHE WAS, FULL SIZE, IN THE FLESH...
...OR CAN ANY-ONE JOIN IN?
ABBY APOLLO....
DAMN STRAIGHT, KIDDO. AND YOU ARE?
ABBY, THIS IS ZACK McKINLEY. THE YOUNG MAN I WAS TELLING YOU ABOUT.
AH, MR. McKINLEY. I'VE HEARD SO MUCH ABOUT YOU.
YOU-- YOU HAVE? BUT HOW DO YOU KNOW--
BELIEVE IT OR NOT, ABBY, HE'S EVEN MORE FASCINATING THAN WE THOUGHT HE'D BE.
FOR EXAMPLE, JUST BEFORE YOU CAME IN...
...HE WAS EXPLAINING HOW HE WAS GOING TO KILL ME.

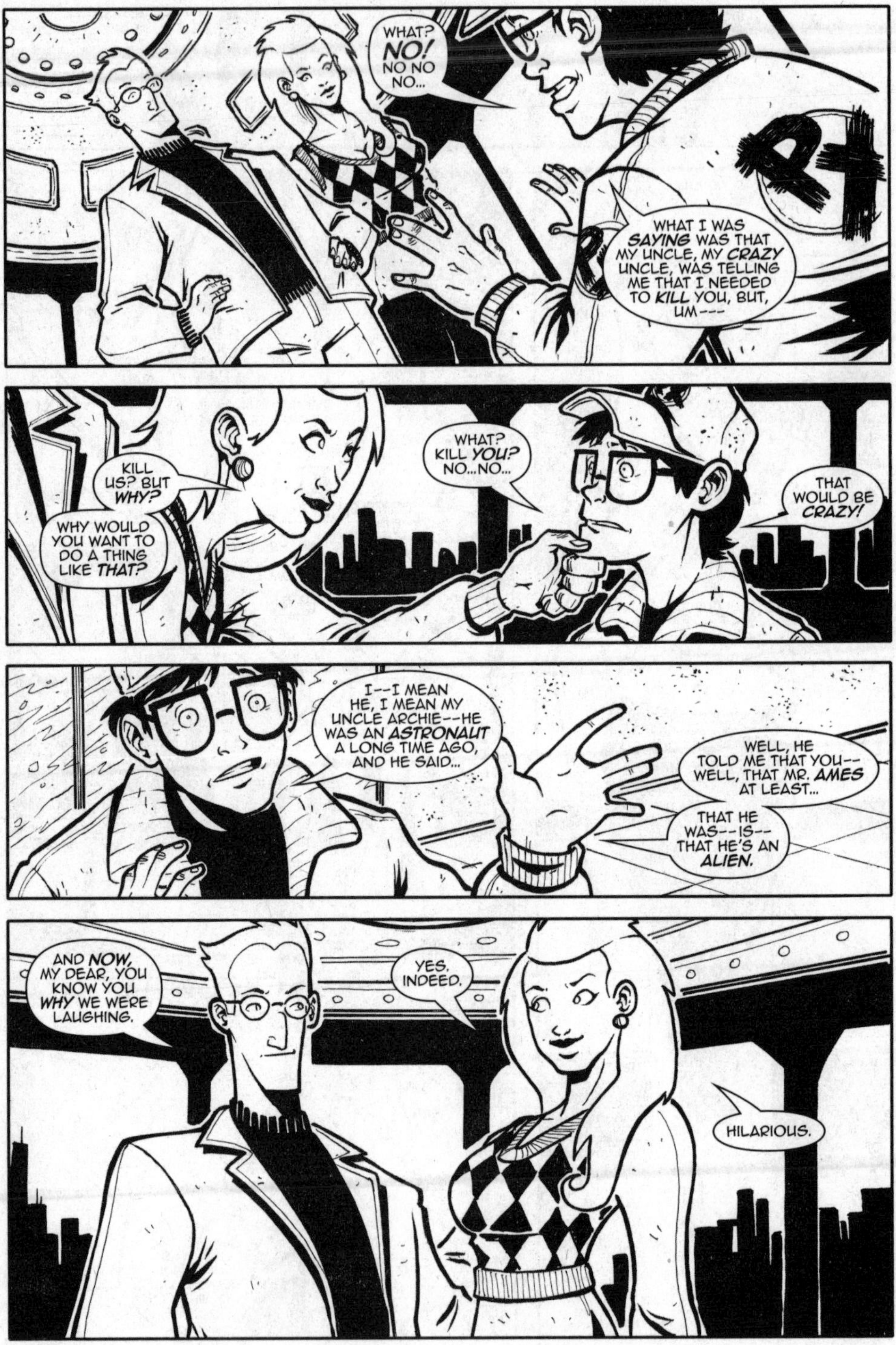
WHAT? NO! NO NO NO...
WHAT I WAS SAYING WAS THAT MY UNCLE, MY CRAZY UNCLE, WAS TELLING ME THAT I NEEDED TO KILL YOU, BUT, UM---
KILL US? BUT WHY?
WHY WOULD YOU WANT TO DO A THING LIKE THAT?
WHAT? KILL YOU? NO...NO...
THAT WOULD BE CRAZY!
I--I MEAN HE, I MEAN MY UNCLE ARCHIE--HE WAS AN ASTRONAUT A LONG TIME AGO, AND HE SAID...
WELL, HE TOLD ME THAT YOU--WELL, THAT MR. AMES AT LEAST...
THAT HE WAS--IS--THAT HE'S AN ALIEN.
AND NOW, MY DEAR, YOU KNOW YOU WHY WE WERE LAUGHING.
YES. INDEED.
HILARIOUS.

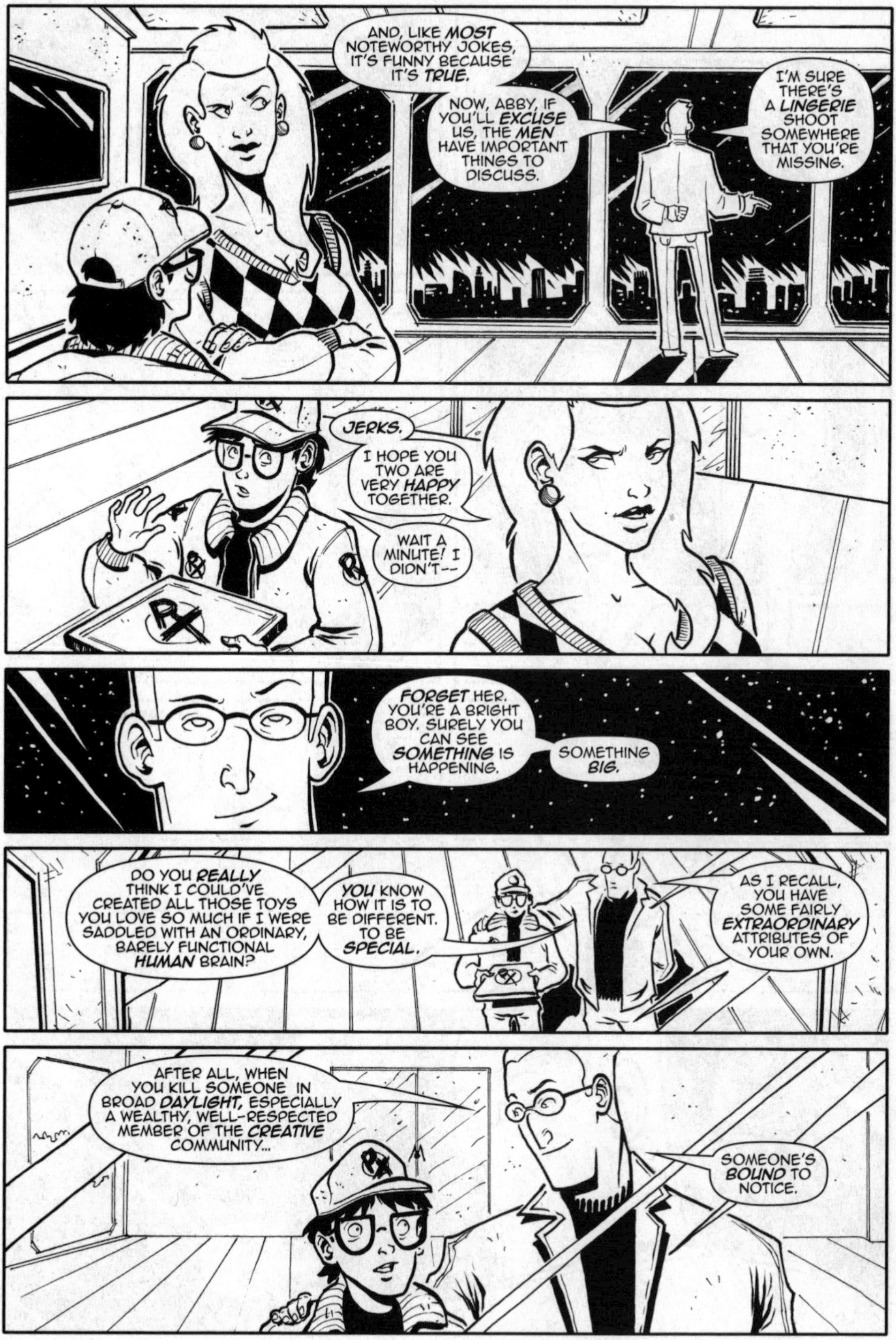
AND, LIKE MOST NOTEWORTHY JOKES, IT'S FUNNY BECAUSE IT'S TRUE.
NOW, ABBY, IF YOU'LL EXCUSE US, THE MEN HAVE IMPORTANT THINGS TO DISCUSS.
I'M SURE THERE'S A LINGERIE SHOOT SOMEWHERE THAT YOU'RE MISSING.
JERKS.
I HOPE YOU TWO ARE VERY HAPPY TOGETHER.
WAIT A MINUTE! I DIDN'T--
FORGET HER. YOU'RE A BRIGHT BOY. SURELY YOU CAN SEE SOMETHING IS HAPPENING.
SOMETHING BIG.
DO YOU REALLY THINK I COULD'VE CREATED ALL THOSE TOYS YOU LOVE SO MUCH IF I WERE SADDLED WITH AN ORDINARY, BARELY FUNCTIONAL HUMAN BRAIN?
YOU KNOW HOW IT IS TO BE DIFFERENT. TO BE SPECIAL.
AS I RECALL, YOU HAVE SOME FAIRLY EXTRAORDINARY ATTRIBUTES OF YOUR OWN.
AFTER ALL, WHEN YOU KILL SOMEONE IN BROAD DAYLIGHT, ESPECIALLY A WEALTHY, WELL-RESPECTED MEMBER OF THE CREATIVE COMMUNITY...
SOMEONE'S BOUND TO NOTICE.

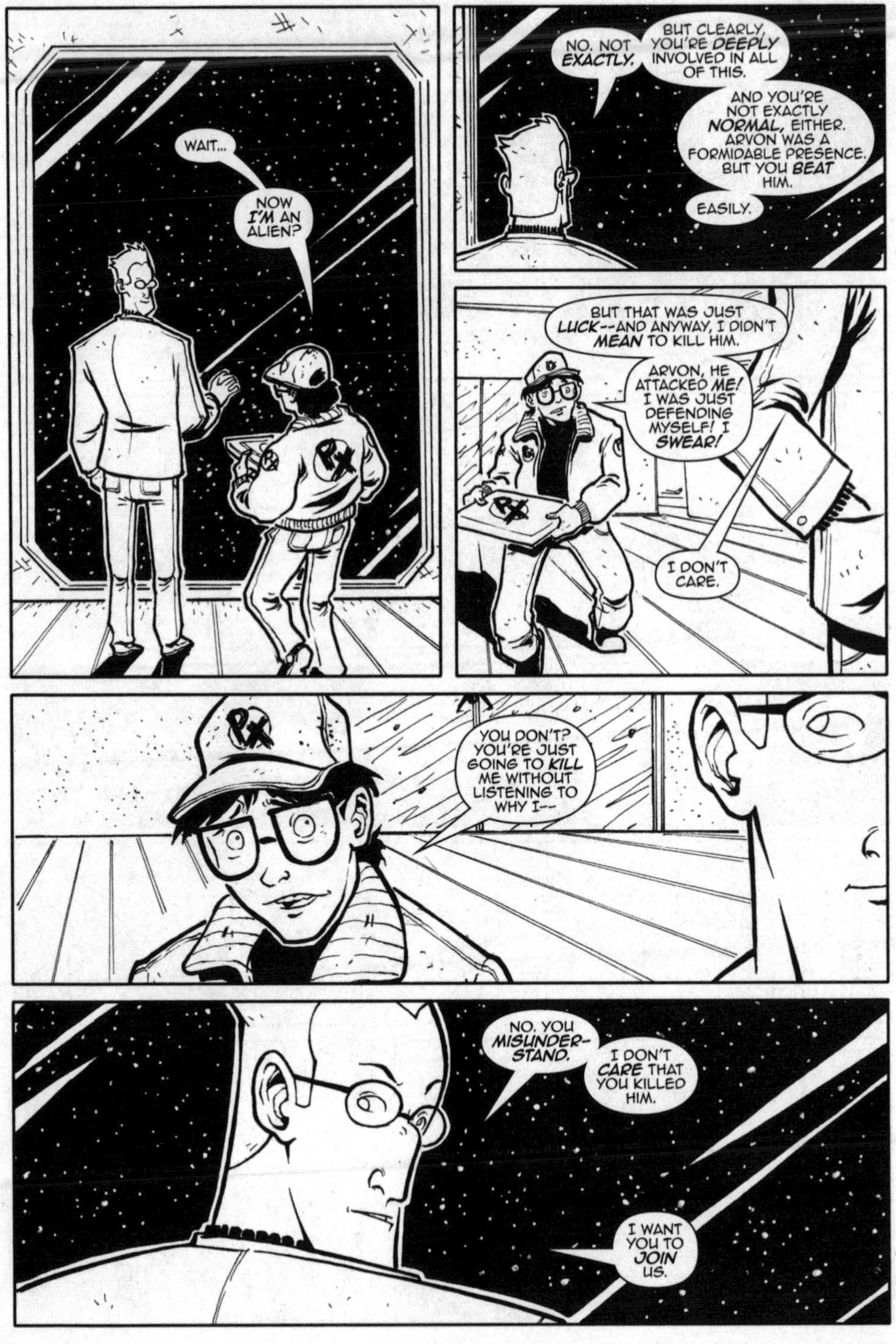
WAIT...
NOW I'M AN ALIEN?
NO. NOT EXACTLY.
BUT CLEARLY, YOU'RE DEEPLY INVOLVED IN ALL OF THIS.
AND YOU'RE NOT EXACTLY NORMAL, EITHER. ARVON WAS A FORMIDABLE PRESENCE. BUT YOU BEAT HIM.
EASILY.
BUT THAT WAS JUST LUCK--AND ANYWAY, I DIDN'T MEAN TO KILL HIM.
ARVON, HE ATTACKED ME! I WAS JUST DEFENDING MYSELF! I SWEAR!
I DON'T CARE.
YOU DON'T? YOU'RE JUST GOING TO KILL ME WITHOUT LISTENING TO WHY I--
NO. YOU MISUNDER-STAND.
I DON'T CARE THAT YOU KILLED HIM.
I WANT YOU TO JOIN US.

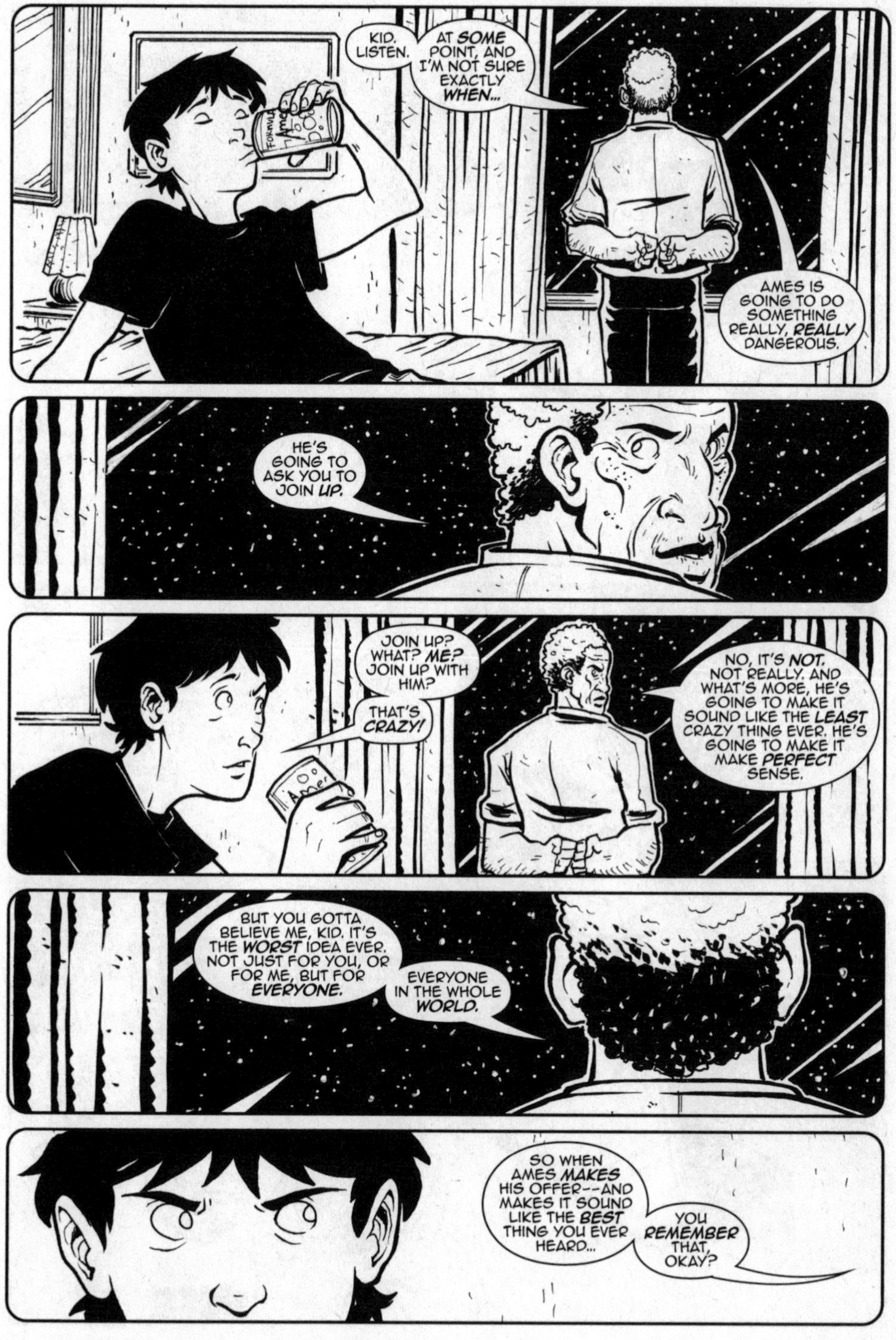
KID. LISTEN.
AT SOME POINT, AND I'M NOT SURE EXACTLY WHEN...
AMES IS GOING TO DO SOMETHING REALLY, REALLY DANGEROUS.
HE'S GOING TO ASK YOU TO JOIN UP.
JOIN UP? WHAT? ME? JOIN UP WITH HIM?
THAT'S CRAZY!
NO, IT'S NOT. NOT REALLY. AND WHAT'S MORE, HE'S GOING TO MAKE IT SOUND LIKE THE LEAST CRAZY THING EVER. HE'S GOING TO MAKE IT MAKE PERFECT SENSE.
BUT YOU GOTTA BELIEVE ME, KID. IT'S THE WORST IDEA EVER. NOT JUST FOR YOU, OR FOR ME, BUT FOR EVERYONE.
EVERYONE IN THE WHOLE WORLD.
SO WHEN AMES MAKES HIS OFFER--AND MAKES IT SOUND LIKE THE BEST THING YOU EVER HEARD...
YOU REMEMBER THAT, OKAY?

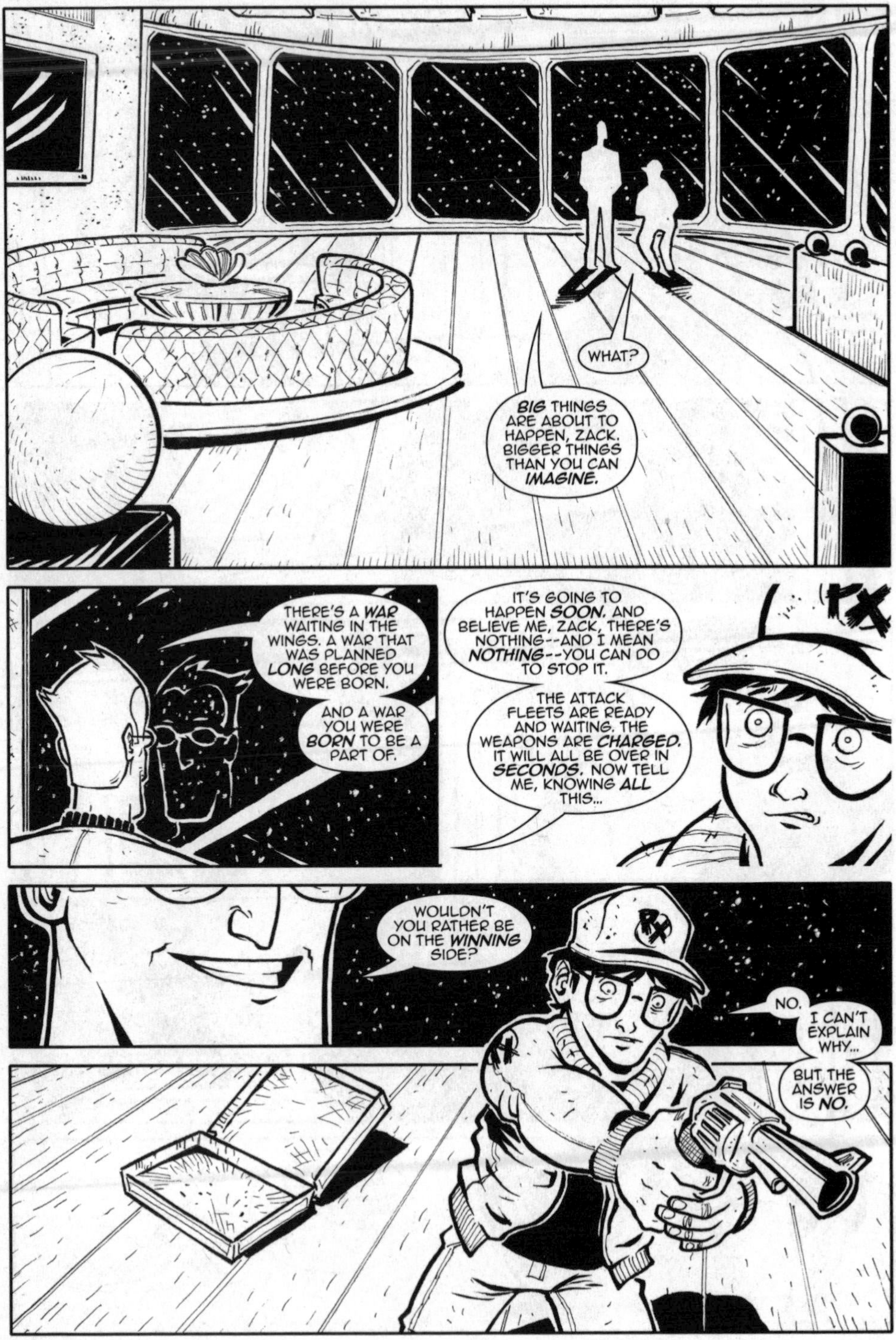

WHAT?
BIG THINGS ARE ABOUT TO HAPPEN, ZACK. BIGGER THINGS THAN YOU CAN IMAGINE.
THERE'S A WAR WAITING IN THE WINGS. A WAR THAT WAS PLANNED LONG BEFORE YOU WERE BORN.
AND A WAR YOU WERE BORN TO BE A PART OF.
IT'S GOING TO HAPPEN SOON. AND BELIEVE ME, ZACK, THERE'S NOTHING--AND I MEAN NOTHING--YOU CAN DO TO STOP IT.
THE ATTACK FLEETS ARE READY AND WAITING. THE WEAPONS ARE CHARGED. IT WILL ALL BE OVER IN SECONDS. NOW TELL ME, KNOWING ALL THIS...
WOULDN'T YOU RATHER BE ON THE WINNING SIDE?
NO.
I CAN'T EXPLAIN WHY...
BUT THE ANSWER IS NO.

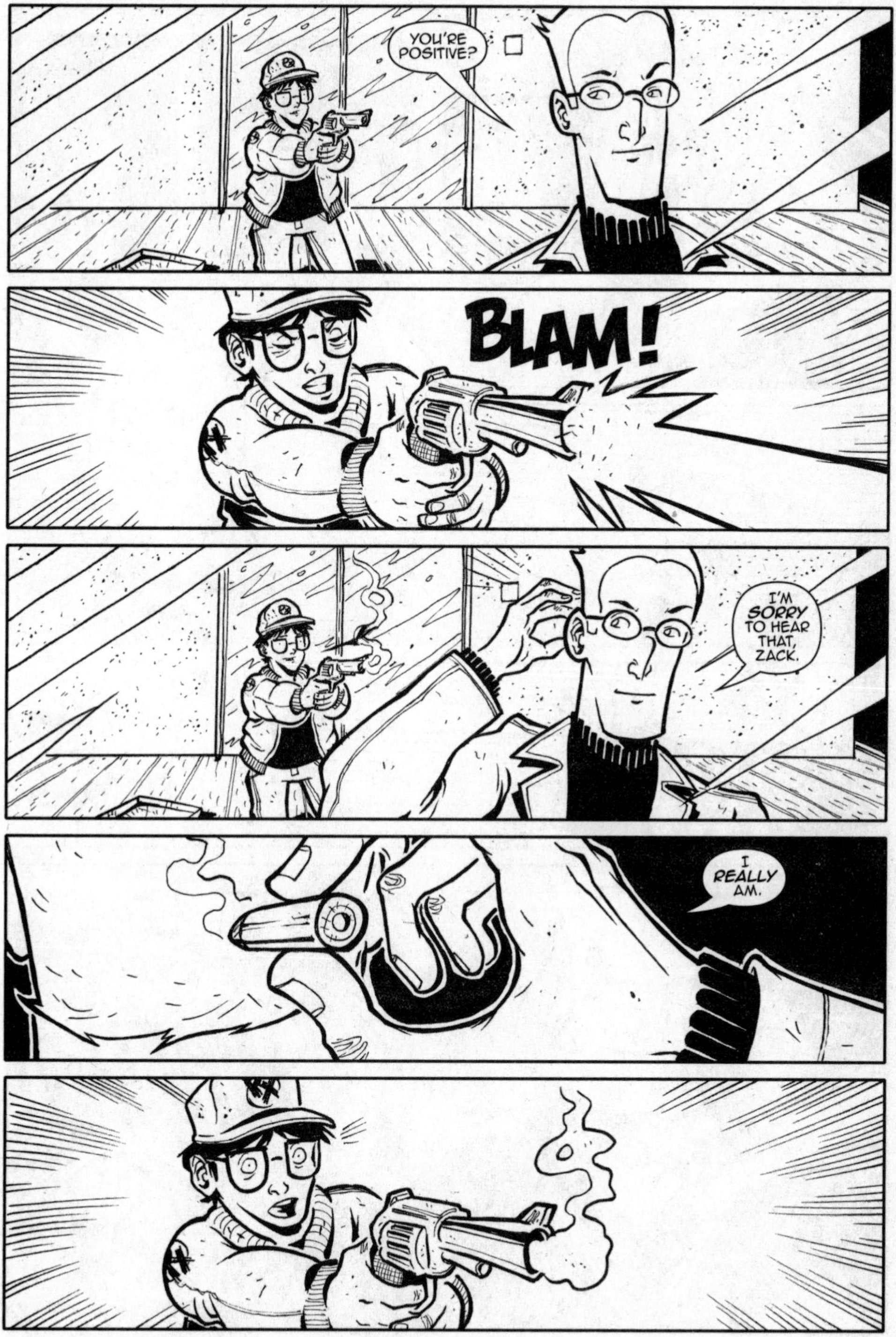
YOU'RE POSITIVE?
BLAM!
I'M SORRY TO HEAR THAT, ZACK.
I REALLY AM.

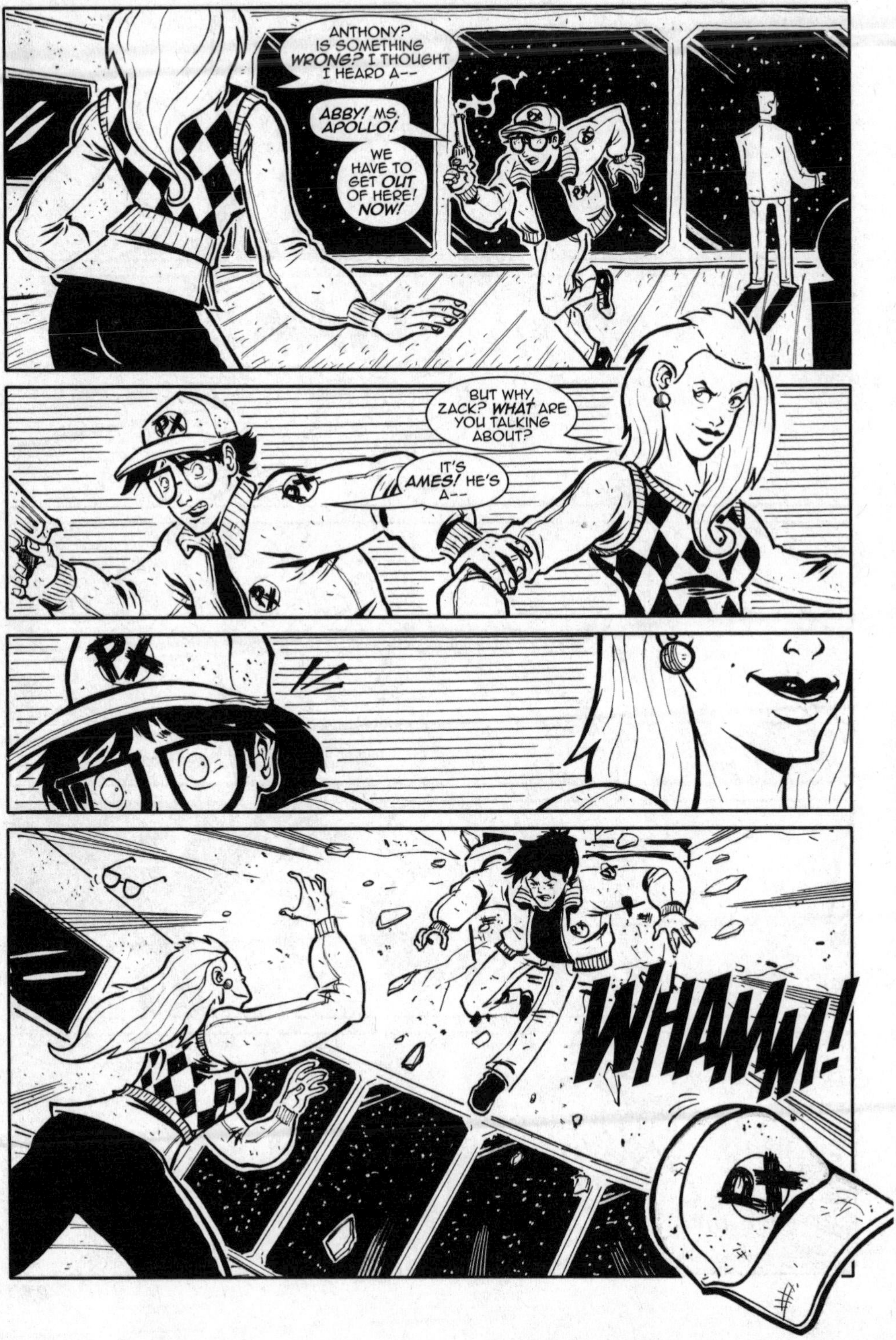
ANTHONY? IS SOMETHING WRONG? I THOUGHT I HEARD A--
ABBY! MS. APOLLO!
WE HAVE TO GET OUT OF HERE! NOW!
BUT WHY, ZACK? WHAT ARE YOU TALKING ABOUT?
IT'S AMES! HE'S A--
WHAMM!

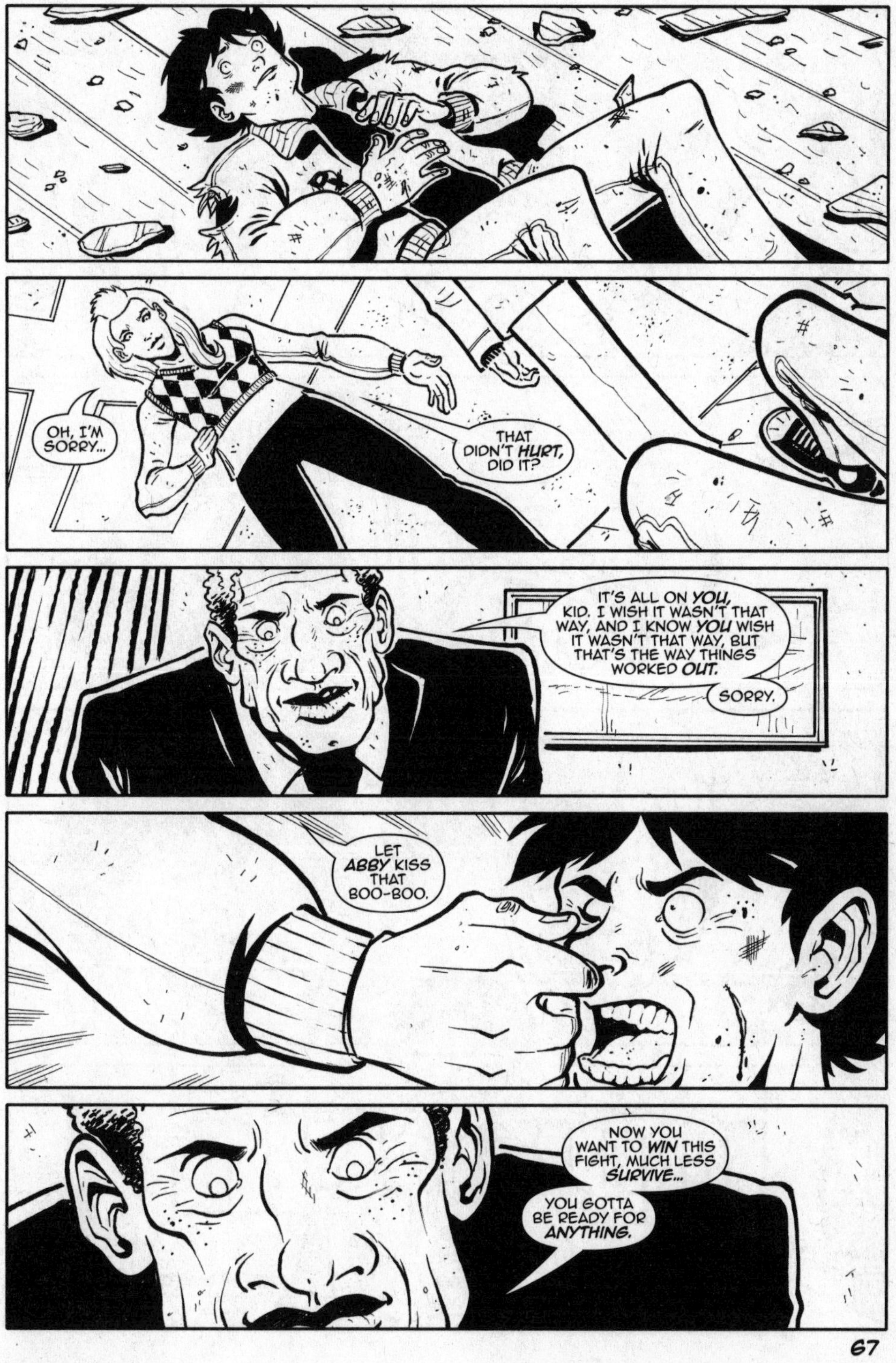
OH, I'M SORRY...
THAT DIDN'T HURT, DID IT?
IT'S ALL ON YOU, KID. I WISH IT WASN'T THAT WAY, AND I KNOW YOU WISH IT WASN'T THAT WAY, BUT THAT'S THE WAY THINGS WORKED OUT.
SORRY.
LET ABBY KISS THAT BOO-BOO.
NOW YOU WANT TO WIN THIS FIGHT, MUCH LESS SURVIVE...
YOU GOTTA BE READY FOR ANYTHING.

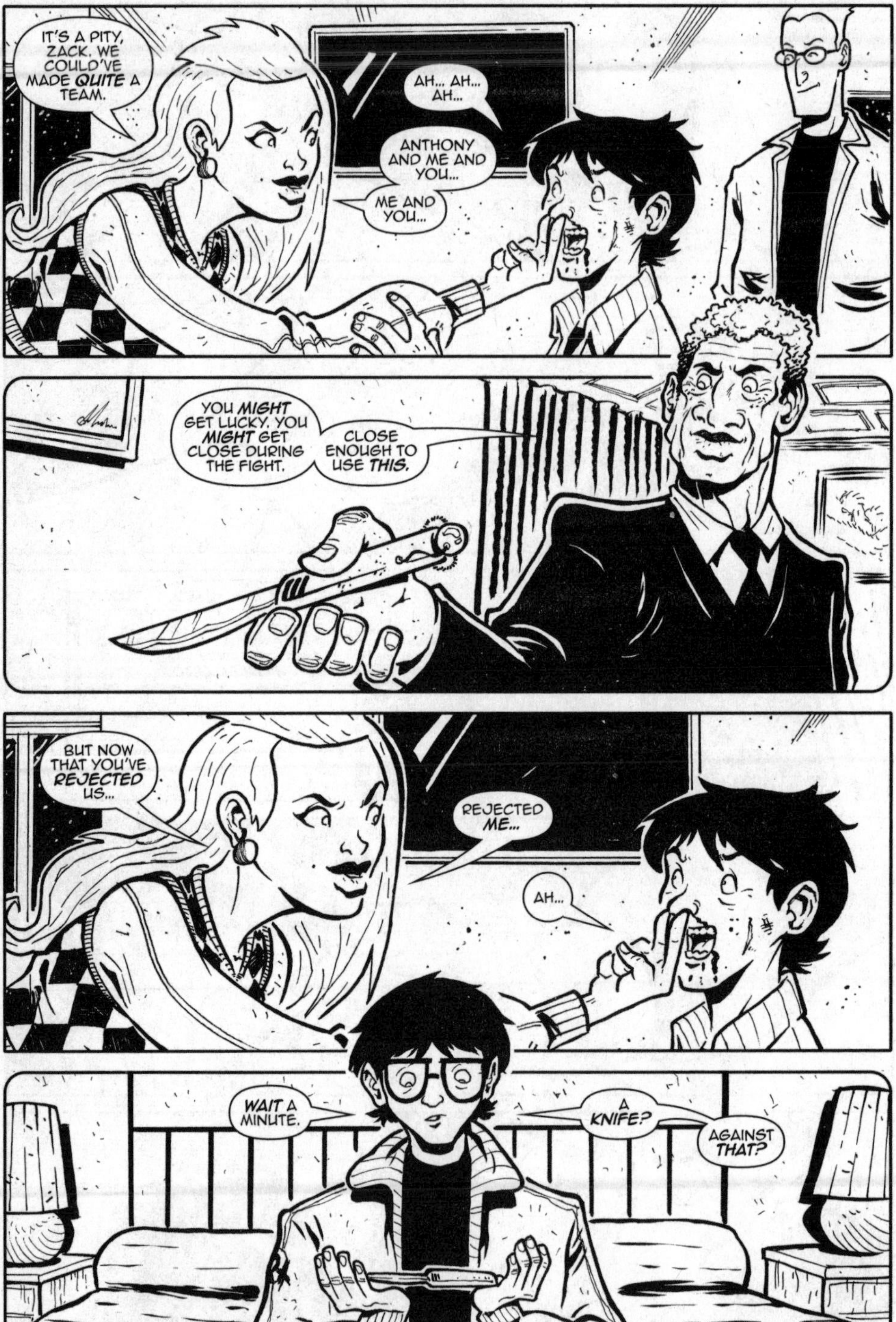
IT'S A PITY, ZACK. WE COULD'VE MADE QUITE A TEAM.
AH... AH... AH...
ANTHONY AND ME AND YOU...
ME AND YOU...
YOU MIGHT GET LUCKY. YOU MIGHT GET CLOSE DURING THE FIGHT.
CLOSE ENOUGH TO USE THIS.
BUT NOW THAT YOU'VE REJECTED US...
REJECTED ME...
AH...
WAIT A MINUTE.
A KNIFE?
AGAINST THAT?

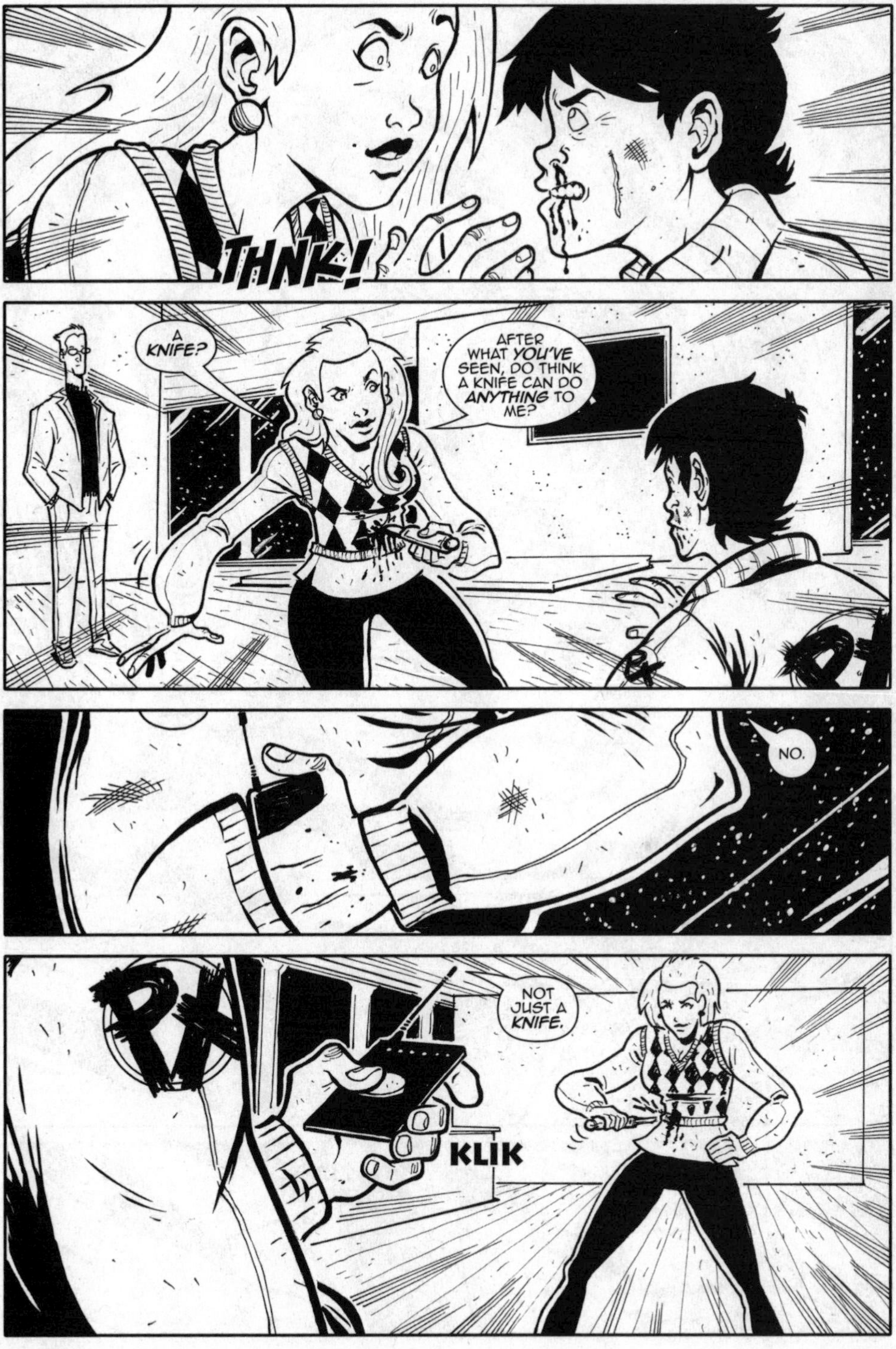
THNK!
A KNIFE?
AFTER WHAT YOU'VE SEEN, DO THINK A KNIFE CAN DO ANYTHING TO ME?
NO.
NOT JUST A KNIFE.
KLIK

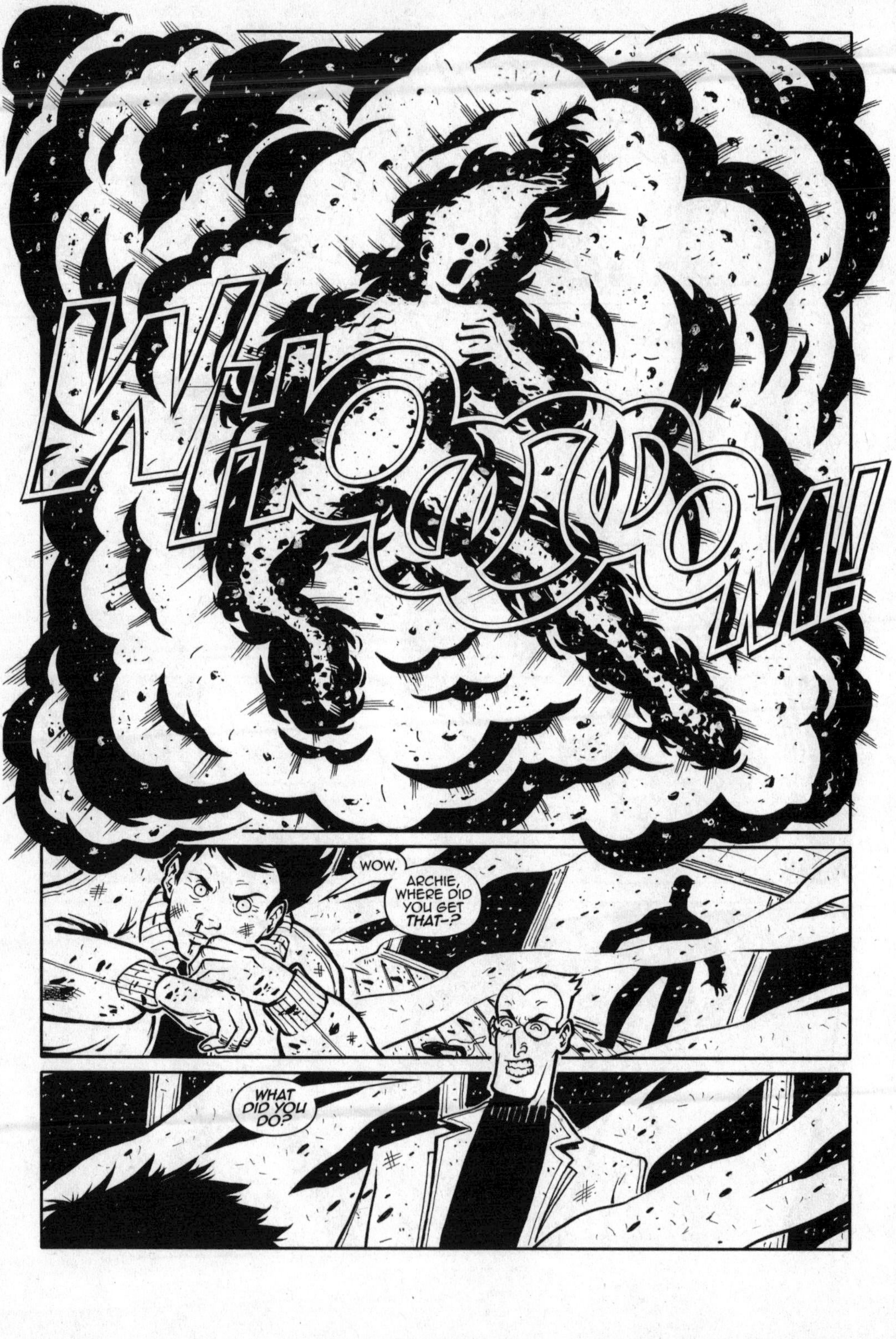
WHOOOOOM!
WOW.
ARCHIE, WHERE DID YOU GET *THAT*-?
WHAT DID YOU DO?

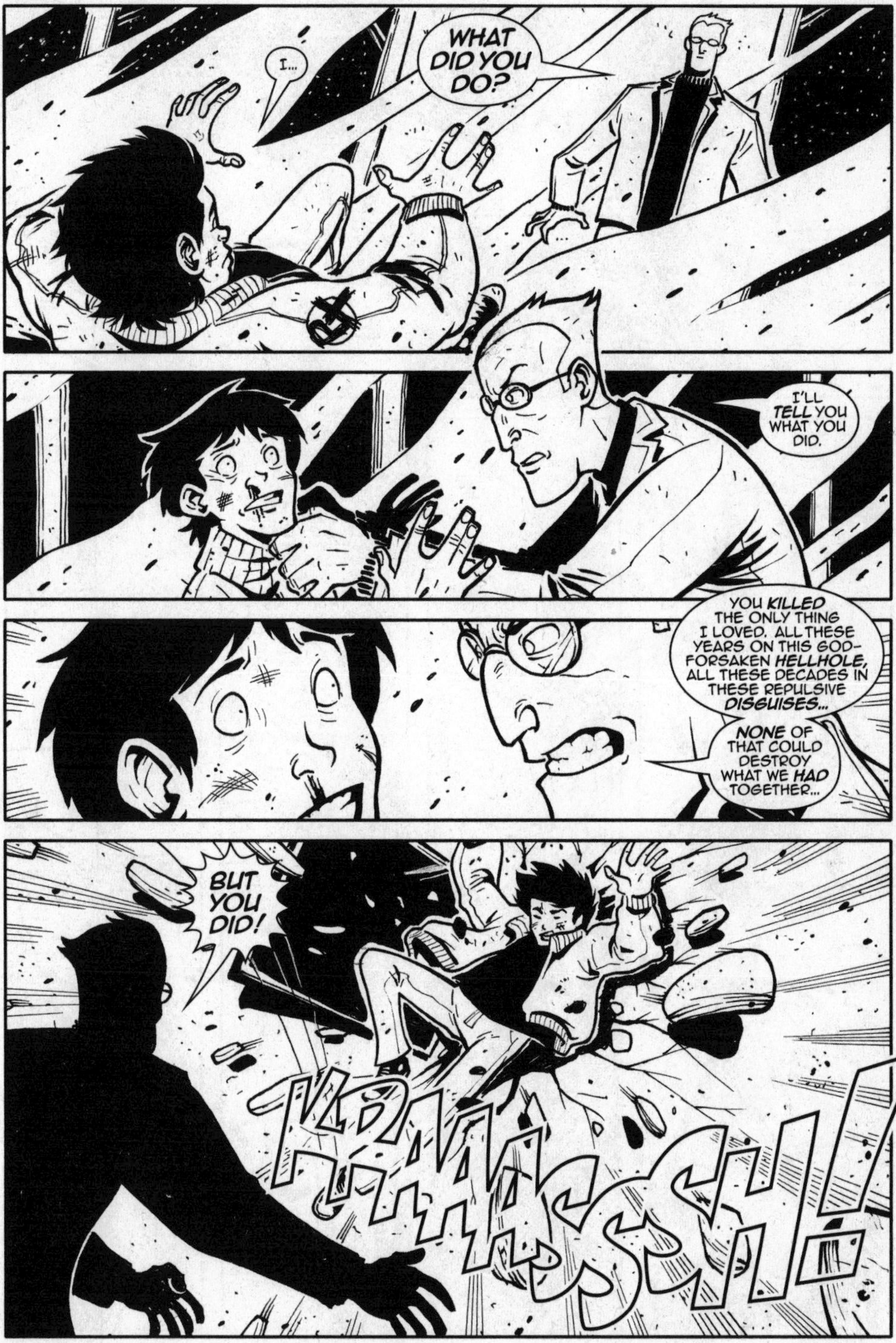
I...
WHAT DID YOU DO?
I'LL TELL YOU WHAT YOU DID.
YOU KILLED THE ONLY THING I LOVED. ALL THESE YEARS ON THIS GOD-FORSAKEN HELLHOLE, ALL THESE DECADES IN THESE REPULSIVE DISGUISES...
NONE OF THAT COULD DESTROY WHAT WE HAD TOGETHER...
BUT YOU DID!
KRAAASSCH!!

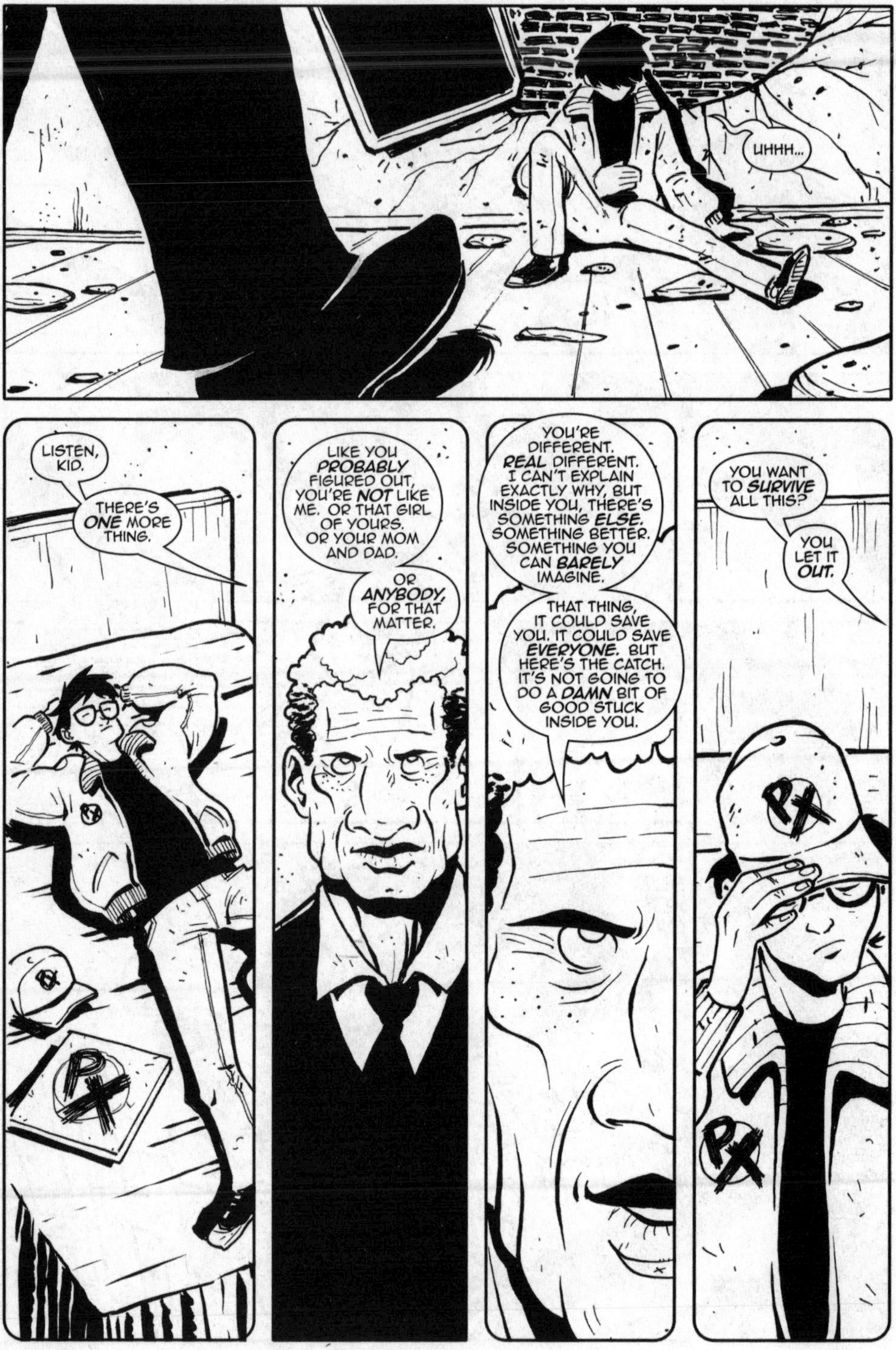
UHHH...
LISTEN, KID.
THERE'S ONE MORE THING.
LIKE YOU PROBABLY FIGURED OUT, YOU'RE NOT LIKE ME. OR THAT GIRL OF YOURS. OR YOUR MOM AND DAD.
OR ANYBODY, FOR THAT MATTER.
YOU'RE DIFFERENT. REAL DIFFERENT. I CAN'T EXPLAIN EXACTLY WHY, BUT INSIDE YOU, THERE'S SOMETHING ELSE. SOMETHING BETTER. SOMETHING YOU CAN BARELY IMAGINE.
THAT THING, IT COULD SAVE YOU. IT COULD SAVE EVERYONE. BUT HERE'S THE CATCH. IT'S NOT GOING TO DO A DAMN BIT OF GOOD STUCK INSIDE YOU.
YOU WANT TO SURVIVE ALL THIS?
YOU LET IT OUT.

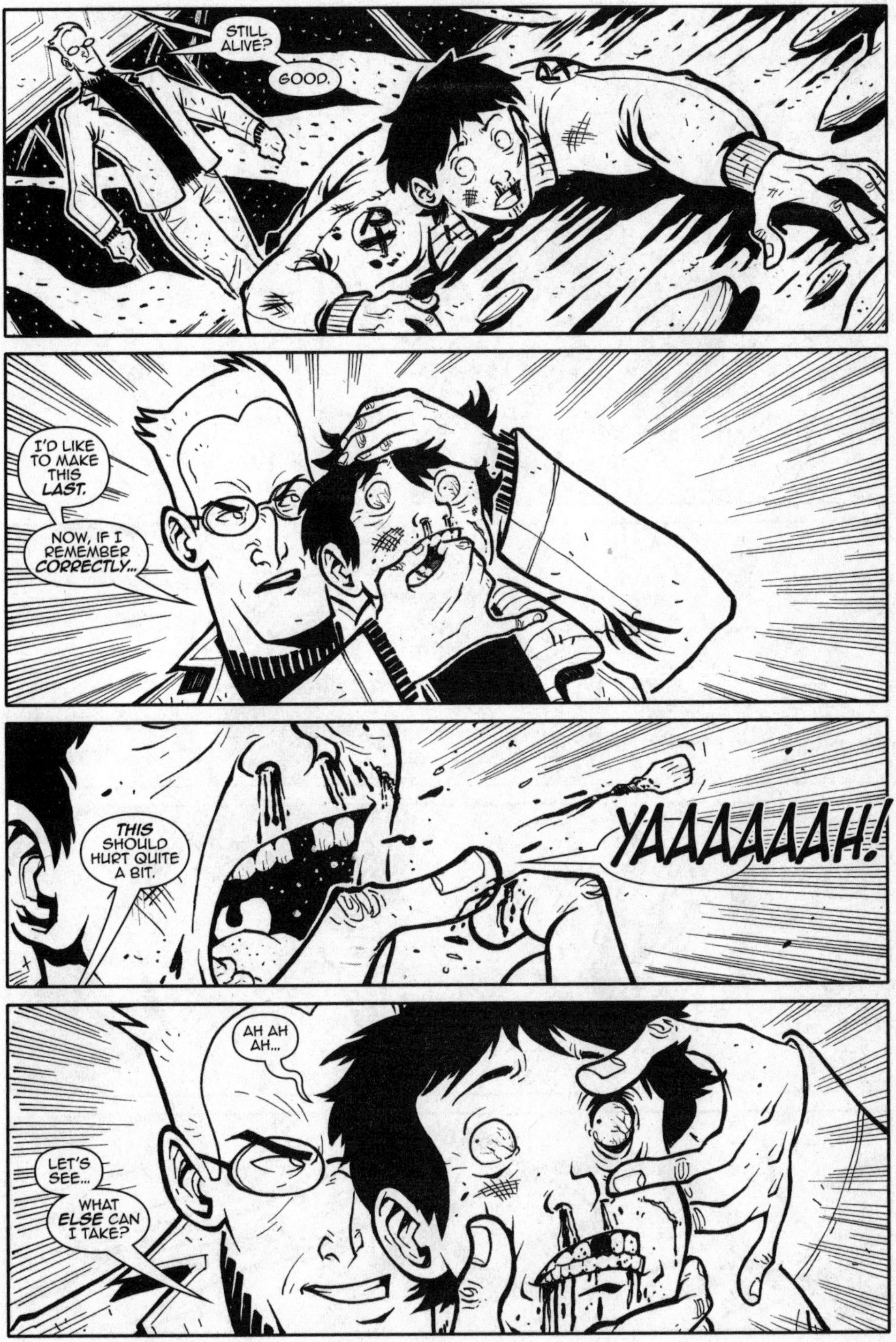
STILL ALIVE?
GOOD.
I'D LIKE TO MAKE THIS LAST.
NOW, IF I REMEMBER CORRECTLY...
THIS SHOULD HURT QUITE A BIT.
YAAAAAAH!
AH AH AH...
LET'S SEE...
WHAT ELSE CAN I TAKE?

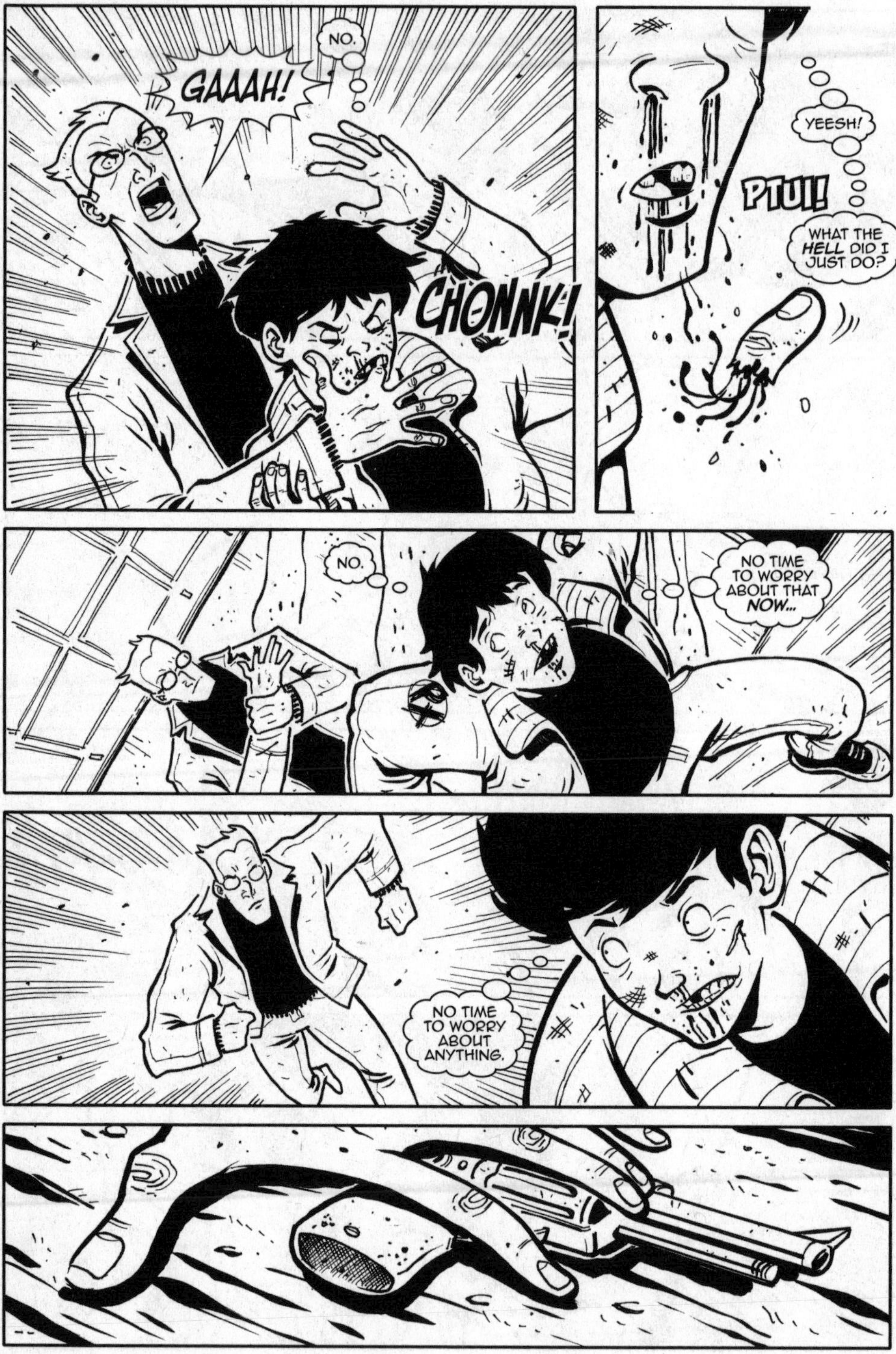

NO.
GAAAH!
CHONNK!
YEESH!
PTUI!
WHAT THE HELL DID I JUST DO?
NO.
NO TIME TO WORRY ABOUT THAT NOW...
NO TIME TO WORRY ABOUT ANYTHING.

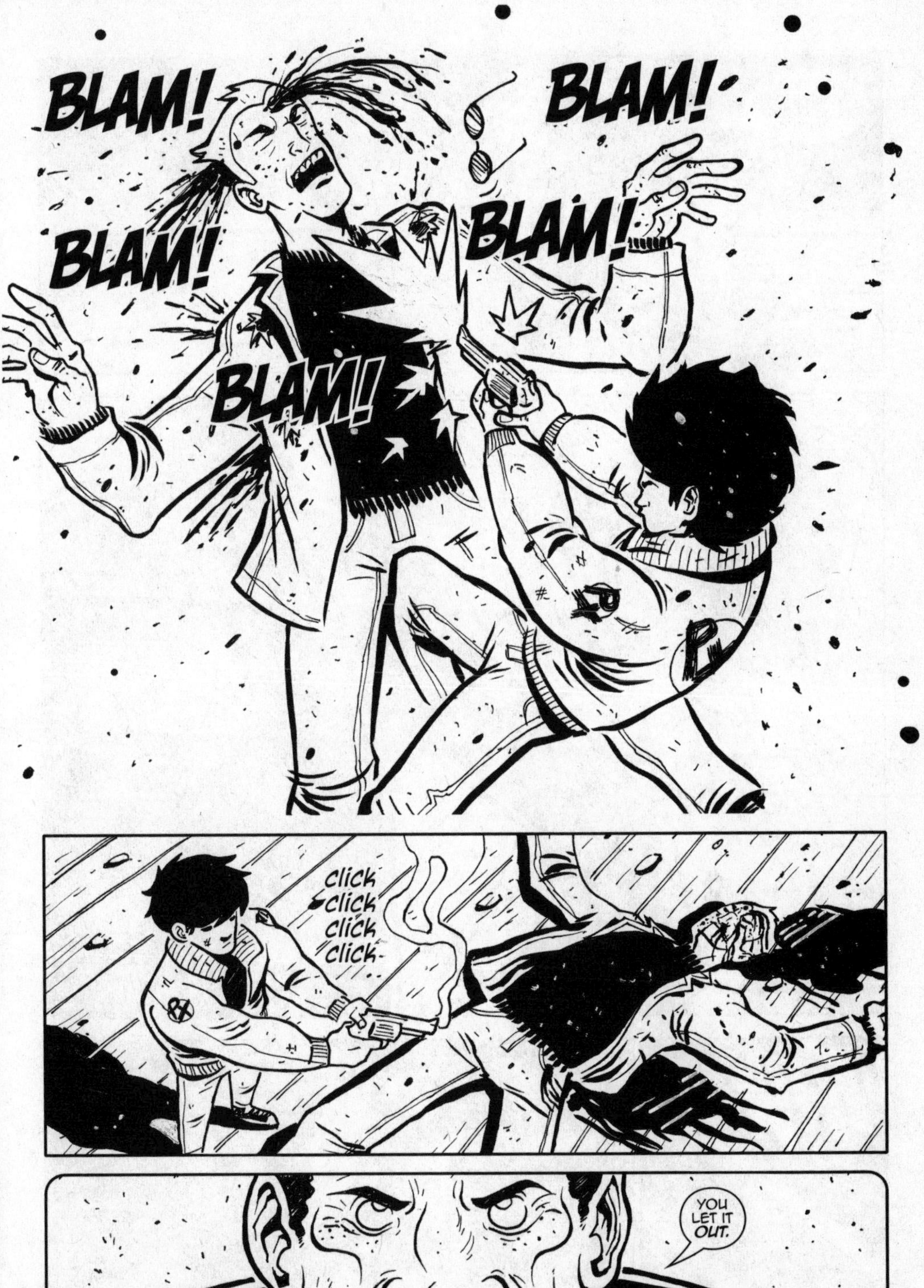
BLAM!
BLAM!
BLAM!
BLAM!
BLAM!
click
click
click
click
YOU LET IT OUT.

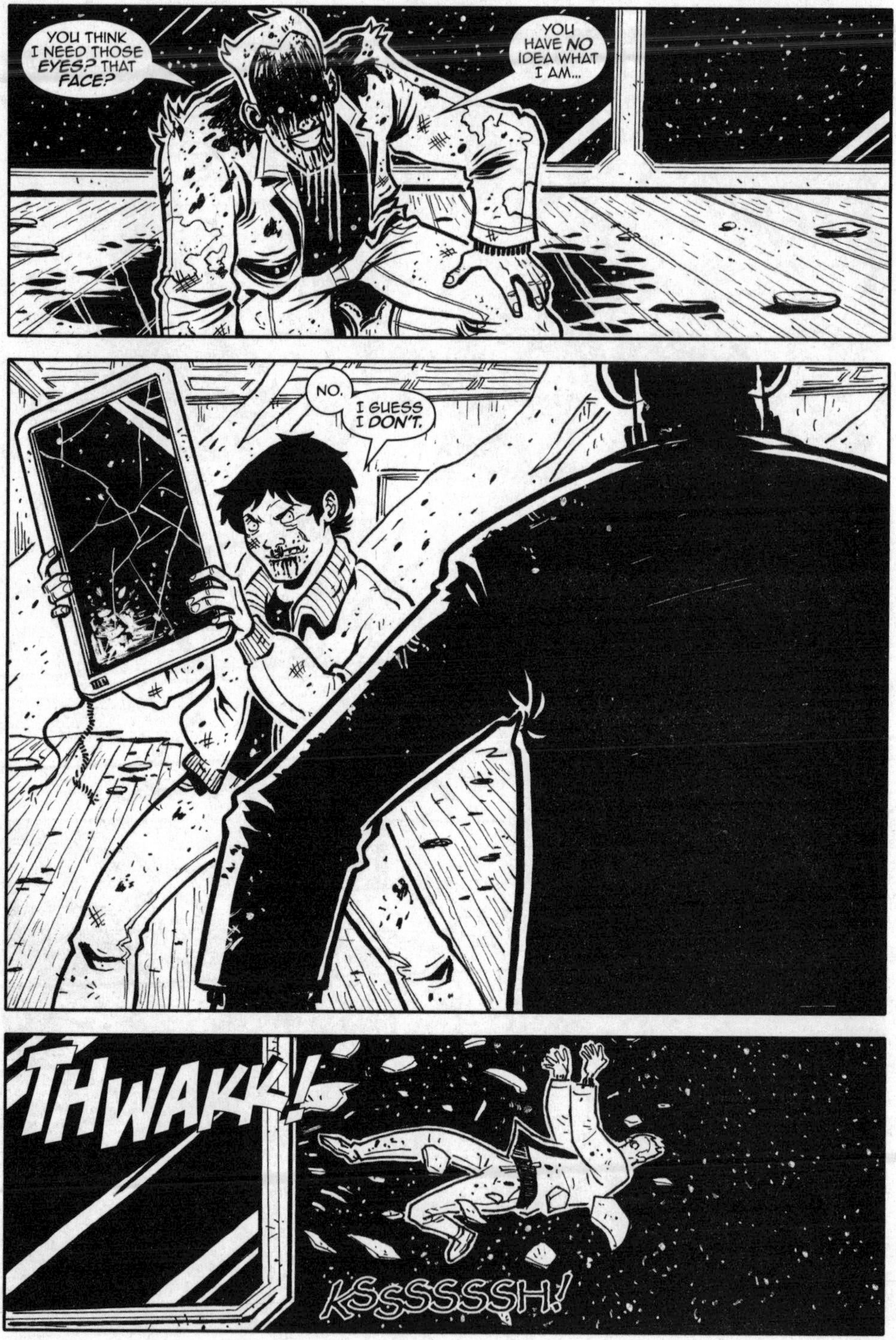
YOU THINK I NEED THOSE EYES? THAT FACE?
YOU HAVE NO IDEA WHAT I AM...
NO.
I GUESS I DON'T.
THWAKK!
KSSSSSSH!

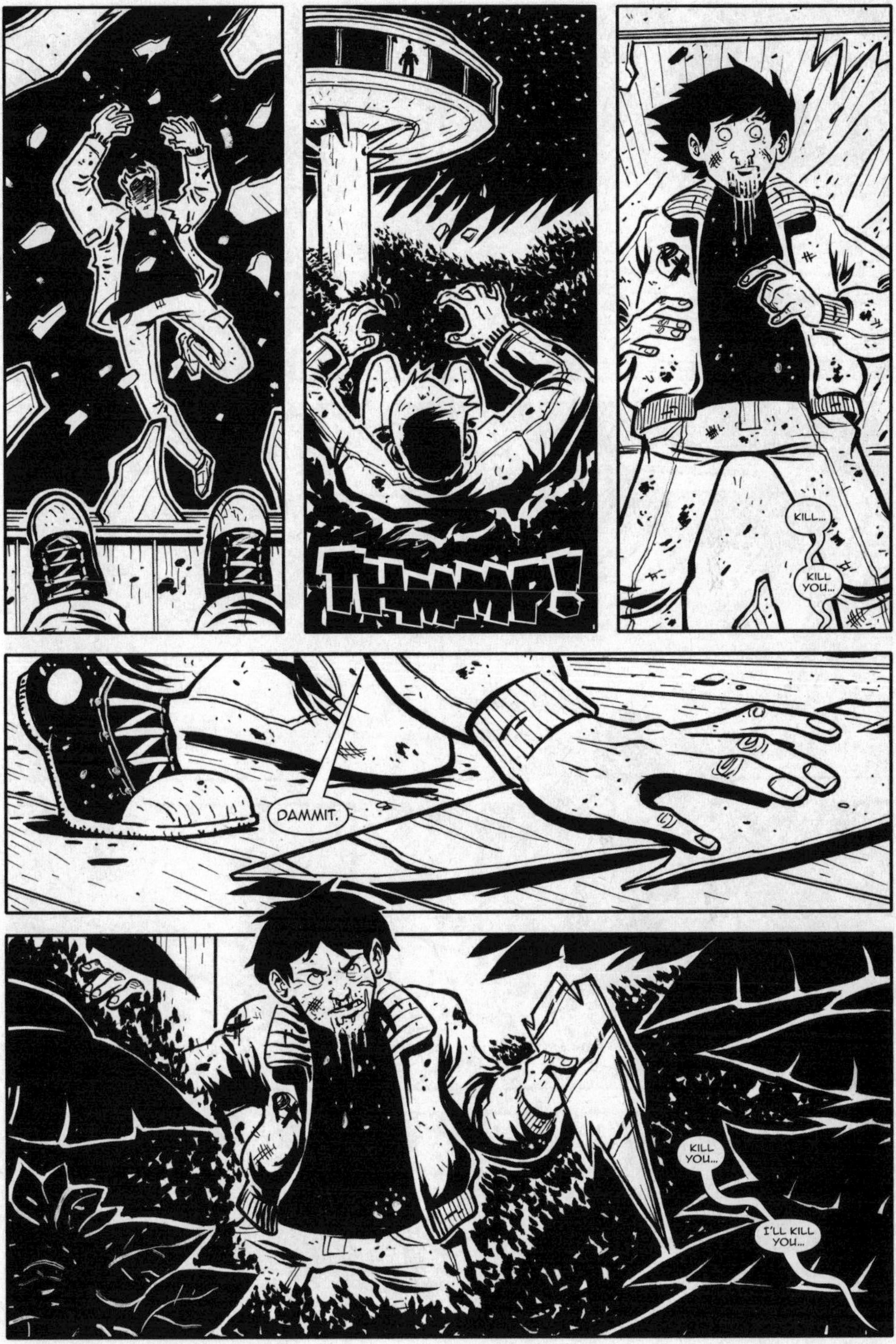
THMMP!
KILL...
KILL YOU...
DAMMIT.
KILL YOU...
I'LL KILL YOU...

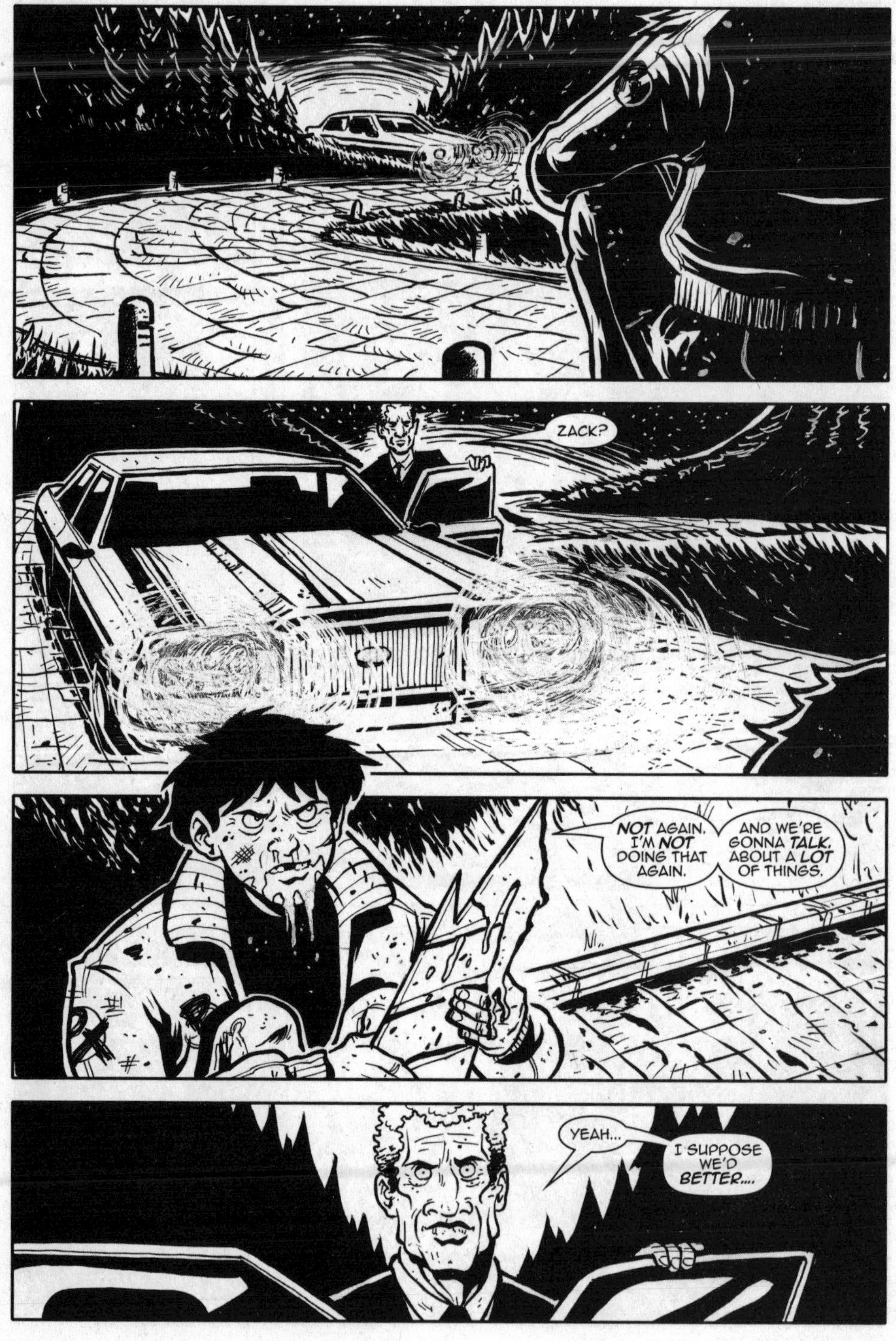
ZACK?
NOT AGAIN. I'M NOT DOING THAT AGAIN.
AND WE'RE GONNA TALK. ABOUT A LOT OF THINGS.
YEAH...
I SUPPOSE WE'D BETTER....

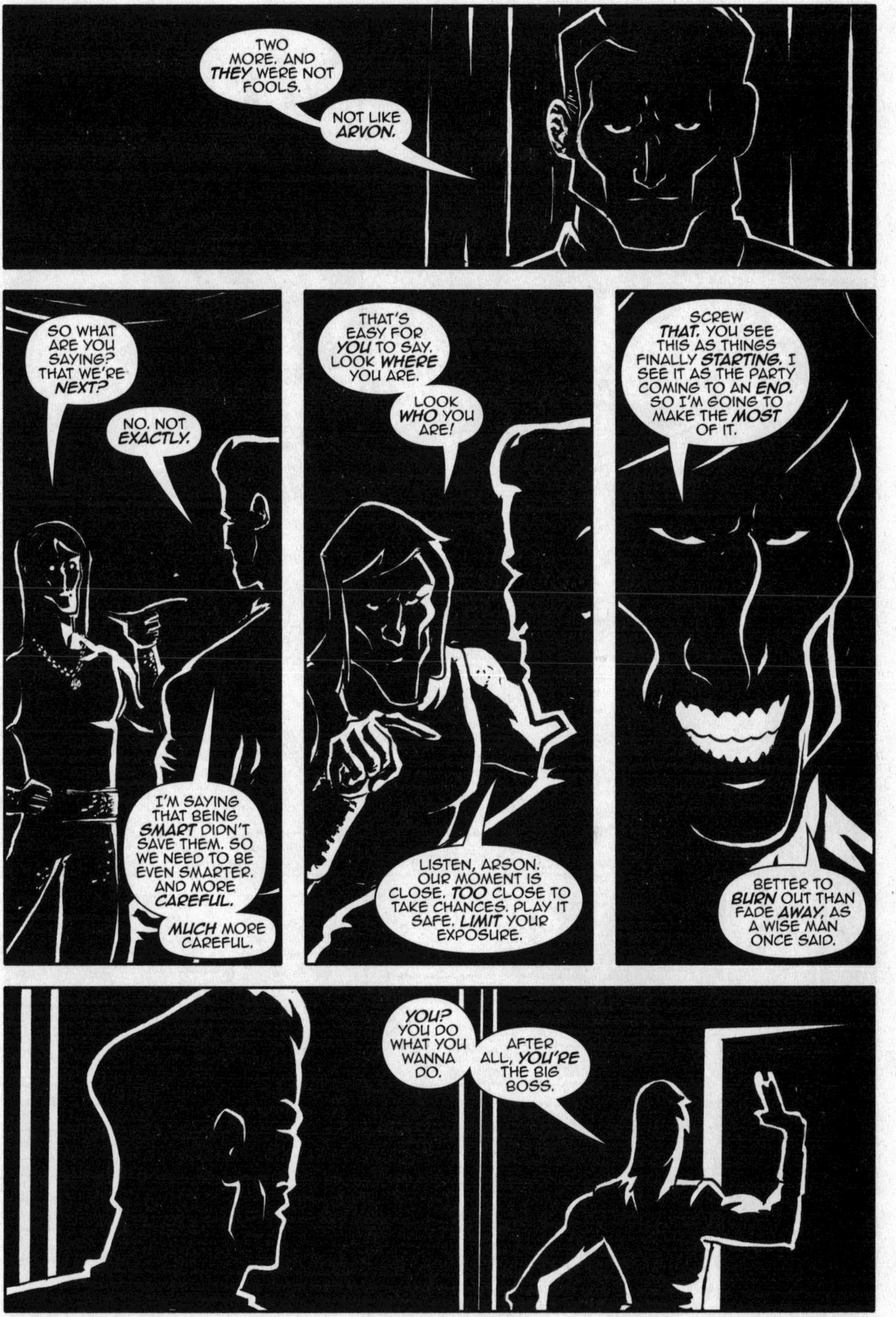
TWO MORE. AND THEY WERE NOT FOOLS.
NOT LIKE ARVON.
SO WHAT ARE YOU SAYING? THAT WE'RE NEXT?
NO. NOT EXACTLY.
I'M SAYING THAT BEING SMART DIDN'T SAVE THEM. SO WE NEED TO BE EVEN SMARTER. AND MORE CAREFUL.
MUCH MORE CAREFUL.
THAT'S EASY FOR YOU TO SAY. LOOK WHERE YOU ARE.
LOOK WHO YOU ARE!
LISTEN, ARSON. OUR MOMENT IS CLOSE. TOO CLOSE TO TAKE CHANCES. PLAY IT SAFE. LIMIT YOUR EXPOSURE.
SCREW THAT. YOU SEE THIS AS THINGS FINALLY STARTING. I SEE IT AS THE PARTY COMING TO AN END. SO I'M GOING TO MAKE THE MOST OF IT.
BETTER TO BURN OUT THAN FADE AWAY, AS A WISE MAN ONCE SAID.
YOU? YOU DO WHAT YOU WANNA DO.
AFTER ALL, YOU'RE THE BIG BOSS.

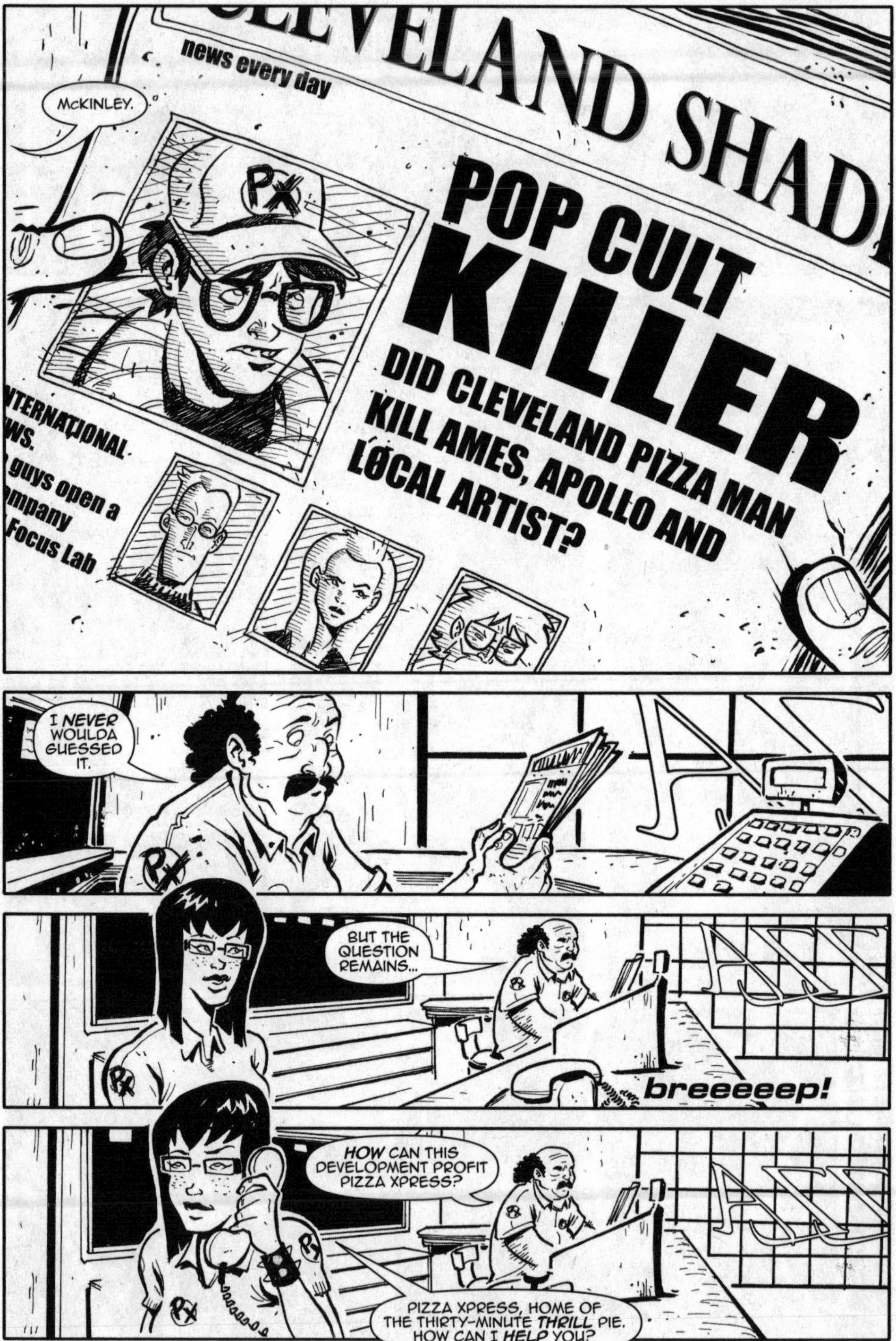

CLEVELAND SHAD
news every day
McKINLEY.
POP CULT KILLER
DID CLEVELAND PIZZA MAN KILL AMES, APOLLO AND LØCAL ARTIST?
NTERNATIONAL
WS.
guys open a
mpany
Focus Lab
I NEVER WOULDA GUESSED IT.
BUT THE QUESTION REMAINS...
breeeeep!
HOW CAN THIS DEVELOPMENT PROFIT PIZZA XPRESS?
PIZZA XPRESS, HOME OF THE THIRTY-MINUTE THRILL PIE. HOW CAN I HELP YOU?

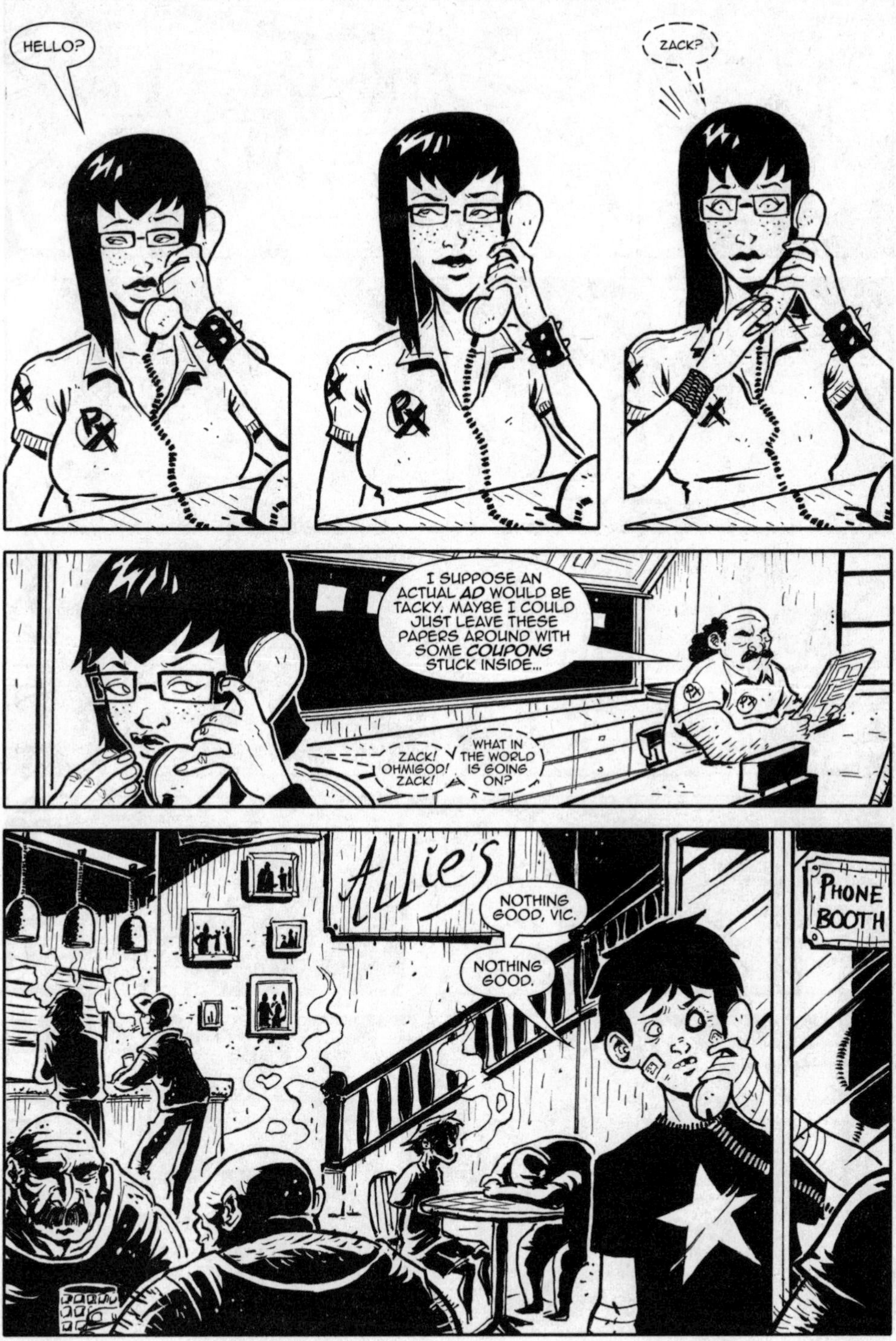
HELLO?
ZACK?
I SUPPOSE AN ACTUAL AD WOULD BE TACKY. MAYBE I COULD JUST LEAVE THESE PAPERS AROUND WITH SOME COUPONS STUCK INSIDE...
ZACK! OHMIGOD! ZACK!
WHAT IN THE WORLD IS GOING ON?
ALLIE'S
PHONE BOOTH
NOTHING GOOD, VIC.
NOTHING GOOD.

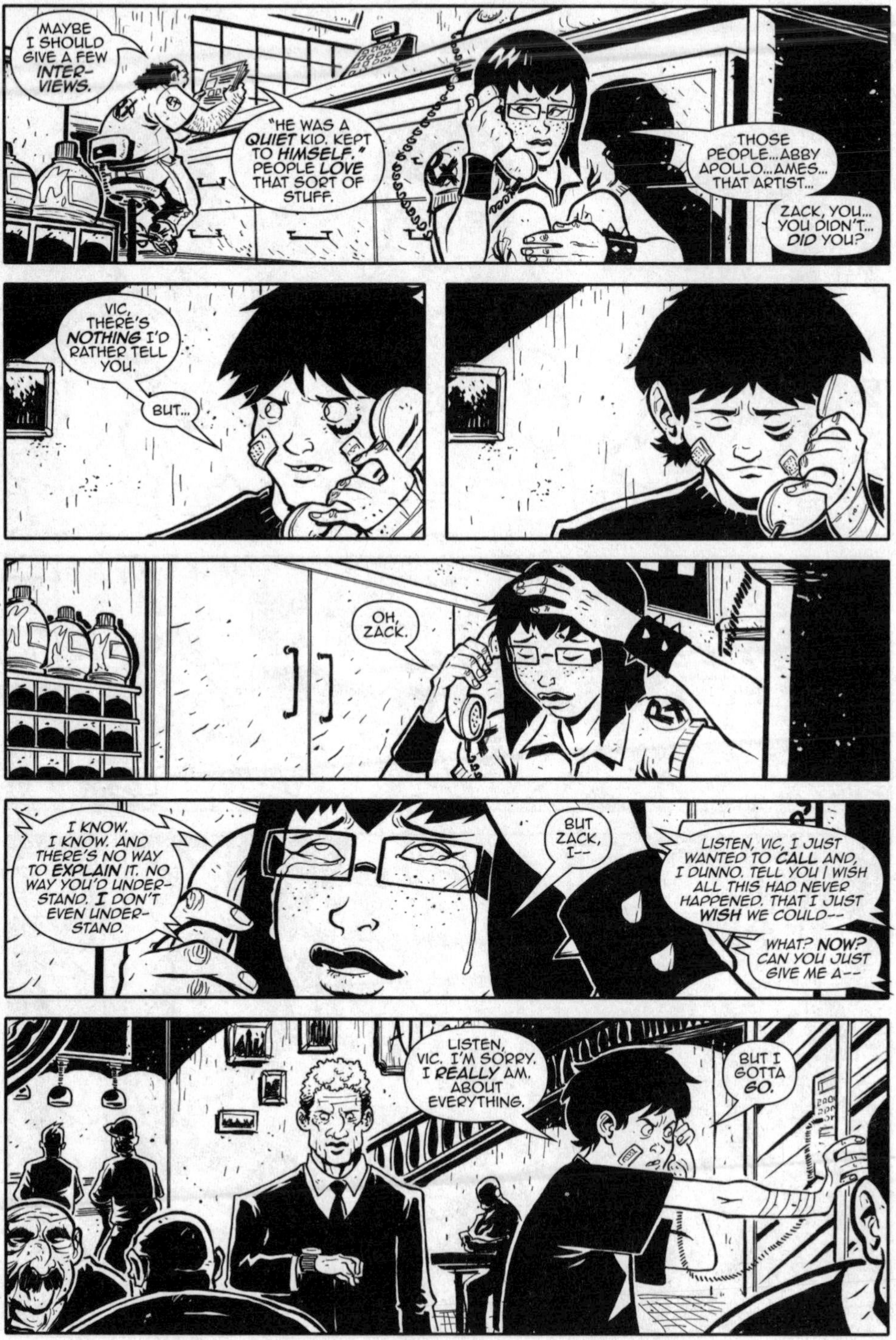
MAYBE I SHOULD GIVE A FEW INTERVIEWS.
"HE WAS A QUIET KID. KEPT TO HIMSELF." PEOPLE LOVE THAT SORT OF STUFF.
THOSE PEOPLE...ABBY APOLLO...AMES... THAT ARTIST...
ZACK, YOU... YOU DIDN'T... DID YOU?
VIC, THERE'S NOTHING I'D RATHER TELL YOU.
BUT...
OH, ZACK.
I KNOW. I KNOW. AND THERE'S NO WAY TO EXPLAIN IT. NO WAY YOU'D UNDERSTAND. I DON'T EVEN UNDERSTAND.
BUT ZACK, I--
LISTEN, VIC, I JUST WANTED TO CALL AND, I DUNNO. TELL YOU I WISH ALL THIS HAD NEVER HAPPENED. THAT I JUST WISH WE COULD--
WHAT? NOW? CAN YOU JUST GIVE ME A--
LISTEN, VIC. I'M SORRY. I REALLY AM. ABOUT EVERYTHING.
BUT I GOTTA GO.

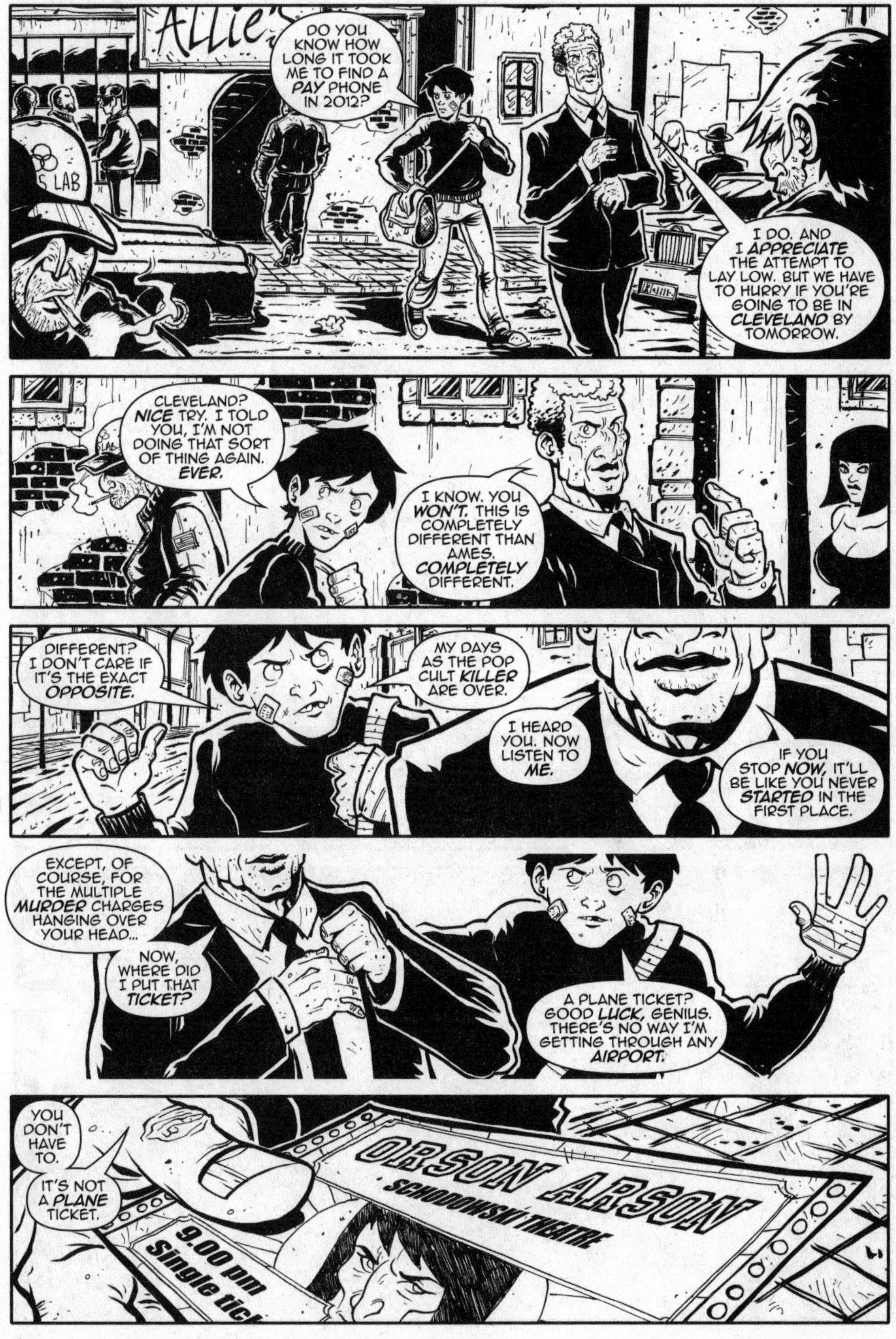
ALLIE'S
S LAB
DO YOU KNOW HOW LONG IT TOOK ME TO FIND A PAY PHONE IN 2012?
I DO. AND I APPRECIATE THE ATTEMPT TO LAY LOW. BUT WE HAVE TO HURRY IF YOU'RE GOING TO BE IN CLEVELAND BY TOMORROW.
CLEVELAND? NICE TRY. I TOLD YOU, I'M NOT DOING THAT SORT OF THING AGAIN. EVER.
I KNOW. YOU WON'T. THIS IS COMPLETELY DIFFERENT THAN AMES. COMPLETELY DIFFERENT.
DIFFERENT? I DON'T CARE IF IT'S THE EXACT OPPOSITE.
MY DAYS AS THE POP CULT KILLER ARE OVER.
I HEARD YOU. NOW LISTEN TO ME.
IF YOU STOP NOW, IT'LL BE LIKE YOU NEVER STARTED IN THE FIRST PLACE.
EXCEPT, OF COURSE, FOR THE MULTIPLE MURDER CHARGES HANGING OVER YOUR HEAD...
NOW, WHERE DID I PUT THAT TICKET?
A PLANE TICKET? GOOD LUCK, GENIUS. THERE'S NO WAY I'M GETTING THROUGH ANY AIRPORT.
YOU DON'T HAVE TO.
IT'S NOT A PLANE TICKET.
ORSON ARSON
SCHODOWSKI THEATRE
9.00 pm
Single tick

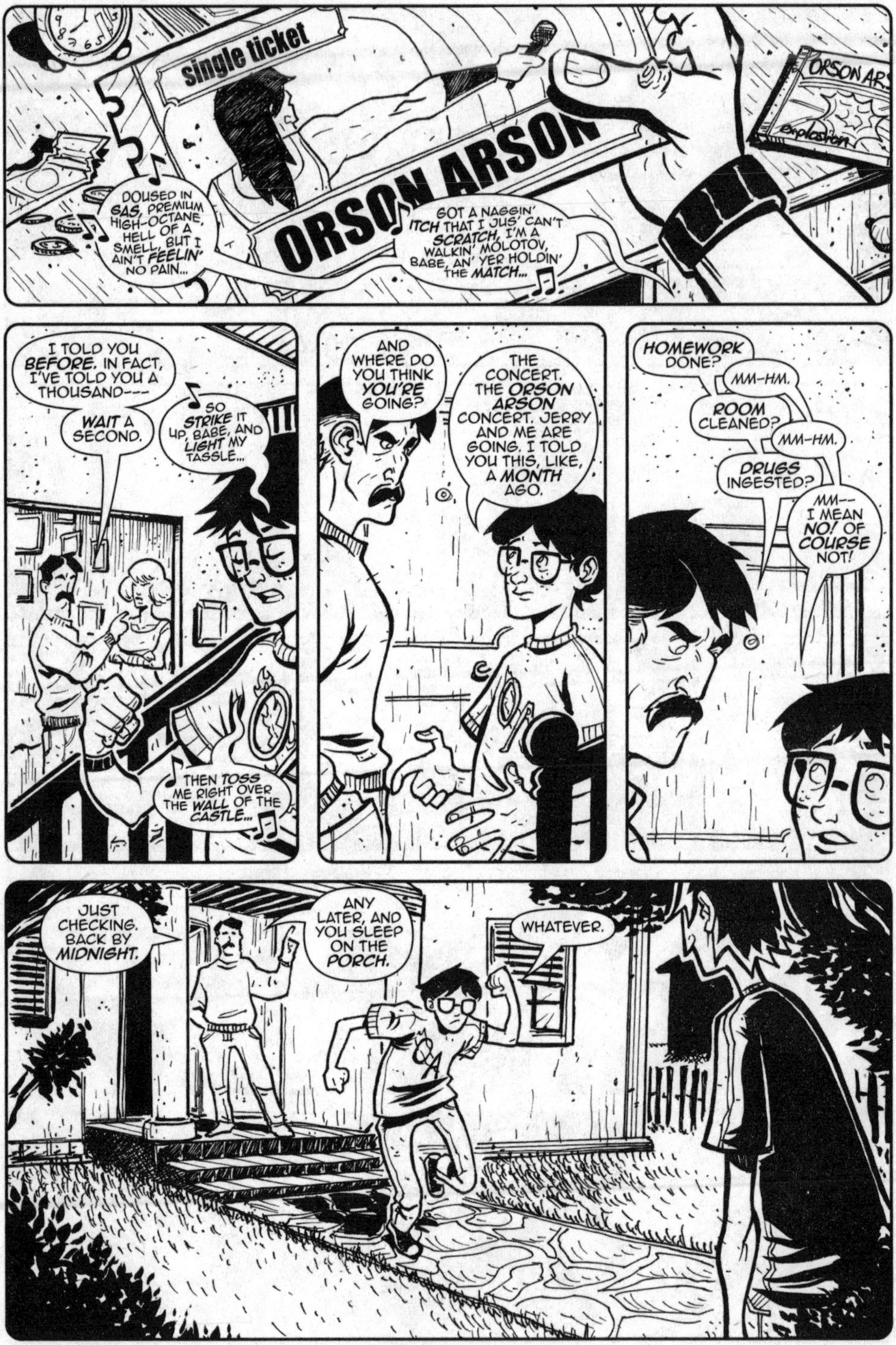
single ticket
ORSON ARSON
ORSON ARS
explosion
DOUSED IN SAS, PREMIUM HIGH-OCTANE HELL OF A SMELL, BUT I AIN'T FEELIN' NO PAIN...
GOT A NAGGIN' ITCH THAT I JUS' CAN'T SCRATCH, I'M A WALKIN' MOLOTOV, BABE, AN' YER HOLDIN' THE MATCH...
I TOLD YOU BEFORE. IN FACT, I'VE TOLD YOU A THOUSAND---
WAIT A SECOND.
SO STRIKE IT UP, BABE, AND LIGHT MY TASSLE...
THEN TOSS ME RIGHT OVER THE WALL OF THE CASTLE...
AND WHERE DO YOU THINK YOU'RE GOING?
THE CONCERT. THE ORSON ARSON CONCERT. JERRY AND ME ARE GOING. I TOLD YOU THIS, LIKE, A MONTH AGO.
HOMEWORK DONE?
MM-HM.
ROOM CLEANED?
MM-HM.
DRUGS INGESTED?
MM-- I MEAN NO! OF COURSE NOT!
JUST CHECKING. BACK BY MIDNIGHT.
ANY LATER, AND YOU SLEEP ON THE PORCH.
WHATEVER.

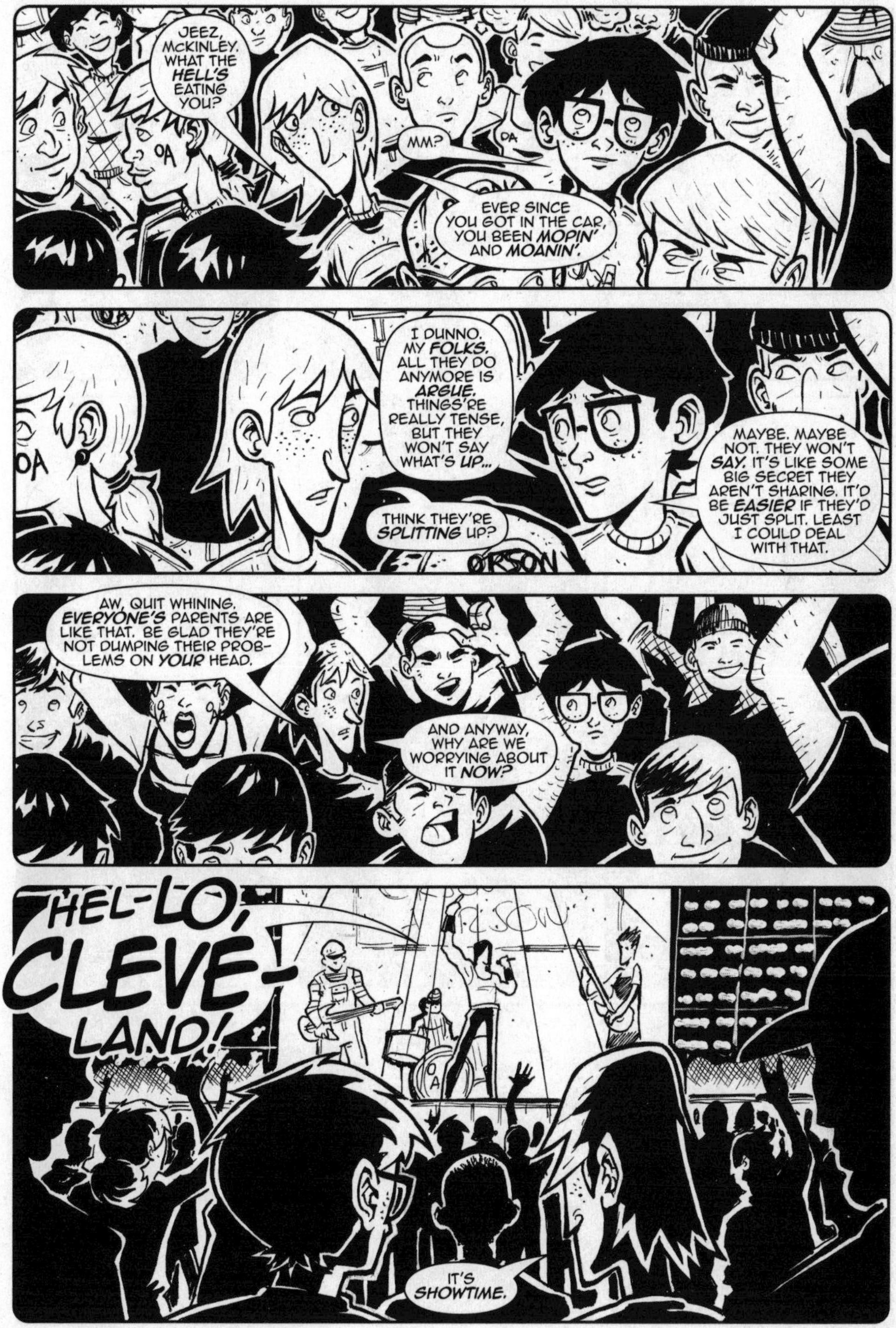

JEEZ, McKINLEY. WHAT THE HELL'S EATING YOU?
MM?
EVER SINCE YOU GOT IN THE CAR, YOU BEEN MOPIN' AND MOANIN'.
I DUNNO. MY FOLKS. ALL THEY DO ANYMORE IS ARGUE. THINGS'RE REALLY TENSE, BUT THEY WON'T SAY WHAT'S UP...
THINK THEY'RE SPLITTING UP?
MAYBE. MAYBE NOT. THEY WON'T SAY. IT'S LIKE SOME BIG SECRET THEY AREN'T SHARING. IT'D BE EASIER IF THEY'D JUST SPLIT. LEAST I COULD DEAL WITH THAT.
ORSON
AW, QUIT WHINING. EVERYONE'S PARENTS ARE LIKE THAT. BE GLAD THEY'RE NOT DUMPING THEIR PROBLEMS ON YOUR HEAD.
AND ANYWAY, WHY ARE WE WORRYING ABOUT IT NOW?
HEL-LO, CLEVE-LAND!
IT'S SHOWTIME.

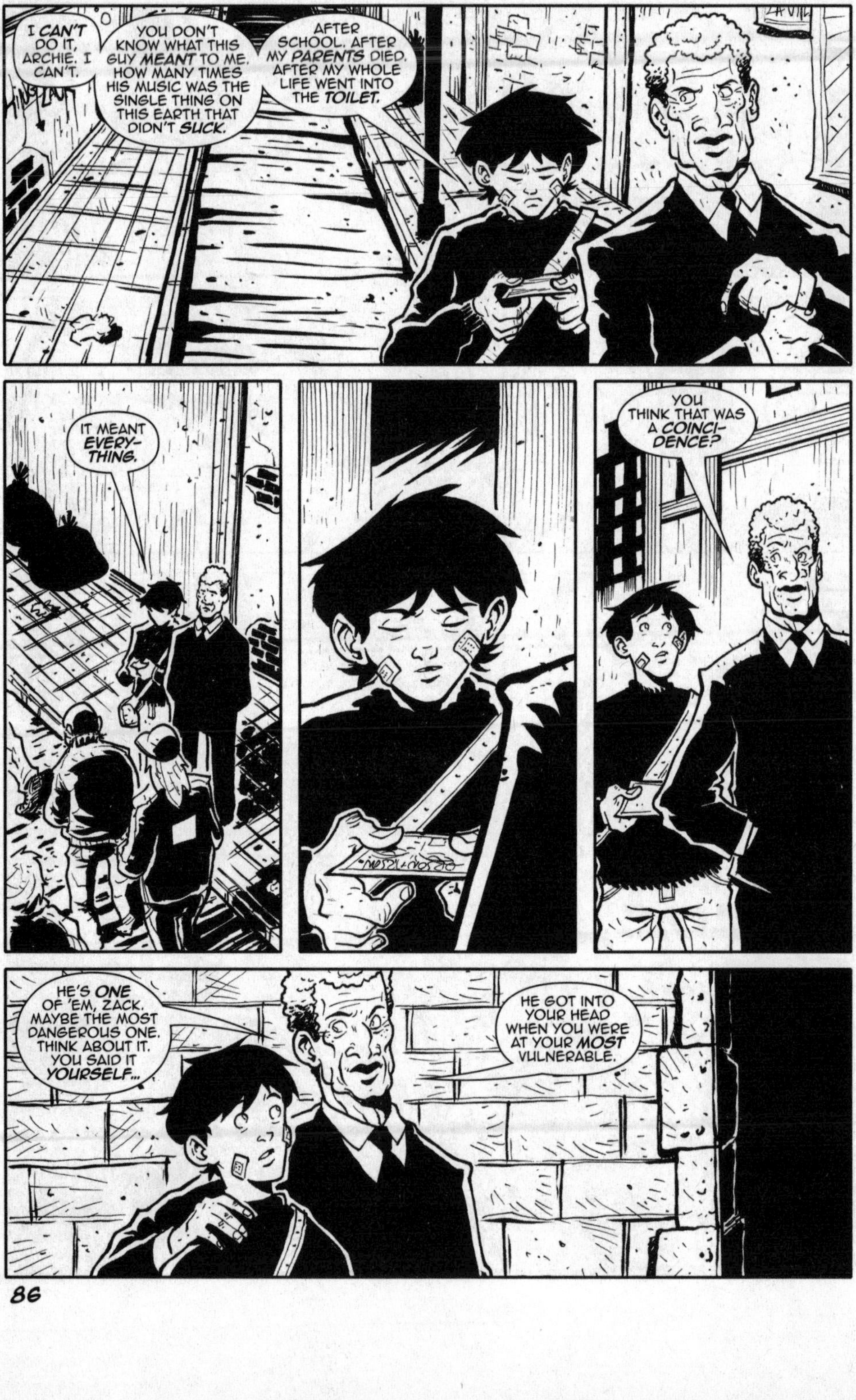
I CAN'T DO IT, ARCHIE. I CAN'T.
YOU DON'T KNOW WHAT THIS GUY MEANT TO ME. HOW MANY TIMES HIS MUSIC WAS THE SINGLE THING ON THIS EARTH THAT DIDN'T SUCK.
AFTER SCHOOL. AFTER MY PARENTS DIED. AFTER MY WHOLE LIFE WENT INTO THE TOILET.
IT MEANT EVERY-THING.
YOU THINK THAT WAS A COINCI-DENCE?
HE'S ONE OF 'EM, ZACK. MAYBE THE MOST DANGEROUS ONE. THINK ABOUT IT. YOU SAID IT YOURSELF...
HE GOT INTO YOUR HEAD WHEN YOU WERE AT YOUR MOST VULNERABLE.

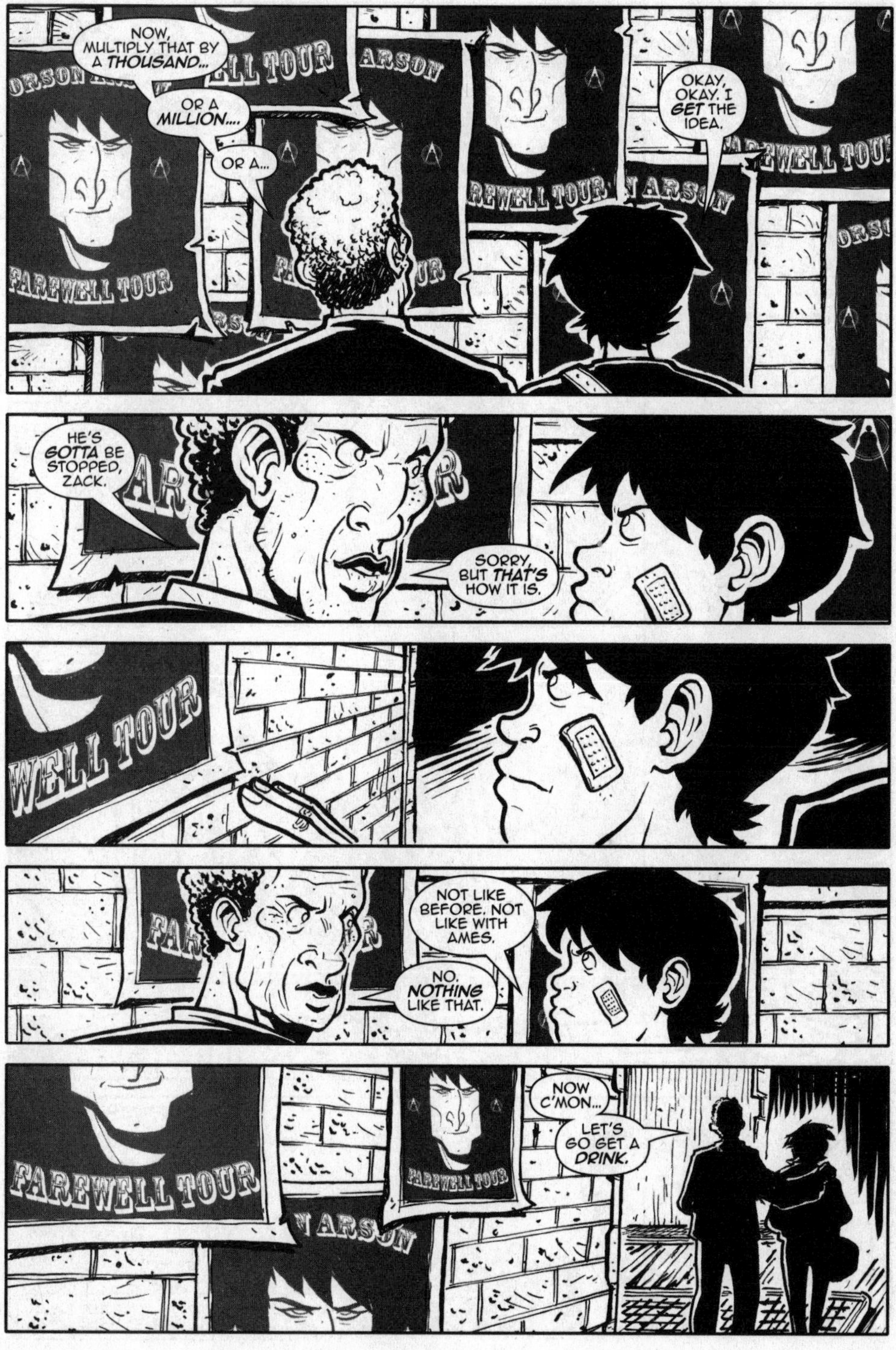
NOW, MULTIPLY THAT BY A THOUSAND...
OR A MILLION....
OR A...
OKAY, OKAY. I GET THE IDEA.
HE'S GOTTA BE STOPPED, ZACK.
SORRY, BUT THAT'S HOW IT IS.
NOT LIKE BEFORE. NOT LIKE WITH AMES.
NO. NOTHING LIKE THAT.
NOW C'MON...
LET'S GO GET A DRINK.

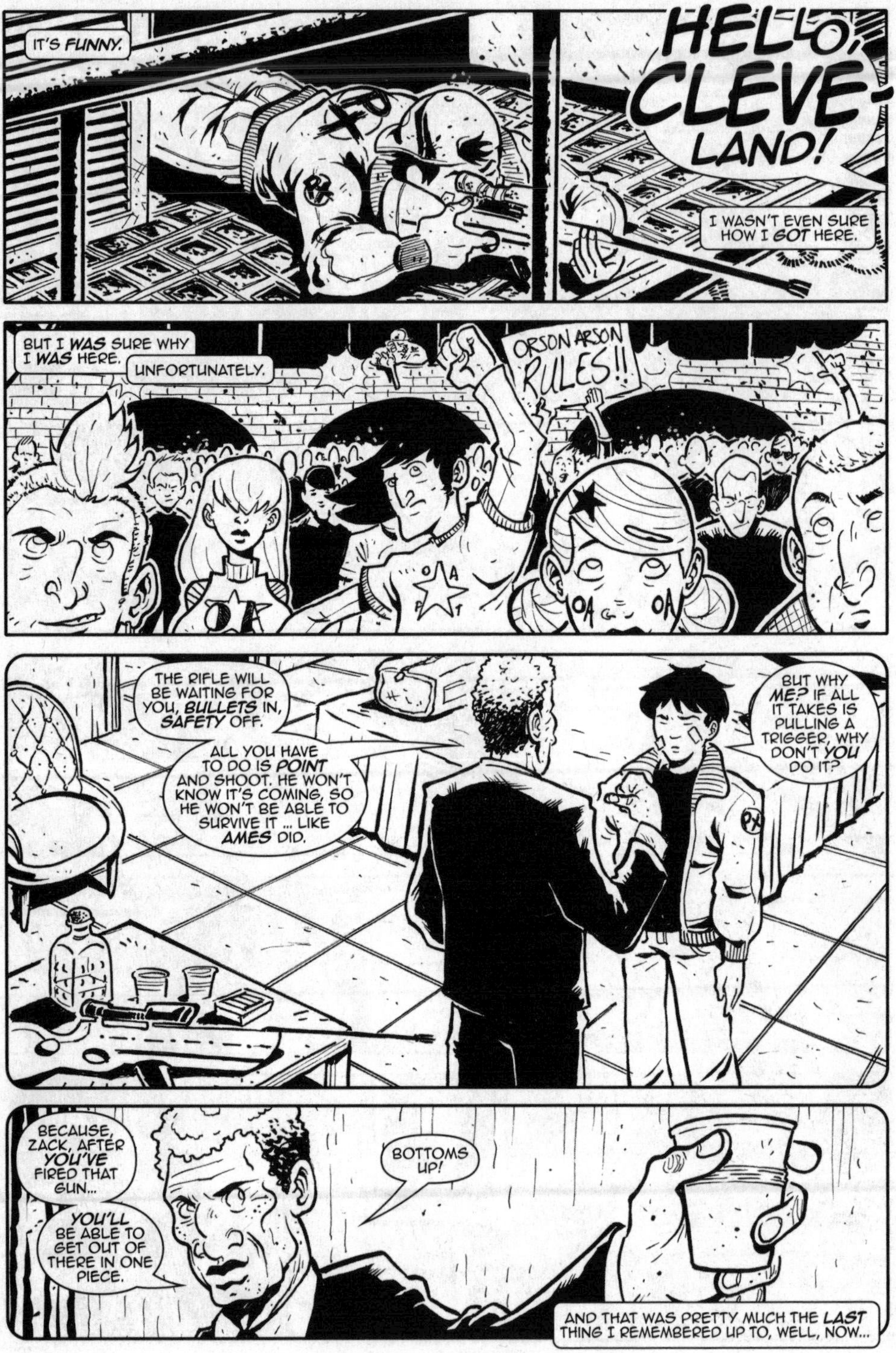
IT'S FUNNY.
HELLO, CLEVE-LAND!
I WASN'T EVEN SURE HOW I GOT HERE.
BUT I WAS SURE WHY I WAS HERE.
UNFORTUNATELY.
ORSON ARSON RULES!!
THE RIFLE WILL BE WAITING FOR YOU, BULLETS IN, SAFETY OFF.
ALL YOU HAVE TO DO IS POINT AND SHOOT. HE WON'T KNOW IT'S COMING, SO HE WON'T BE ABLE TO SURVIVE IT ... LIKE AMES DID.
BUT WHY ME? IF ALL IT TAKES IS PULLING A TRIGGER, WHY DON'T YOU DO IT?
BECAUSE, ZACK, AFTER YOU'VE FIRED THAT GUN...
YOU'LL BE ABLE TO GET OUT OF THERE IN ONE PIECE.
BOTTOMS UP!
AND THAT WAS PRETTY MUCH THE LAST THING I REMEMBERED UP TO, WELL, NOW...

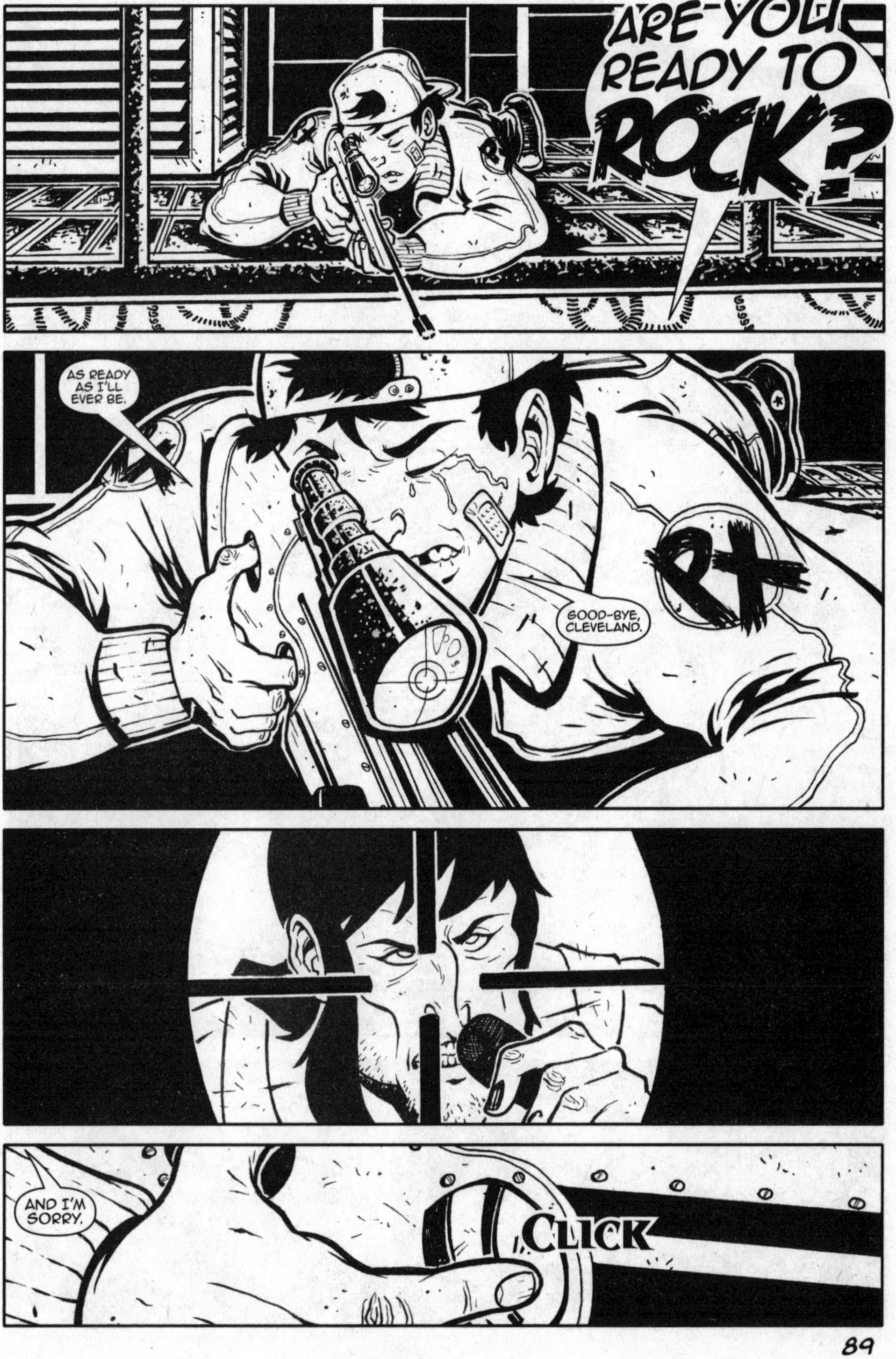
ARE YOU READY TO ROCK?
AS READY AS I'LL EVER BE.
GOOD-BYE, CLEVELAND.
AND I'M SORRY.
CLICK

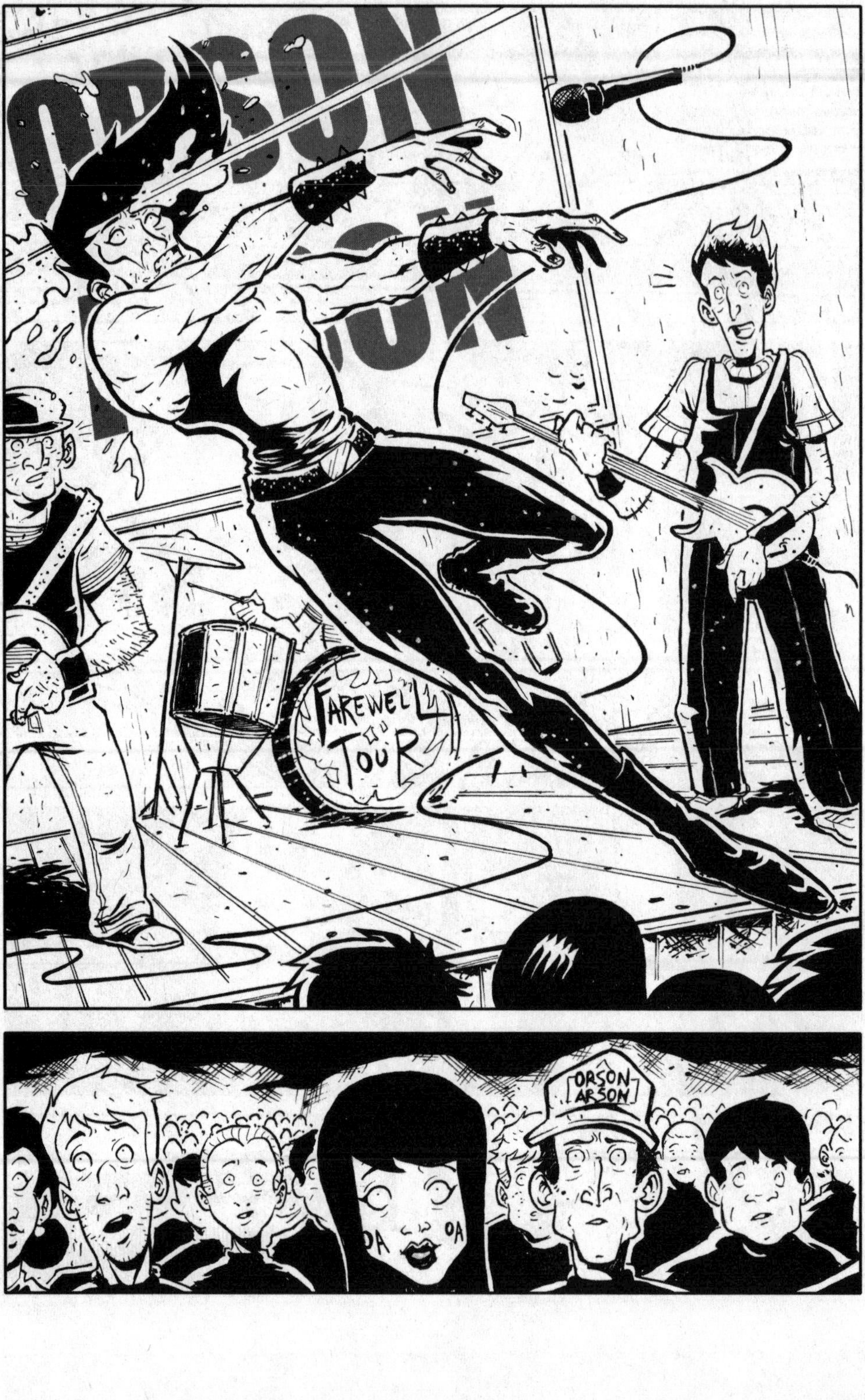
ORSON
FAREWELL TOUR
ORSON ARSON
OA
OA

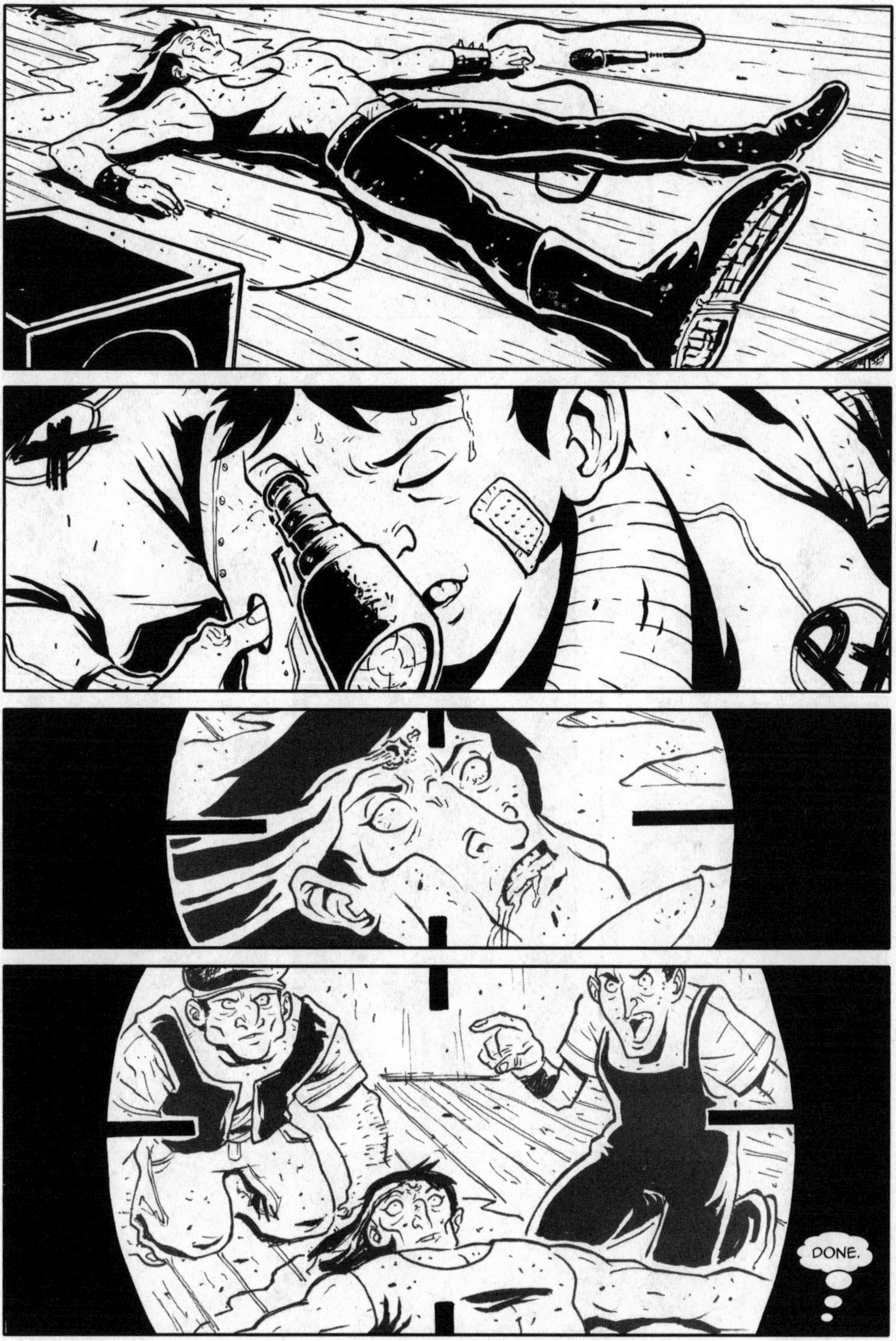
DONE.

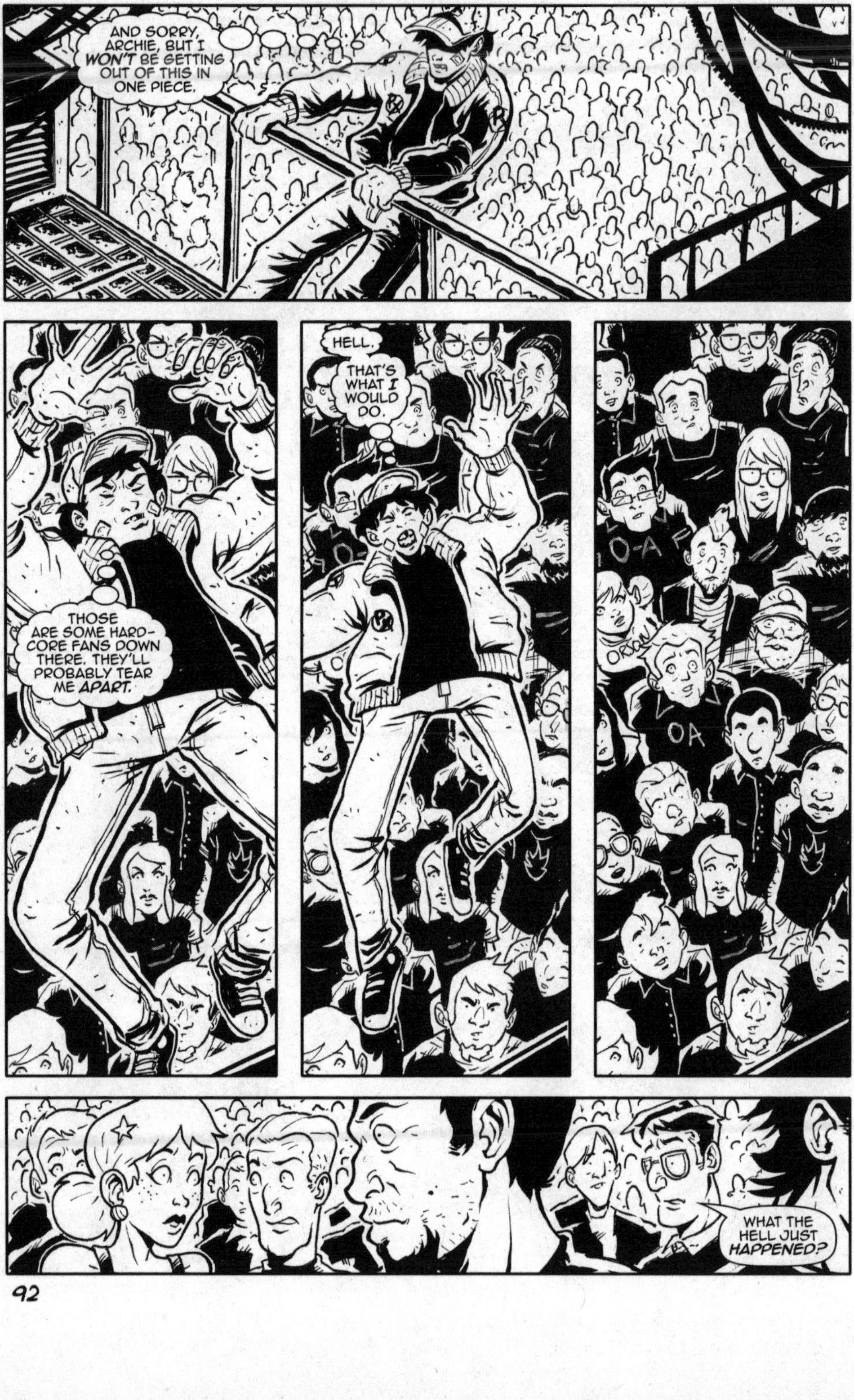
AND SORRY, ARCHIE, BUT I WON'T BE GETTING OUT OF THIS IN ONE PIECE.
THOSE ARE SOME HARD-CORE FANS DOWN THERE. THEY'LL PROBABLY TEAR ME APART.
HELL.
THAT'S WHAT I WOULD DO.
WHAT THE HELL JUST HAPPENED?

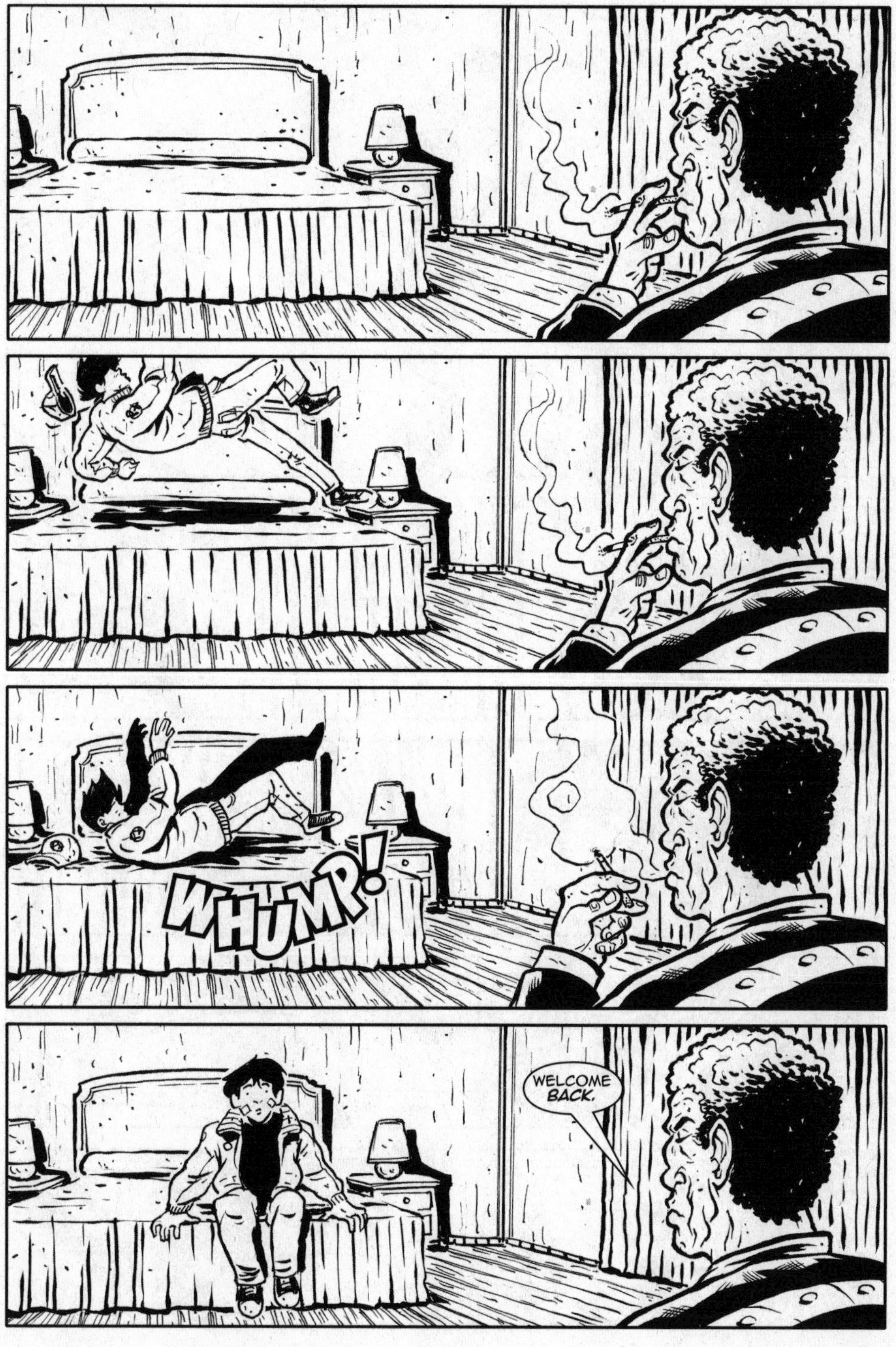
WHUMP!
WELCOME BACK.

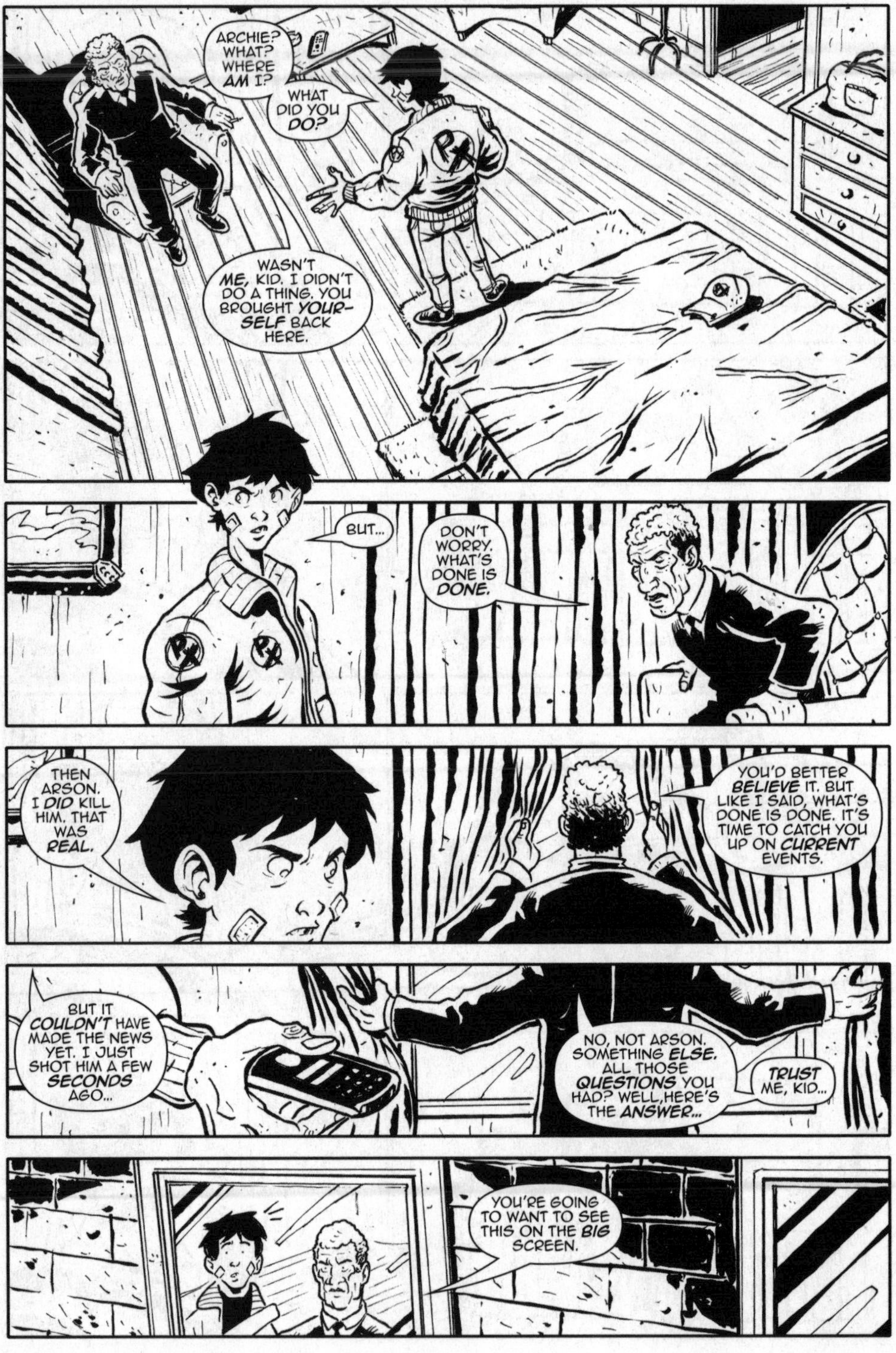
ARCHIE? WHAT? WHERE AM I?
WHAT DID YOU DO?
WASN'T ME, KID. I DIDN'T DO A THING. YOU BROUGHT YOURSELF BACK HERE.
BUT...
DON'T WORRY. WHAT'S DONE IS DONE.
THEN ARSON. I DID KILL HIM. THAT WAS REAL.
YOU'D BETTER BELIEVE IT. BUT LIKE I SAID, WHAT'S DONE IS DONE. IT'S TIME TO CATCH YOU UP ON CURRENT EVENTS.
BUT IT COULDN'T HAVE MADE THE NEWS YET. I JUST SHOT HIM A FEW SECONDS AGO...
NO, NOT ARSON. SOMETHING ELSE. ALL THOSE QUESTIONS YOU HAD? WELL, HERE'S THE ANSWER...
TRUST ME, KID...
YOU'RE GOING TO WANT TO SEE THIS ON THE BIG SCREEN.

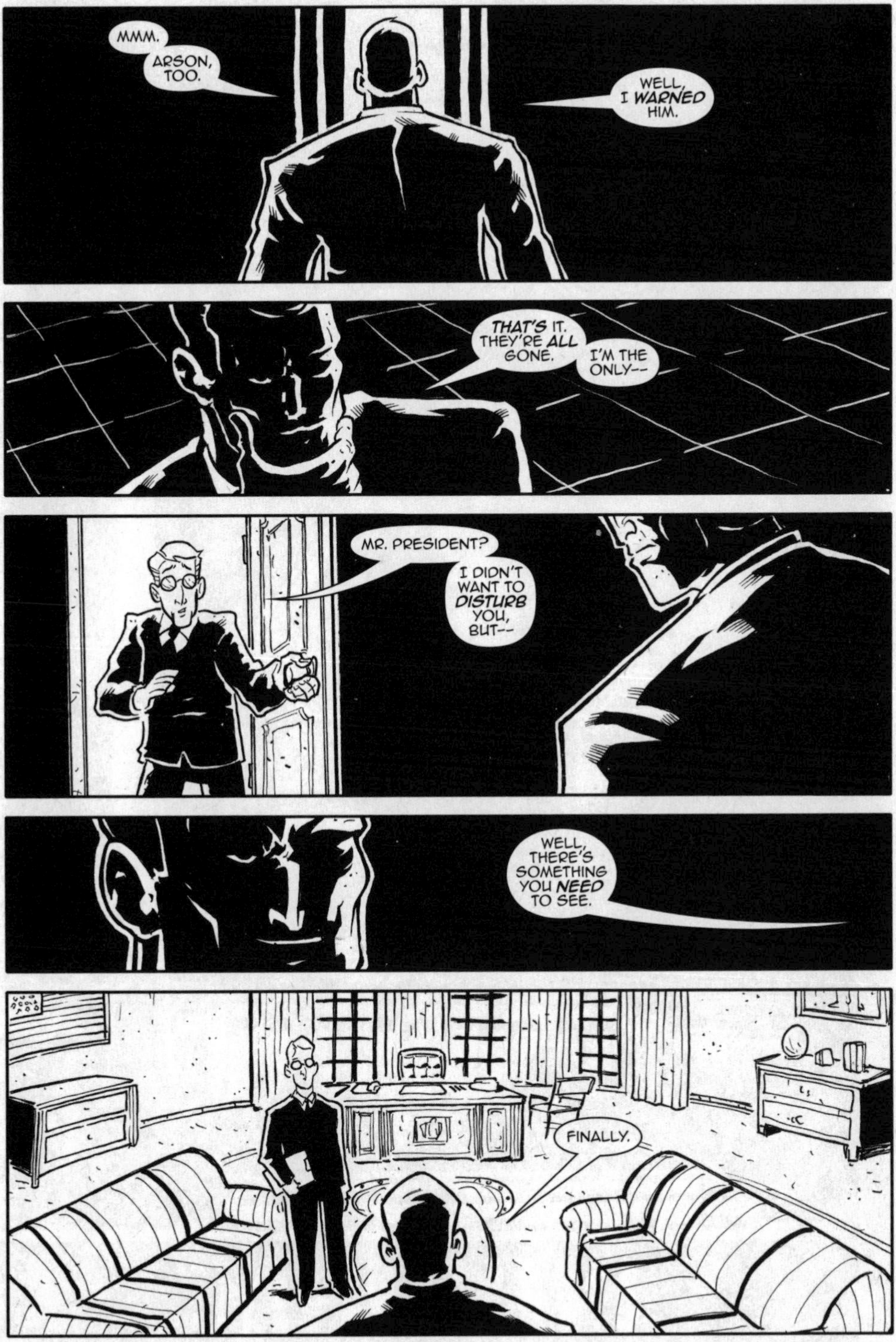
MMM.
ARSON, TOO.
WELL, I *WARNED* HIM.
THAT'S IT. THEY'RE *ALL* GONE.
I'M THE ONLY--
MR. PRESIDENT?
I DIDN'T WANT TO *DISTURB* YOU, BUT--
WELL, THERE'S SOMETHING YOU *NEED* TO SEE.
FINALLY.

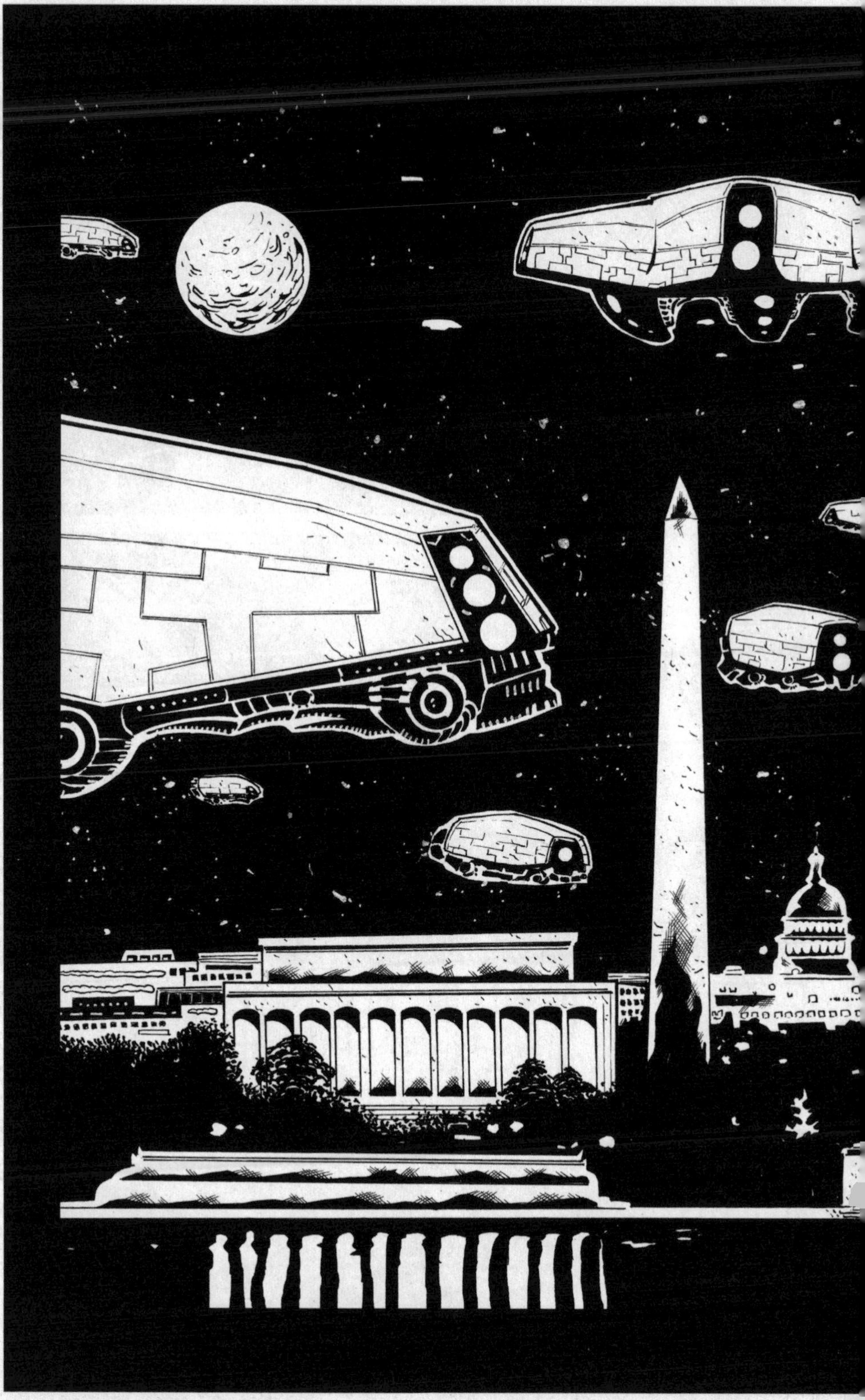

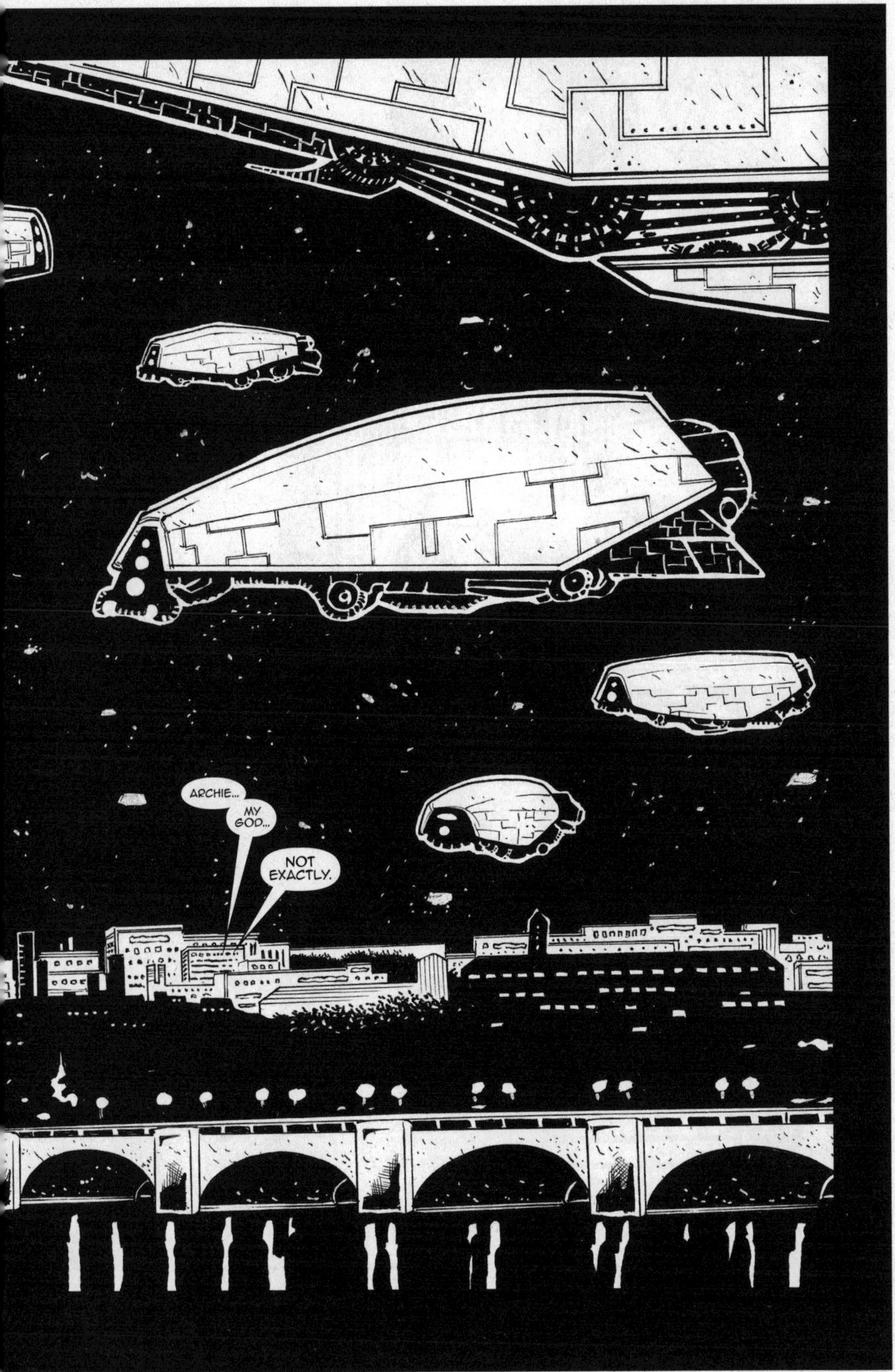
ARCHIE...
MY GOD...
NOT EXACTLY.

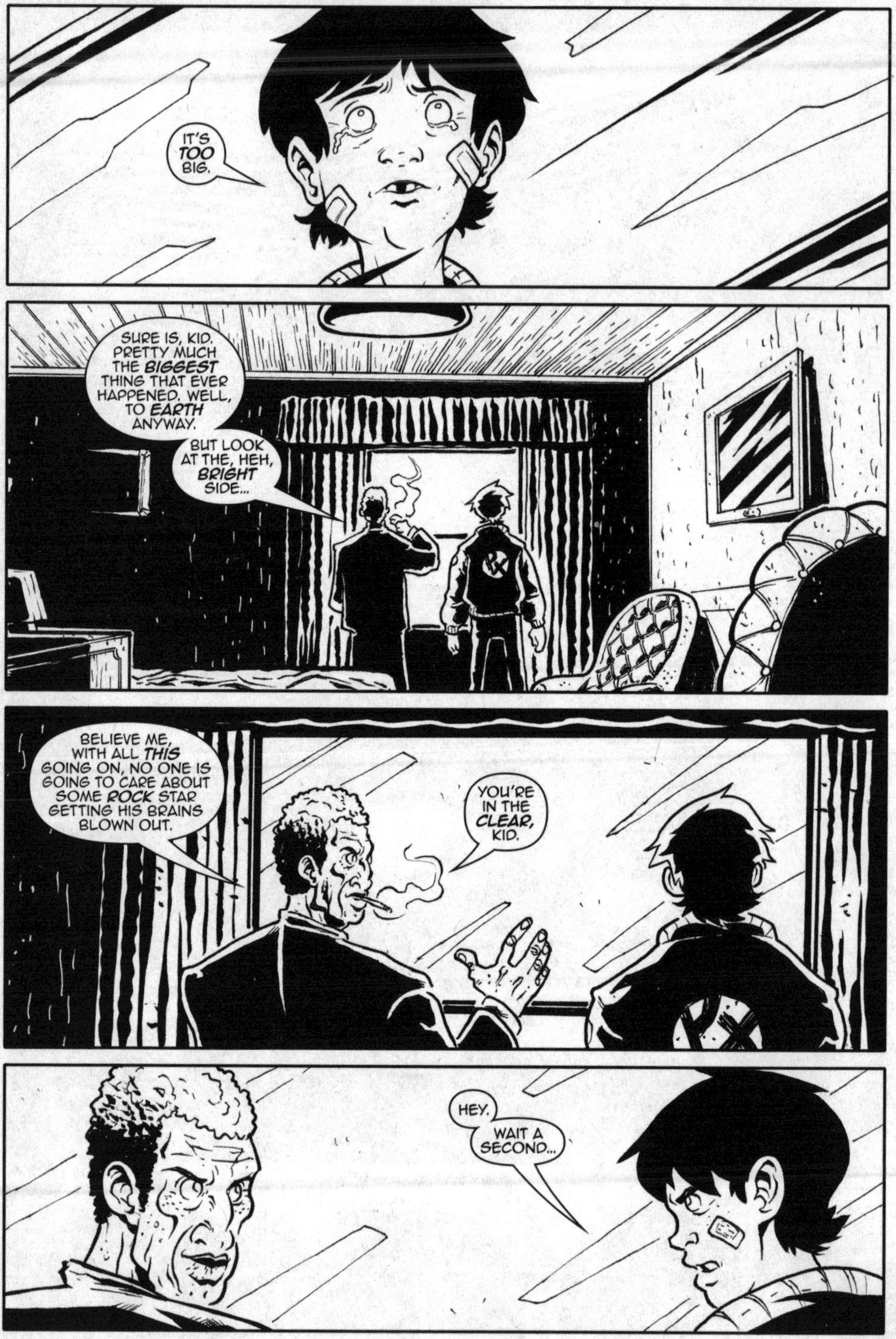
IT'S TOO BIG.
SURE IS, KID. PRETTY MUCH THE BIGGEST THING THAT EVER HAPPENED. WELL, TO EARTH ANYWAY.
BUT LOOK AT THE, HEH, BRIGHT SIDE...
BELIEVE ME, WITH ALL THIS GOING ON, NO ONE IS GOING TO CARE ABOUT SOME ROCK STAR GETTING HIS BRAINS BLOWN OUT.
YOU'RE IN THE CLEAR, KID.
HEY.
WAIT A SECOND...

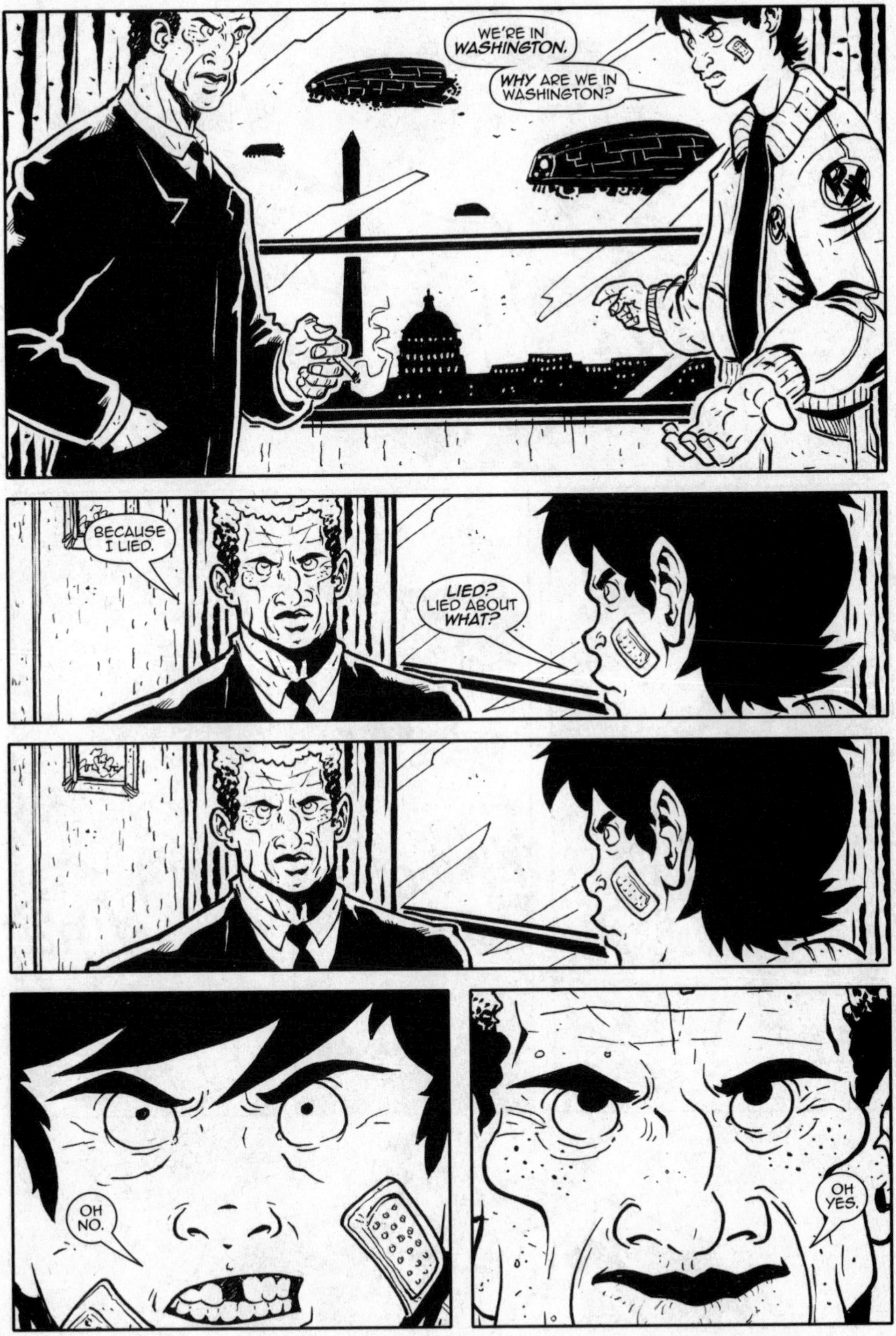
WE'RE IN WASHINGTON.
WHY ARE WE IN WASHINGTON?
BECAUSE I LIED.
LIED? LIED ABOUT WHAT?
OH NO.
OH YES.

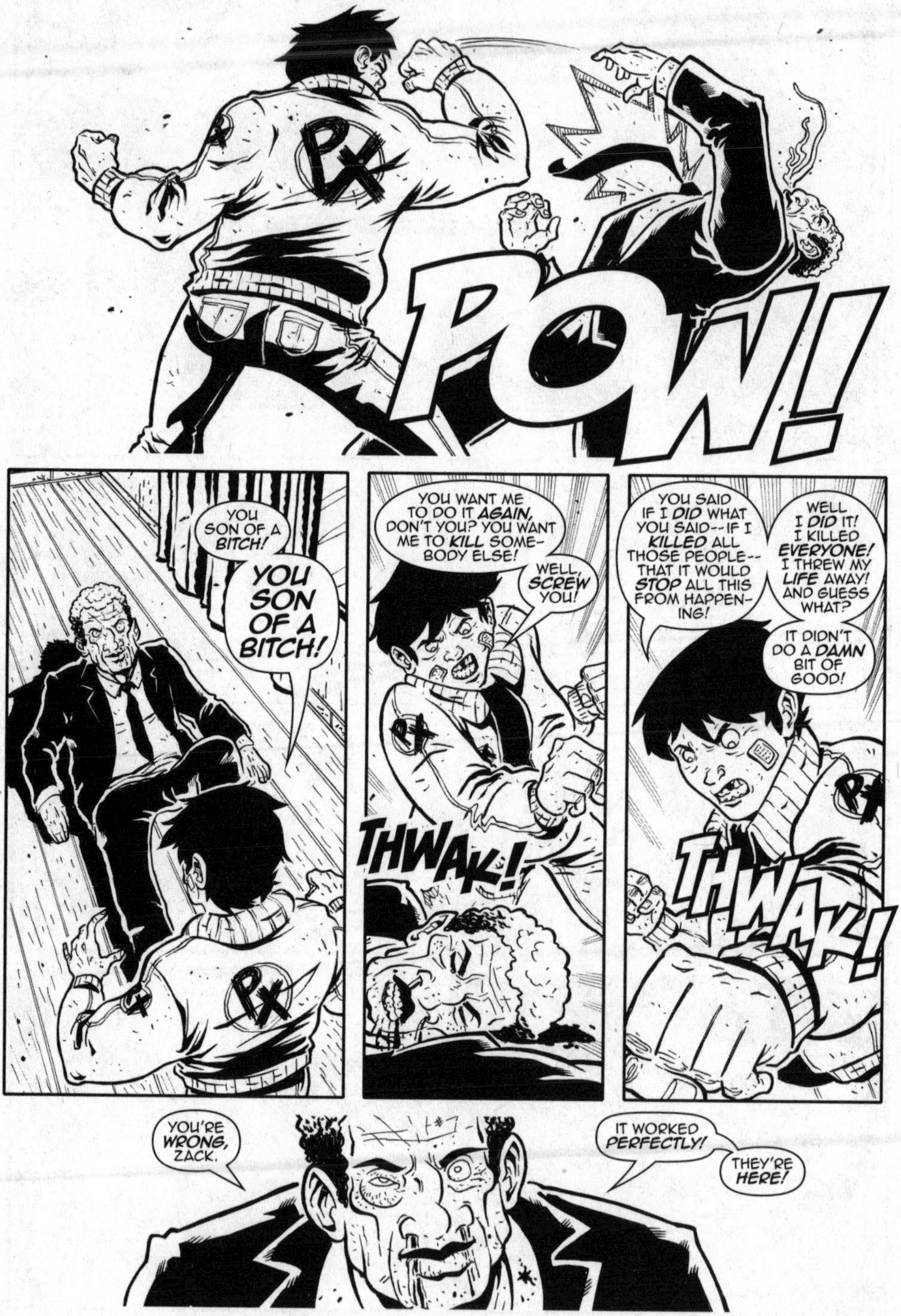
POW!
YOU SON OF A BITCH!
YOU SON OF A BITCH!
YOU WANT ME TO DO IT AGAIN, DON'T YOU? YOU WANT ME TO KILL SOMEBODY ELSE!
WELL, SCREW YOU!
THWAK!
YOU SAID IF I DID WHAT YOU SAID--IF I KILLED ALL THOSE PEOPLE--THAT IT WOULD STOP ALL THIS FROM HAPPENING!
WELL I DID IT! I KILLED EVERYONE! I THREW MY LIFE AWAY! AND GUESS WHAT?
IT DIDN'T DO A DAMN BIT OF GOOD!
THWAK!
YOU'RE WRONG, ZACK.
IT WORKED PERFECTLY!
THEY'RE HERE!

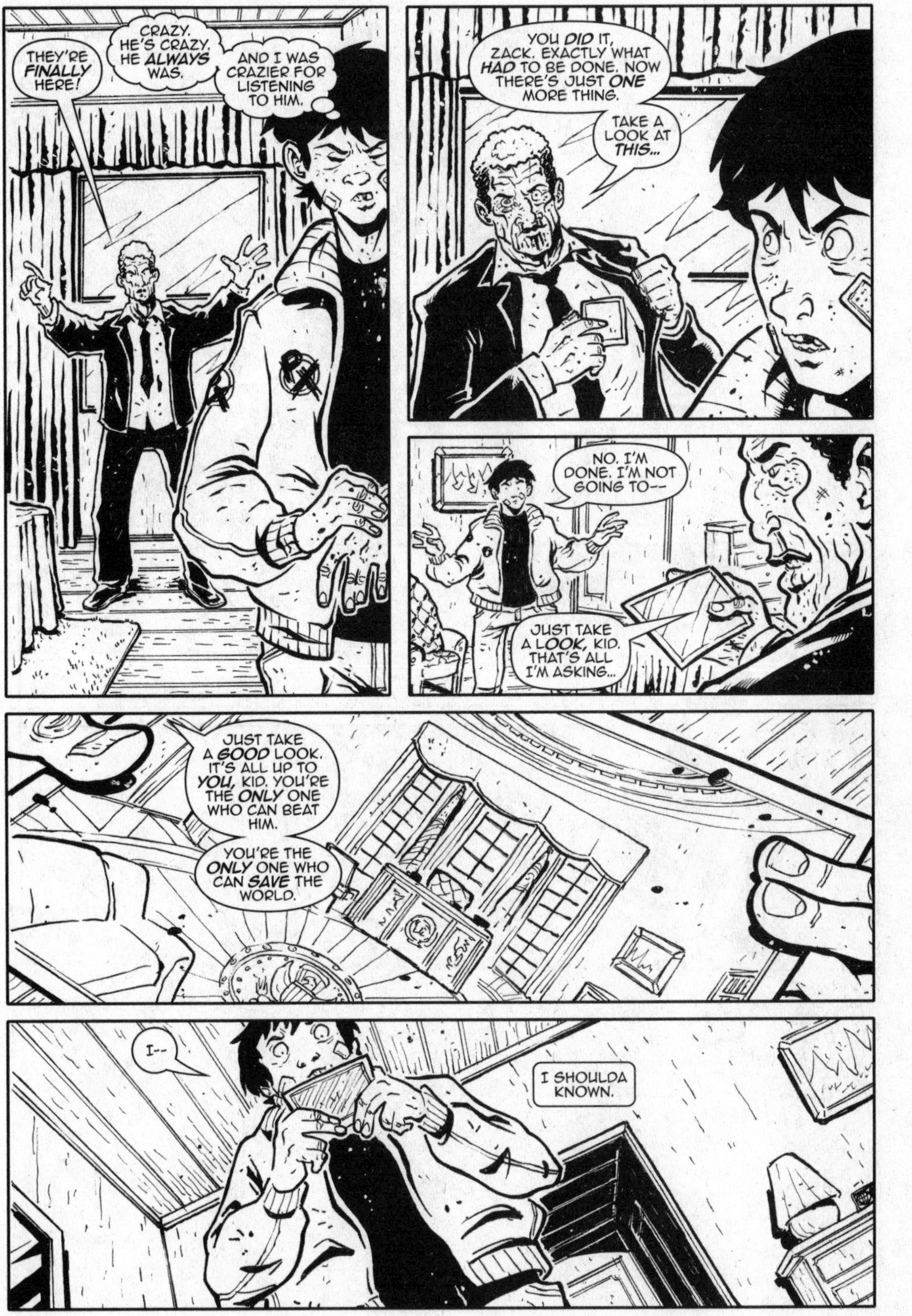
THEY'RE *FINALLY* HERE!
CRAZY. HE'S CRAZY. HE *ALWAYS* WAS.
AND I WAS CRAZIER FOR LISTENING TO HIM.
YOU *DID* IT, ZACK. EXACTLY WHAT *HAD* TO BE DONE. NOW THERE'S JUST *ONE* MORE THING.
TAKE A LOOK AT *THIS*...
NO. I'M DONE. I'M NOT GOING TO--
JUST TAKE A *LOOK*, KID. THAT'S ALL I'M ASKING...
JUST TAKE A *GOOD* LOOK. IT'S ALL UP TO *YOU*, KID. YOU'RE THE *ONLY* ONE WHO CAN BEAT HIM.
YOU'RE THE *ONLY* ONE WHO CAN *SAVE* THE WORLD.
I--
I SHOULDA KNOWN.

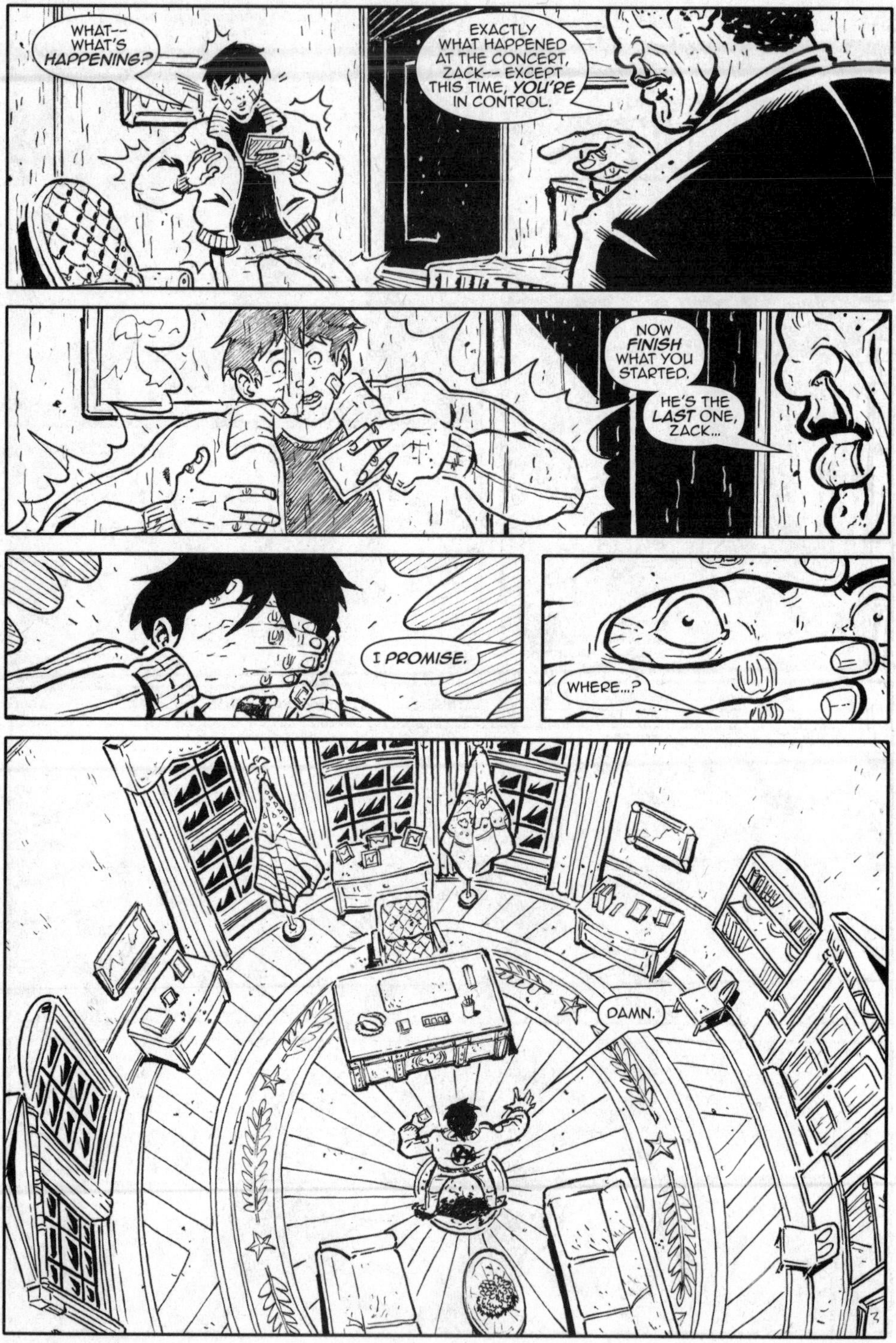
WHAT-- WHAT'S *HAPPENING?*
EXACTLY WHAT HAPPENED AT THE CONCERT, ZACK-- EXCEPT THIS TIME, *YOU'RE* IN CONTROL.
NOW *FINISH* WHAT YOU STARTED.
HE'S THE *LAST* ONE, ZACK...
I *PROMISE.*
WHERE...?
DAMN.

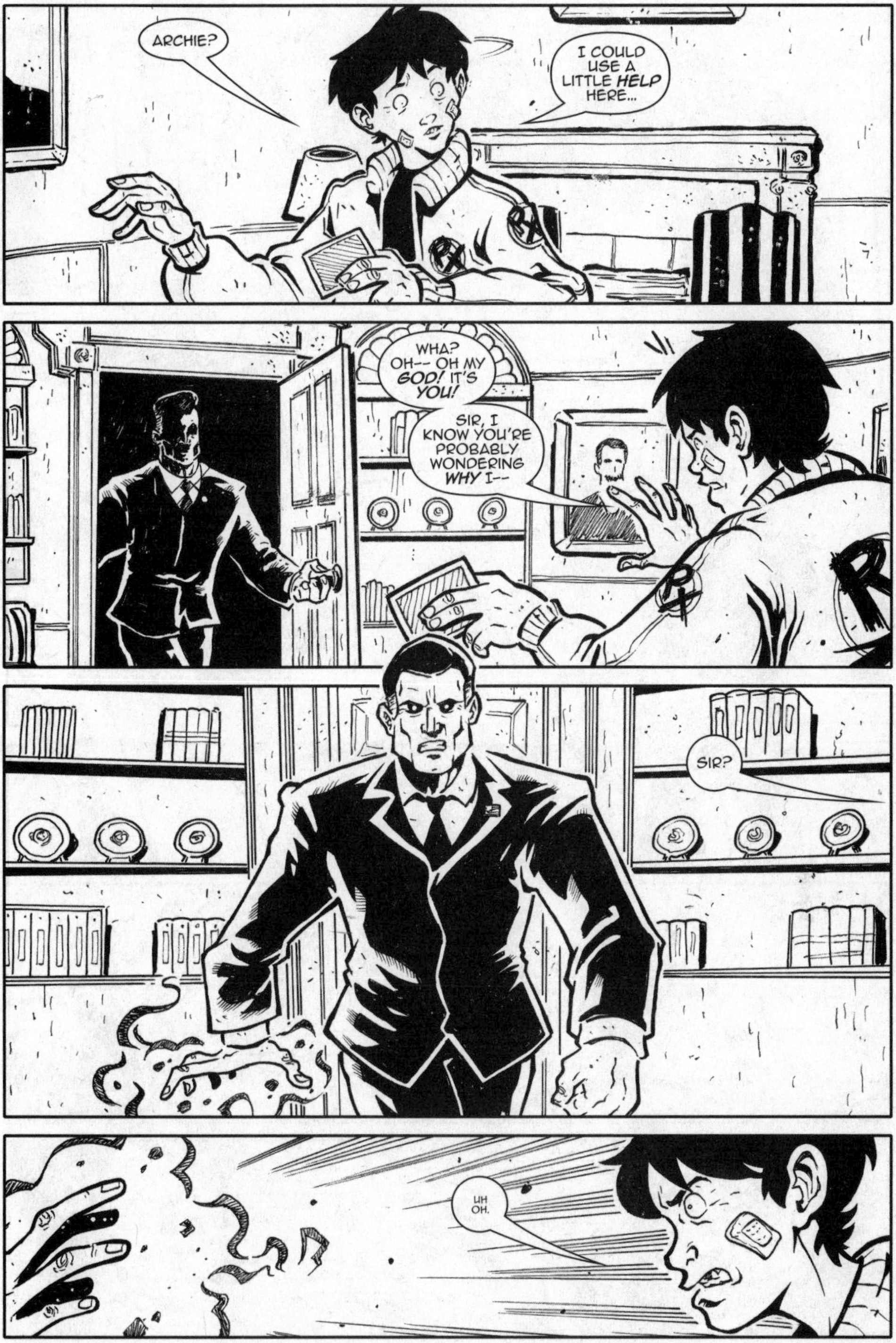
ARCHIE?
I COULD USE A LITTLE HELP HERE...
WHA? OH-- OH MY GOD! IT'S YOU!
SIR, I KNOW YOU'RE PROBABLY WONDERING WHY I--
SIR?
UH OH.

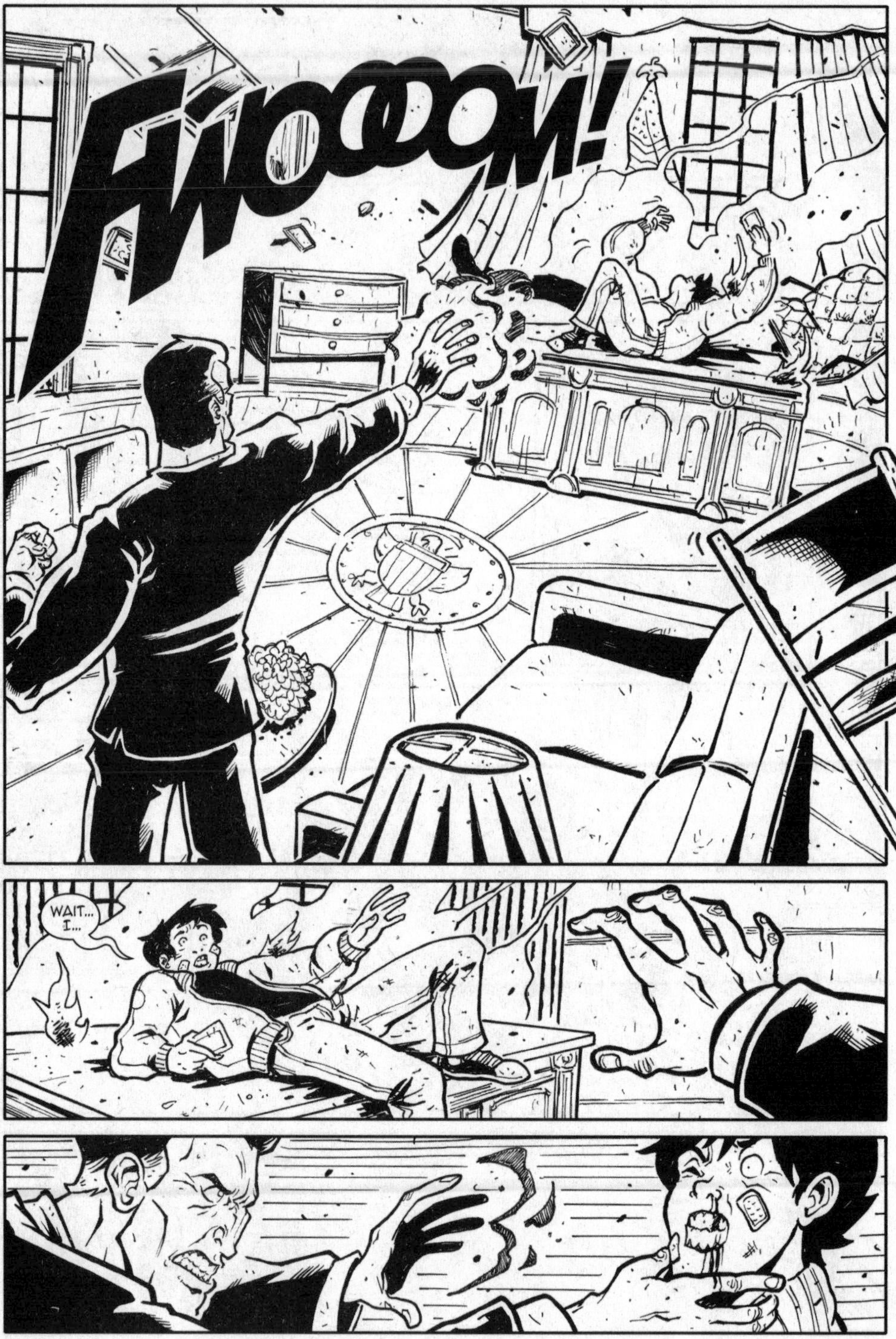
FWOOOM!
WAIT... I...

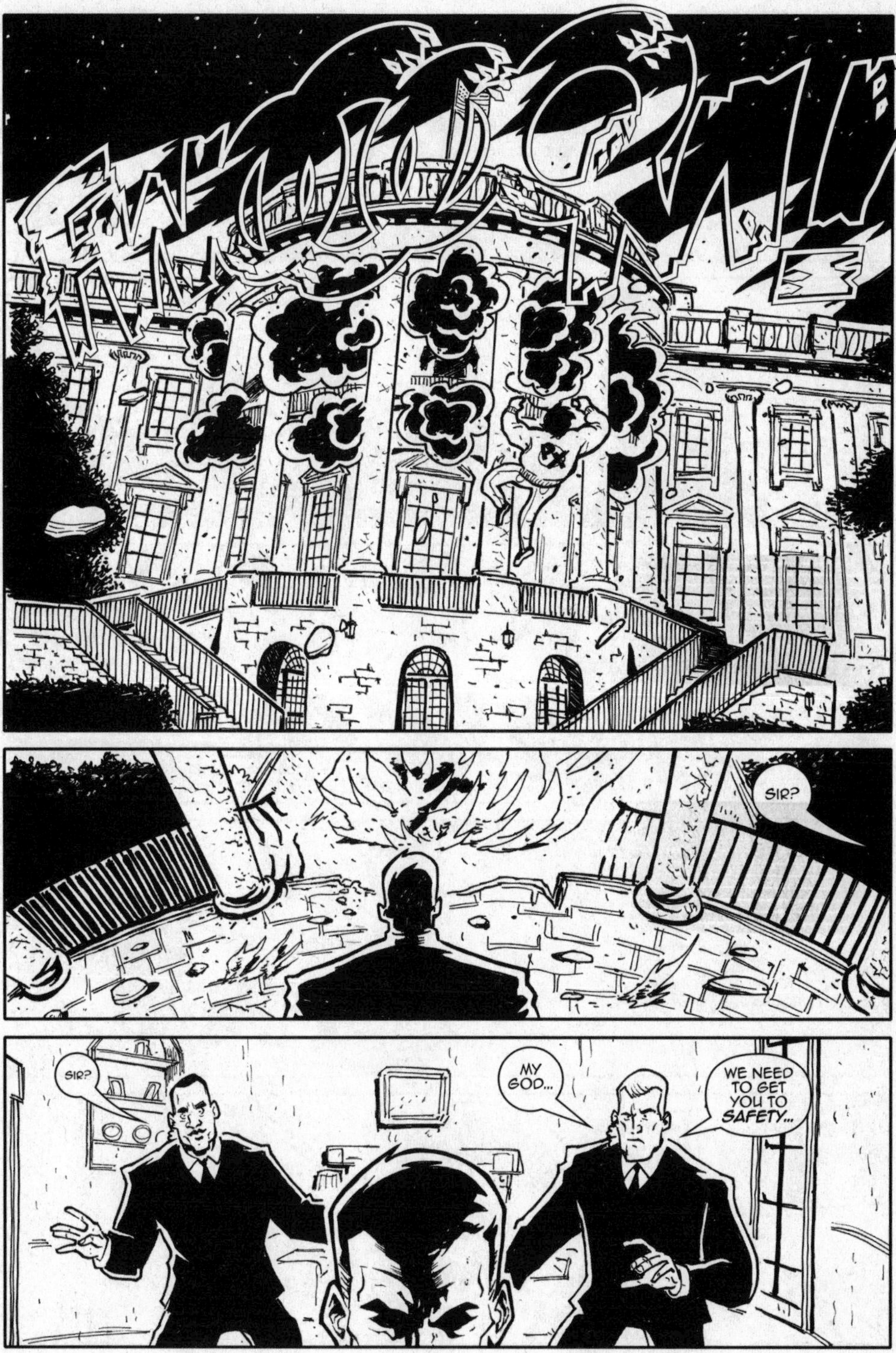
SIR?
SIR?
MY GOD...
WE NEED TO GET YOU TO SAFETY...

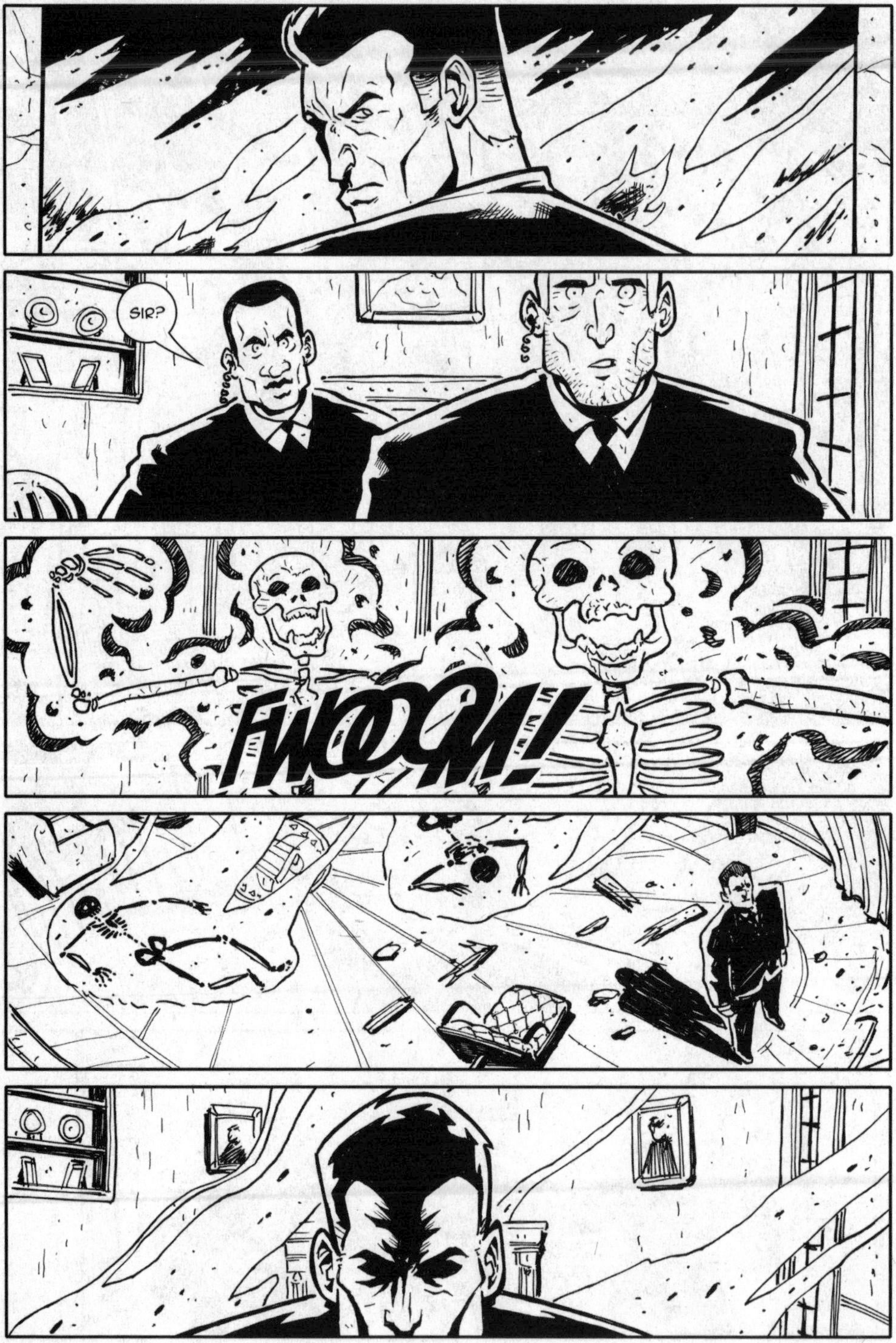
SIR?
FWOOM!

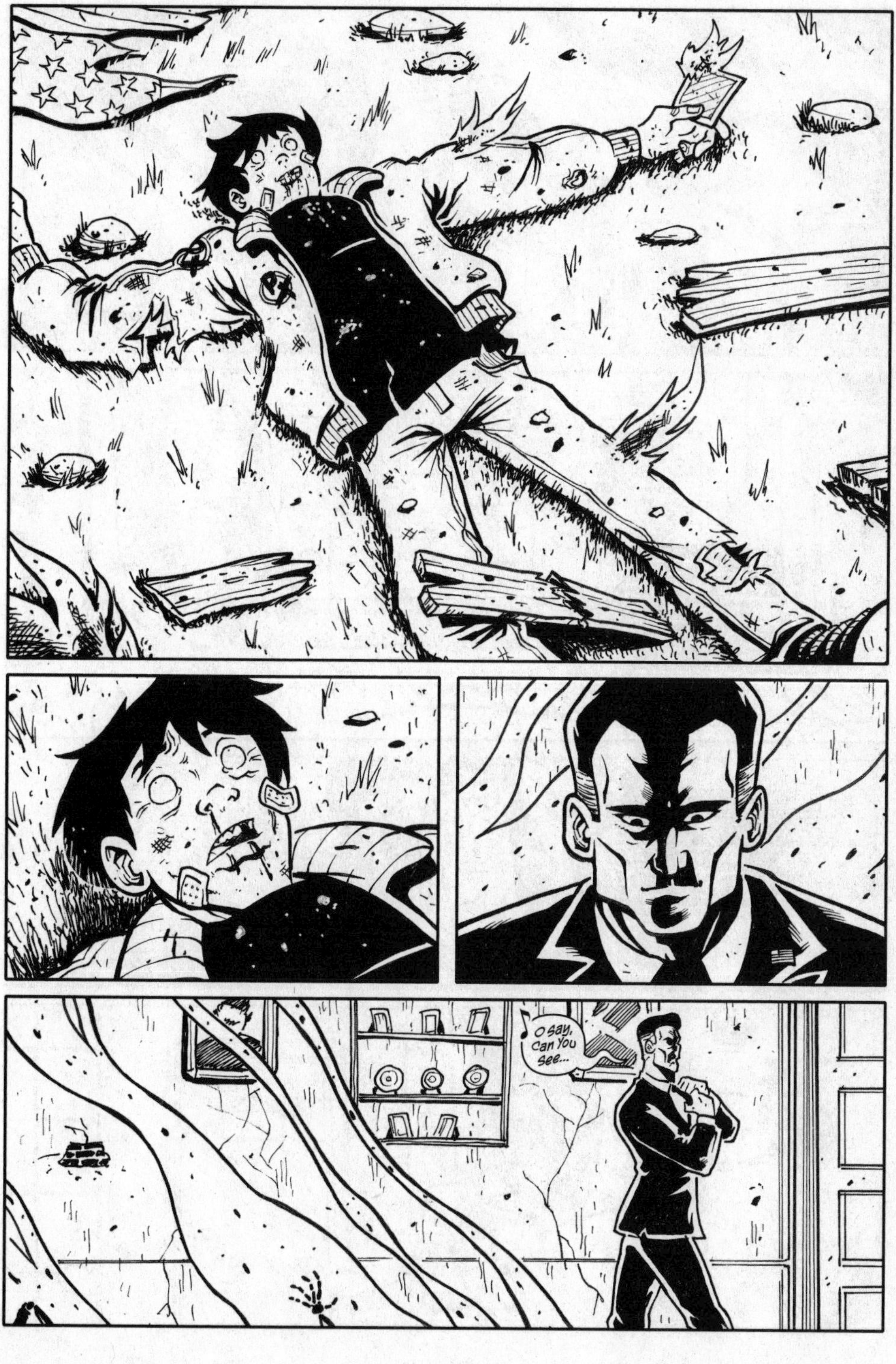
O say, Can You see...

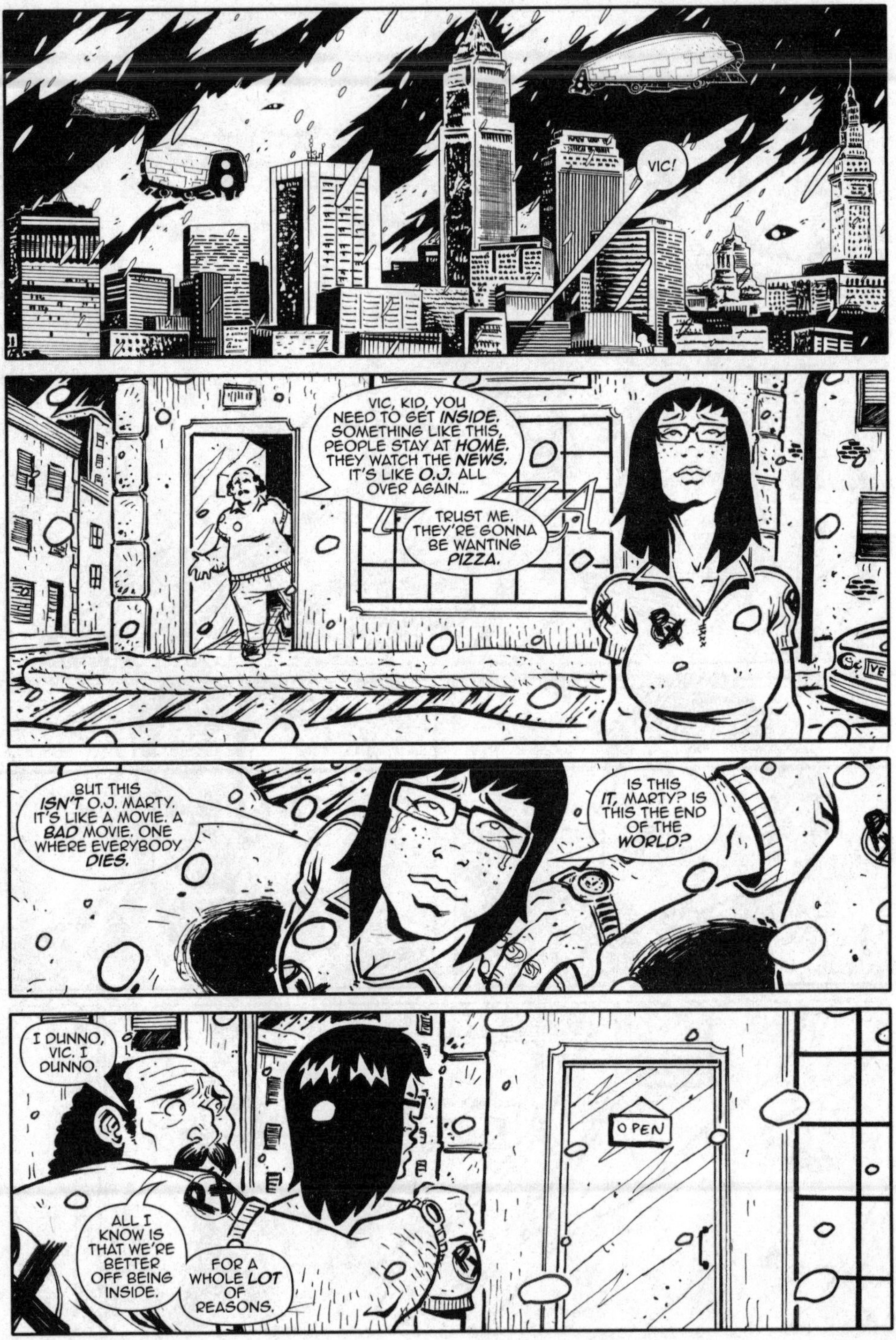
VIC!
VIC, KID, YOU NEED TO GET INSIDE. SOMETHING LIKE THIS, PEOPLE STAY AT HOME. THEY WATCH THE NEWS. IT'S LIKE O.J. ALL OVER AGAIN...
TRUST ME. THEY'RE GONNA BE WANTING PIZZA.
BUT THIS ISN'T O.J. MARTY. IT'S LIKE A MOVIE. A BAD MOVIE. ONE WHERE EVERYBODY DIES.
IS THIS IT, MARTY? IS THIS THE END OF THE WORLD?
I DUNNO, VIC. I DUNNO.
OPEN
ALL I KNOW IS THAT WE'RE BETTER OFF BEING INSIDE.
FOR A WHOLE LOT OF REASONS.

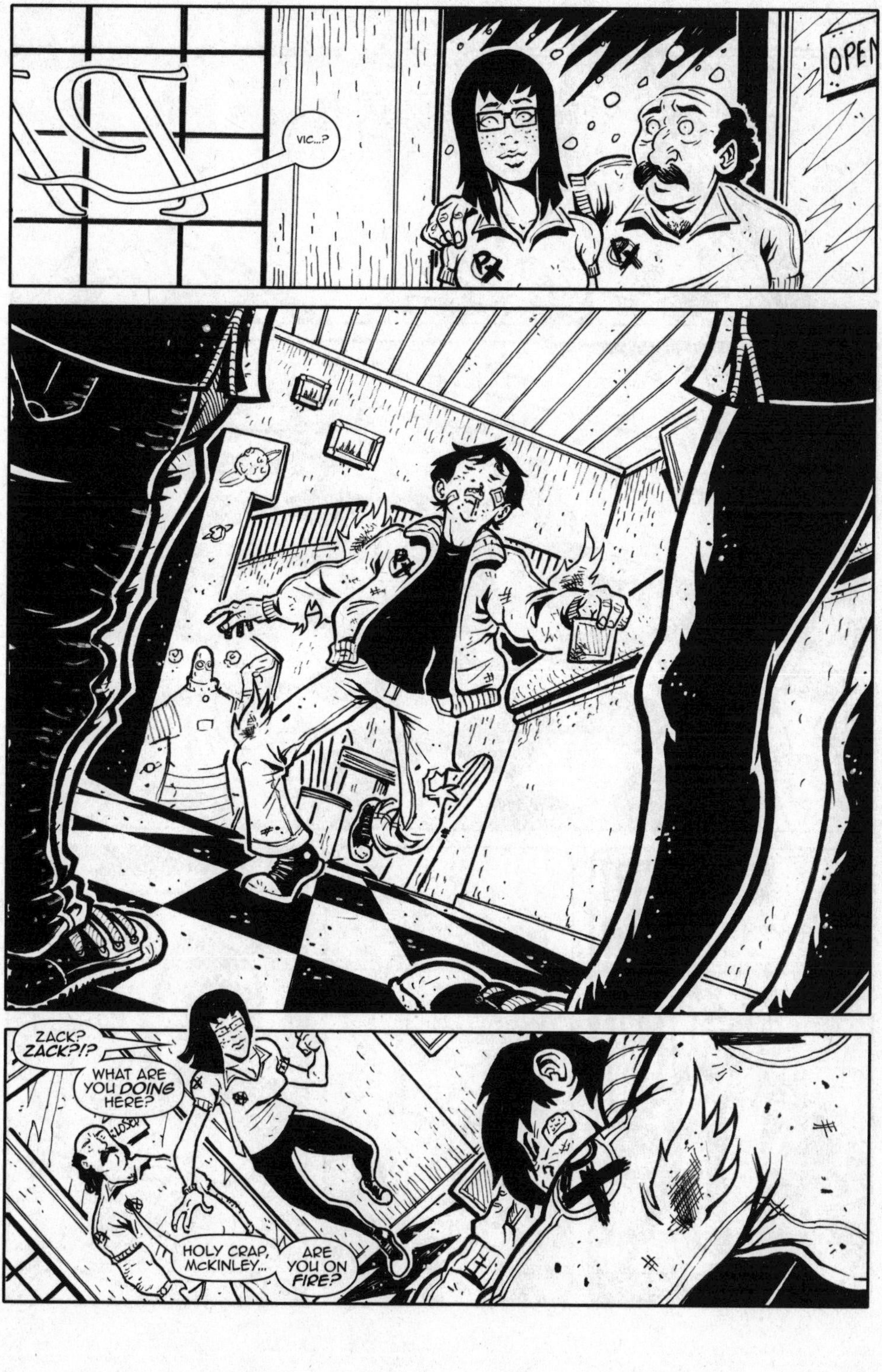
OPEN
VIC...?
ZACK? ZACK?!?
WHAT ARE YOU DOING HERE?
HOLY CRAP, McKINLEY...
ARE YOU ON FIRE?

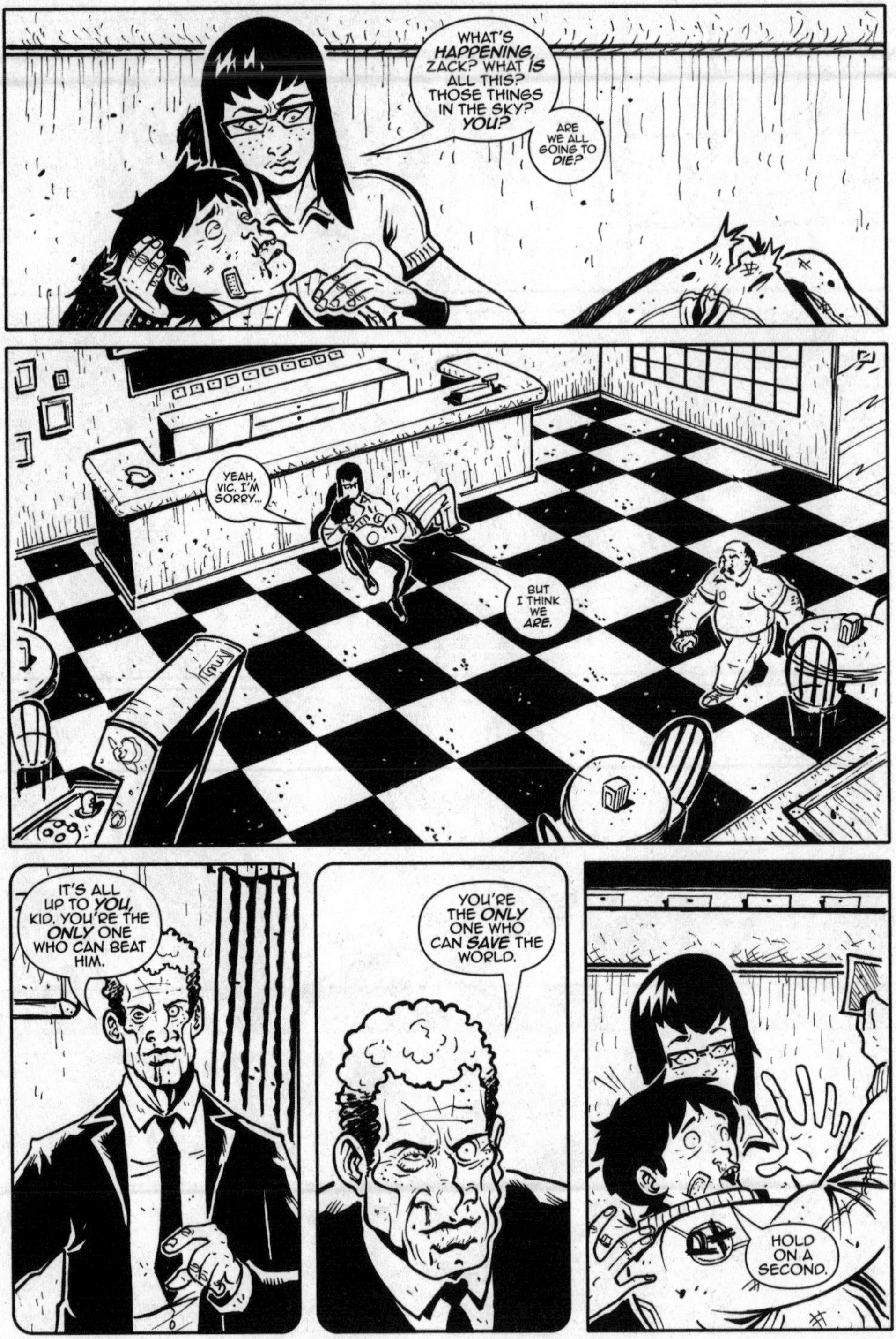
WHAT'S HAPPENING, ZACK? WHAT IS ALL THIS? THOSE THINGS IN THE SKY? YOU?
ARE WE ALL GOING TO DIE?
YEAH, VIC. I'M SORRY...
BUT I THINK WE ARE.
IT'S ALL UP TO YOU, KID. YOU'RE THE ONLY ONE WHO CAN BEAT HIM.
YOU'RE THE ONLY ONE WHO CAN SAVE THE WORLD.
HOLD ON A SECOND.

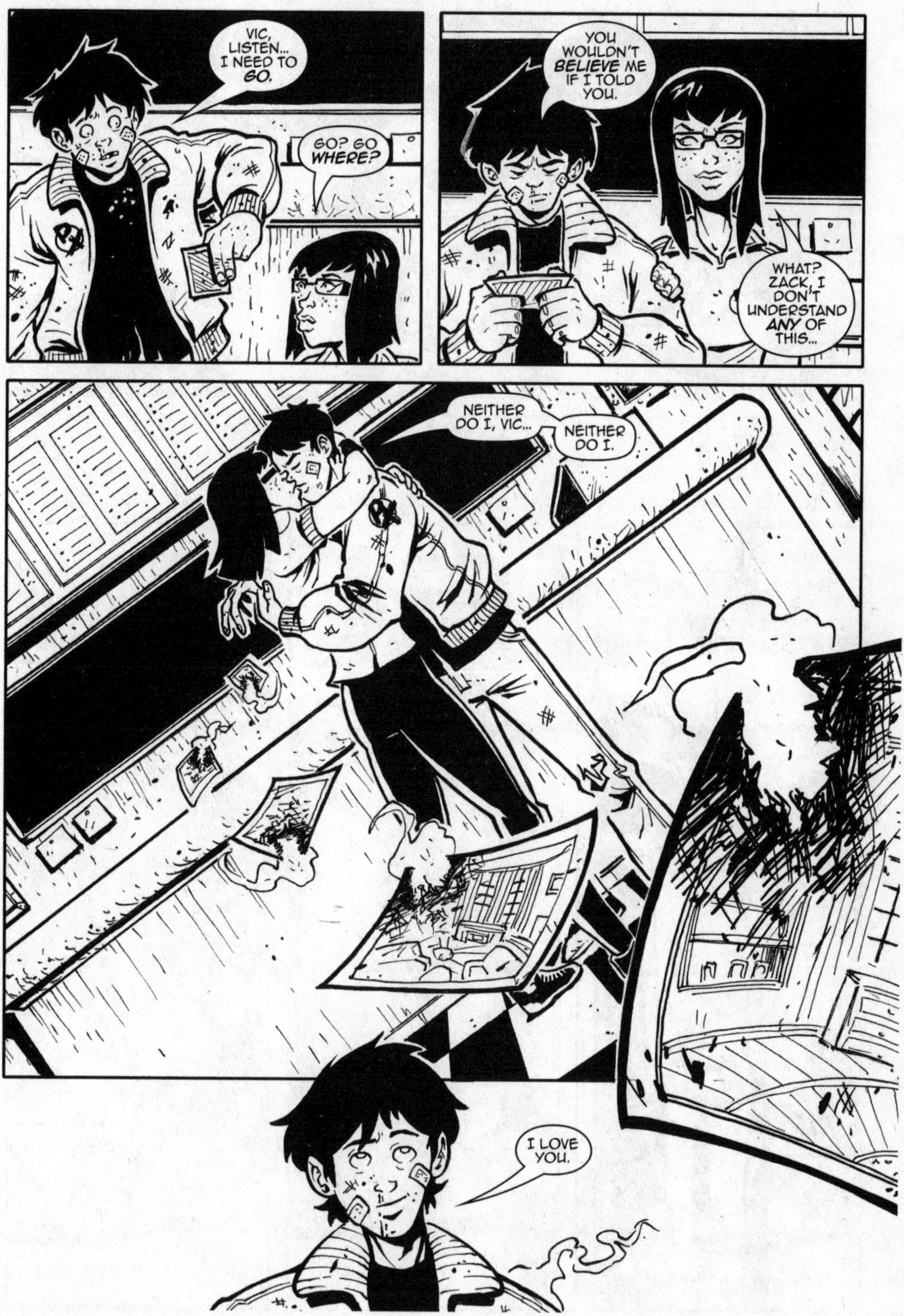
VIC, LISTEN... I NEED TO GO.
GO? GO WHERE?
YOU WOULDN'T BELIEVE ME IF I TOLD YOU.
WHAT? ZACK, I DON'T UNDERSTAND ANY OF THIS...
NEITHER DO I, VIC...
NEITHER DO I.
I LOVE YOU.

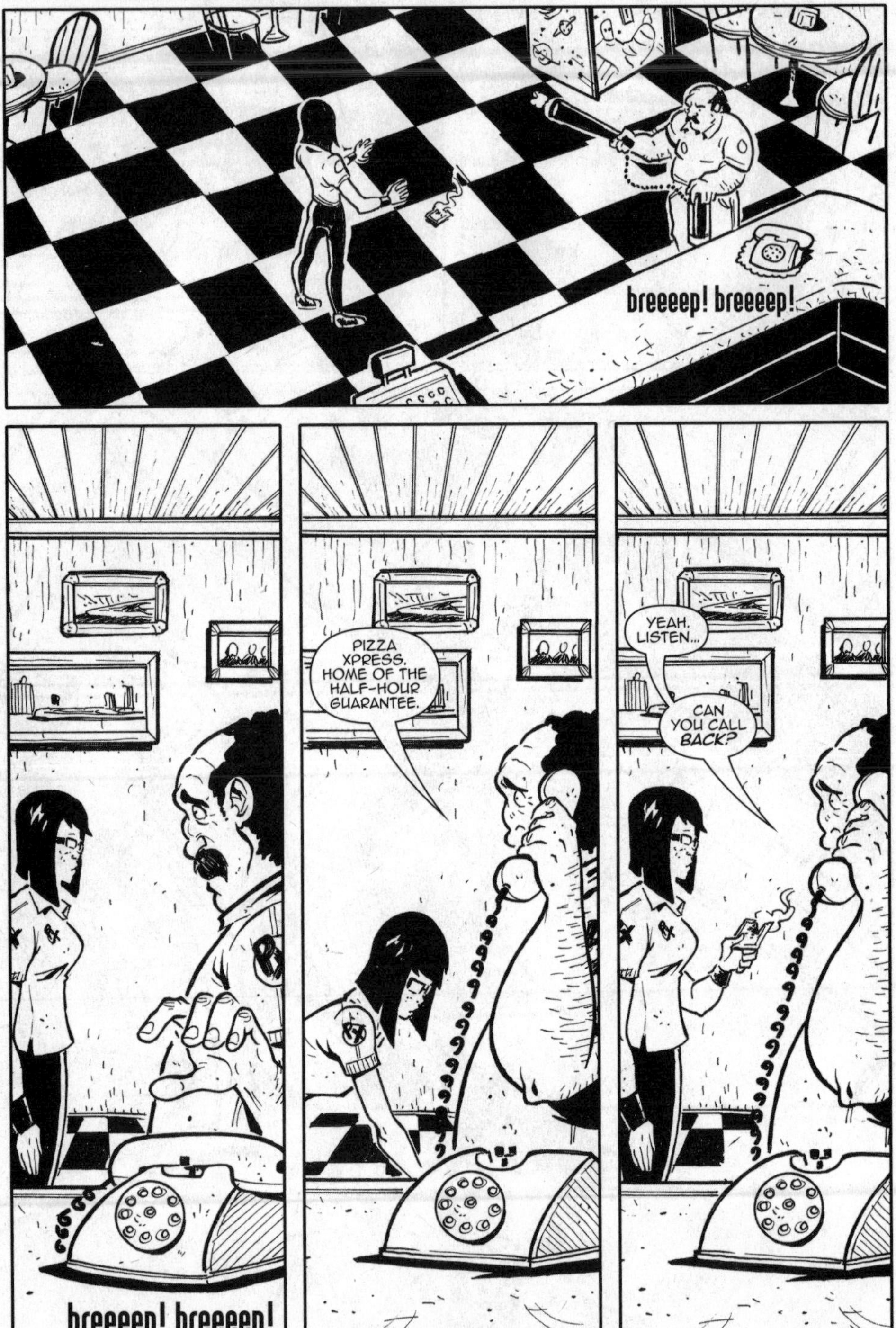
breeeep! breeeep!
breeeep! breeeep!
PIZZA XPRESS. HOME OF THE HALF-HOUR GUARANTEE.
YEAH. LISTEN...
CAN YOU CALL BACK?

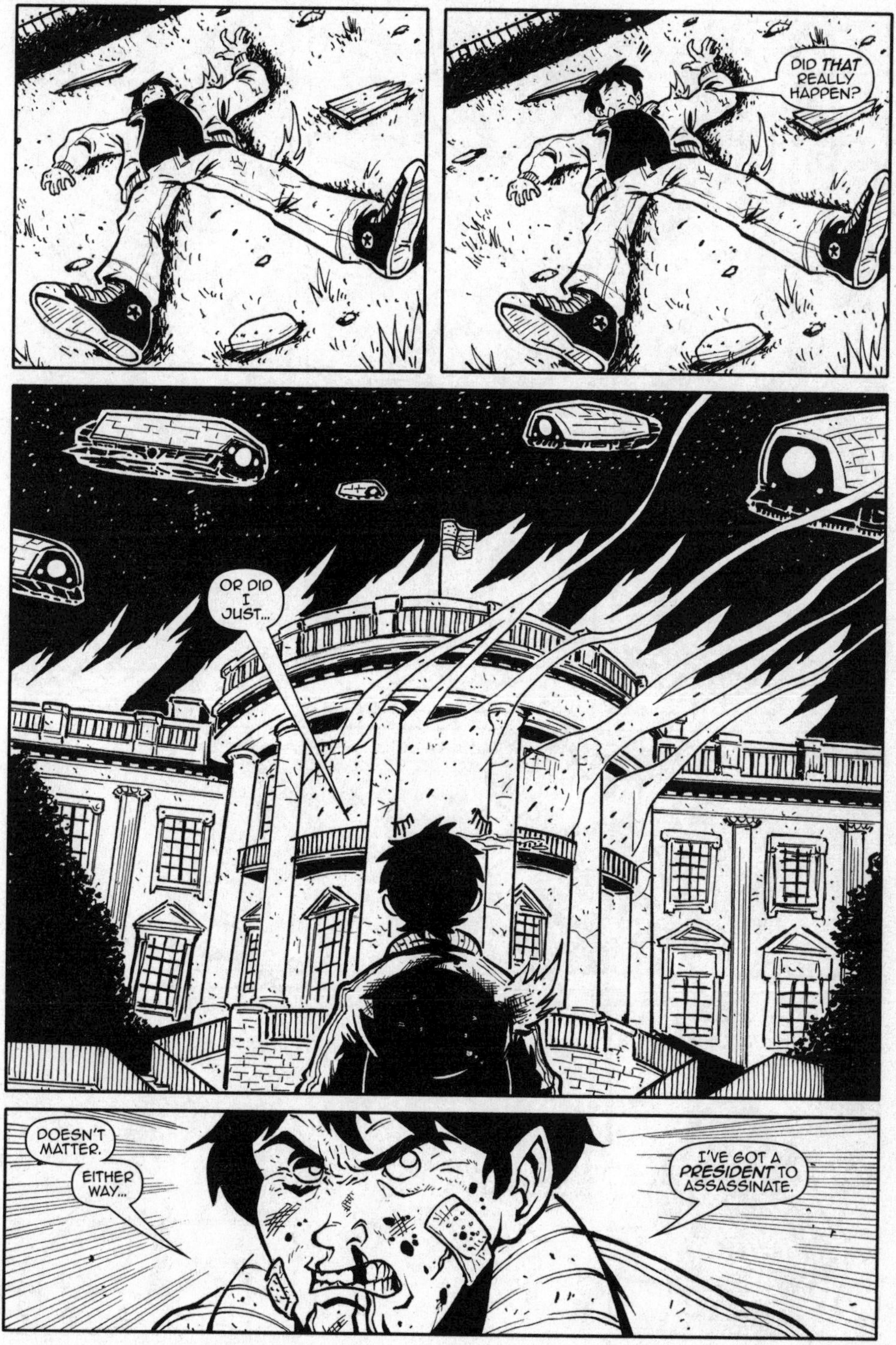
DID THAT REALLY HAPPEN?
OR DID I JUST...
DOESN'T MATTER.
EITHER WAY...
I'VE GOT A PRESIDENT TO ASSASSINATE.

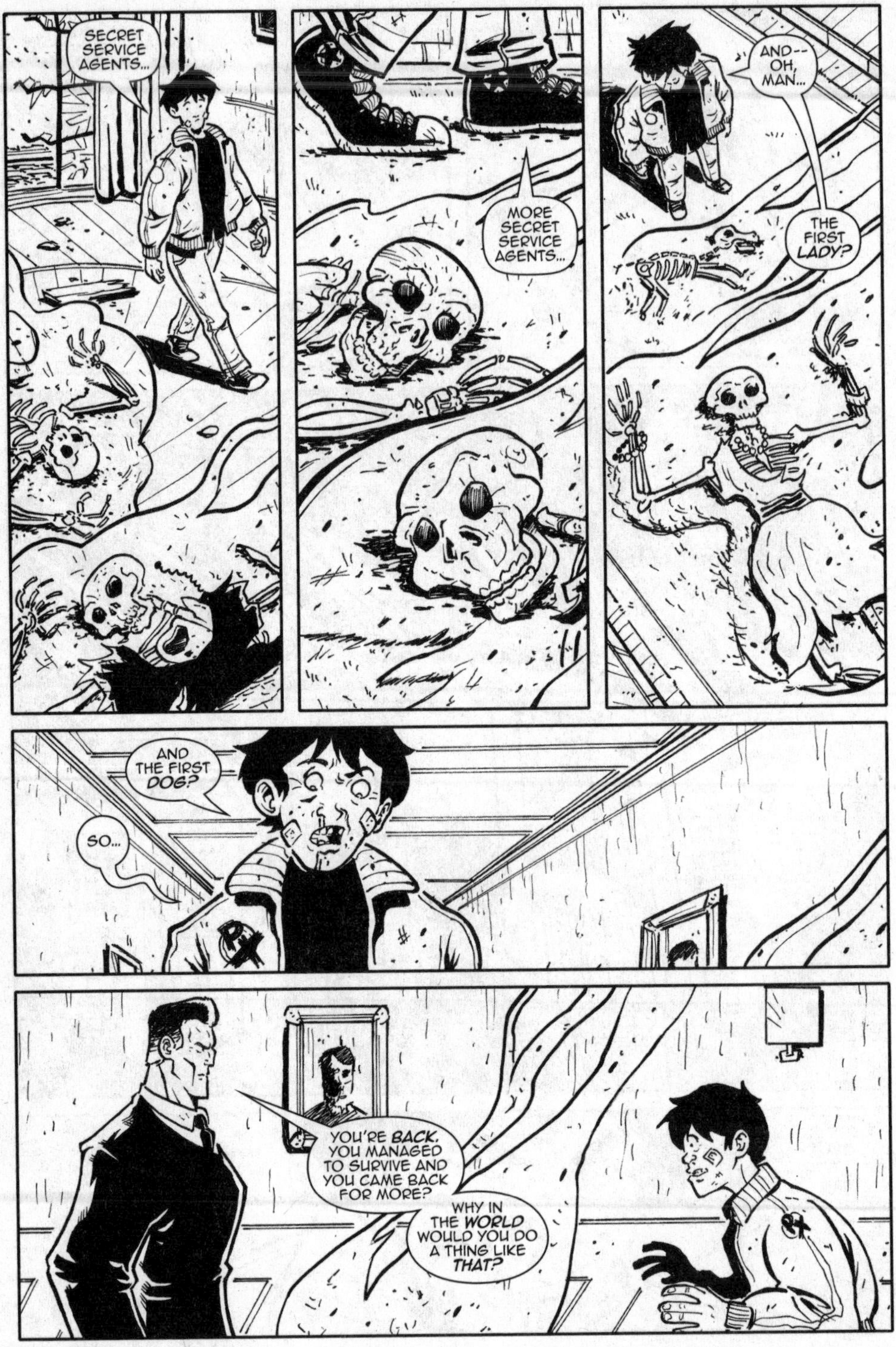
SECRET SERVICE AGENTS...
MORE SECRET SERVICE AGENTS...
AND-- OH, MAN...
THE FIRST LADY?
AND THE FIRST DOG?
SO...
YOU'RE BACK. YOU MANAGED TO SURVIVE AND YOU CAME BACK FOR MORE?
WHY IN THE WORLD WOULD YOU DO A THING LIKE THAT?

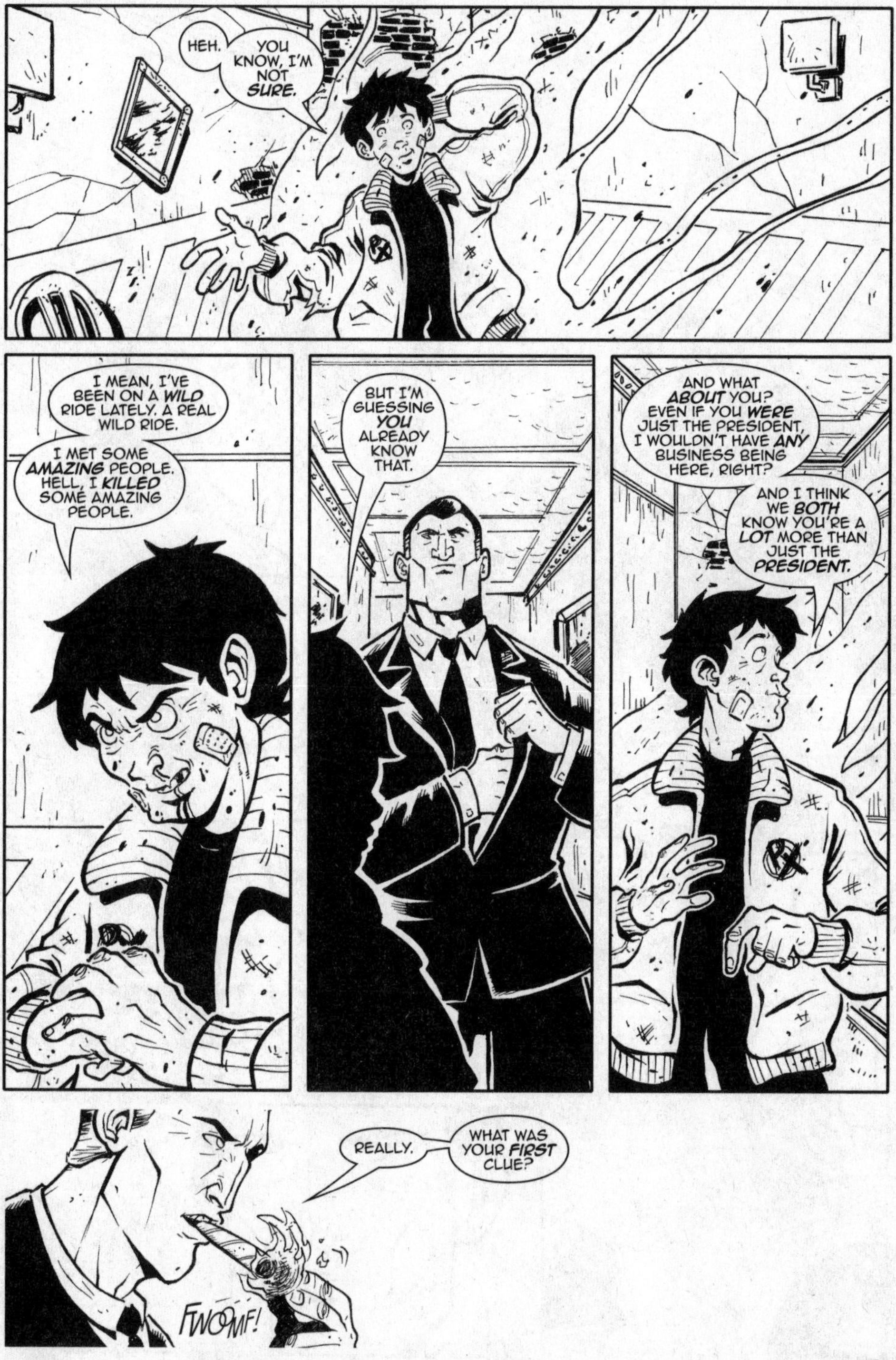
HEH.
YOU KNOW, I'M NOT SURE.
I MEAN, I'VE BEEN ON A WILD RIDE LATELY. A REAL WILD RIDE.
I MET SOME AMAZING PEOPLE. HELL, I KILLED SOME AMAZING PEOPLE.
BUT I'M GUESSING YOU ALREADY KNOW THAT.
AND WHAT ABOUT YOU? EVEN IF YOU WERE JUST THE PRESIDENT, I WOULDN'T HAVE ANY BUSINESS BEING HERE, RIGHT?
AND I THINK WE BOTH KNOW YOU'RE A LOT MORE THAN JUST THE PRESIDENT.
REALLY.
WHAT WAS YOUR FIRST CLUE?
FWOOMF!

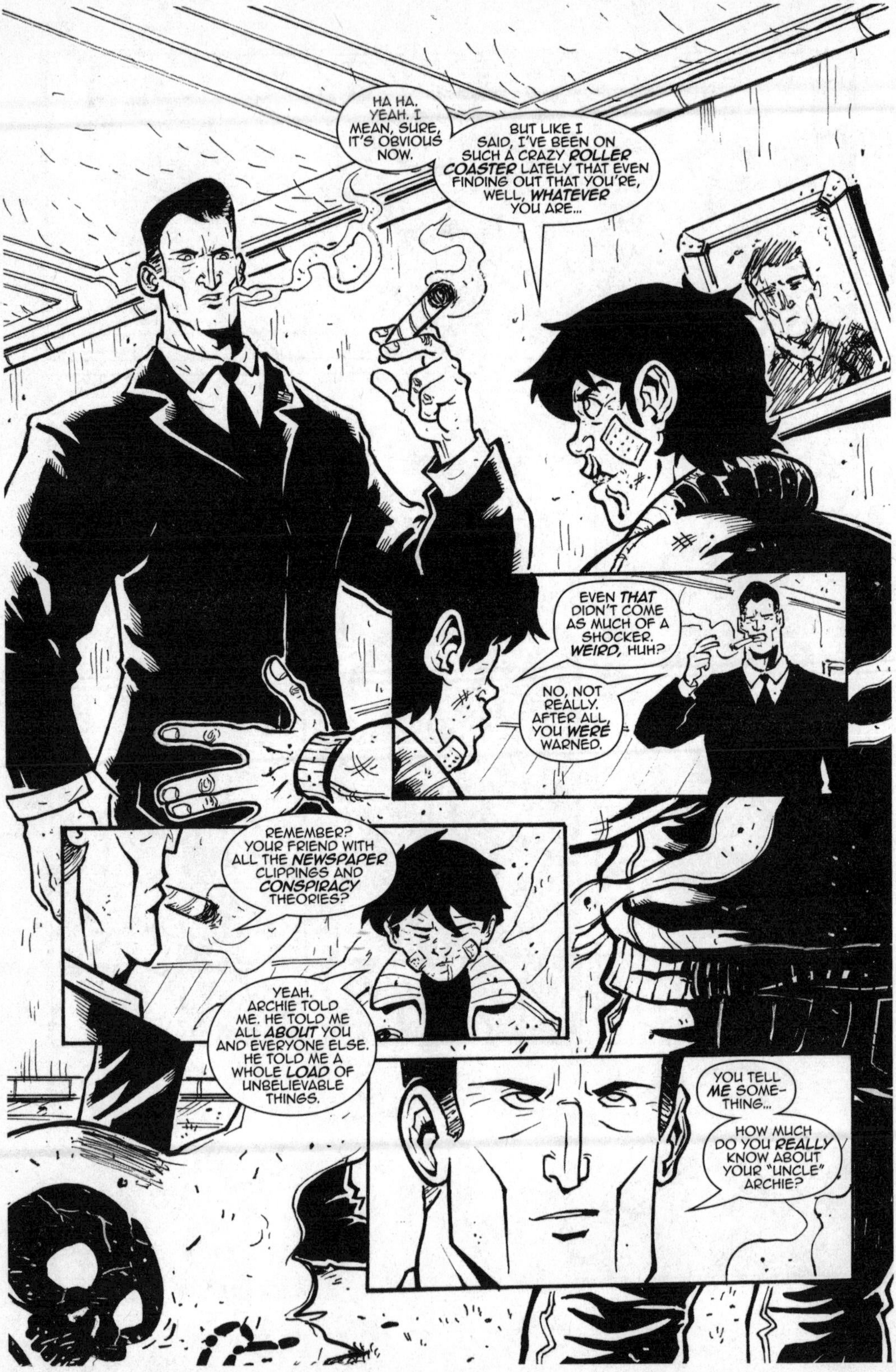
HA HA. YEAH. I MEAN, SURE, IT'S OBVIOUS NOW.
BUT LIKE I SAID, I'VE BEEN ON SUCH A CRAZY ROLLER COASTER LATELY THAT EVEN FINDING OUT THAT YOU'RE, WELL, WHATEVER YOU ARE...
EVEN THAT DIDN'T COME AS MUCH OF A SHOCKER. WEIRD, HUH?
NO, NOT REALLY. AFTER ALL, YOU WERE WARNED.
REMEMBER? YOUR FRIEND WITH ALL THE NEWSPAPER CLIPPINGS AND CONSPIRACY THEORIES?
YEAH. ARCHIE TOLD ME. HE TOLD ME ALL ABOUT YOU AND EVERYONE ELSE. HE TOLD ME A WHOLE LOAD OF UNBELIEVABLE THINGS.
YOU TELL ME SOME-THING...
HOW MUCH DO YOU REALLY KNOW ABOUT YOUR "UNCLE" ARCHIE?

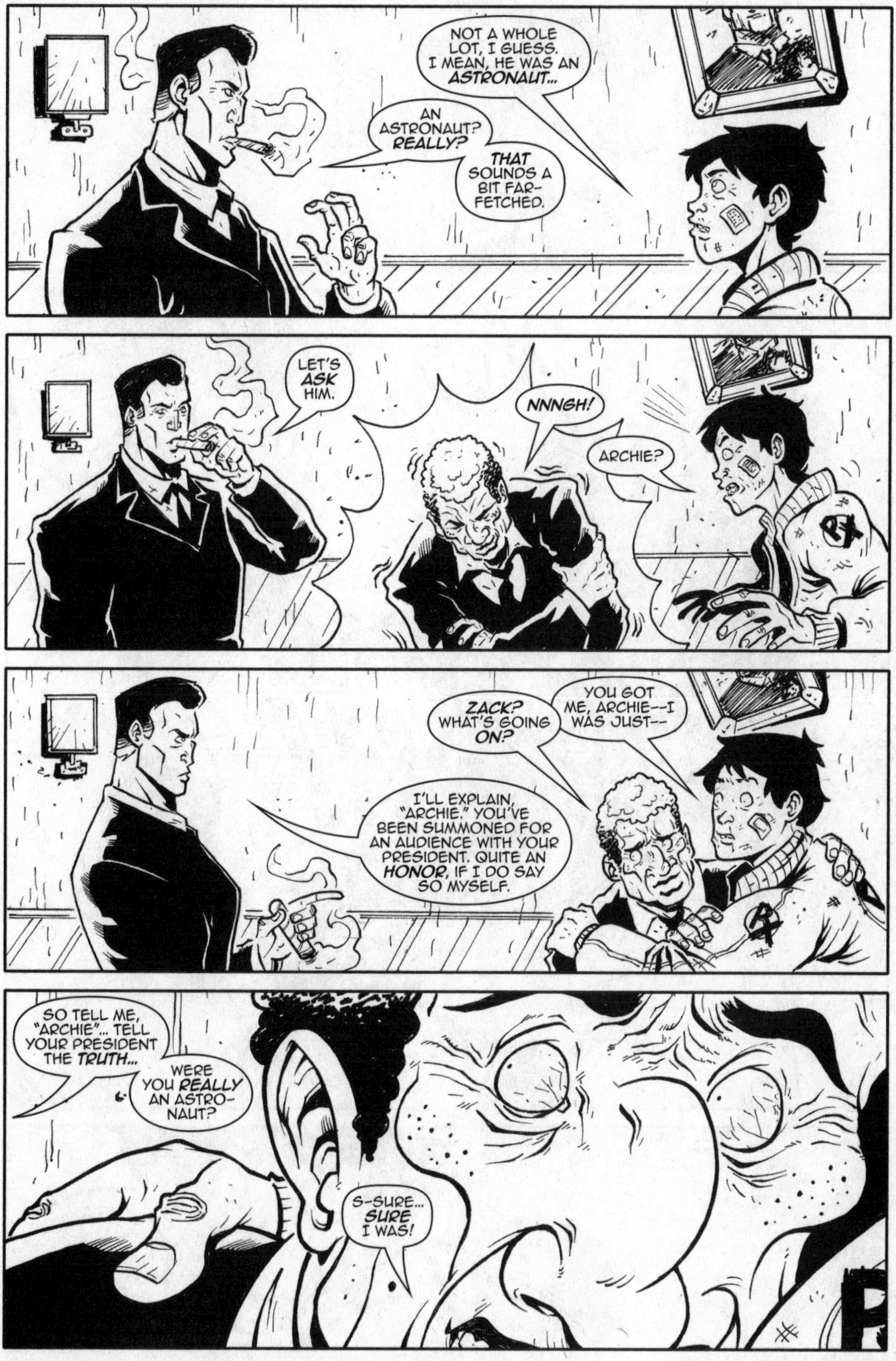
NOT A WHOLE LOT, I GUESS. I MEAN, HE WAS AN ASTRONAUT...
AN ASTRONAUT? REALLY?
THAT SOUNDS A BIT FAR-FETCHED.
LET'S ASK HIM.
NNNGH!
ARCHIE?
ZACK? WHAT'S GOING ON?
YOU GOT ME, ARCHIE--I WAS JUST--
I'LL EXPLAIN, "ARCHIE." YOU'VE BEEN SUMMONED FOR AN AUDIENCE WITH YOUR PRESIDENT. QUITE AN HONOR, IF I DO SAY SO MYSELF.
SO TELL ME, "ARCHIE"... TELL YOUR PRESIDENT THE TRUTH...
WERE YOU REALLY AN ASTRONAUT?
S-SURE... SURE I WAS!

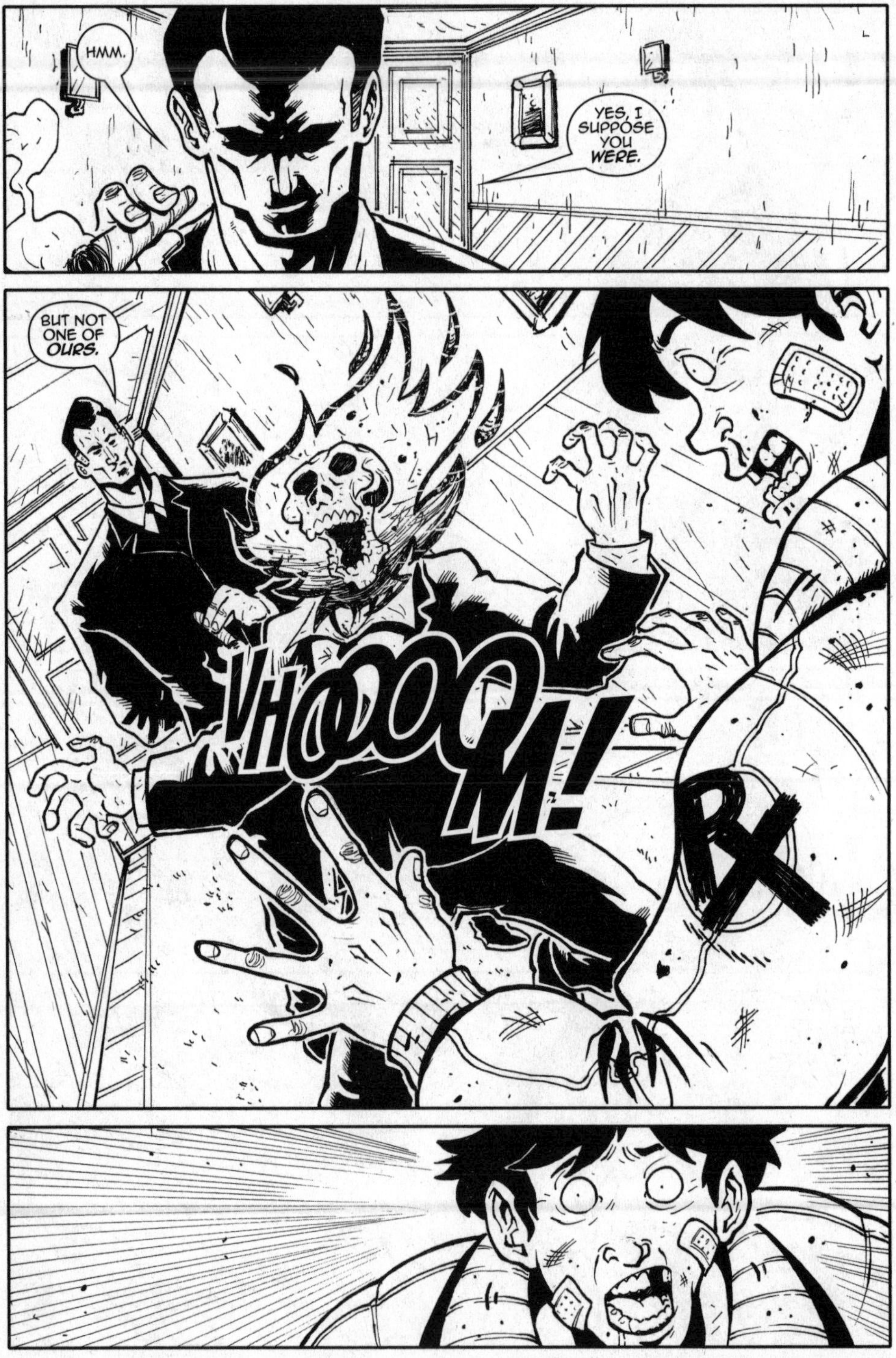
HMM.
YES, I SUPPOSE YOU WERE.
BUT NOT ONE OF OURS.
VHOOOM!
RX

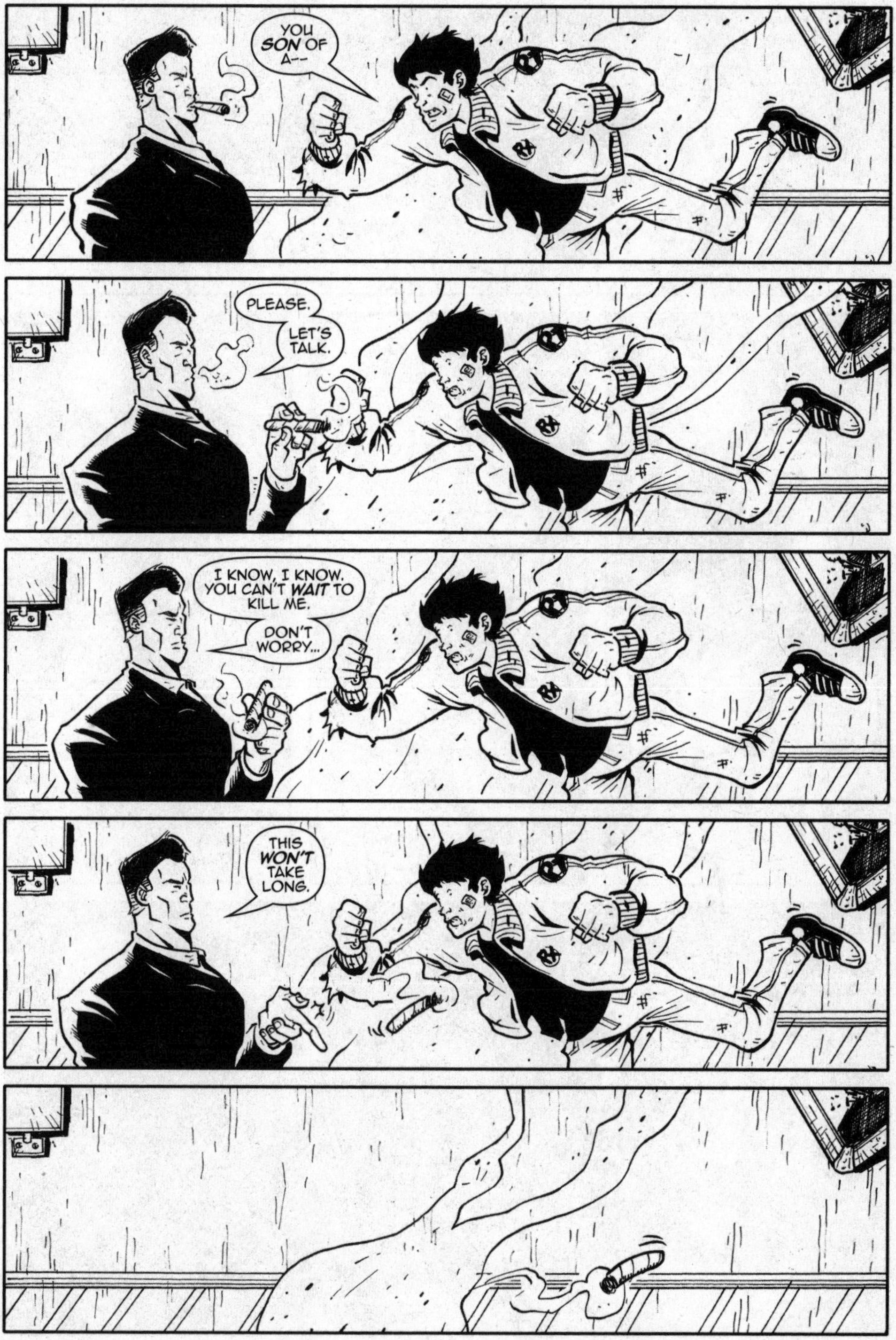
YOU SON OF A--
PLEASE.
LET'S TALK.
I KNOW, I KNOW. YOU CAN'T WAIT TO KILL ME.
DON'T WORRY...
THIS WON'T TAKE LONG.

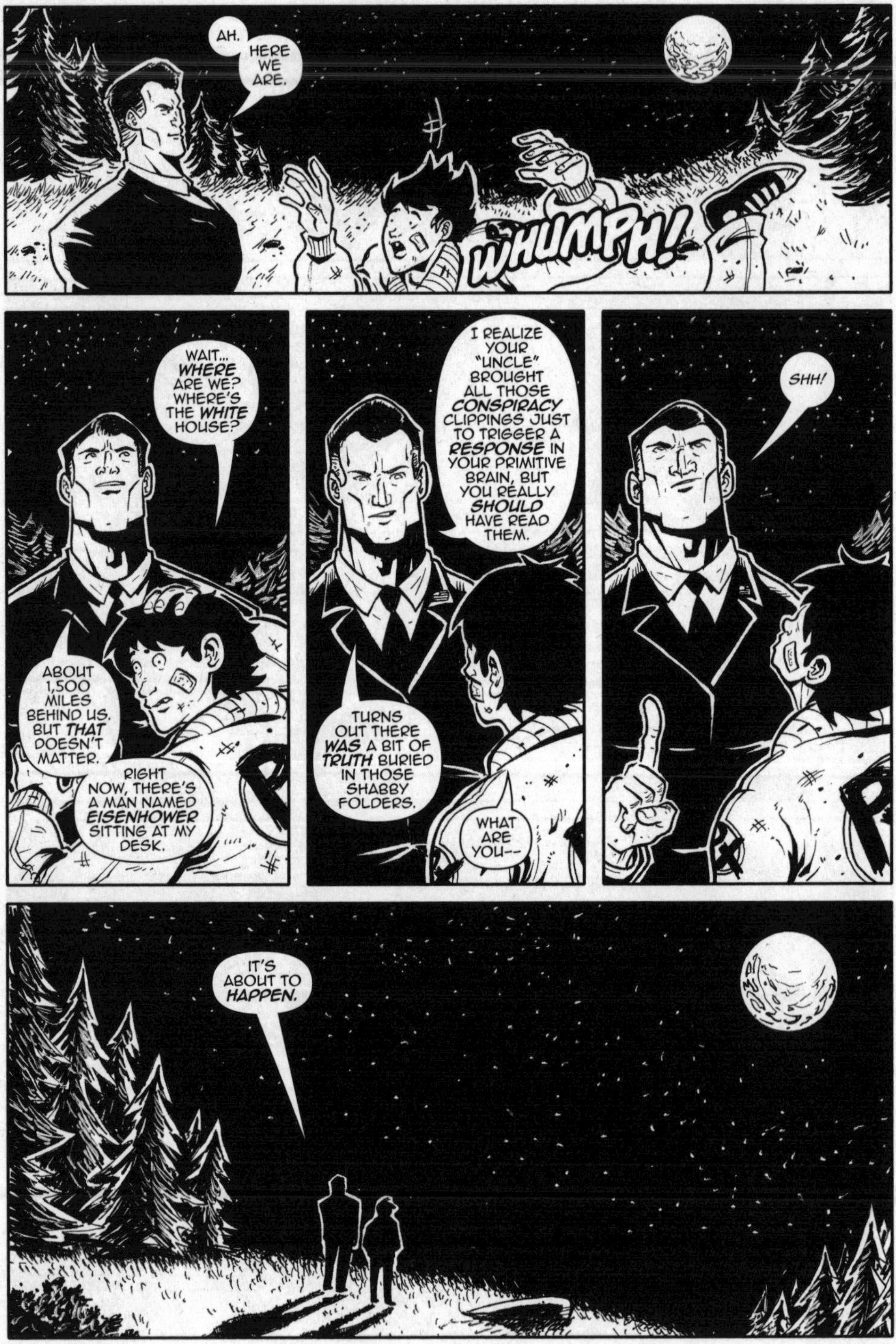
AH. HERE WE ARE.
WHUMPH!
WAIT... WHERE ARE WE? WHERE'S THE WHITE HOUSE?
ABOUT 1,500 MILES BEHIND US. BUT THAT DOESN'T MATTER.
RIGHT NOW, THERE'S A MAN NAMED EISENHOWER SITTING AT MY DESK.
I REALIZE YOUR "UNCLE" BROUGHT ALL THOSE CONSPIRACY CLIPPINGS JUST TO TRIGGER A RESPONSE IN YOUR PRIMITIVE BRAIN, BUT YOU REALLY SHOULD HAVE READ THEM.
TURNS OUT THERE WAS A BIT OF TRUTH BURIED IN THOSE SHABBY FOLDERS.
WHAT ARE YOU--
SHH!
IT'S ABOUT TO HAPPEN.

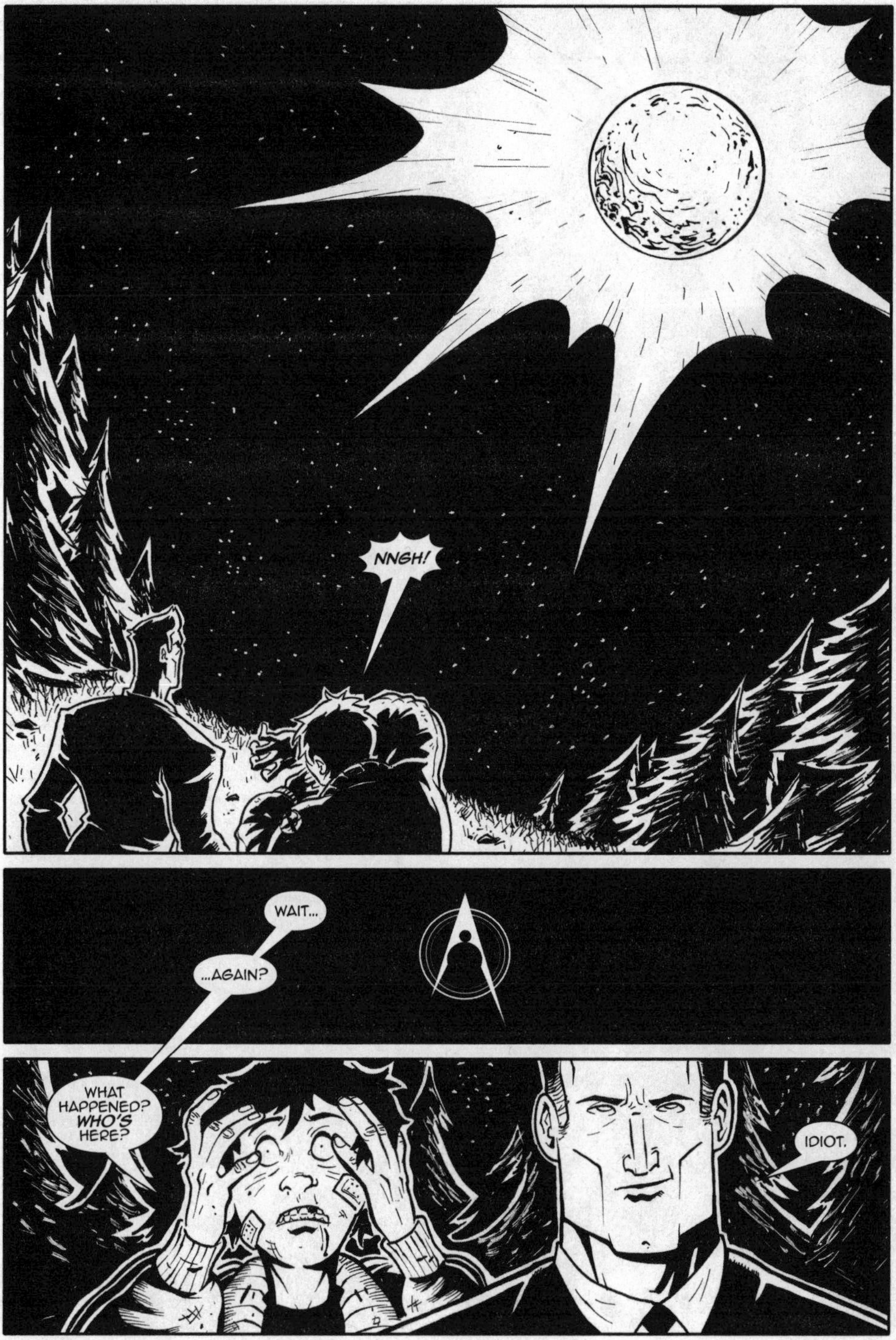
NNGH!
WAIT...
...AGAIN?
WHAT HAPPENED? WHO'S HERE?
IDIOT.

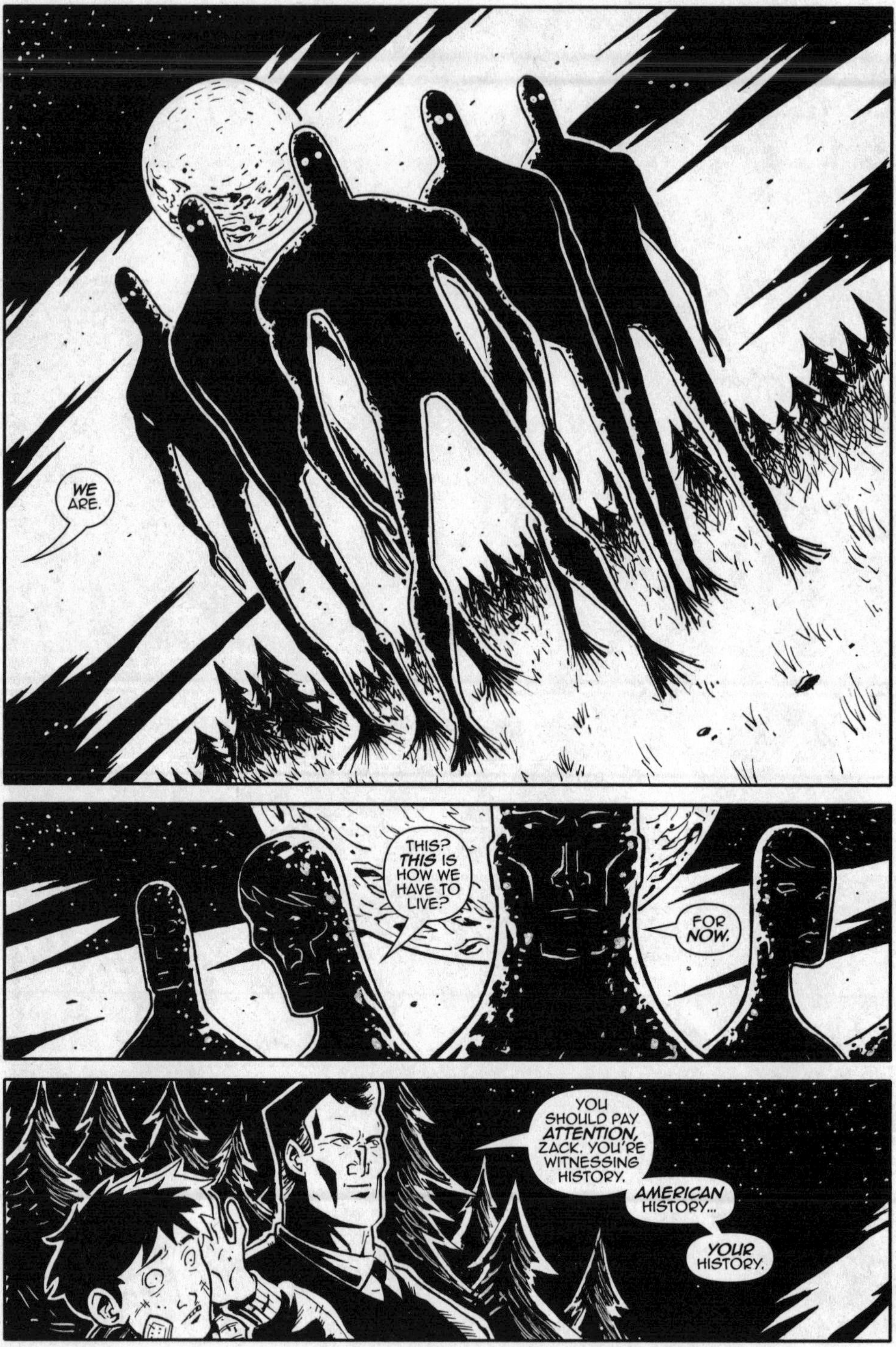
WE ARE.
THIS? THIS IS HOW WE HAVE TO LIVE?
FOR NOW.
YOU SHOULD PAY ATTENTION, ZACK. YOU'RE WITNESSING HISTORY.
AMERICAN HISTORY...
YOUR HISTORY.

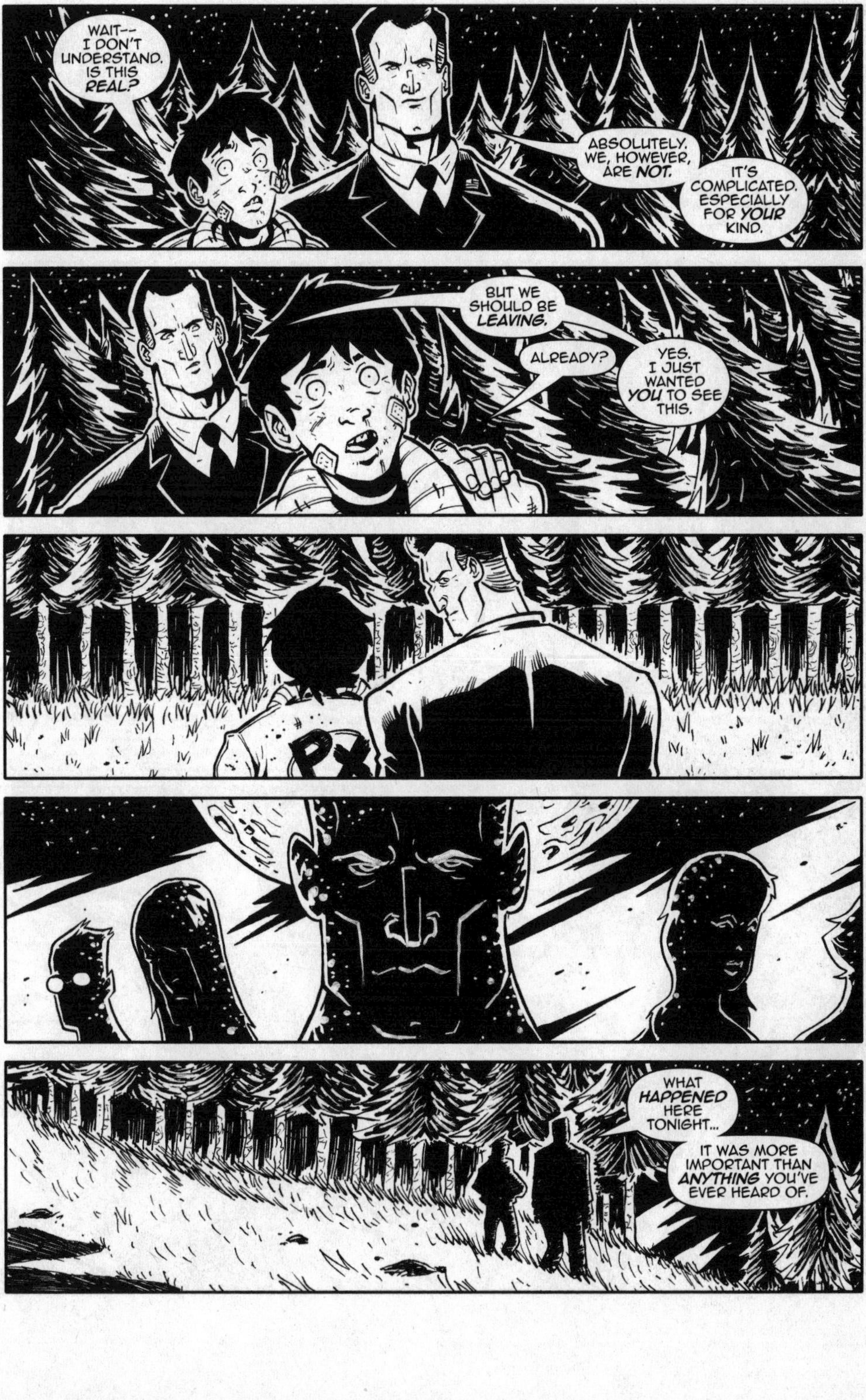
WAIT-- I DON'T UNDERSTAND. IS THIS REAL?
ABSOLUTELY. WE, HOWEVER, ARE NOT.
IT'S COMPLICATED. ESPECIALLY FOR YOUR KIND.
BUT WE SHOULD BE LEAVING.
ALREADY?
YES. I JUST WANTED YOU TO SEE THIS.
WHAT HAPPENED HERE TONIGHT...
IT WAS MORE IMPORTANT THAN ANYTHING YOU'VE EVER HEARD OF.

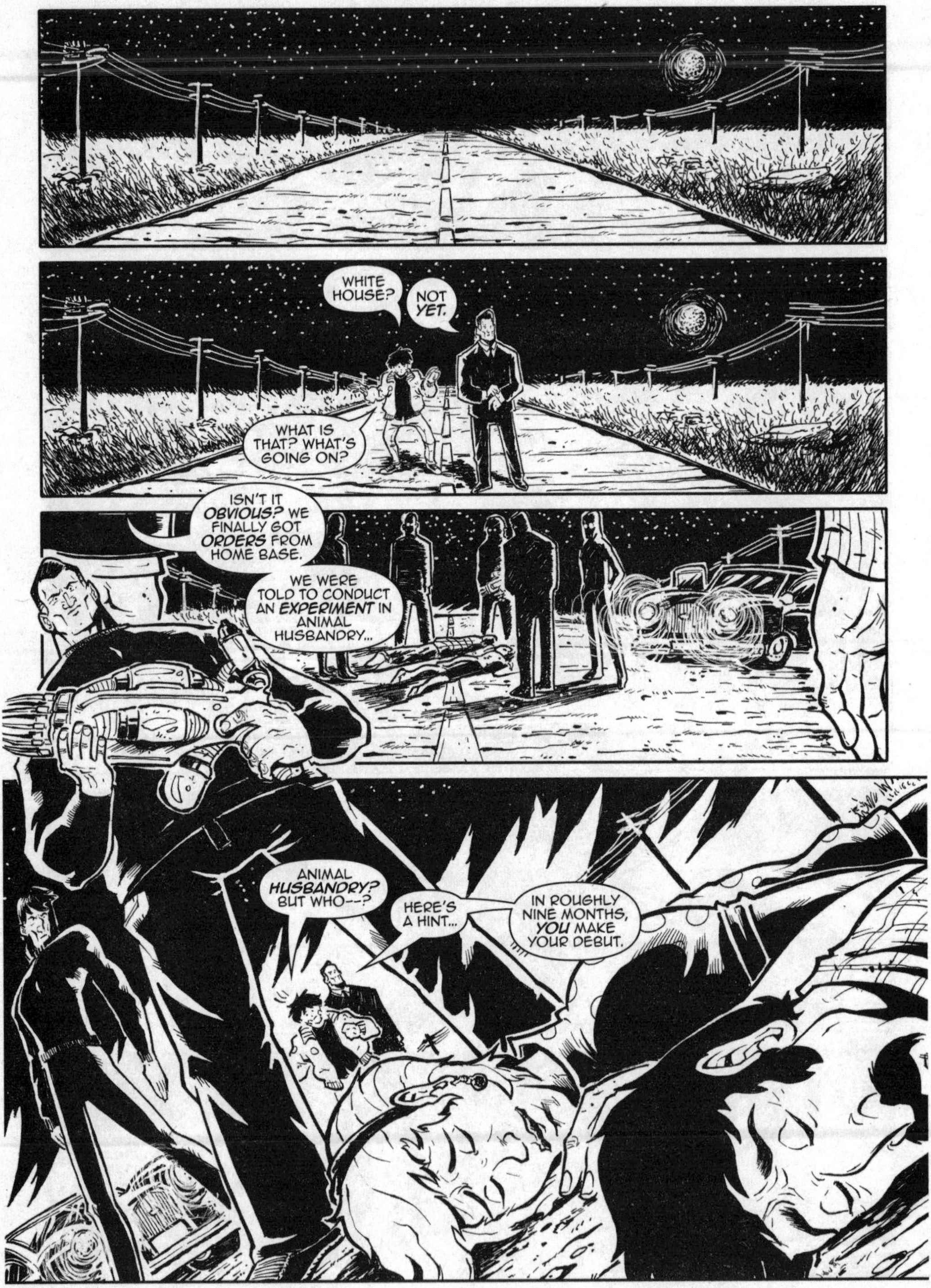
WHITE HOUSE?
NOT YET.
WHAT IS THAT? WHAT'S GOING ON?
ISN'T IT OBVIOUS? WE FINALLY GOT ORDERS FROM HOME BASE.
WE WERE TOLD TO CONDUCT AN EXPERIMENT IN ANIMAL HUSBANDRY...
ANIMAL HUSBANDRY? BUT WHO--?
HERE'S A HINT...
IN ROUGHLY NINE MONTHS, YOU MAKE YOUR DEBUT.

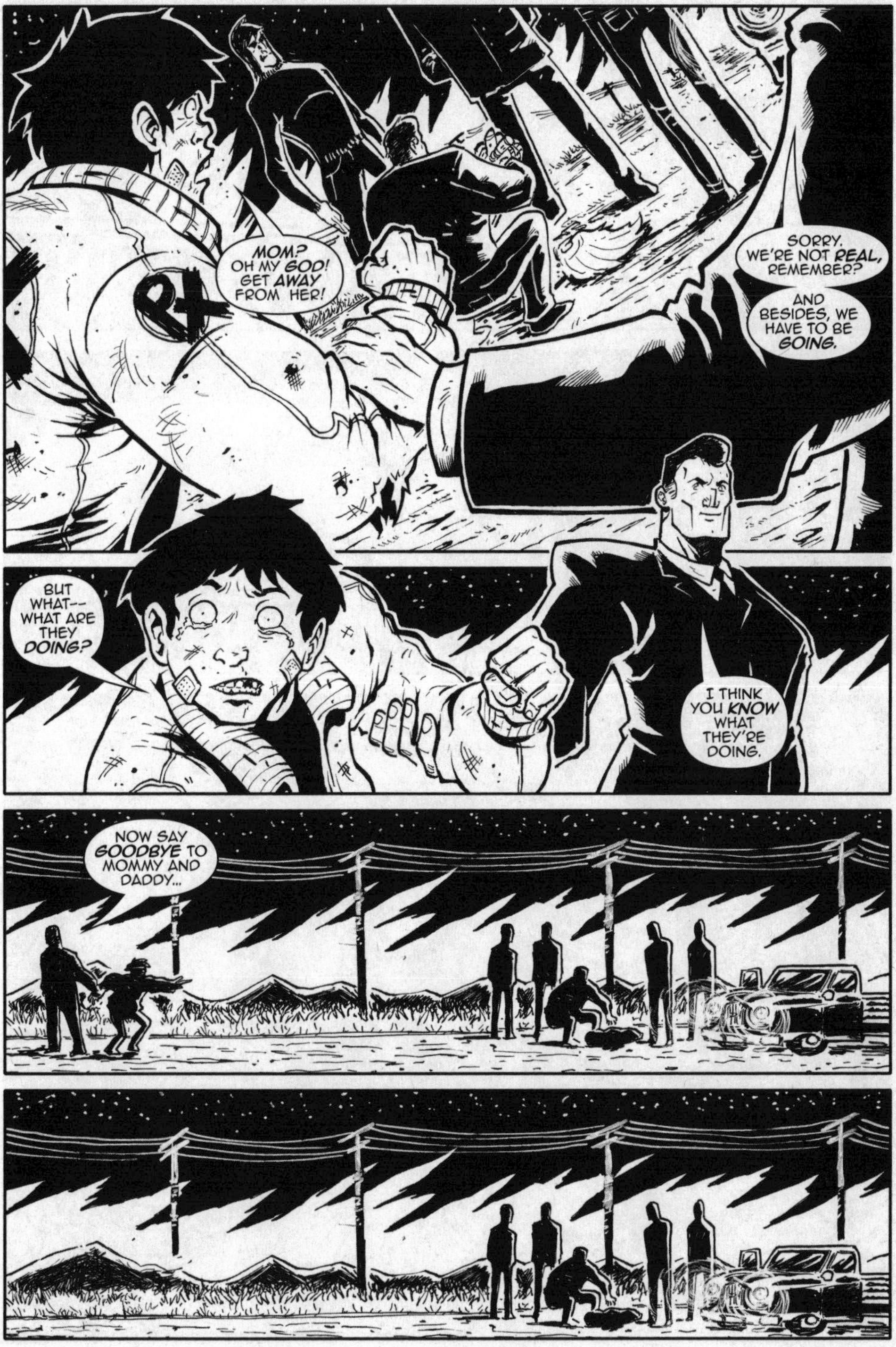
MOM? OH MY GOD! GET AWAY FROM HER!
SORRY. WE'RE NOT REAL, REMEMBER?
AND BESIDES, WE HAVE TO BE GOING.
BUT WHAT-- WHAT ARE THEY DOING?
I THINK YOU KNOW WHAT THEY'RE DOING.
NOW SAY GOODBYE TO MOMMY AND DADDY...

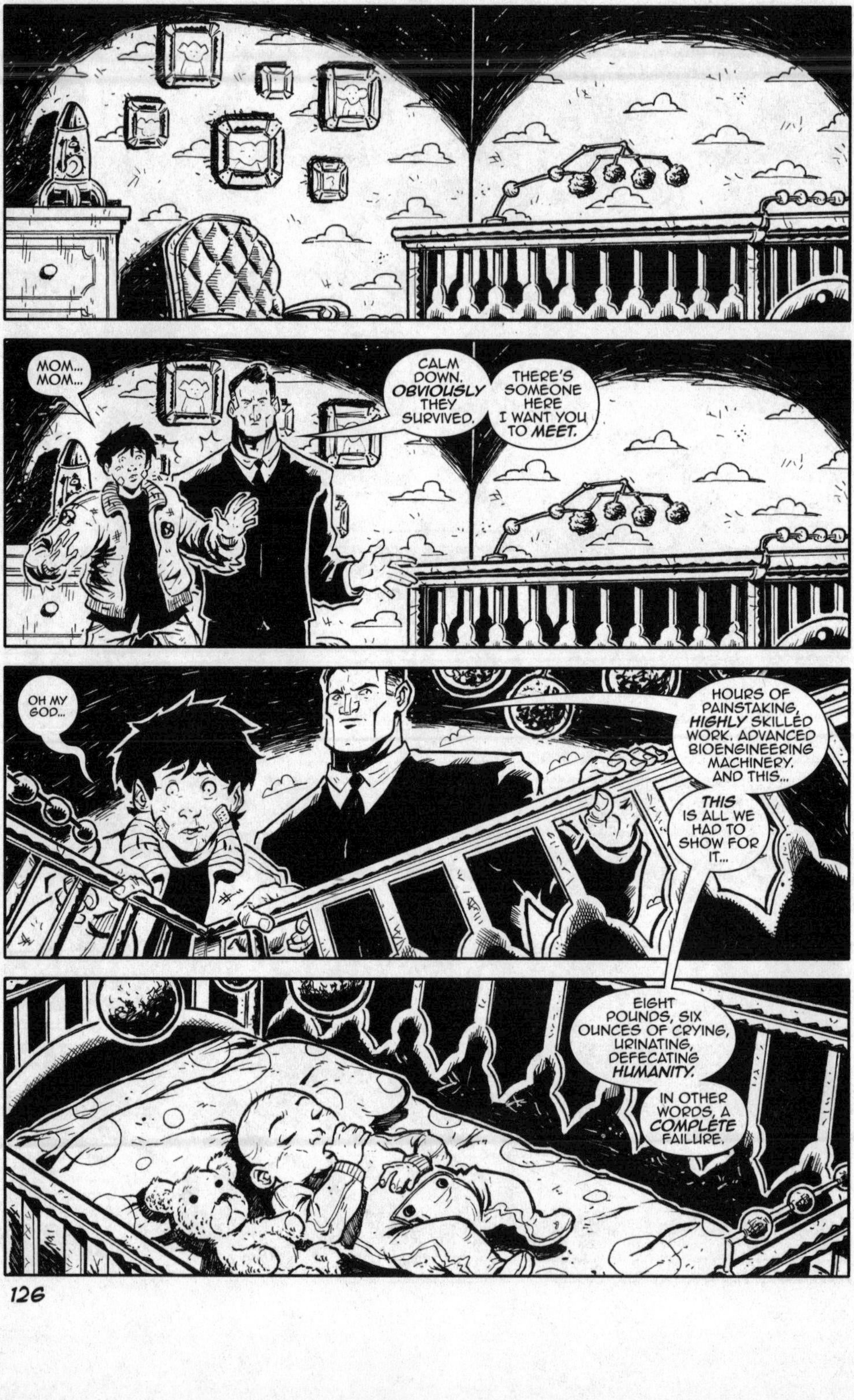
MOM... MOM...
CALM DOWN. OBVIOUSLY THEY SURVIVED.
THERE'S SOMEONE HERE I WANT YOU TO MEET.
OH MY GOD...
HOURS OF PAINSTAKING, HIGHLY SKILLED WORK. ADVANCED BIOENGINEERING MACHINERY. AND THIS...
THIS IS ALL WE HAD TO SHOW FOR IT...
EIGHT POUNDS, SIX OUNCES OF CRYING, URINATING, DEFECATING HUMANITY.
IN OTHER WORDS, A COMPLETE FAILURE.

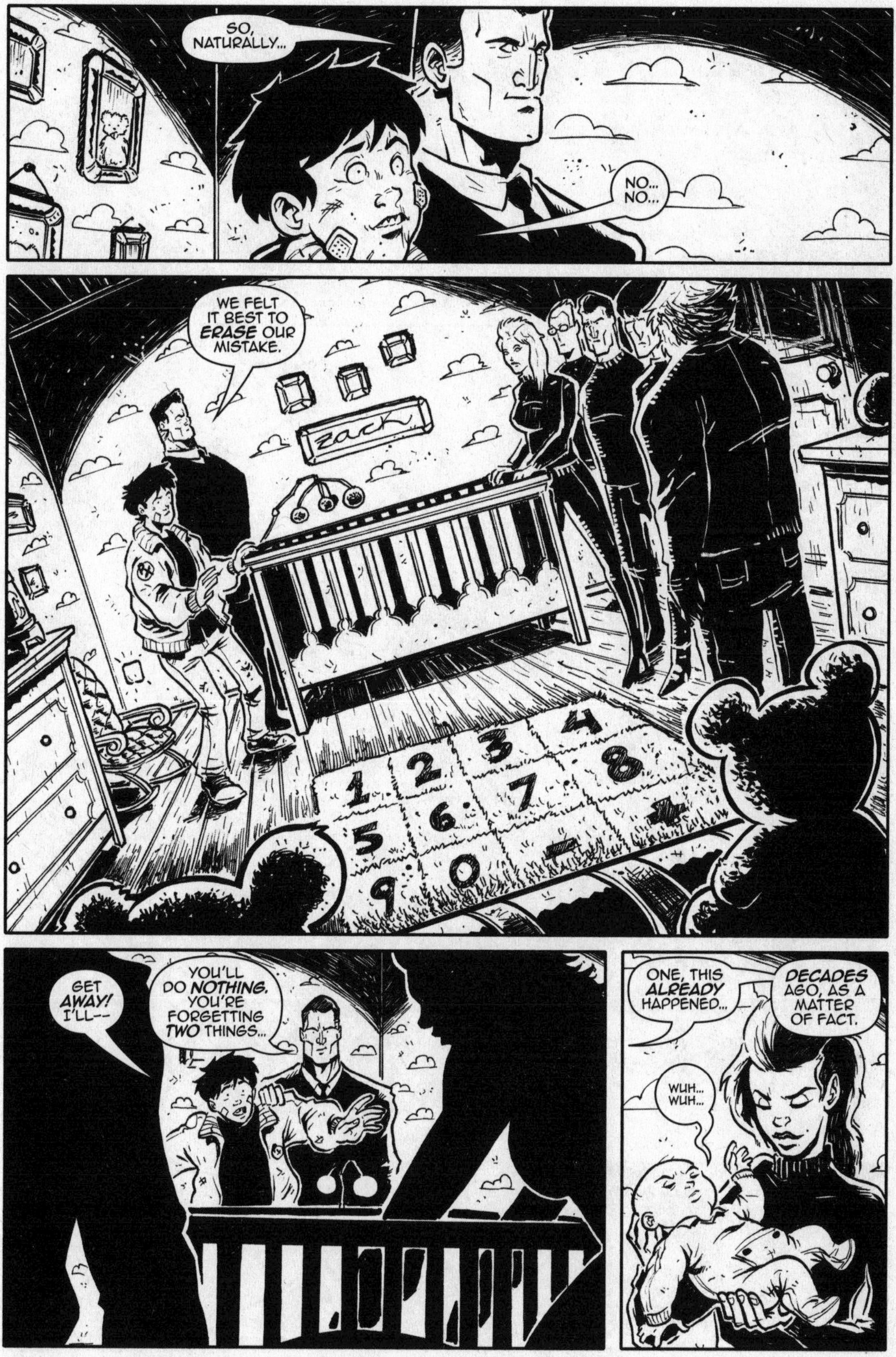
SO, NATURALLY...
NO... NO...
WE FELT IT BEST TO ERASE OUR MISTAKE.
ZACH
1 2 3 4 5 6 7 8 9 0
GET AWAY! I'LL--
YOU'LL DO NOTHING. YOU'RE FORGETTING TWO THINGS...
ONE, THIS ALREADY HAPPENED...
DECADES AGO, AS A MATTER OF FACT.
WUH... WUH...

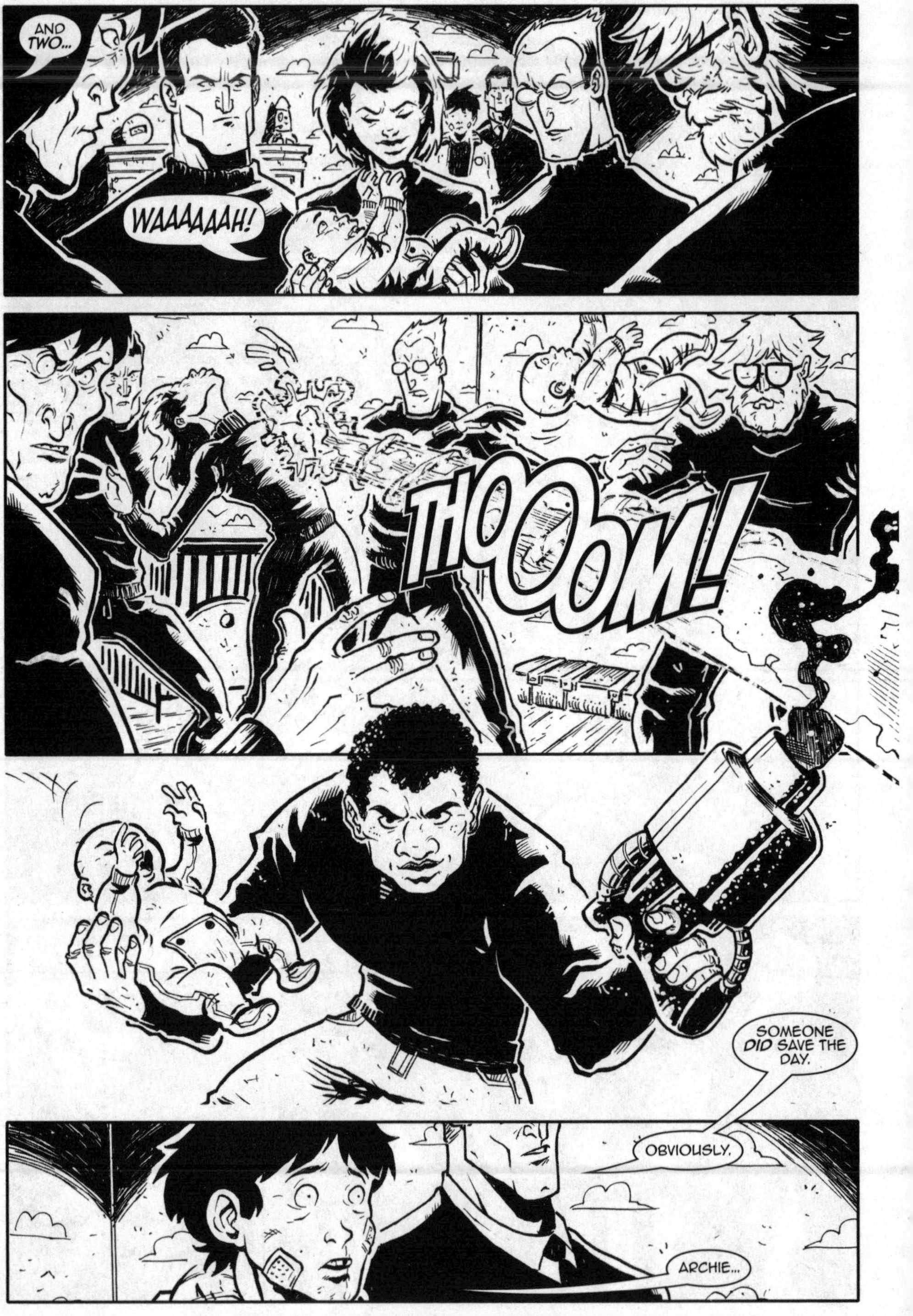
AND TWO...
WAAAAAAH!
THOOOOM!
SOMEONE DID SAVE THE DAY.
OBVIOUSLY.
ARCHIE...

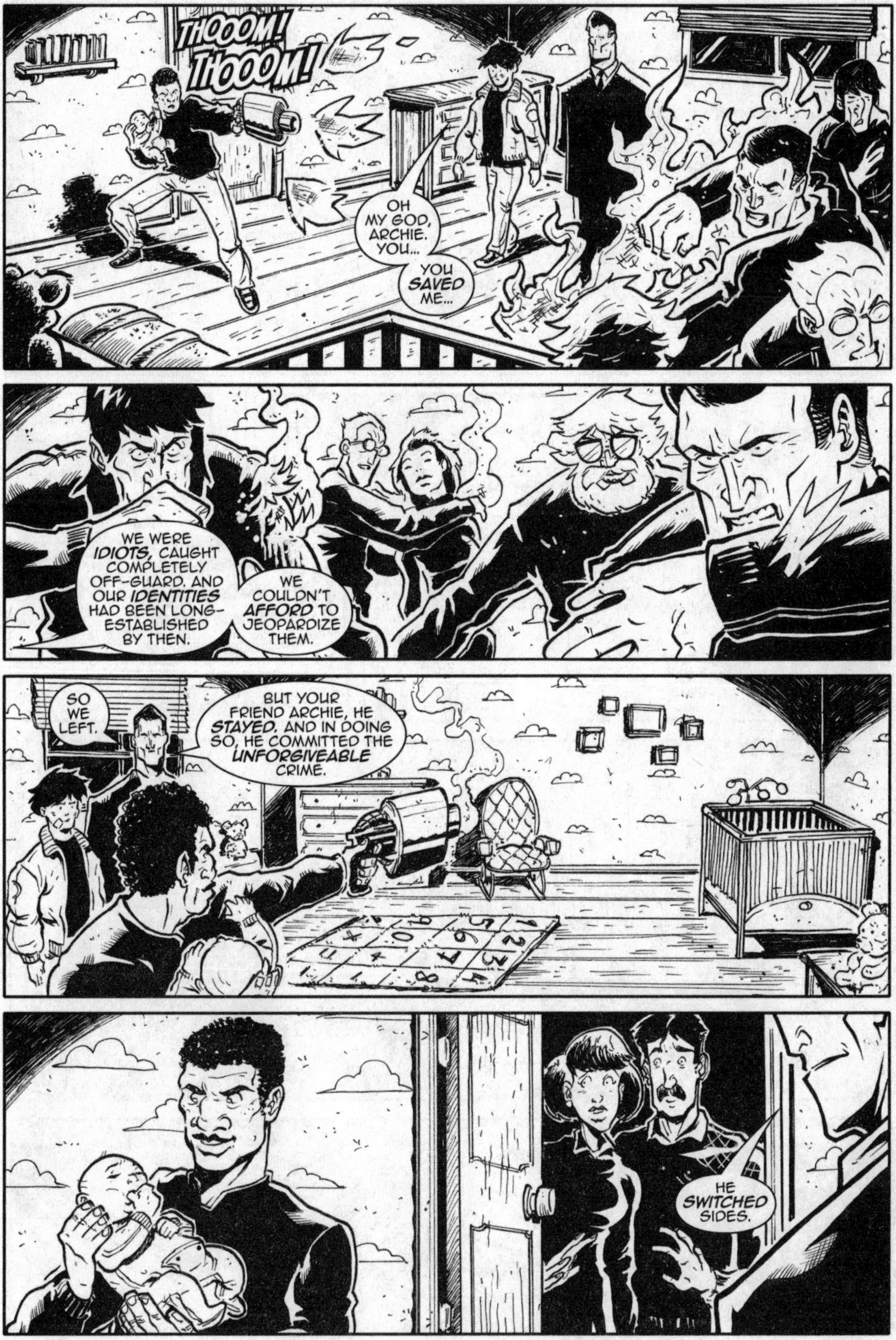
THOOOM! THOOOM!
OH MY GOD, ARCHIE. YOU...
YOU SAVED ME...
WE WERE IDIOTS, CAUGHT COMPLETELY OFF-GUARD. AND OUR IDENTITIES HAD BEEN LONG-ESTABLISHED BY THEN.
WE COULDN'T AFFORD TO JEOPARDIZE THEM.
SO WE LEFT.
BUT YOUR FRIEND ARCHIE, HE STAYED. AND IN DOING SO, HE COMMITTED THE UNFORGIVEABLE CRIME.
HE SWITCHED SIDES.

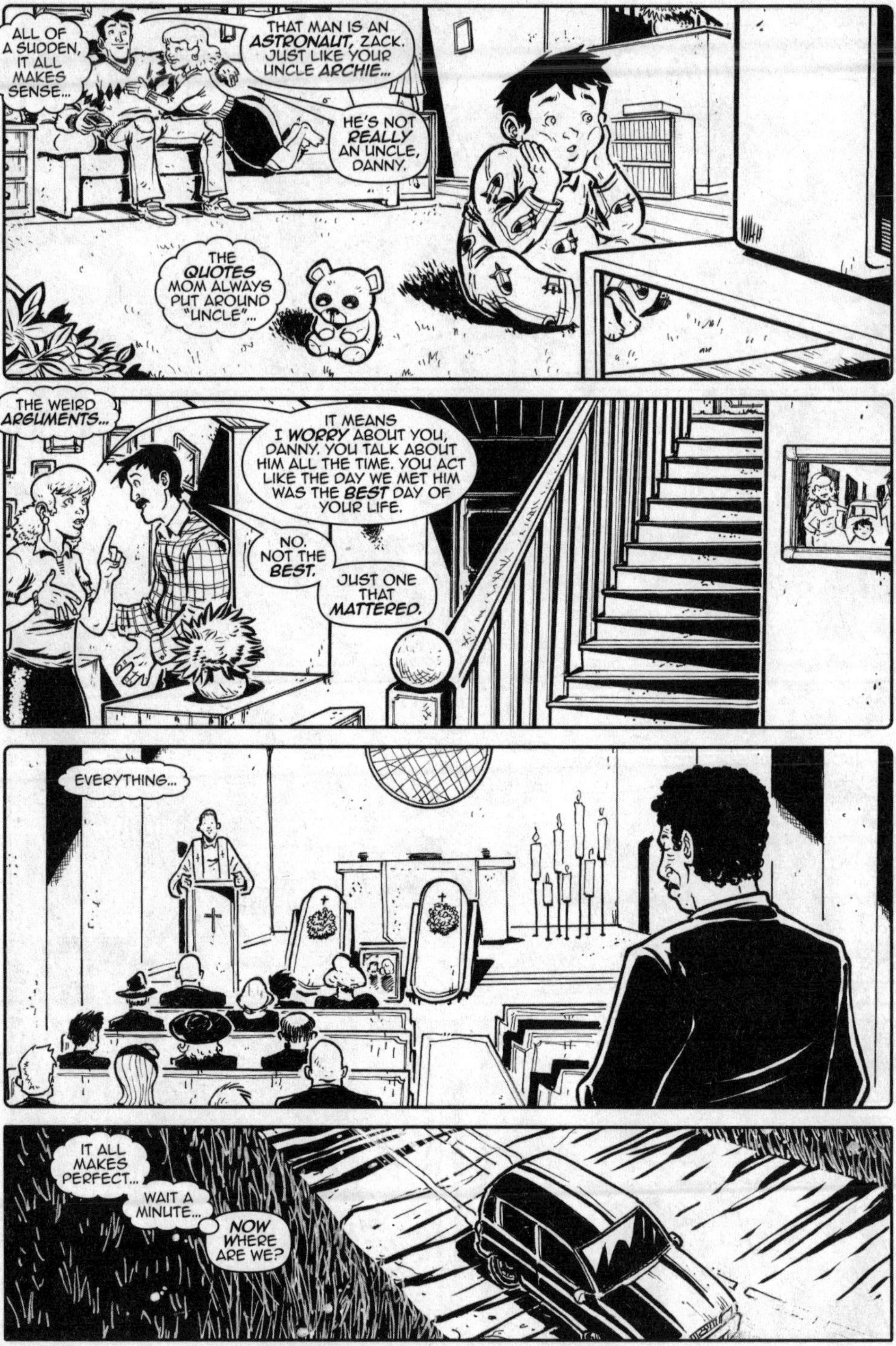
ALL OF A SUDDEN, IT ALL MAKES SENSE...
THAT MAN IS AN ASTRONAUT, ZACK. JUST LIKE YOUR UNCLE ARCHIE...
HE'S NOT REALLY AN UNCLE, DANNY.
THE QUOTES MOM ALWAYS PUT AROUND "UNCLE"...
THE WEIRD ARGUMENTS...
IT MEANS I WORRY ABOUT YOU, DANNY. YOU TALK ABOUT HIM ALL THE TIME. YOU ACT LIKE THE DAY WE MET HIM WAS THE BEST DAY OF YOUR LIFE.
NO. NOT THE BEST.
JUST ONE THAT MATTERED.
EVERYTHING...
IT ALL MAKES PERFECT...
WAIT A MINUTE...
NOW WHERE ARE WE?

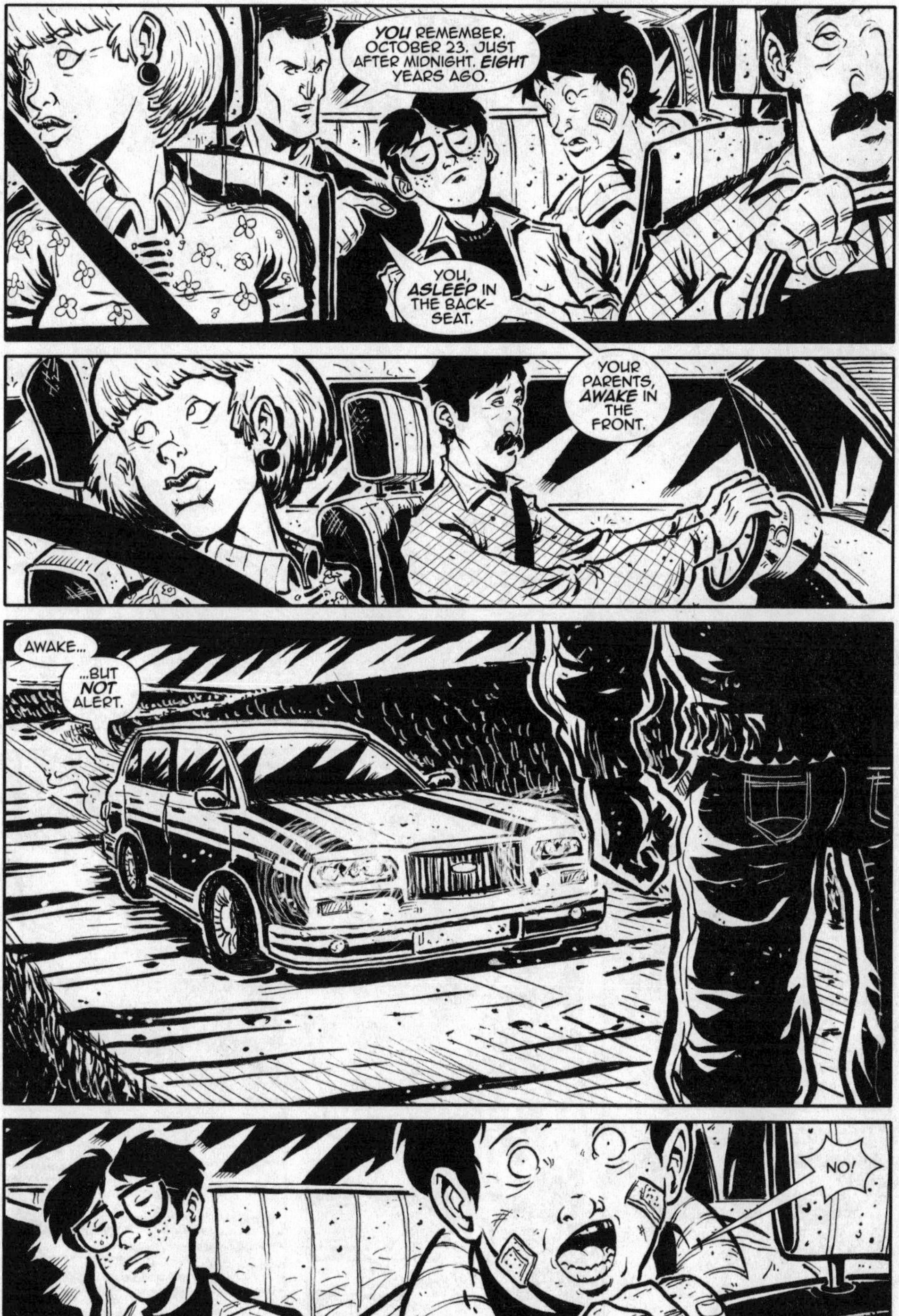
YOU REMEMBER. OCTOBER 23. JUST AFTER MIDNIGHT. EIGHT YEARS AGO.
YOU, ASLEEP IN THE BACK-SEAT.
YOUR PARENTS, AWAKE IN THE FRONT.
AWAKE...
...BUT NOT ALERT.
NO!

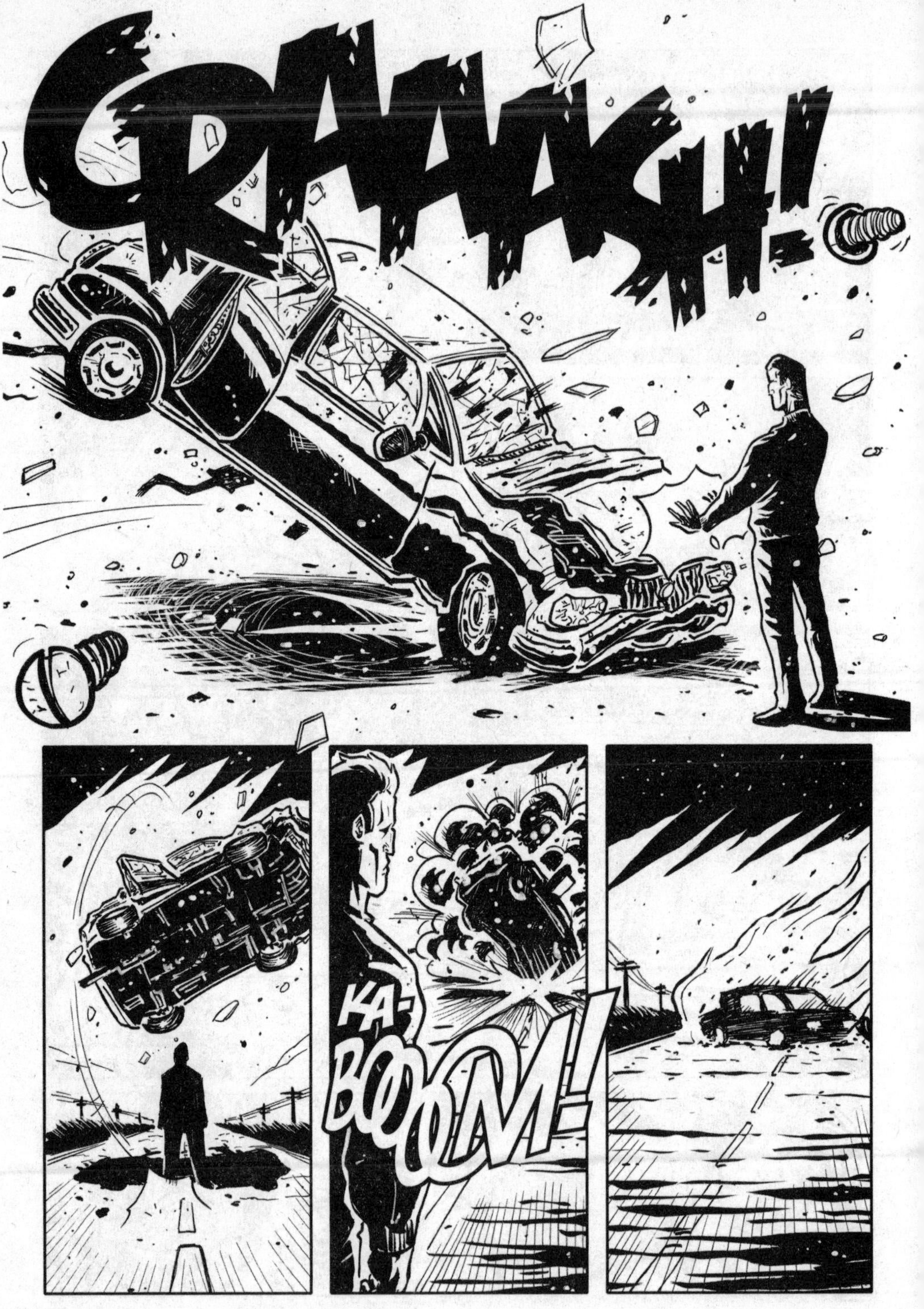
CRAAASH!
KA-BOOOM!

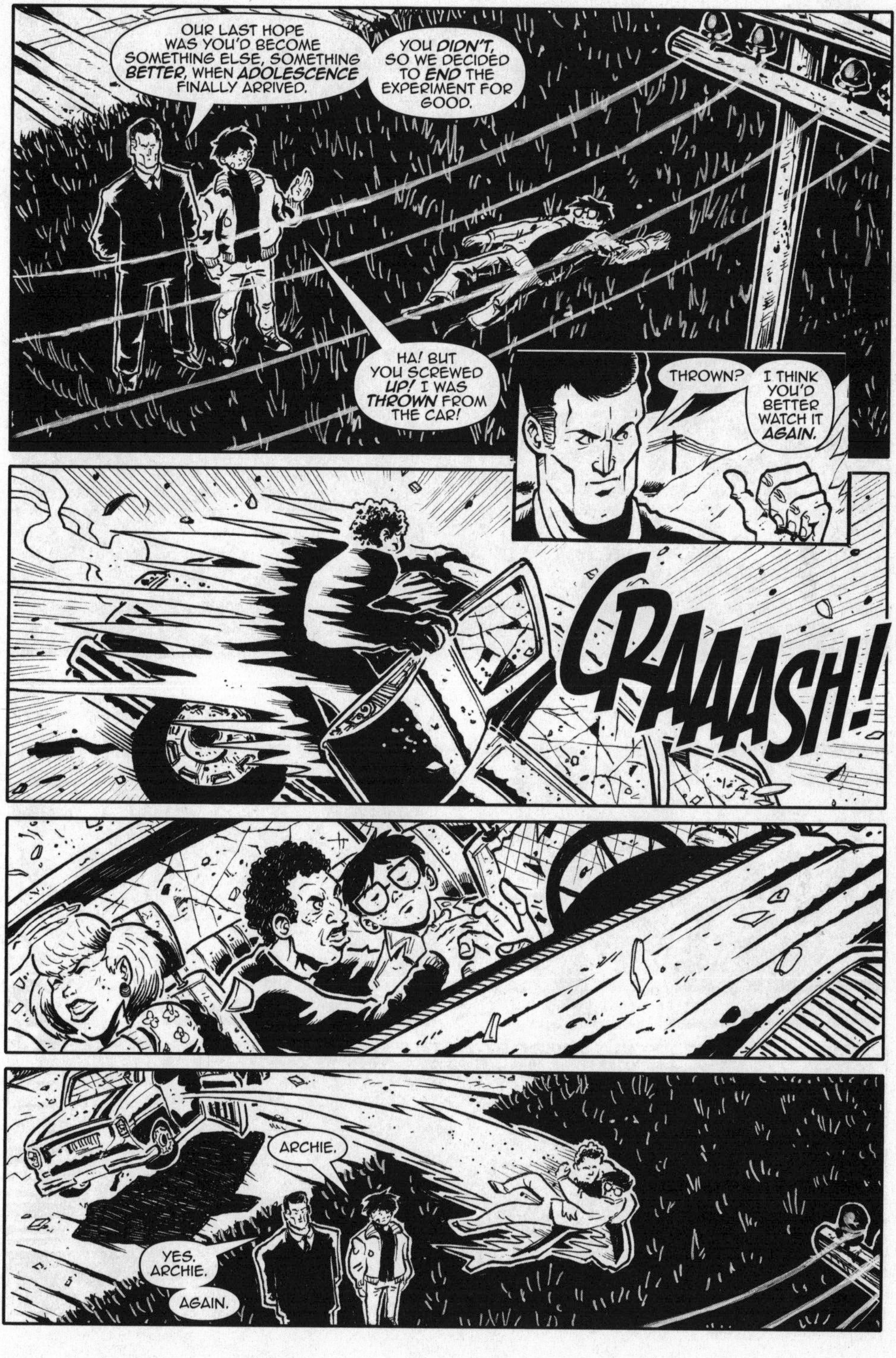
OUR LAST HOPE WAS YOU'D BECOME SOMETHING ELSE, SOMETHING BETTER, WHEN ADOLESCENCE FINALLY ARRIVED.
YOU DIDN'T, SO WE DECIDED TO END THE EXPERIMENT FOR GOOD.
HA! BUT YOU SCREWED UP! I WAS THROWN FROM THE CAR!
THROWN?
I THINK YOU'D BETTER WATCH IT AGAIN.
CRAAAASH!
ARCHIE.
YES. ARCHIE.
AGAIN.

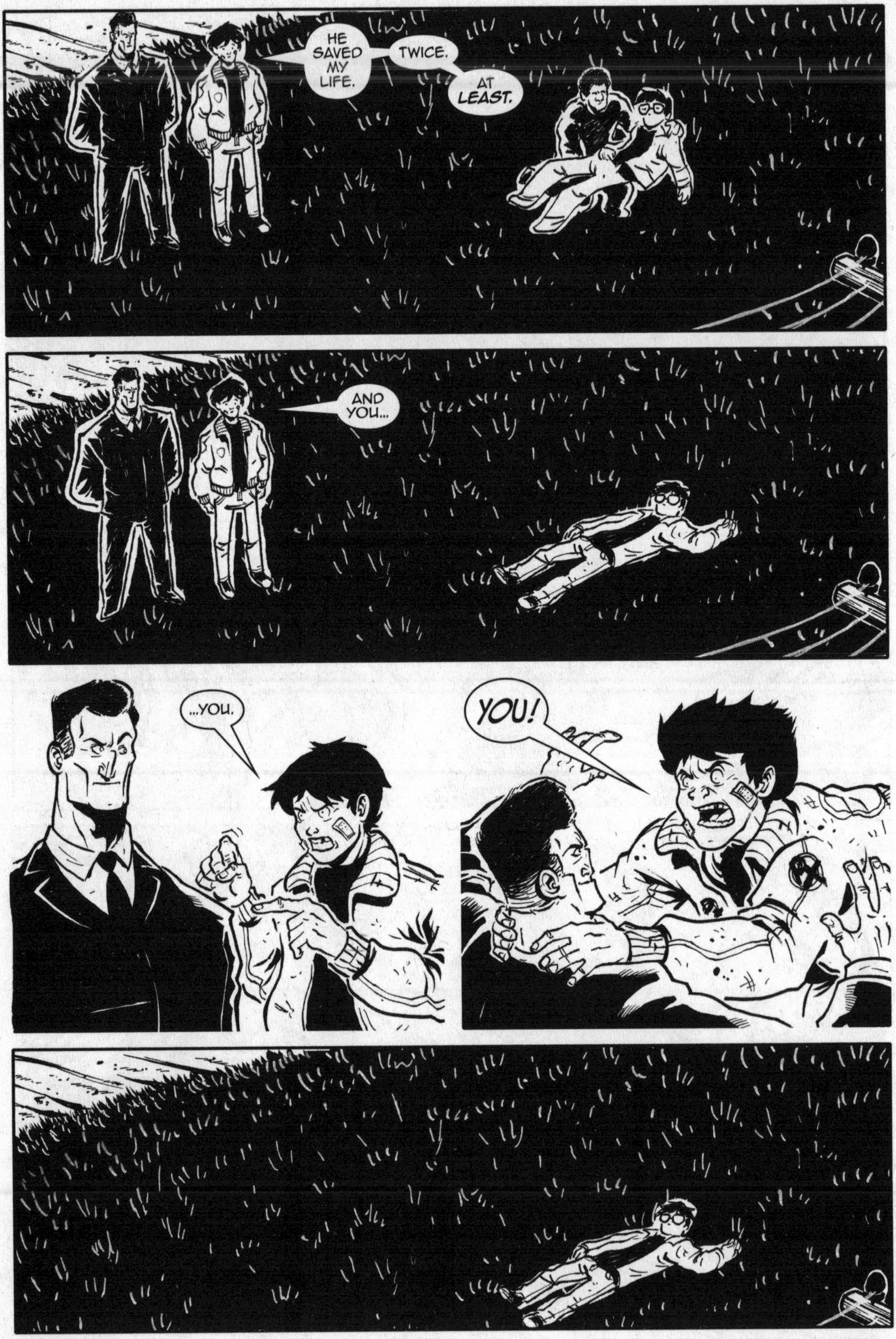
HE SAVED MY LIFE.
TWICE.
AT LEAST.
AND YOU...
...YOU.
YOU!

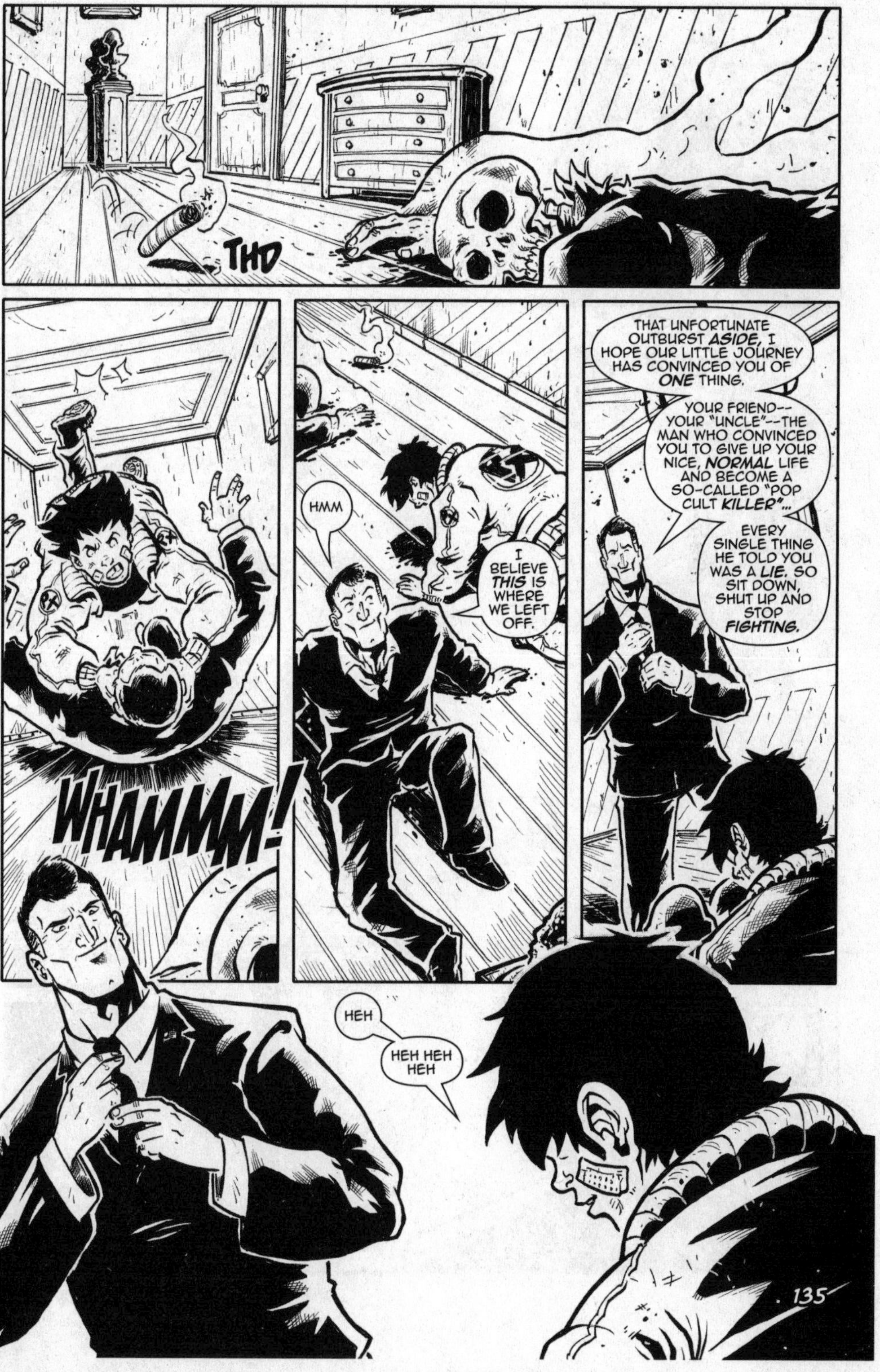
THD
WHAMMM!
HMM
I BELIEVE THIS IS WHERE WE LEFT OFF.
THAT UNFORTUNATE OUTBURST ASIDE, I HOPE OUR LITTLE JOURNEY HAS CONVINCED YOU OF ONE THING.
YOUR FRIEND-- YOUR "UNCLE"--THE MAN WHO CONVINCED YOU TO GIVE UP YOUR NICE, NORMAL LIFE AND BECOME A SO-CALLED "POP CULT KILLER"...
EVERY SINGLE THING HE TOLD YOU WAS A LIE. SO SIT DOWN, SHUT UP AND STOP FIGHTING.
HEH
HEH HEH HEH

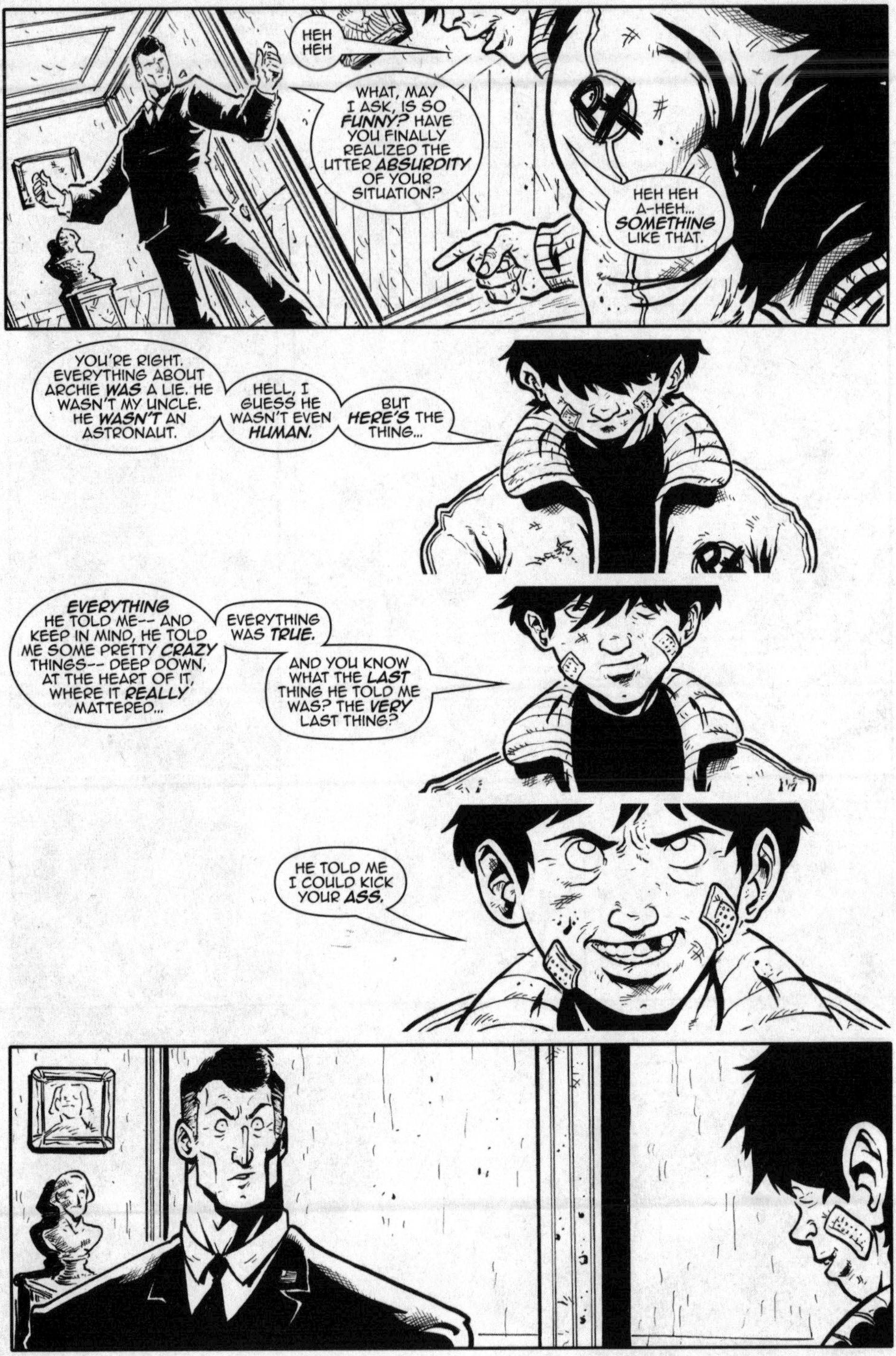
HEH
HEH
WHAT, MAY I ASK, IS SO FUNNY? HAVE YOU FINALLY REALIZED THE UTTER ABSURDITY OF YOUR SITUATION?
HEH HEH A-HEH... SOMETHING LIKE THAT.
YOU'RE RIGHT. EVERYTHING ABOUT ARCHIE WAS A LIE. HE WASN'T MY UNCLE. HE WASN'T AN ASTRONAUT.
HELL, I GUESS HE WASN'T EVEN HUMAN.
BUT HERE'S THE THING...
EVERYTHING HE TOLD ME-- AND KEEP IN MIND, HE TOLD ME SOME PRETTY CRAZY THINGS-- DEEP DOWN, AT THE HEART OF IT, WHERE IT REALLY MATTERED...
EVERYTHING WAS TRUE.
AND YOU KNOW WHAT THE LAST THING HE TOLD ME WAS? THE VERY LAST THING?
HE TOLD ME I COULD KICK YOUR ASS.

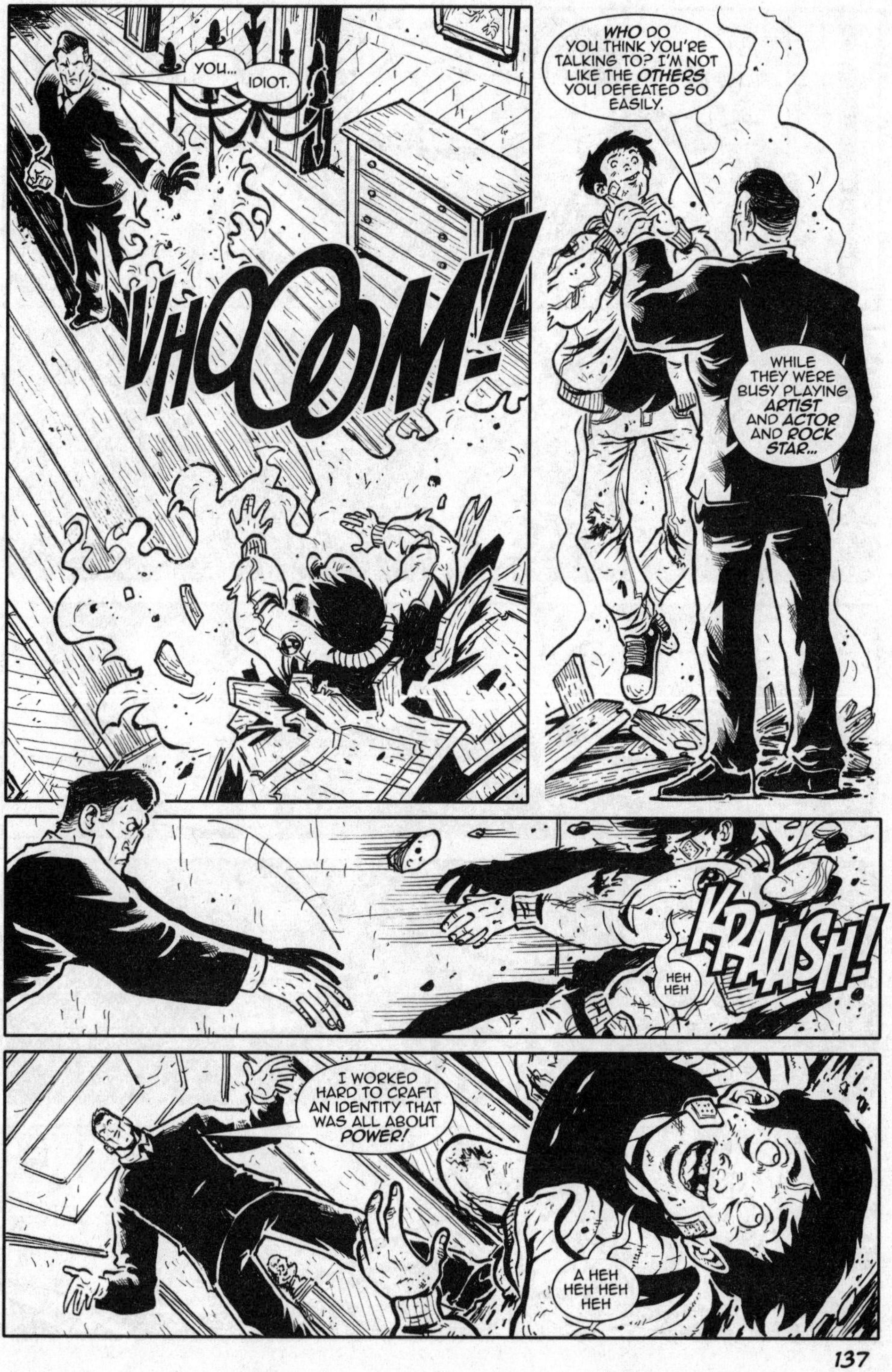
YOU... IDIOT.
VHOOOM!
WHO DO YOU THINK YOU'RE TALKING TO? I'M NOT LIKE THE OTHERS YOU DEFEATED SO EASILY.
WHILE THEY WERE BUSY PLAYING ARTIST AND ACTOR AND ROCK STAR...
KRAASH!
HEH HEH
I WORKED HARD TO CRAFT AN IDENTITY THAT WAS ALL ABOUT POWER!
A HEH HEH HEH HEH HEH

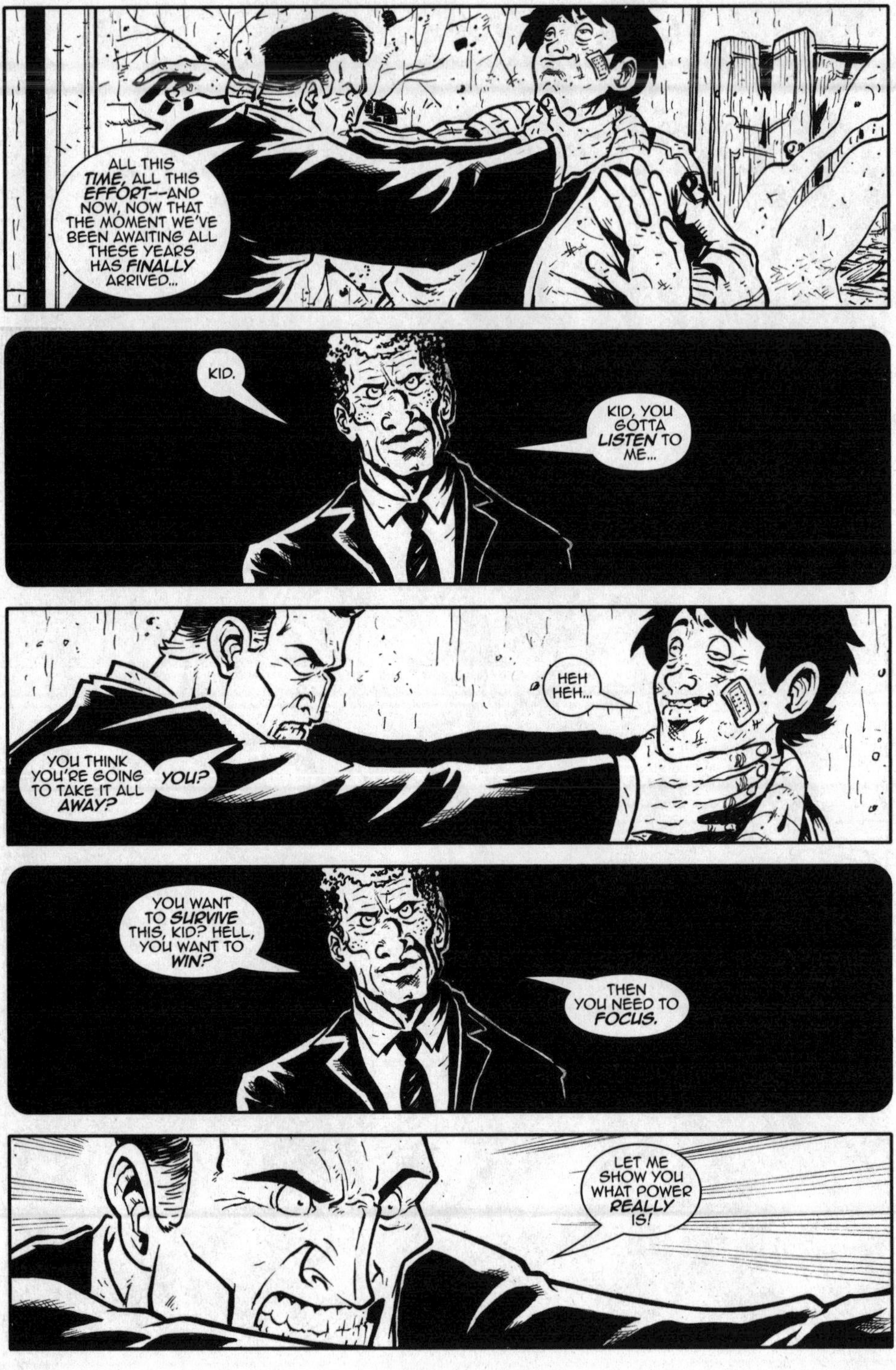
ALL THIS TIME, ALL THIS EFFORT--AND NOW, NOW THAT THE MOMENT WE'VE BEEN AWAITING ALL THESE YEARS HAS FINALLY ARRIVED...
KID.
KID, YOU GOTTA LISTEN TO ME...
HEH HEH...
YOU THINK YOU'RE GOING TO TAKE IT ALL AWAY?
YOU?
YOU WANT TO SURVIVE THIS, KID? HELL, YOU WANT TO WIN?
THEN YOU NEED TO FOCUS.
LET ME SHOW YOU WHAT POWER REALLY IS!

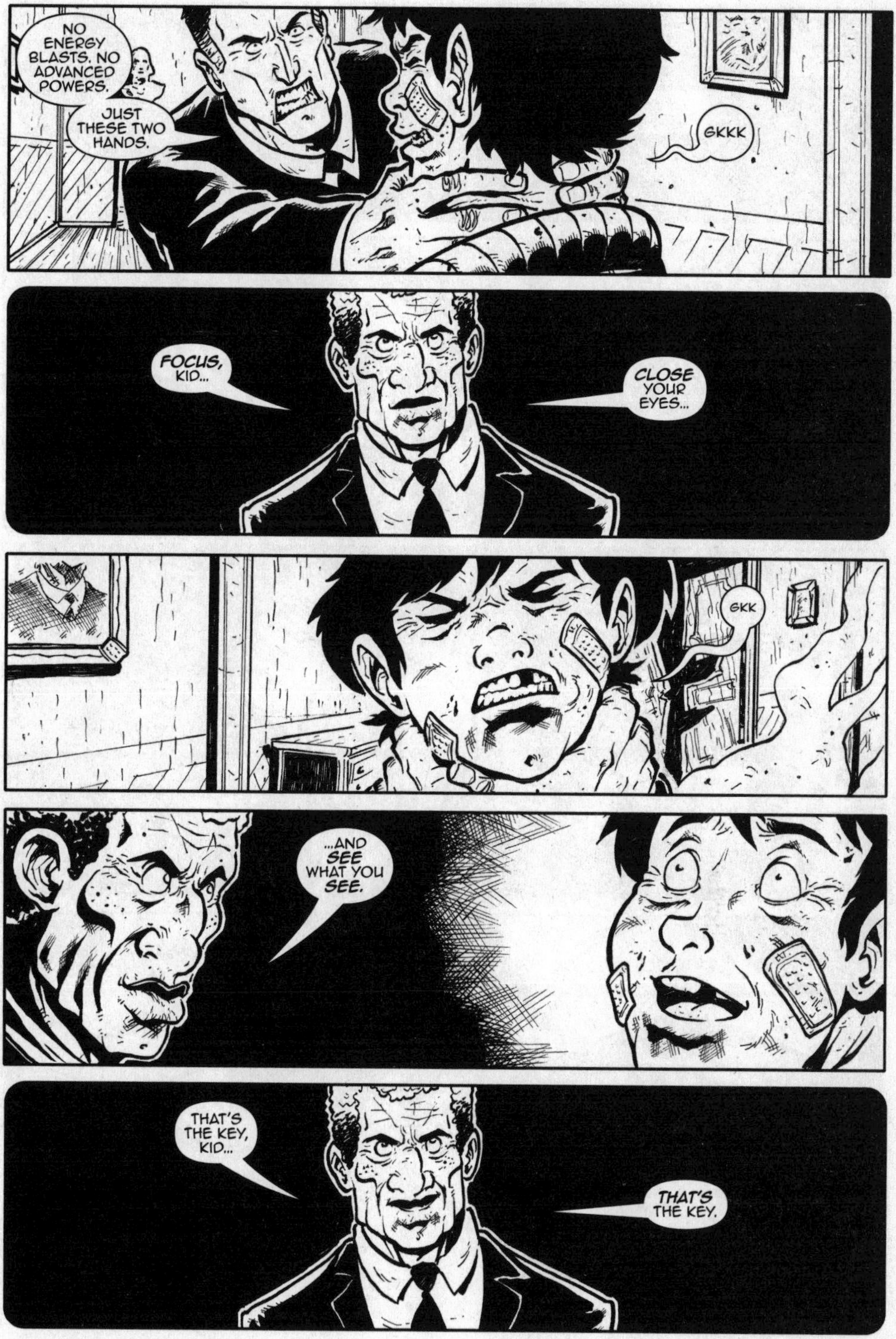
NO ENERGY BLASTS. NO ADVANCED POWERS.
JUST THESE TWO HANDS.
GKKK
FOCUS, KID...
CLOSE YOUR EYES...
GKK
...AND SEE WHAT YOU SEE.
THAT'S THE KEY, KID...
THAT'S THE KEY.

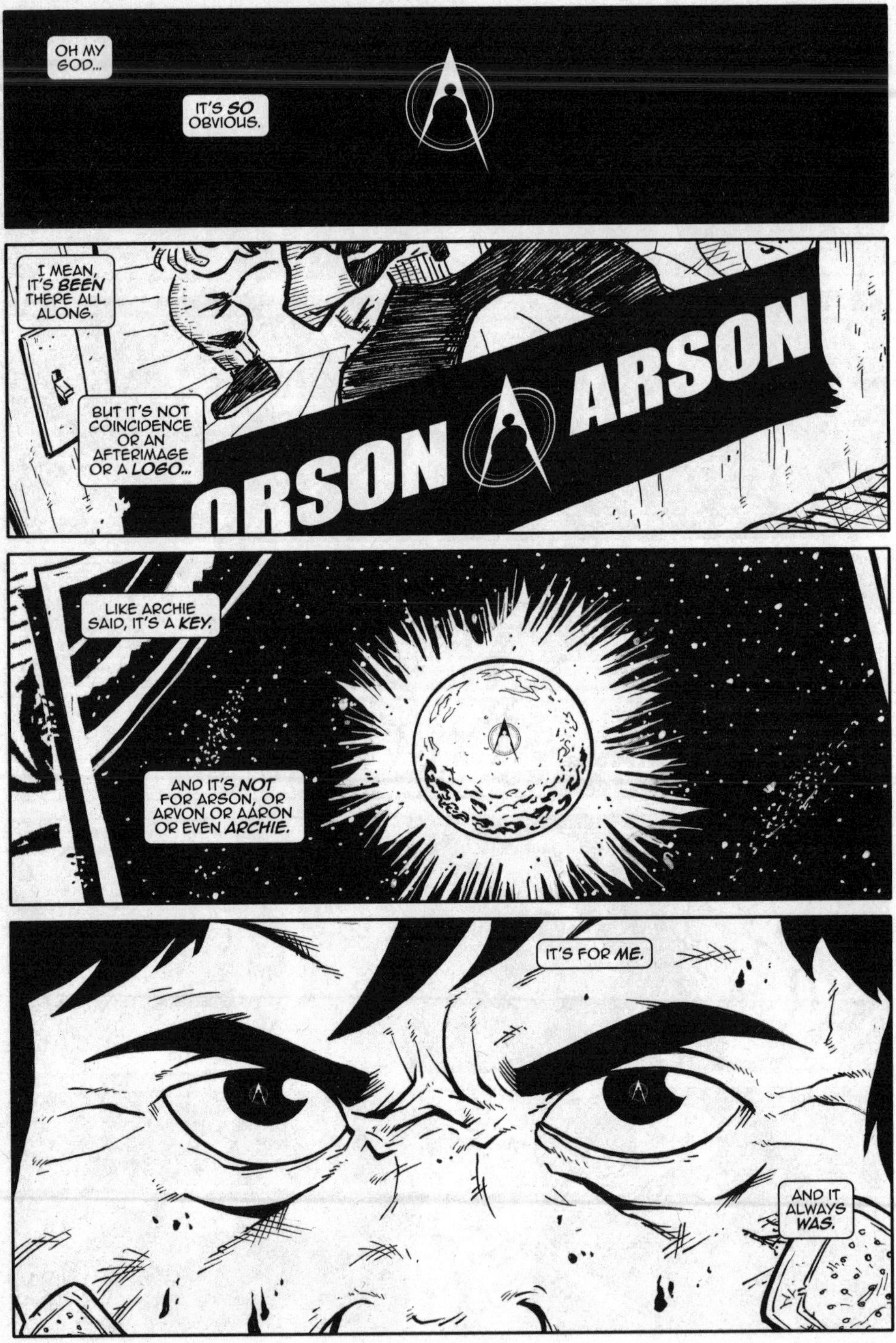
OH MY GOD...
IT'S SO OBVIOUS.
I MEAN, IT'S BEEN THERE ALL ALONG.
ORSON ARSON
BUT IT'S NOT COINCIDENCE OR AN AFTERIMAGE OR A LOGO...
LIKE ARCHIE SAID, IT'S A KEY.
AND IT'S NOT FOR ARSON, OR ARVON OR AÁRON OR EVEN ARCHIE.
IT'S FOR ME.
AND IT ALWAYS WAS.

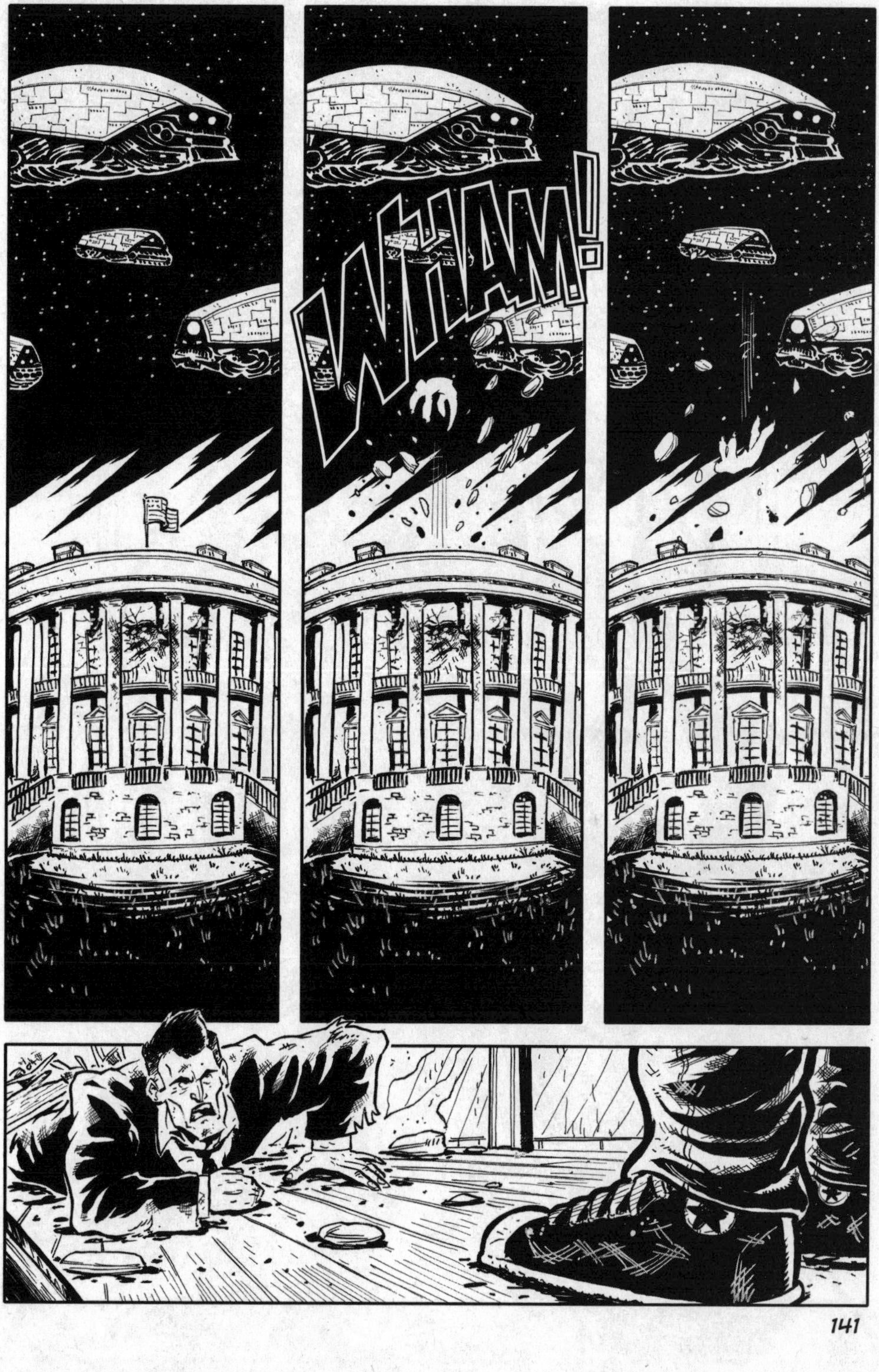
WHAM!

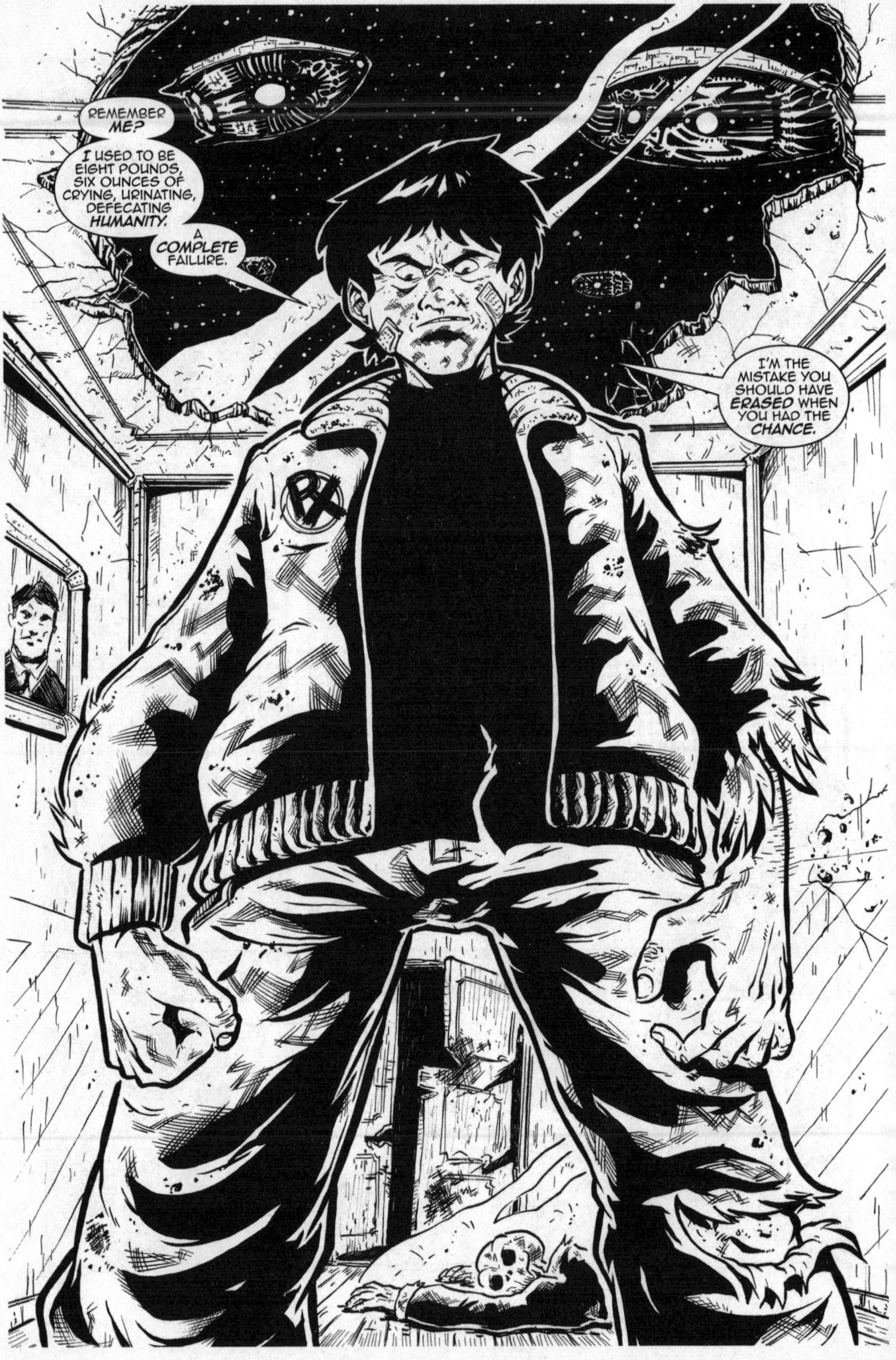
REMEMBER ME?
I USED TO BE EIGHT POUNDS, SIX OUNCES OF CRYING, URINATING, DEFECATING HUMANITY.
A COMPLETE FAILURE.
I'M THE MISTAKE YOU SHOULD HAVE ERASED WHEN YOU HAD THE CHANCE.

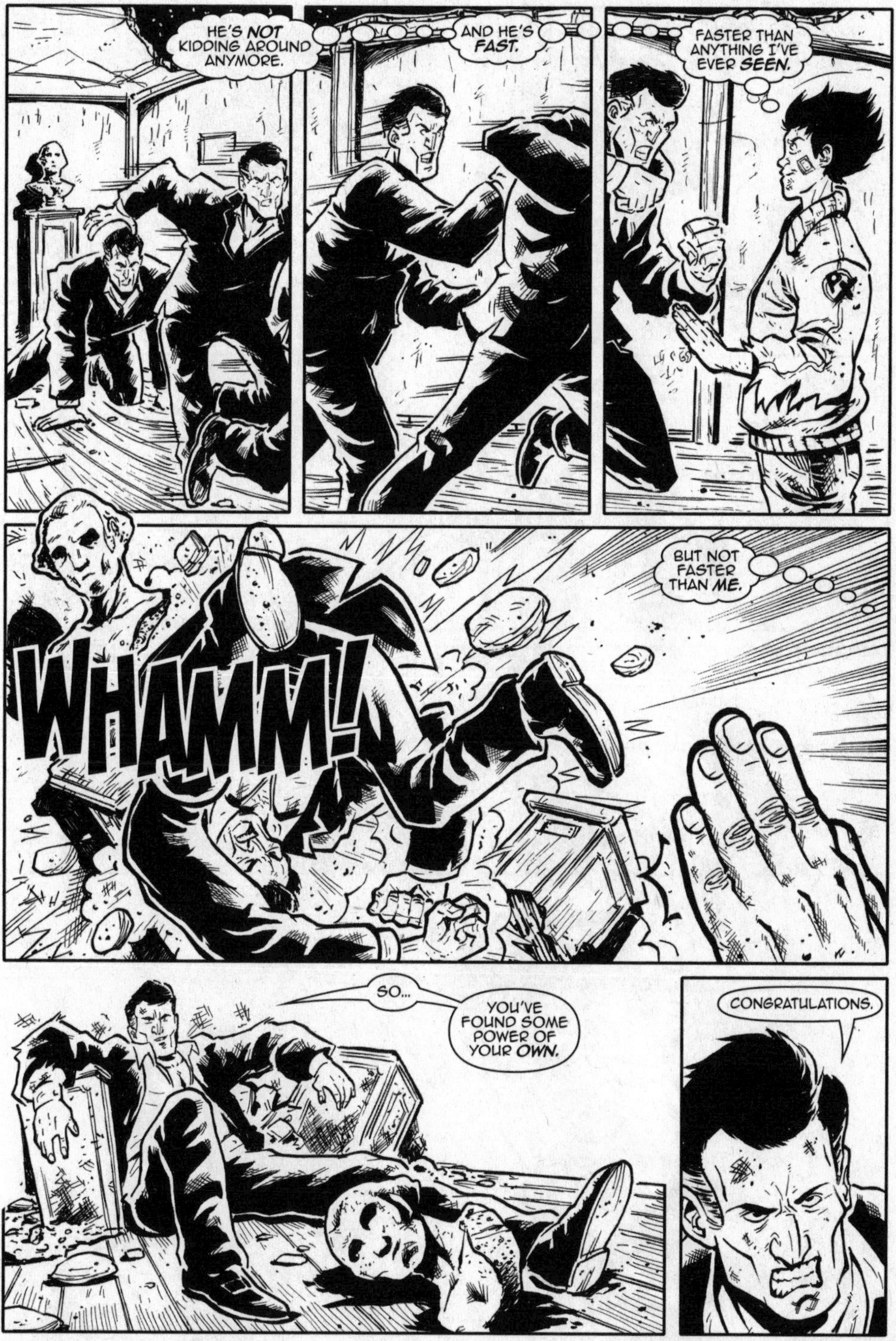
HE'S NOT KIDDING AROUND ANYMORE.
AND HE'S FAST.
FASTER THAN ANYTHING I'VE EVER SEEN.
BUT NOT FASTER THAN ME.
WHAMM!
SO...
YOU'VE FOUND SOME POWER OF YOUR OWN.
CONGRATULATIONS.

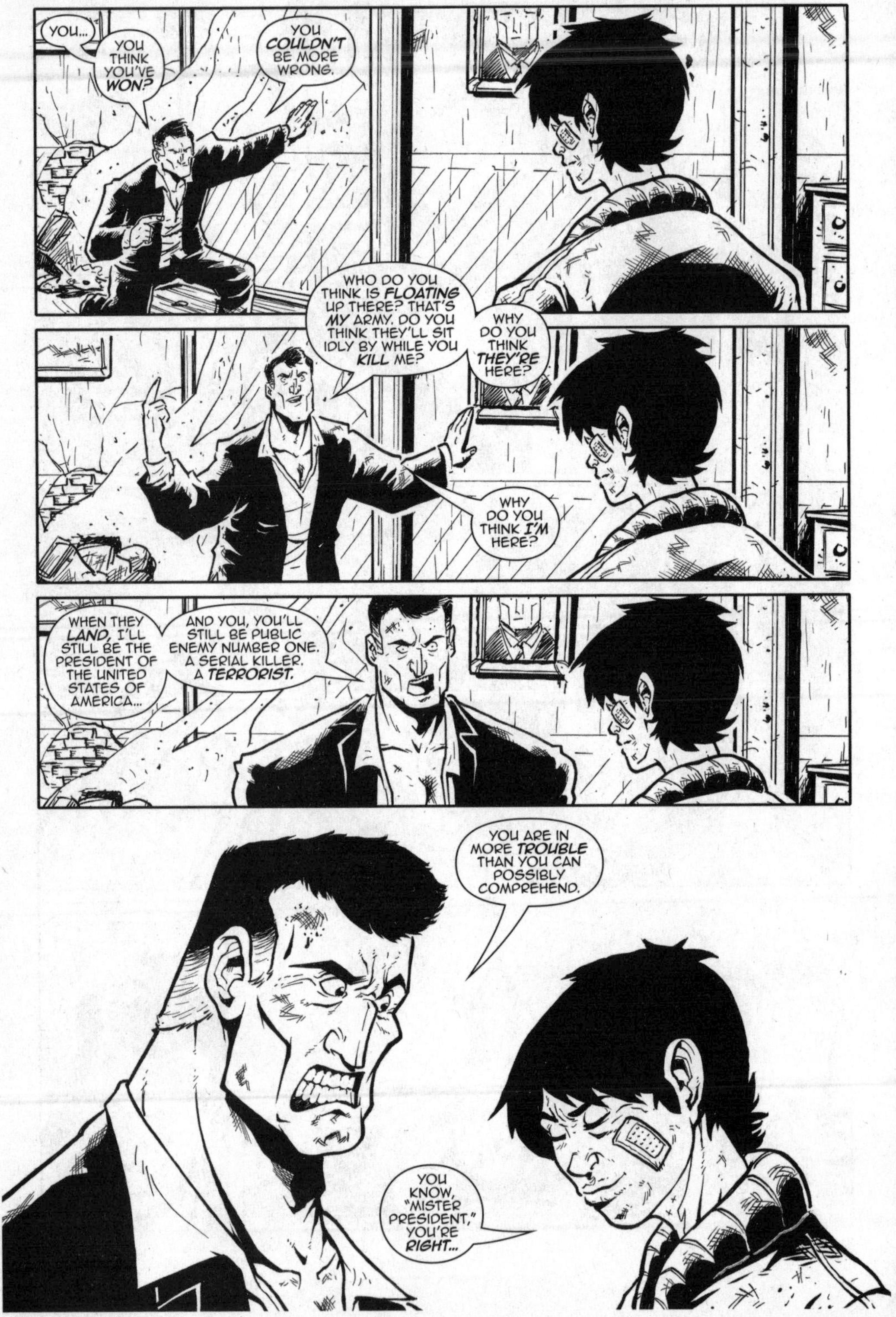
YOU...
YOU THINK YOU'VE WON?
YOU COULDN'T BE MORE WRONG.
WHO DO YOU THINK IS FLOATING UP THERE? THAT'S MY ARMY. DO YOU THINK THEY'LL SIT IDLY BY WHILE YOU KILL ME?
WHY DO YOU THINK THEY'RE HERE?
WHY DO YOU THINK I'M HERE?
WHEN THEY LAND, I'LL STILL BE THE PRESIDENT OF THE UNITED STATES OF AMERICA...
AND YOU, YOU'LL STILL BE PUBLIC ENEMY NUMBER ONE. A SERIAL KILLER. A TERRORIST.
YOU ARE IN MORE TROUBLE THAN YOU CAN POSSIBLY COMPREHEND.
YOU KNOW, "MISTER PRESIDENT," YOU'RE RIGHT...

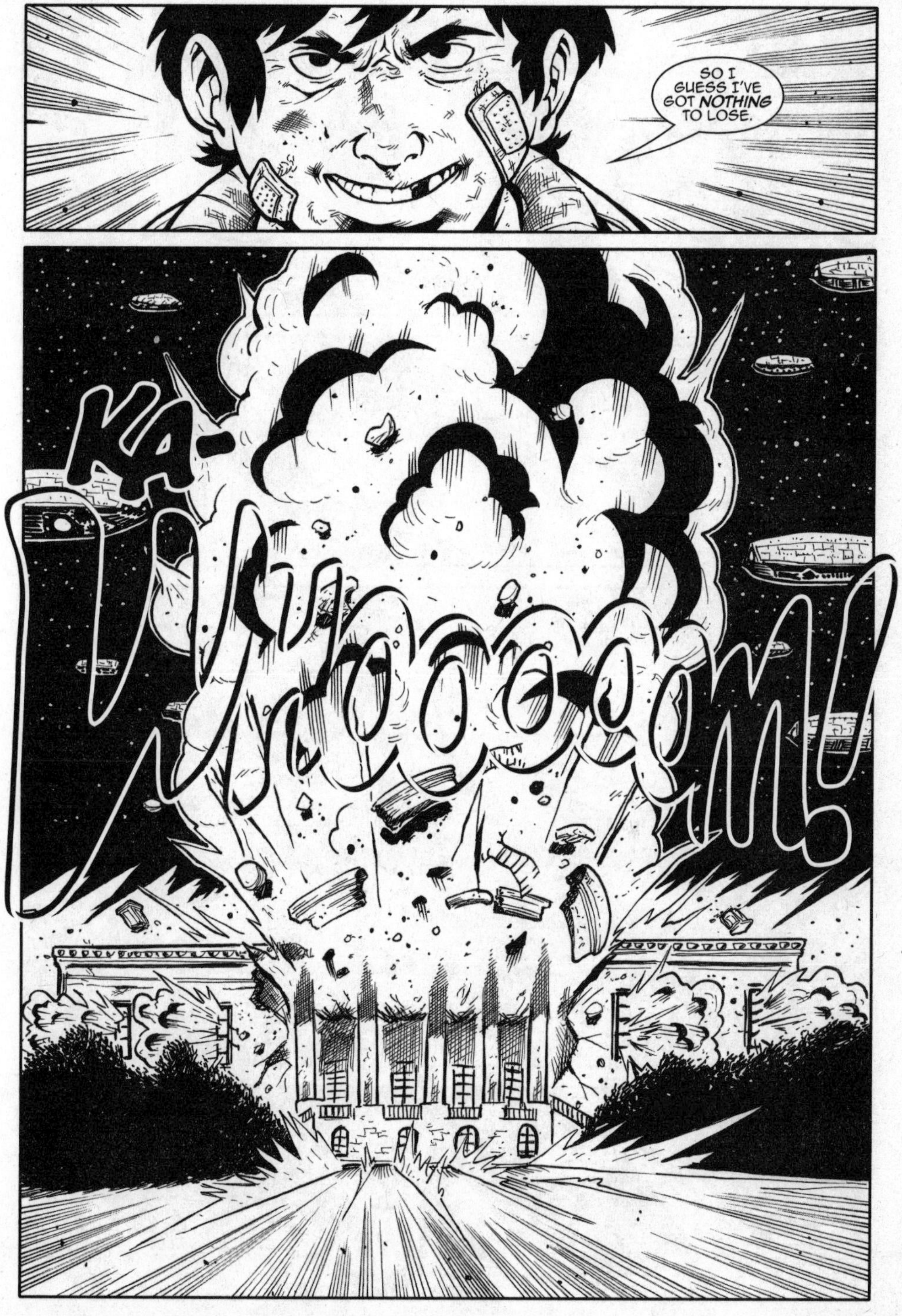
SO I GUESS I'VE GOT *NOTHING* TO LOSE.
KA-
VROOOOOM!

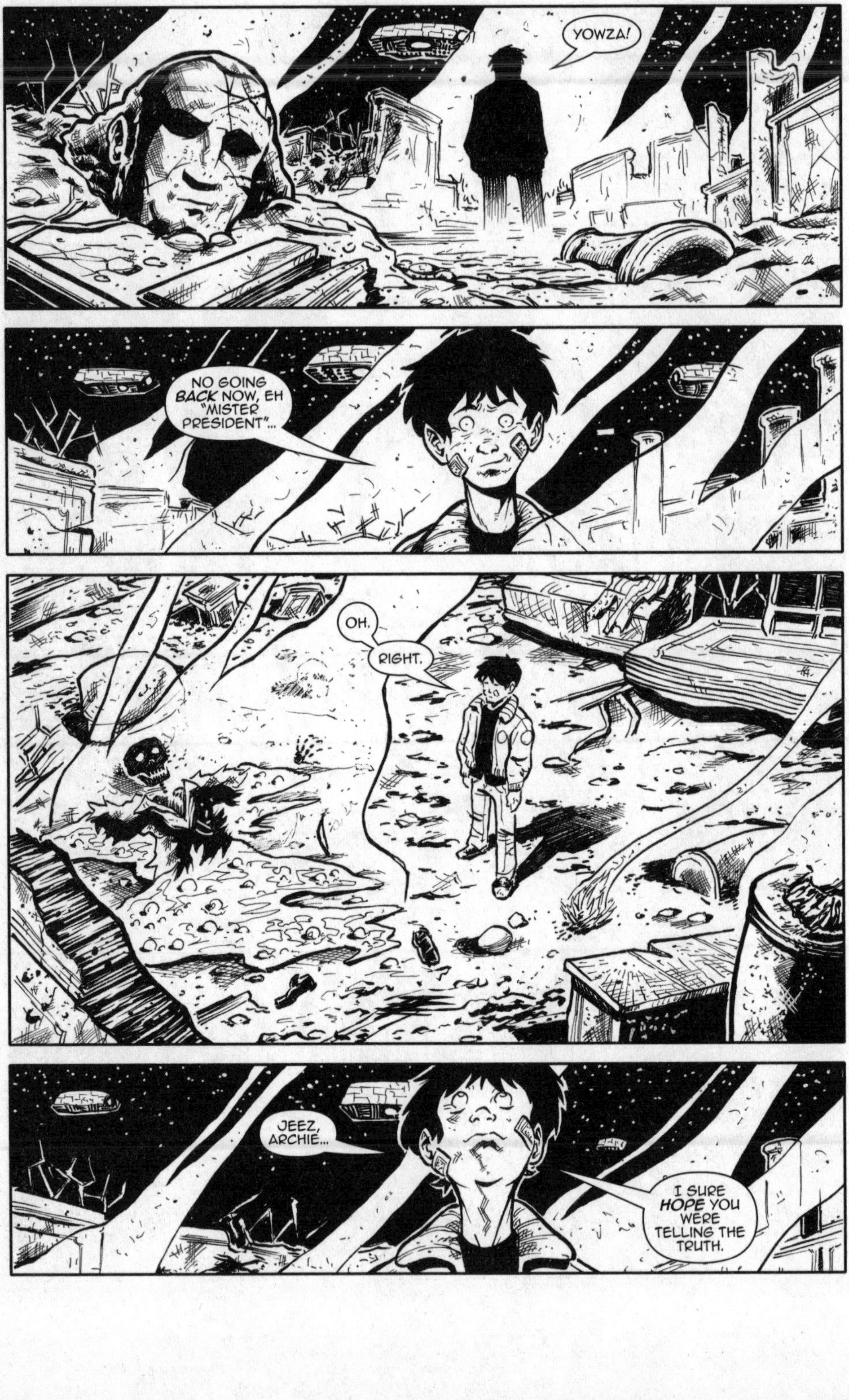
YOWZA!
NO GOING BACK NOW, EH "MISTER PRESIDENT"...
OH.
RIGHT.
JEEZ, ARCHIE...
I SURE HOPE YOU WERE TELLING THE TRUTH.

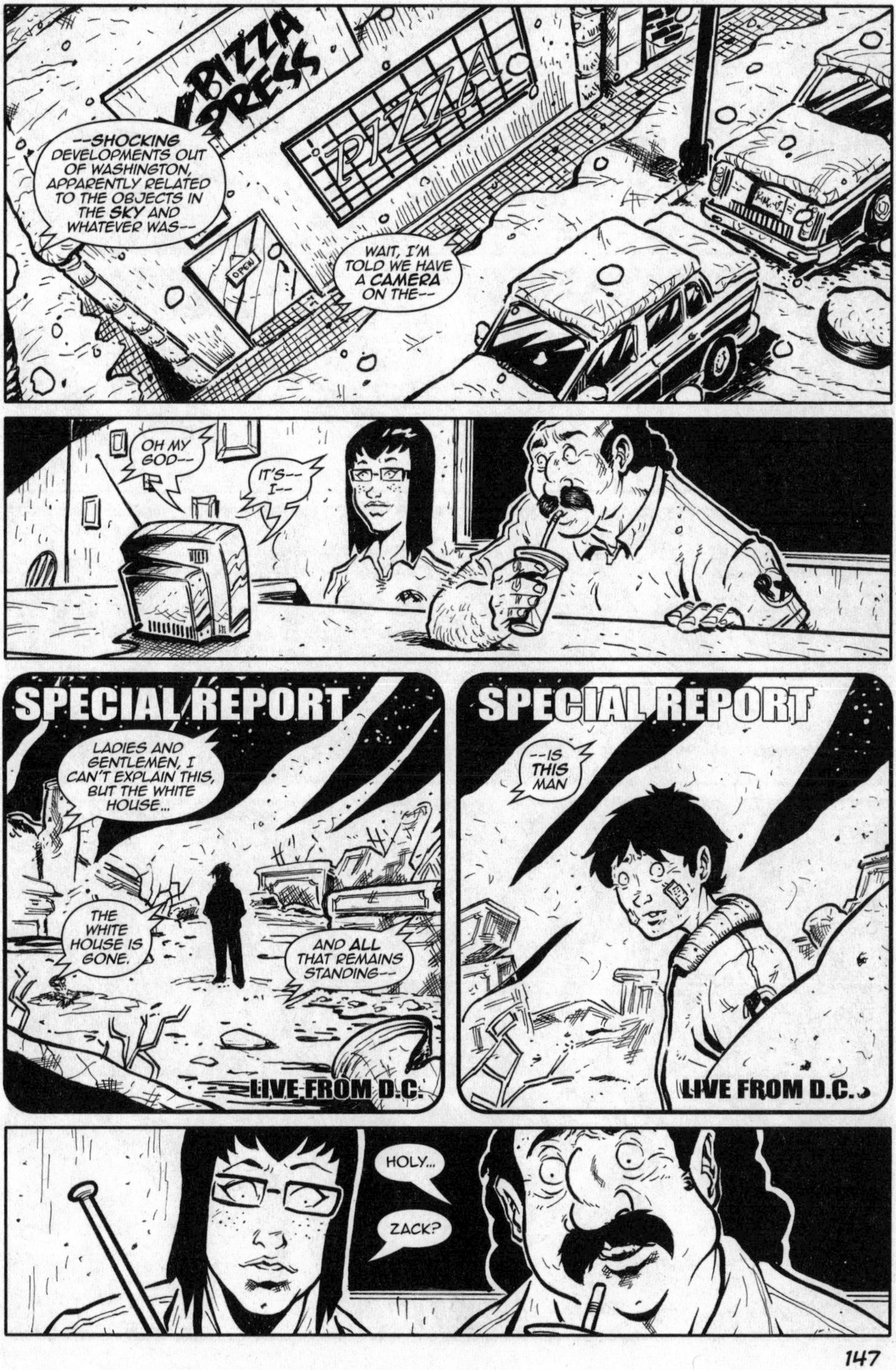

PIZZA PRESS
PIZZA
--SHOCKING DEVELOPMENTS OUT OF WASHINGTON, APPARENTLY RELATED TO THE OBJECTS IN THE SKY AND WHATEVER WAS--
WAIT, I'M TOLD WE HAVE A CAMERA ON THE--
OH MY GOD--
IT'S-- I--
SPECIAL REPORT
LADIES AND GENTLEMEN, I CAN'T EXPLAIN THIS, BUT THE WHITE HOUSE...
THE WHITE HOUSE IS GONE.
AND ALL THAT REMAINS STANDING--
LIVE FROM D.C.
SPECIAL REPORT
--IS THIS MAN
LIVE FROM D.C.
HOLY...
ZACK?

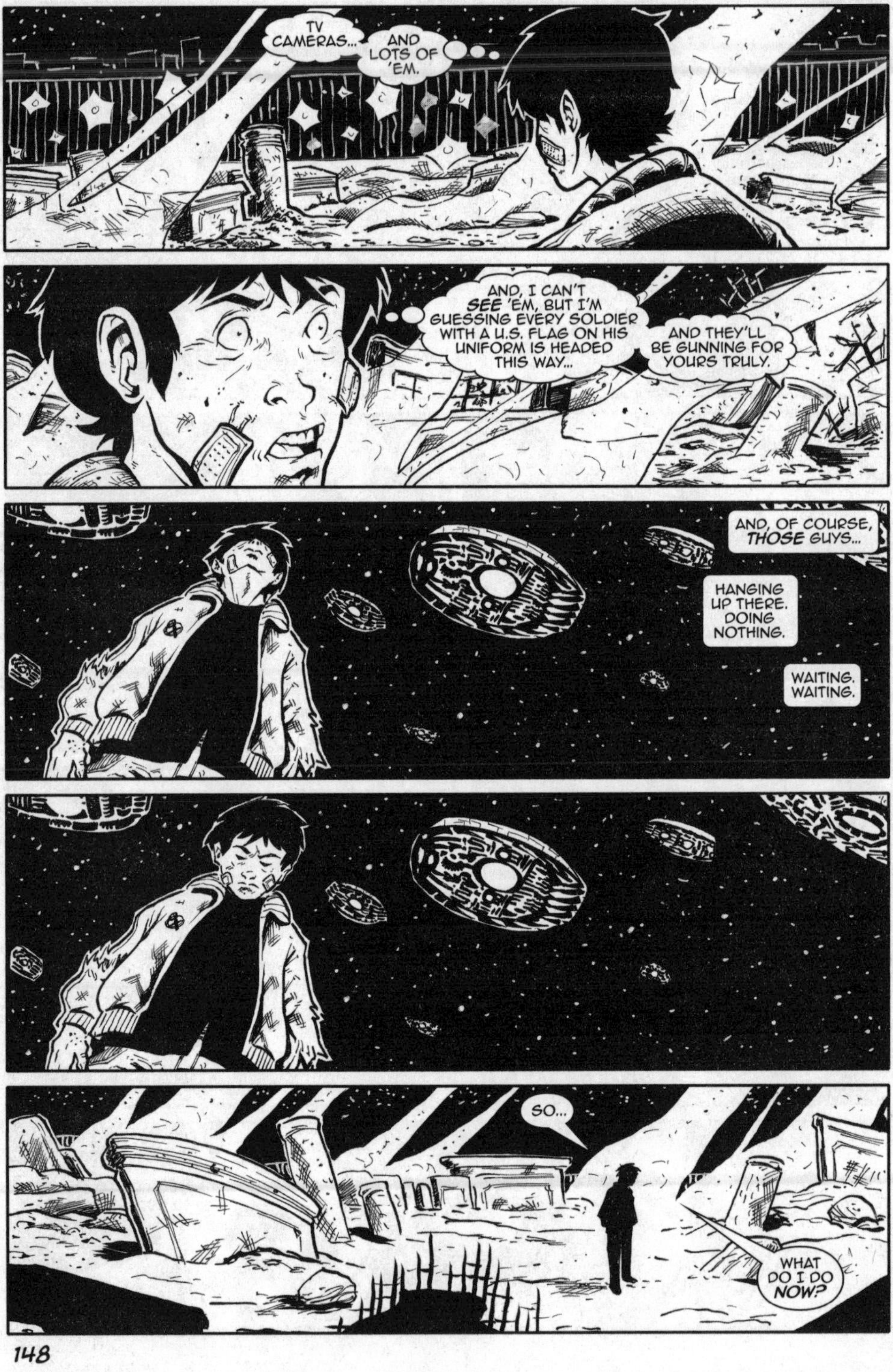
TV CAMERAS...
AND LOTS OF 'EM.
AND, I CAN'T SEE 'EM, BUT I'M GUESSING EVERY SOLDIER WITH A U.S. FLAG ON HIS UNIFORM IS HEADED THIS WAY...
AND THEY'LL BE GUNNING FOR YOURS TRULY.
AND, OF COURSE, THOSE GUYS...
HANGING UP THERE. DOING NOTHING.
WAITING. WAITING.
SO...
WHAT DO I DO NOW?

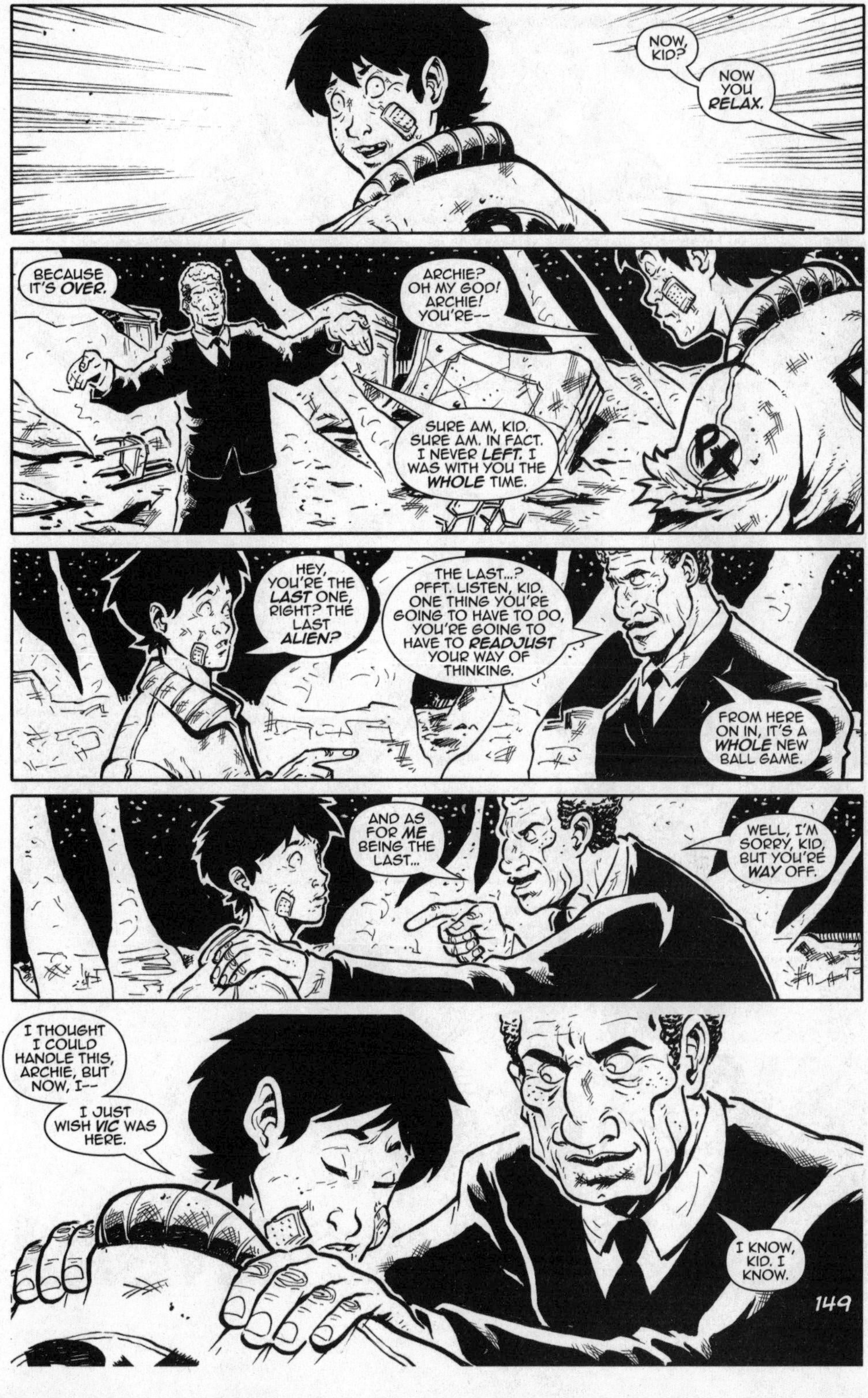
NOW, KID?
NOW YOU RELAX.
BECAUSE IT'S OVER.
ARCHIE? OH MY GOD! ARCHIE! YOU'RE--
SURE AM, KID. SURE AM. IN FACT. I NEVER LEFT. I WAS WITH YOU THE WHOLE TIME.
HEY, YOU'RE THE LAST ONE, RIGHT? THE LAST ALIEN?
THE LAST...? PFFT. LISTEN, KID. ONE THING YOU'RE GOING TO HAVE TO DO, YOU'RE GOING TO HAVE TO READJUST YOUR WAY OF THINKING.
FROM HERE ON IN, IT'S A WHOLE NEW BALL GAME.
AND AS FOR ME BEING THE LAST...
WELL, I'M SORRY, KID, BUT YOU'RE WAY OFF.
I THOUGHT I COULD HANDLE THIS, ARCHIE, BUT NOW, I--
I JUST WISH VIC WAS HERE.
I KNOW, KID. I KNOW.

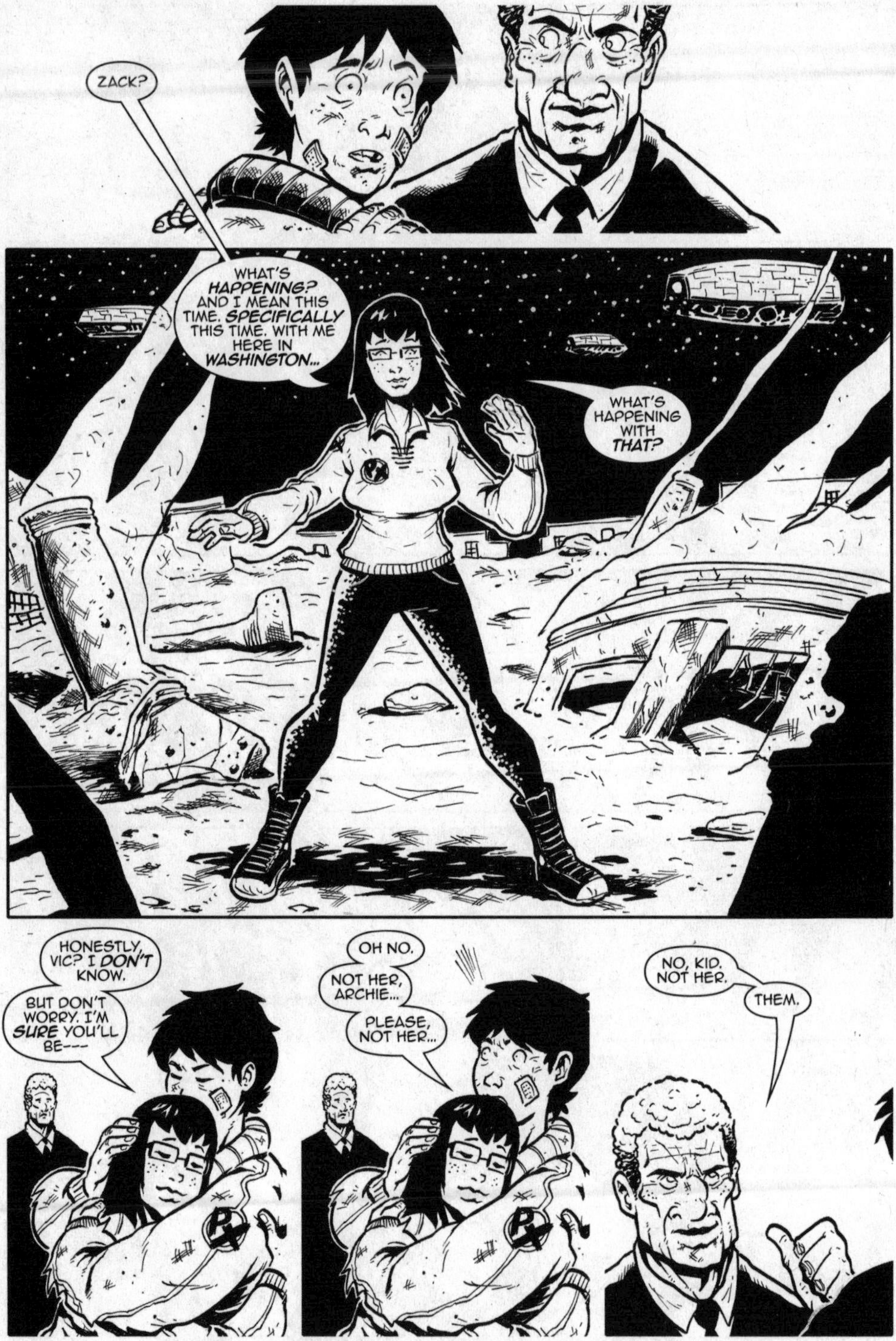
ZACK?
WHAT'S HAPPENING? AND I MEAN THIS TIME. SPECIFICALLY THIS TIME. WITH ME HERE IN WASHINGTON...
WHAT'S HAPPENING WITH THAT?
HONESTLY, VIC? I DON'T KNOW.
BUT DON'T WORRY. I'M SURE YOU'LL BE---
OH NO.
NOT HER, ARCHIE...
PLEASE, NOT HER...
NO, KID. NOT HER.
THEM.

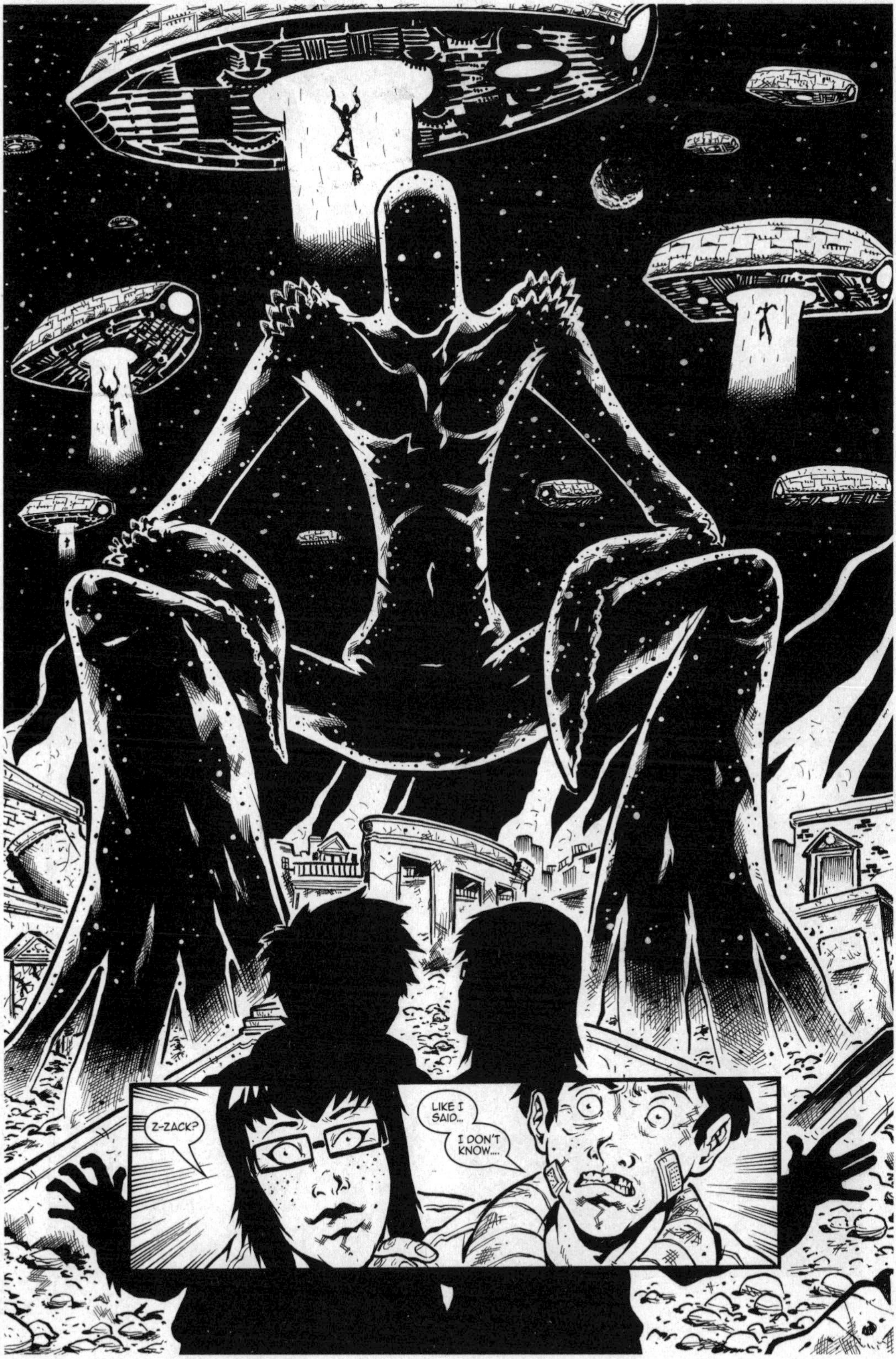
Z-ZACK?
LIKE I SAID...
I DON'T KNOW....

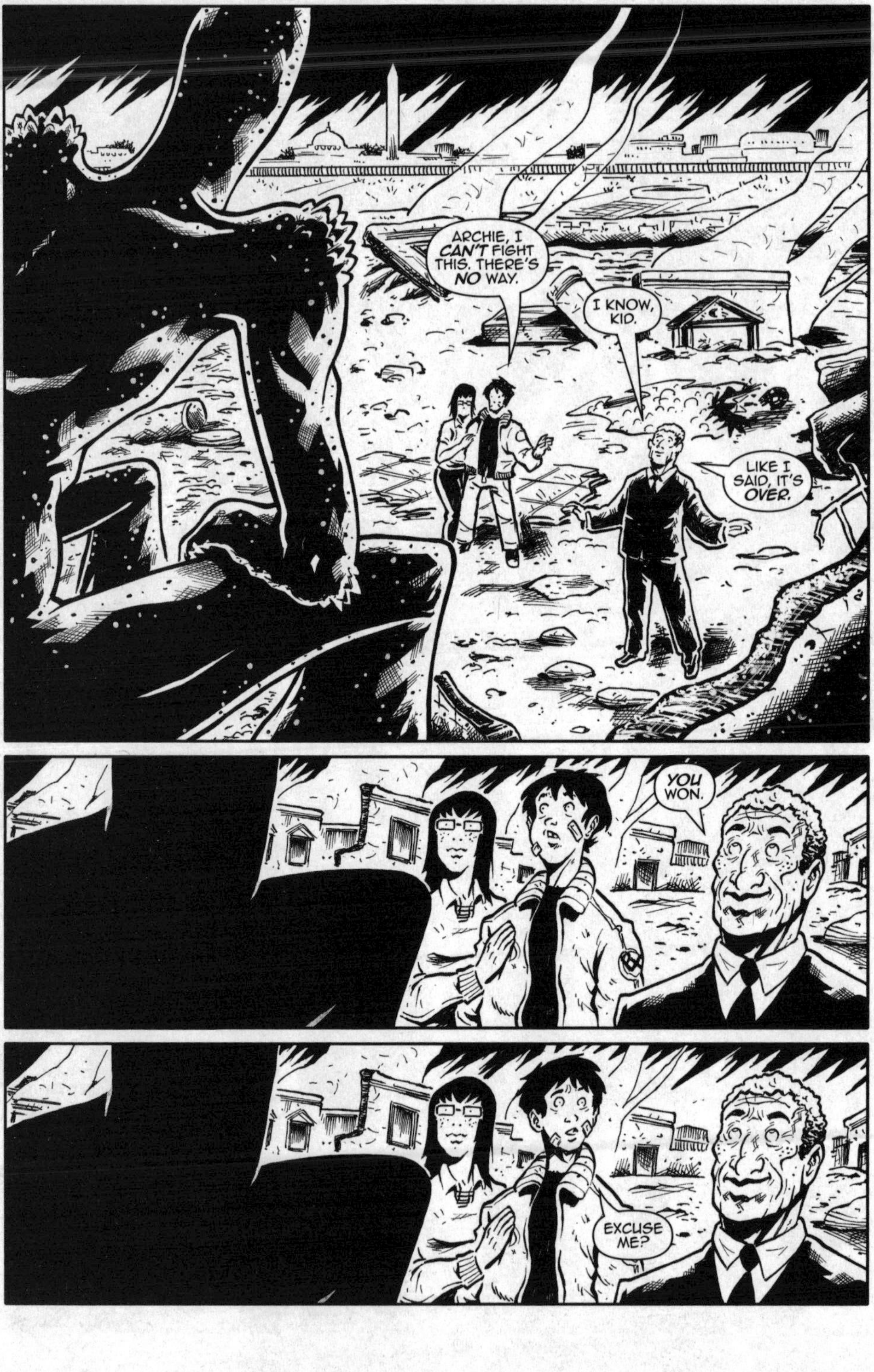
ARCHIE, I CAN'T FIGHT THIS. THERE'S NO WAY.
I KNOW, KID.
LIKE I SAID, IT'S OVER.
YOU WON.
EXCUSE ME?

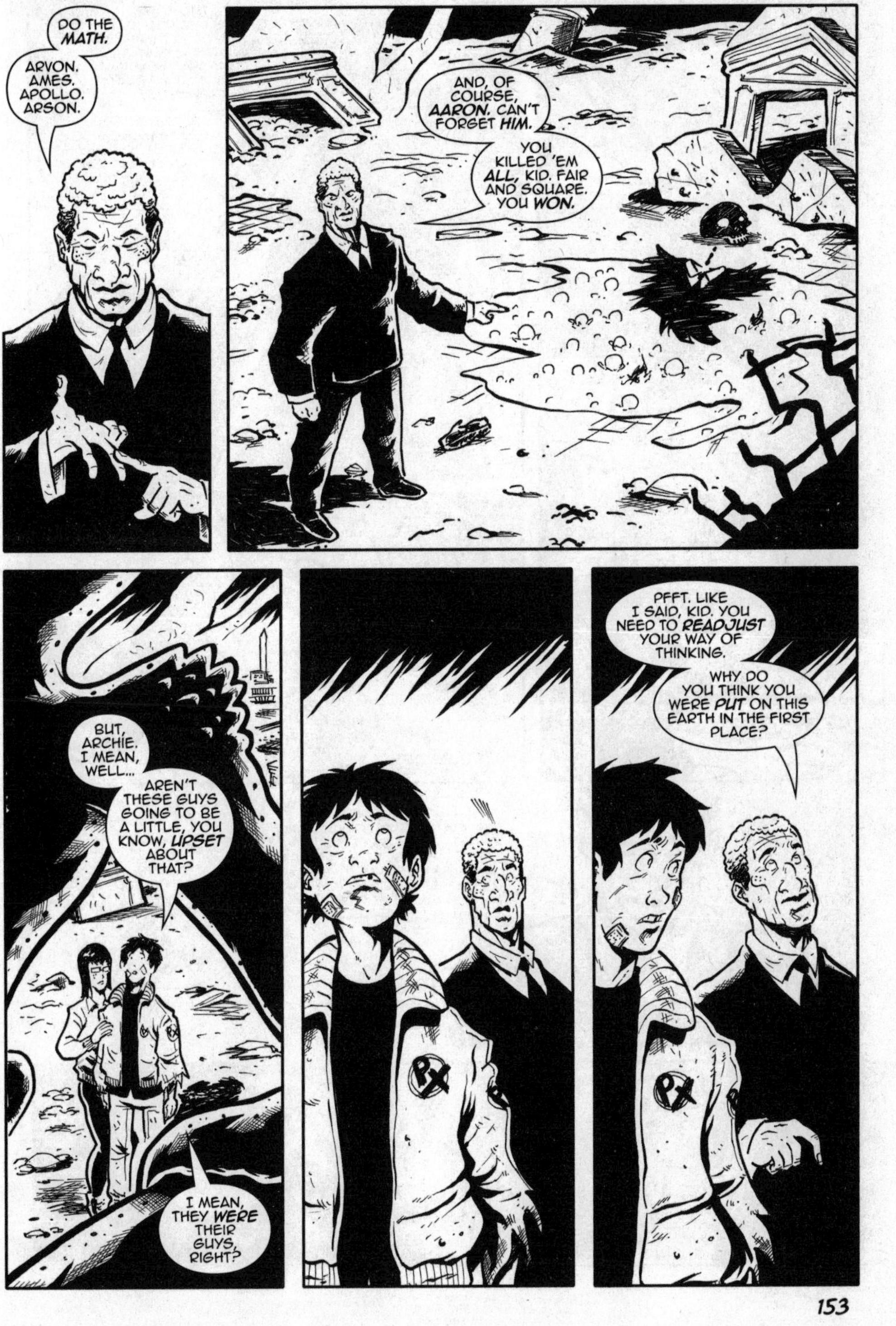
DO THE MATH.
ARVON. AMES. APOLLO. ARSON.
AND, OF COURSE, AARON. CAN'T FORGET HIM.
YOU KILLED 'EM ALL, KID. FAIR AND SQUARE. YOU WON.
BUT, ARCHIE. I MEAN, WELL...
AREN'T THESE GUYS GOING TO BE A LITTLE, YOU KNOW, UPSET ABOUT THAT?
I MEAN, THEY WERE THEIR GUYS, RIGHT?
PFFT. LIKE I SAID, KID. YOU NEED TO READJUST YOUR WAY OF THINKING.
WHY DO YOU THINK YOU WERE PUT ON THIS EARTH IN THE FIRST PLACE?

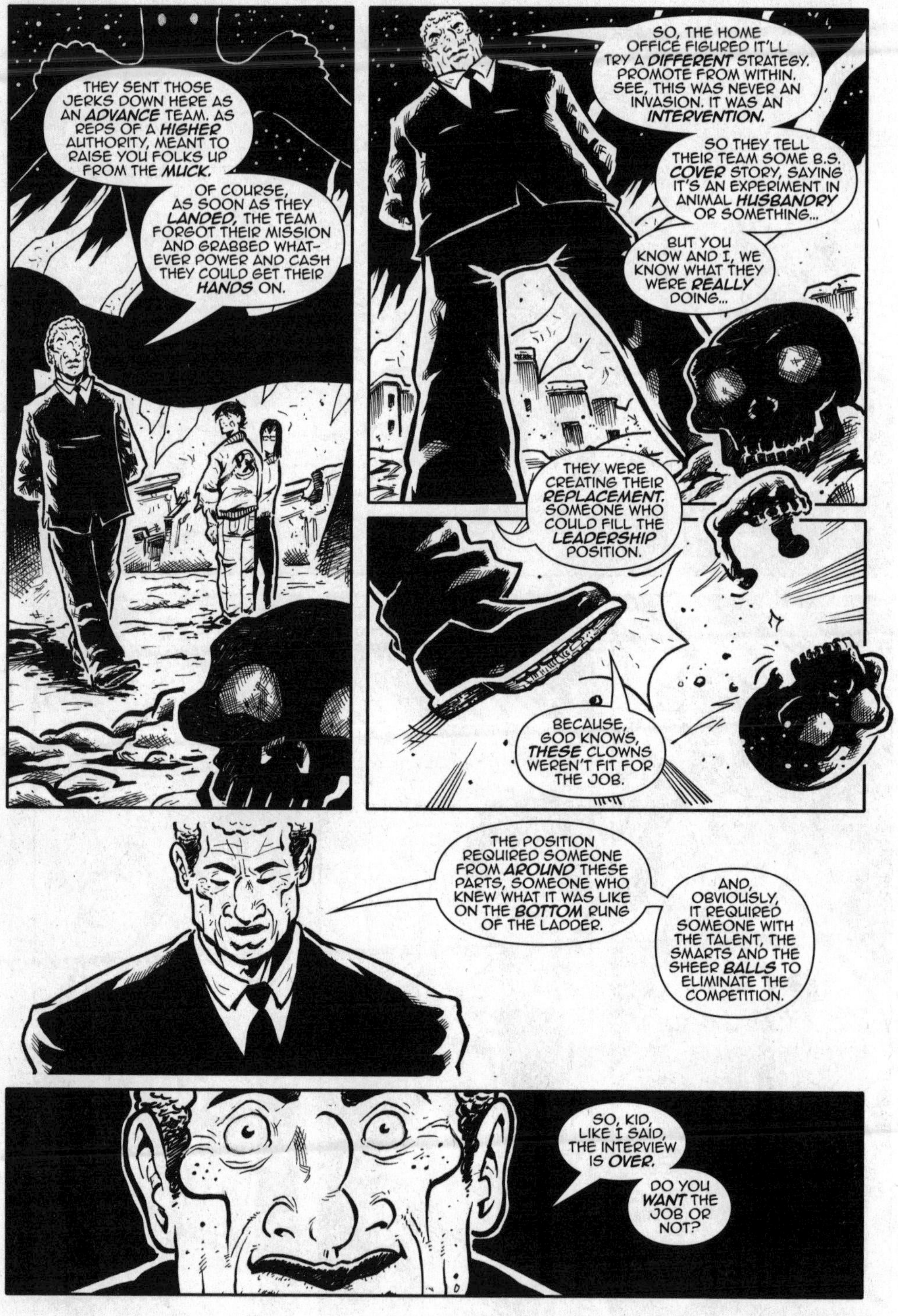
THEY SENT THOSE JERKS DOWN HERE AS AN ADVANCE TEAM. AS REPS OF A HIGHER AUTHORITY, MEANT TO RAISE YOU FOLKS UP FROM THE MUCK.
OF COURSE, AS SOON AS THEY LANDED, THE TEAM FORGOT THEIR MISSION AND GRABBED WHATEVER POWER AND CASH THEY COULD GET THEIR HANDS ON.
SO, THE HOME OFFICE FIGURED IT'LL TRY A DIFFERENT STRATEGY. PROMOTE FROM WITHIN. SEE, THIS WAS NEVER AN INVASION. IT WAS AN INTERVENTION.
SO THEY TELL THEIR TEAM SOME B.S. COVER STORY, SAYING IT'S AN EXPERIMENT IN ANIMAL HUSBANDRY OR SOMETHING...
BUT YOU KNOW AND I, WE KNOW WHAT THEY WERE REALLY DOING...
THEY WERE CREATING THEIR REPLACEMENT. SOMEONE WHO COULD FILL THE LEADERSHIP POSITION.
BECAUSE, GOD KNOWS, THESE CLOWNS WEREN'T FIT FOR THE JOB.
THE POSITION REQUIRED SOMEONE FROM AROUND THESE PARTS, SOMEONE WHO KNEW WHAT IT WAS LIKE ON THE BOTTOM RUNG OF THE LADDER.
AND, OBVIOUSLY, IT REQUIRED SOMEONE WITH THE TALENT, THE SMARTS AND THE SHEER BALLS TO ELIMINATE THE COMPETITION.
SO, KID, LIKE I SAID, THE INTERVIEW IS OVER.
DO YOU WANT THE JOB OR NOT?

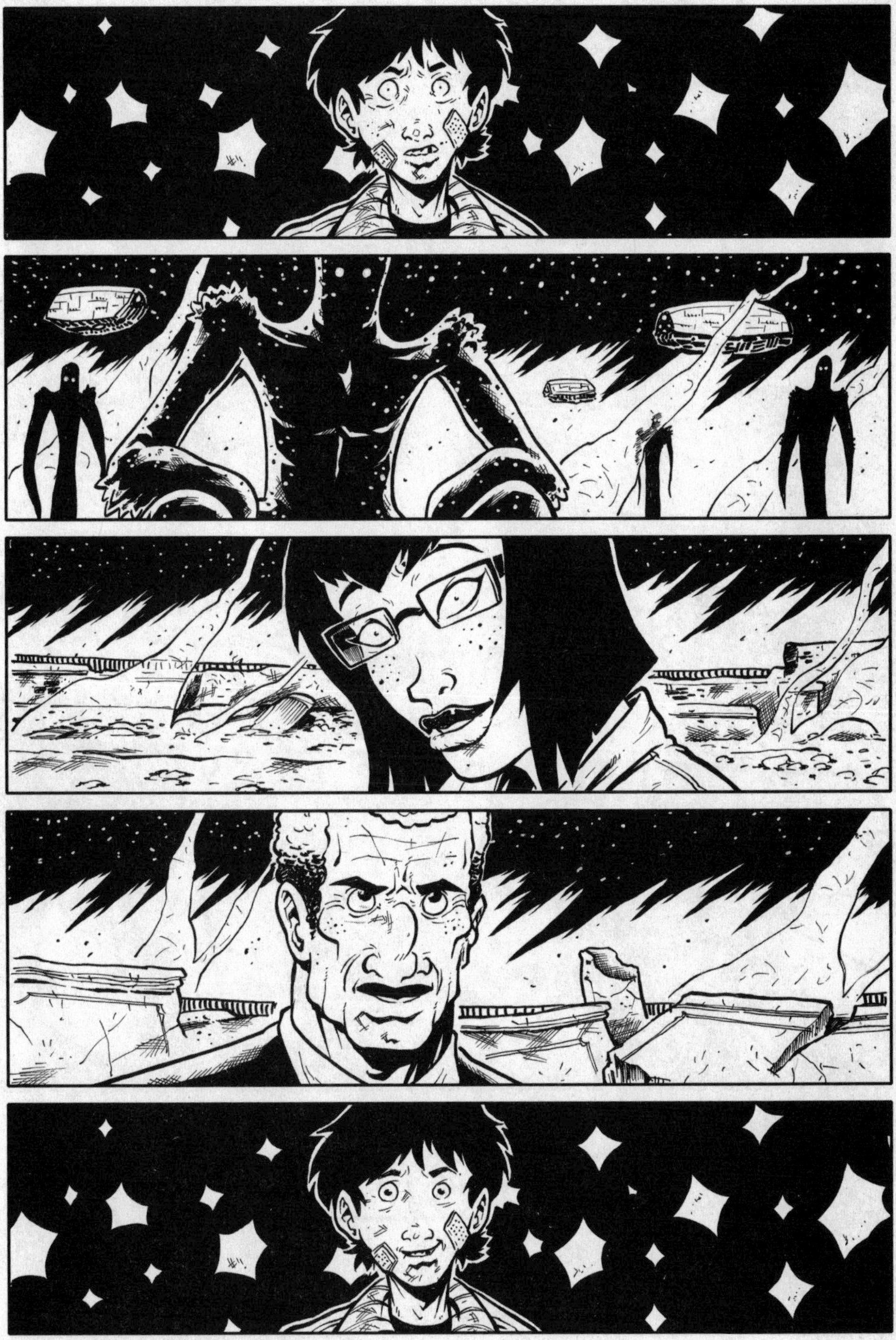

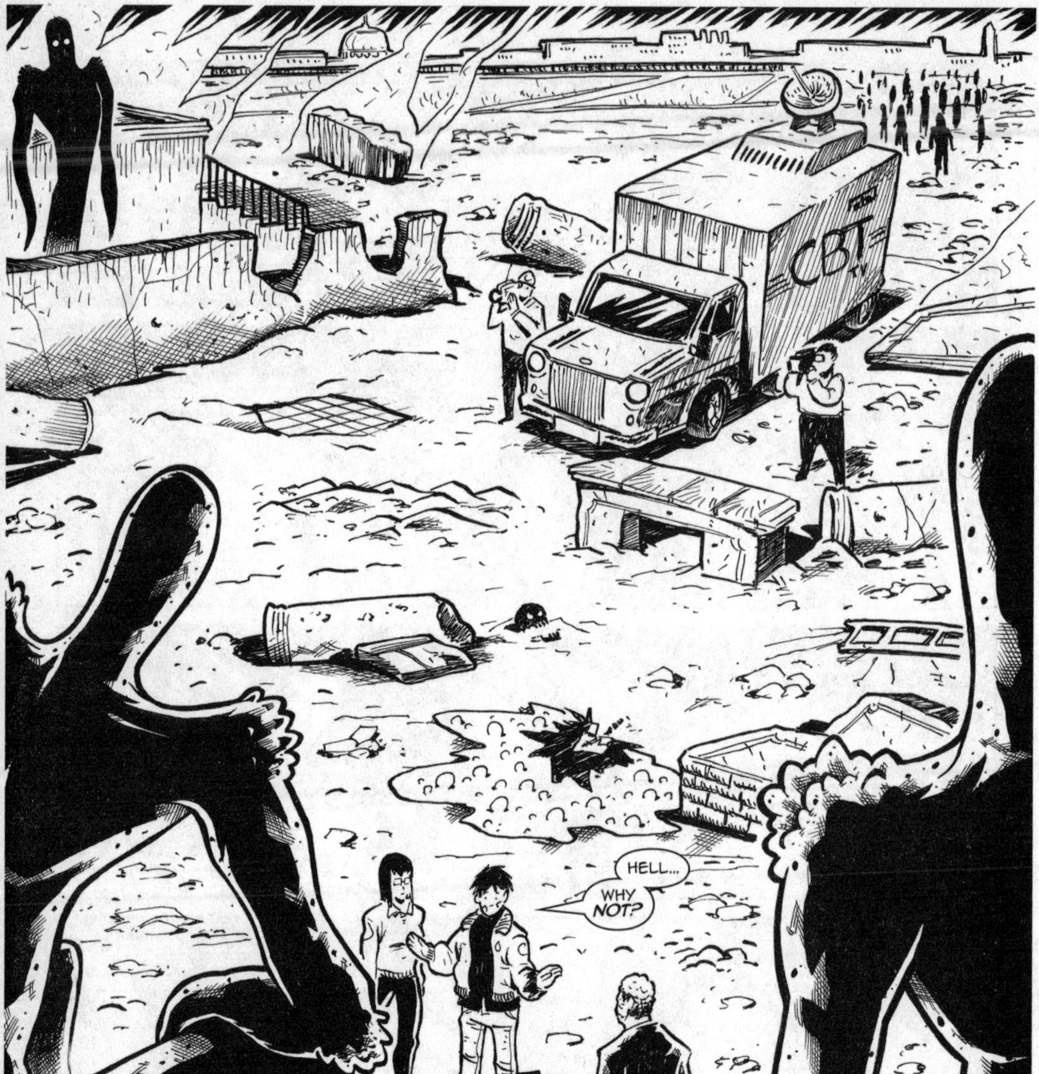
CBT TV
HELL...
WHY NOT?

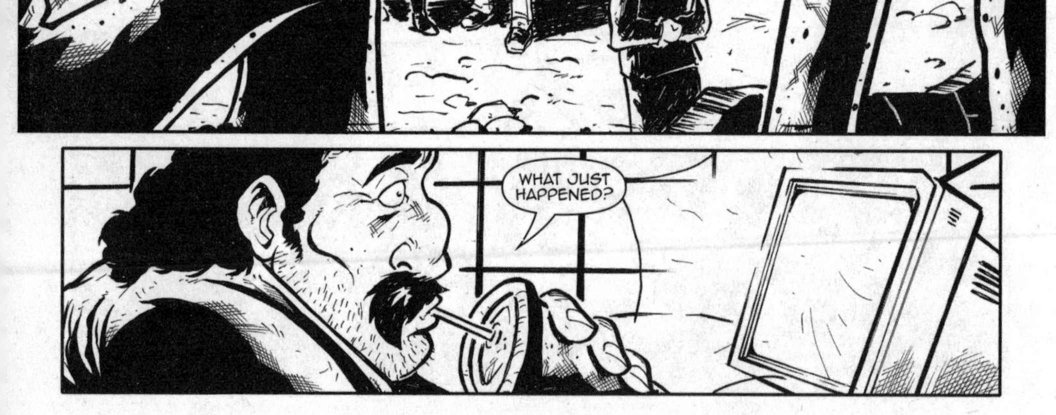
WHAT JUST HAPPENED?

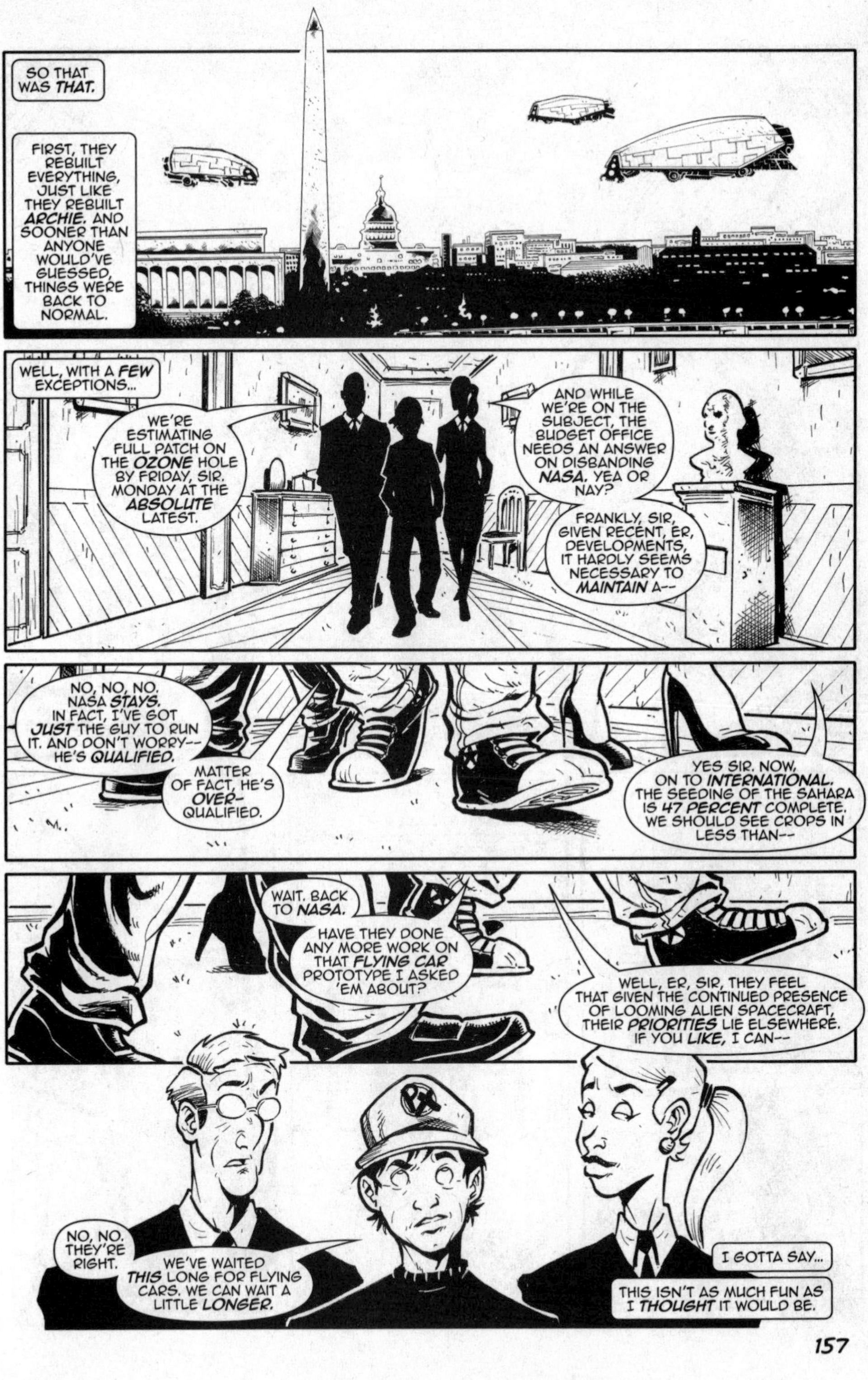
SO THAT WAS THAT.
FIRST, THEY REBUILT EVERYTHING, JUST LIKE THEY REBUILT ARCHIE. AND SOONER THAN ANYONE WOULD'VE GUESSED, THINGS WERE BACK TO NORMAL.
WELL, WITH A FEW EXCEPTIONS...
WE'RE ESTIMATING FULL PATCH ON THE OZONE HOLE BY FRIDAY, SIR. MONDAY AT THE ABSOLUTE LATEST.
AND WHILE WE'RE ON THE SUBJECT, THE BUDGET OFFICE NEEDS AN ANSWER ON DISBANDING NASA. YEA OR NAY?
FRANKLY, SIR, GIVEN RECENT, ER, DEVELOPMENTS, IT HARDLY SEEMS NECESSARY TO MAINTAIN A--
NO, NO, NO. NASA STAYS. IN FACT, I'VE GOT JUST THE GUY TO RUN IT. AND DON'T WORRY-- HE'S QUALIFIED.
MATTER OF FACT, HE'S OVER-QUALIFIED.
YES SIR. NOW, ON TO INTERNATIONAL. THE SEEDING OF THE SAHARA IS 47 PERCENT COMPLETE. WE SHOULD SEE CROPS IN LESS THAN--
WAIT. BACK TO NASA.
HAVE THEY DONE ANY MORE WORK ON THAT FLYING CAR PROTOTYPE I ASKED 'EM ABOUT?
WELL, ER, SIR, THEY FEEL THAT GIVEN THE CONTINUED PRESENCE OF LOOMING ALIEN SPACECRAFT, THEIR PRIORITIES LIE ELSEWHERE. IF YOU LIKE, I CAN--
NO, NO. THEY'RE RIGHT.
WE'VE WAITED THIS LONG FOR FLYING CARS. WE CAN WAIT A LITTLE LONGER.
I GOTTA SAY...
THIS ISN'T AS MUCH FUN AS I THOUGHT IT WOULD BE.

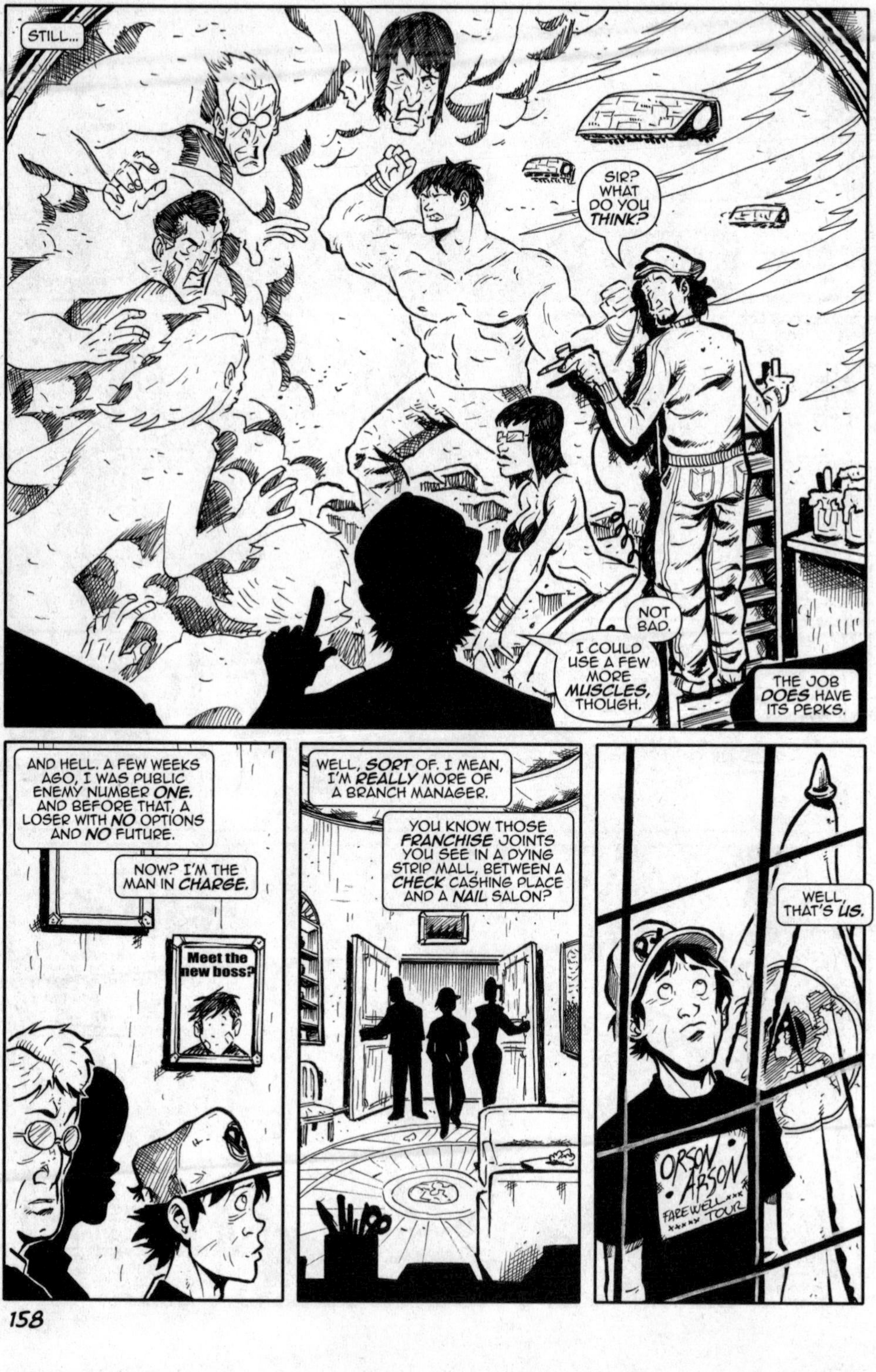
STILL...
SIR? WHAT DO YOU THINK?
NOT BAD.
I COULD USE A FEW MORE MUSCLES, THOUGH.
THE JOB DOES HAVE ITS PERKS.
AND HELL. A FEW WEEKS AGO, I WAS PUBLIC ENEMY NUMBER ONE. AND BEFORE THAT, A LOSER WITH NO OPTIONS AND NO FUTURE.
NOW? I'M THE MAN IN CHARGE.
Meet the new boss?
WELL, SORT OF. I MEAN, I'M REALLY MORE OF A BRANCH MANAGER.
YOU KNOW THOSE FRANCHISE JOINTS YOU SEE IN A DYING STRIP MALL, BETWEEN A CHECK CASHING PLACE AND A NAIL SALON?
WELL, THAT'S US.
ORSON ARSON FAREWELL TOUR

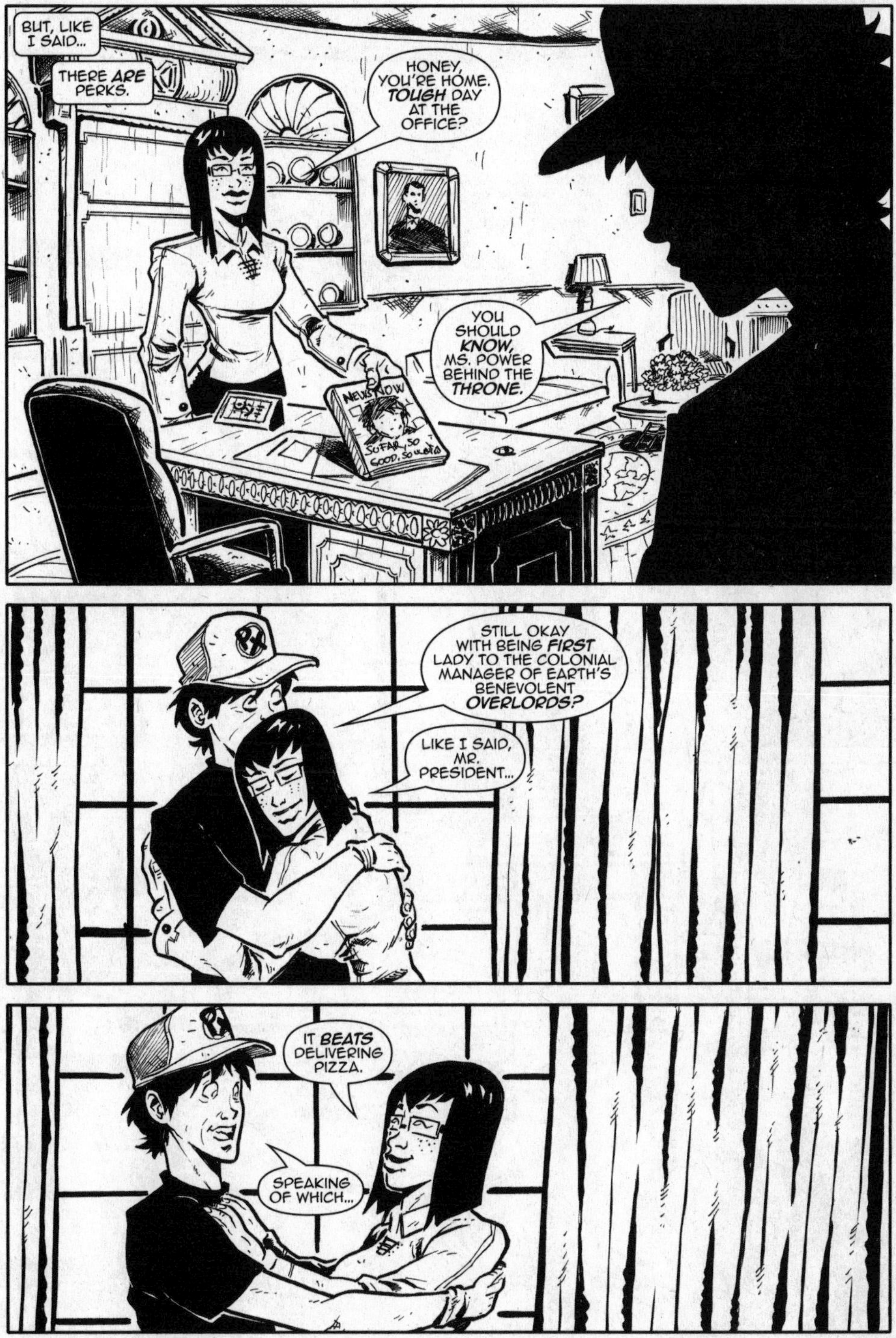
BUT, LIKE I SAID...
THERE *ARE* PERKS.
HONEY, YOU'RE HOME. *TOUGH* DAY AT THE OFFICE?
YOU SHOULD *KNOW,* MS. POWER BEHIND THE *THRONE.*
STILL OKAY WITH BEING *FIRST* LADY TO THE COLONIAL MANAGER OF EARTH'S BENEVOLENT *OVERLORDS?*
LIKE I SAID, MR. PRESIDENT...
IT *BEATS* DELIVERING PIZZA.
SPEAKING OF WHICH...

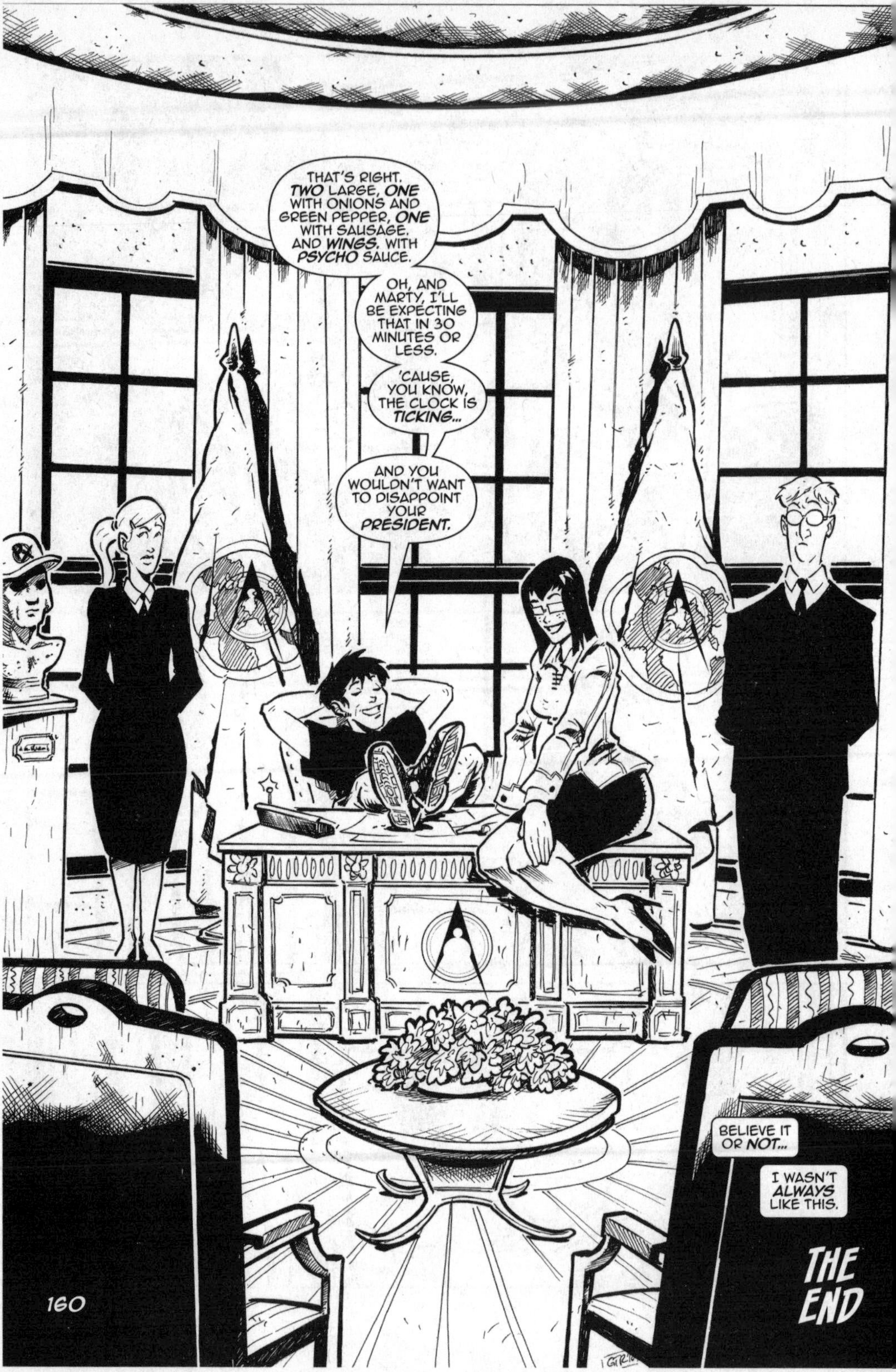
THAT'S RIGHT. TWO LARGE, ONE WITH ONIONS AND GREEN PEPPER, ONE WITH SAUSAGE, AND WINGS. WITH PSYCHO SAUCE.
OH, AND MARTY, I'LL BE EXPECTING THAT IN 30 MINUTES OR LESS.
'CAUSE, YOU KNOW, THE CLOCK IS TICKING...
AND YOU WOULDN'T WANT TO DISAPPOINT YOUR PRESIDENT.
BELIEVE IT OR NOT...
I WASN'T ALWAYS LIKE THIS.
THE END

Germán Torres's

character design sketches for

THE ADVANCE TEAM

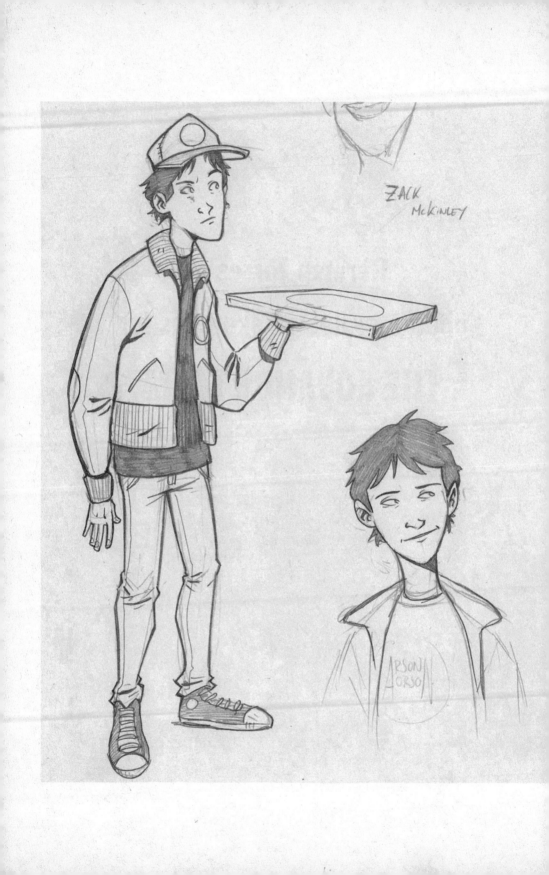

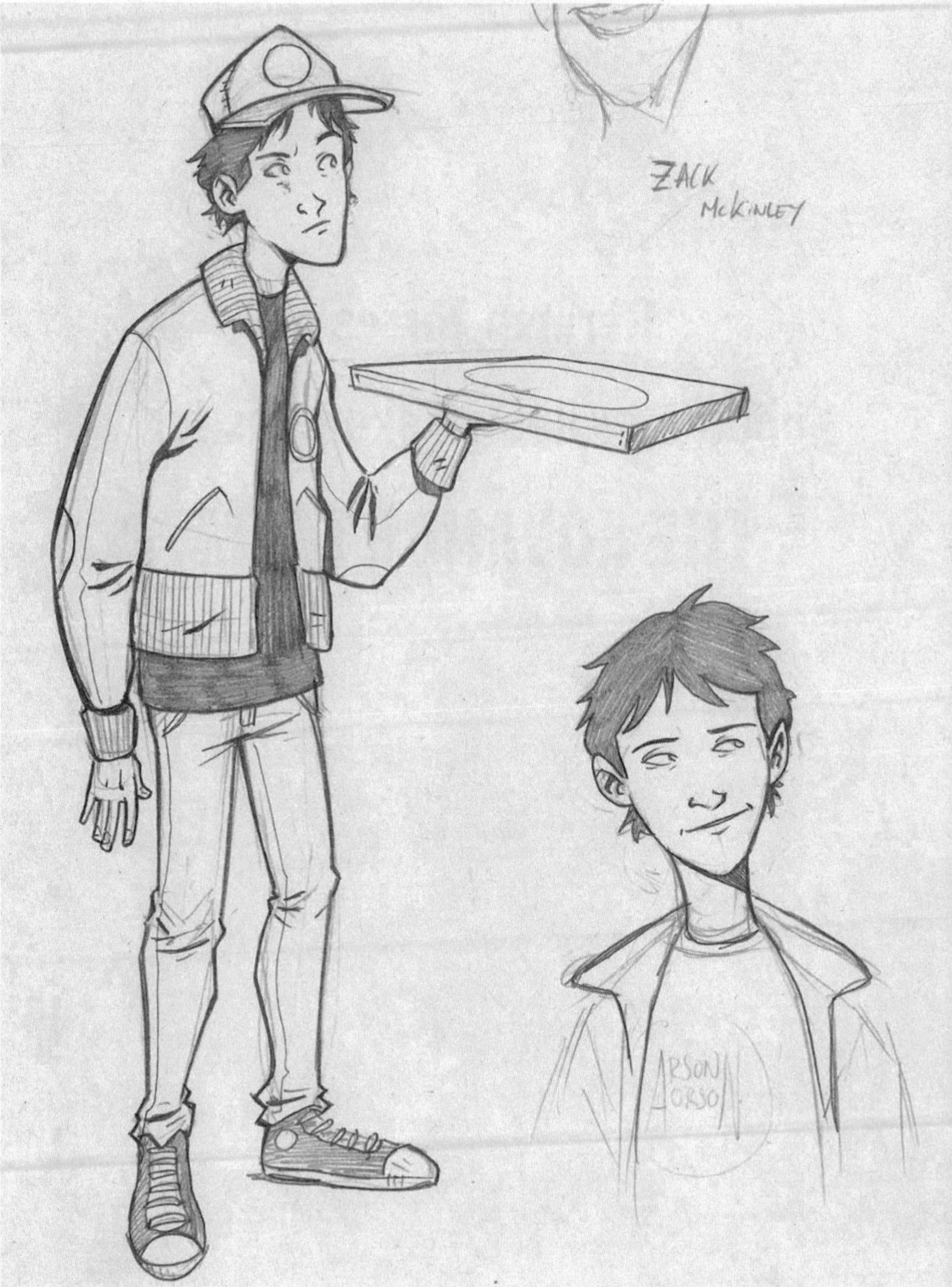
ZACK
McKINLEY

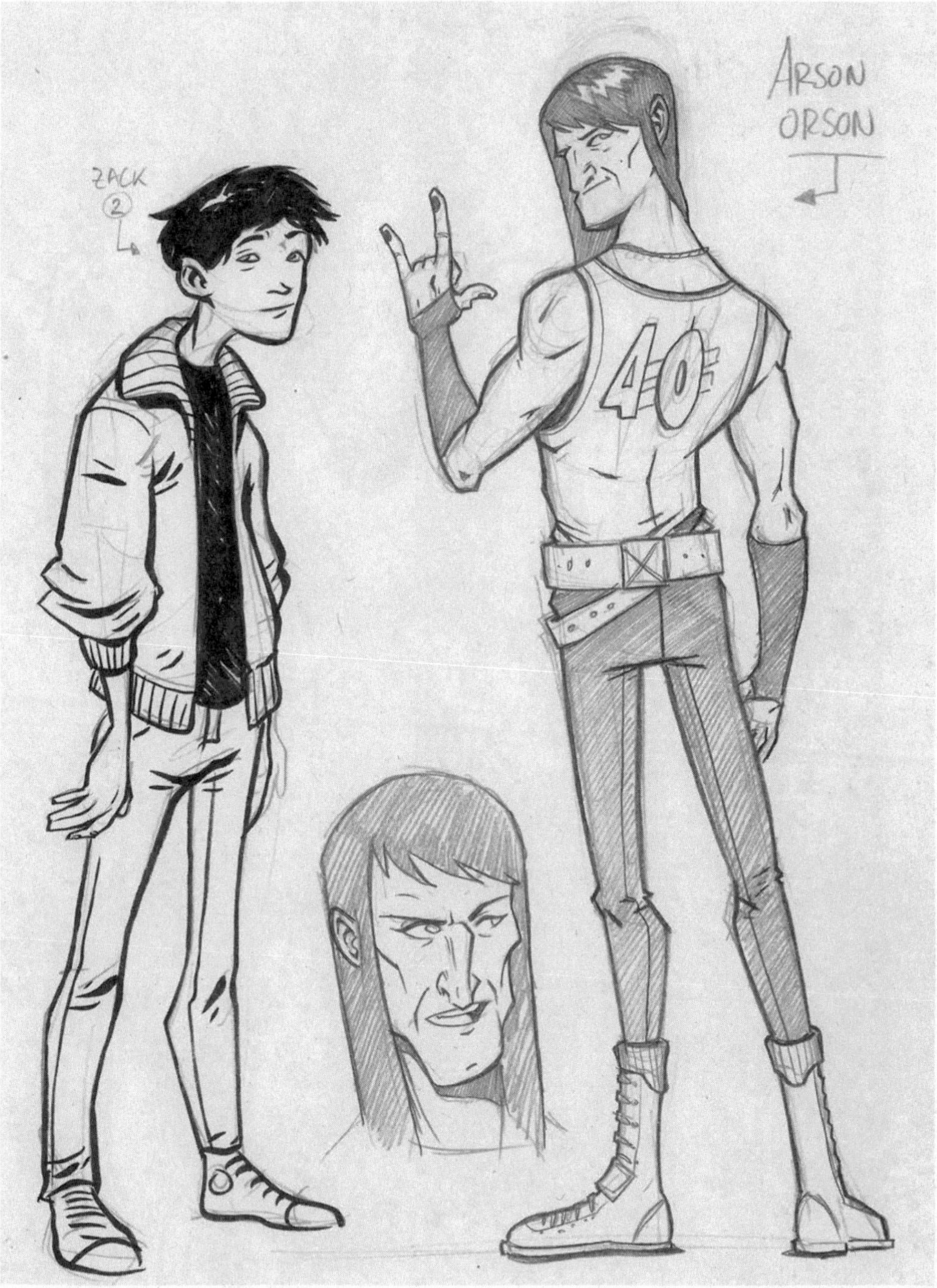
ZACK
2
ARSON
ORSON
40

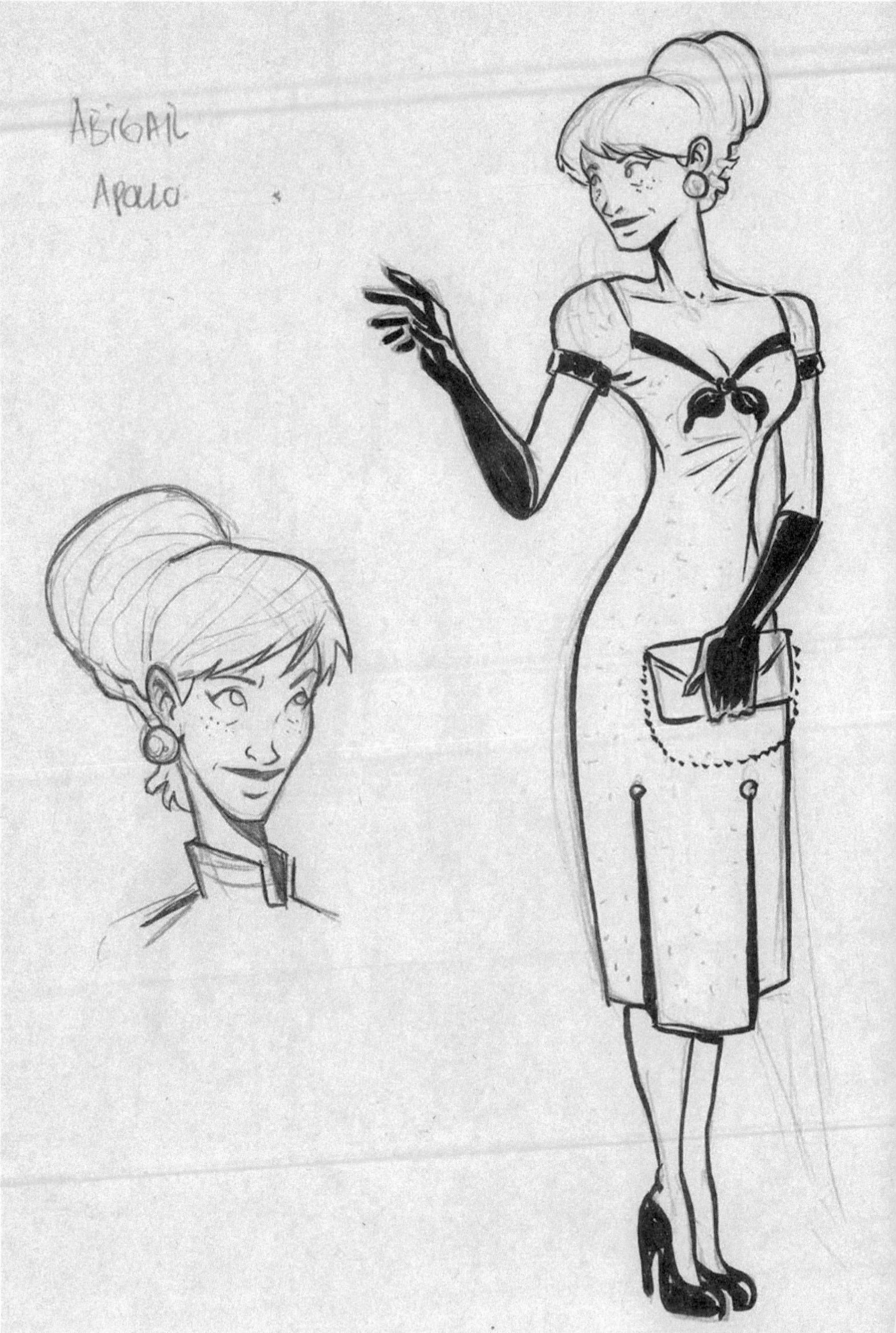
ABIGAIL
Apollo

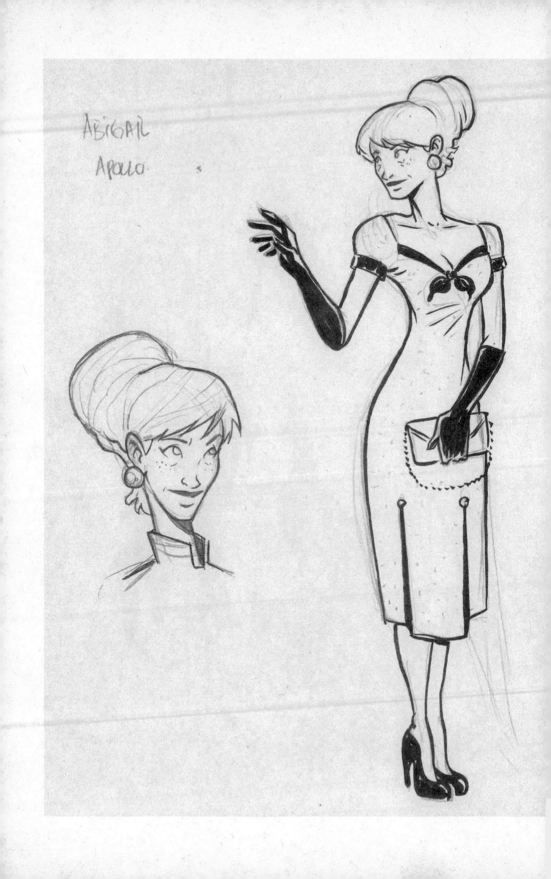

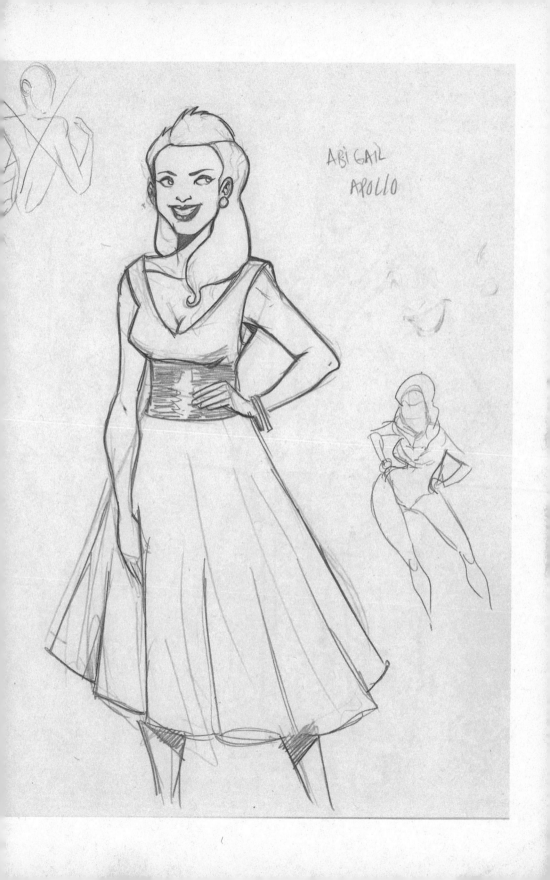

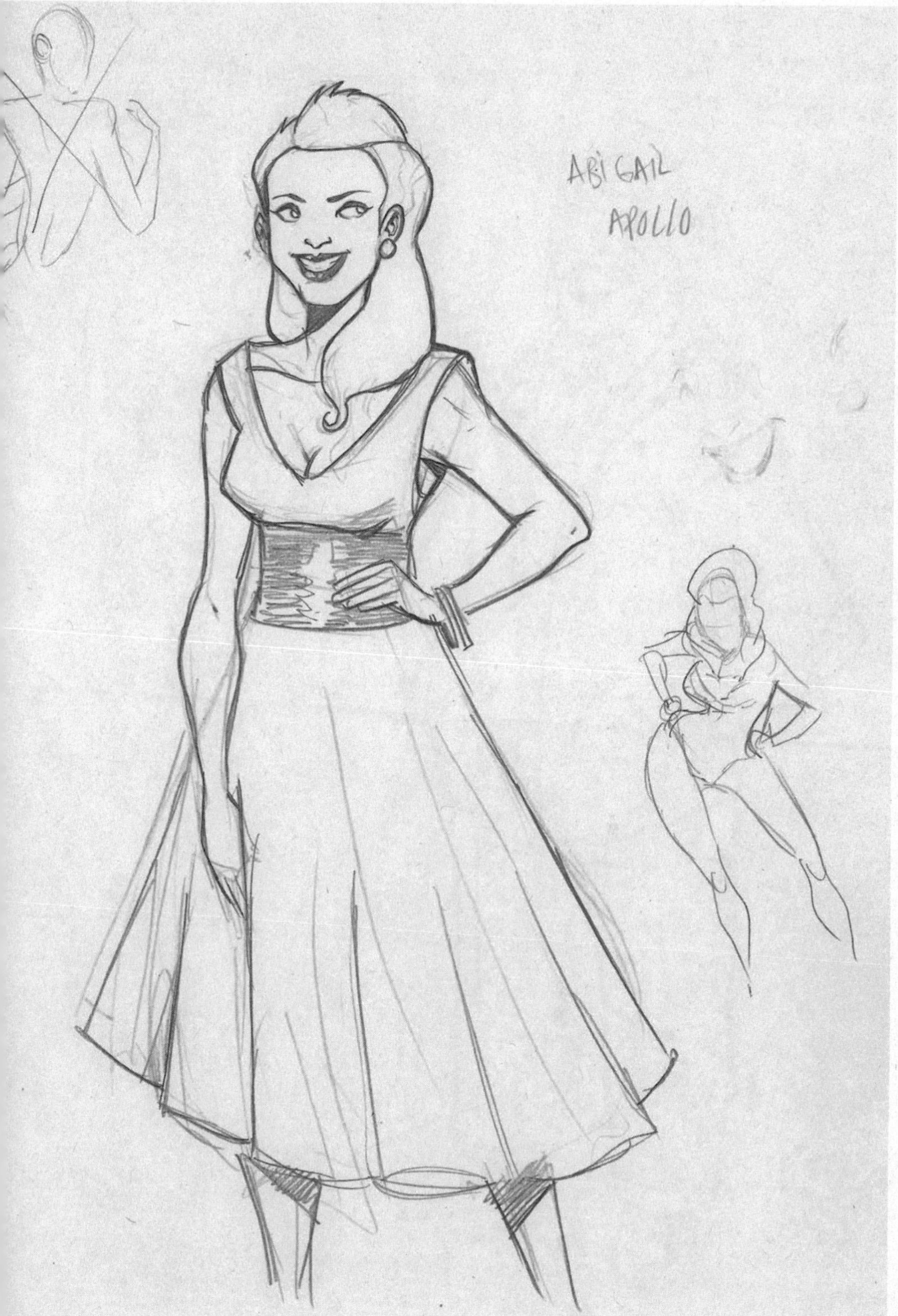
ABIGAIL
APOLLO

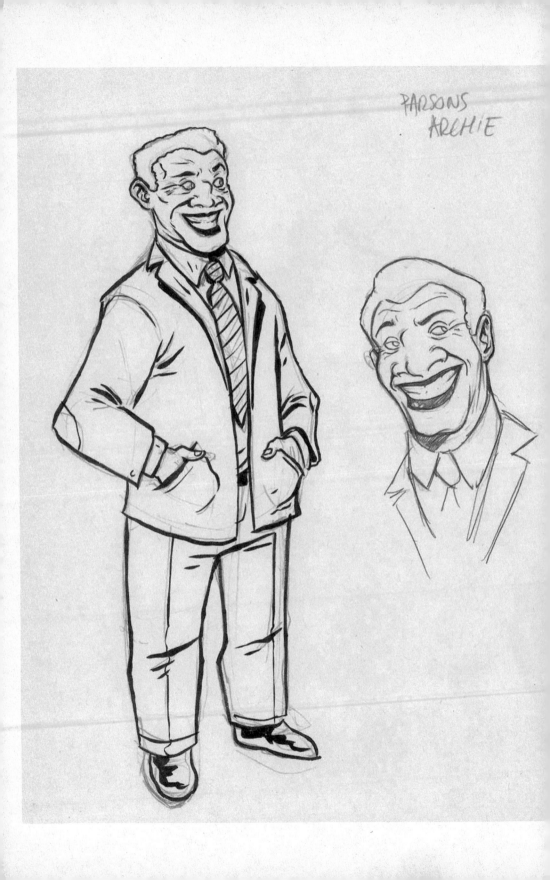

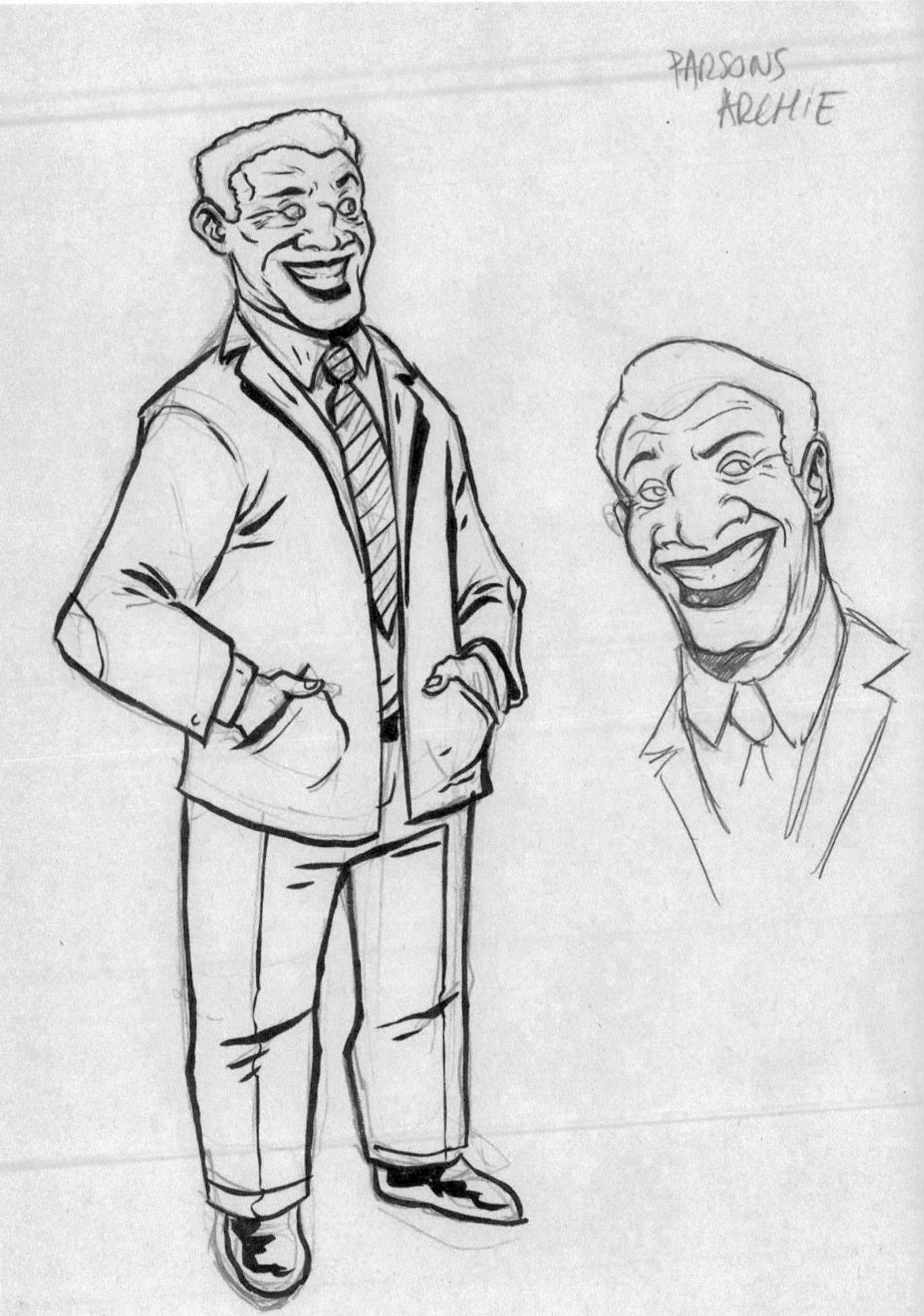
PARSONS
ARCHIE

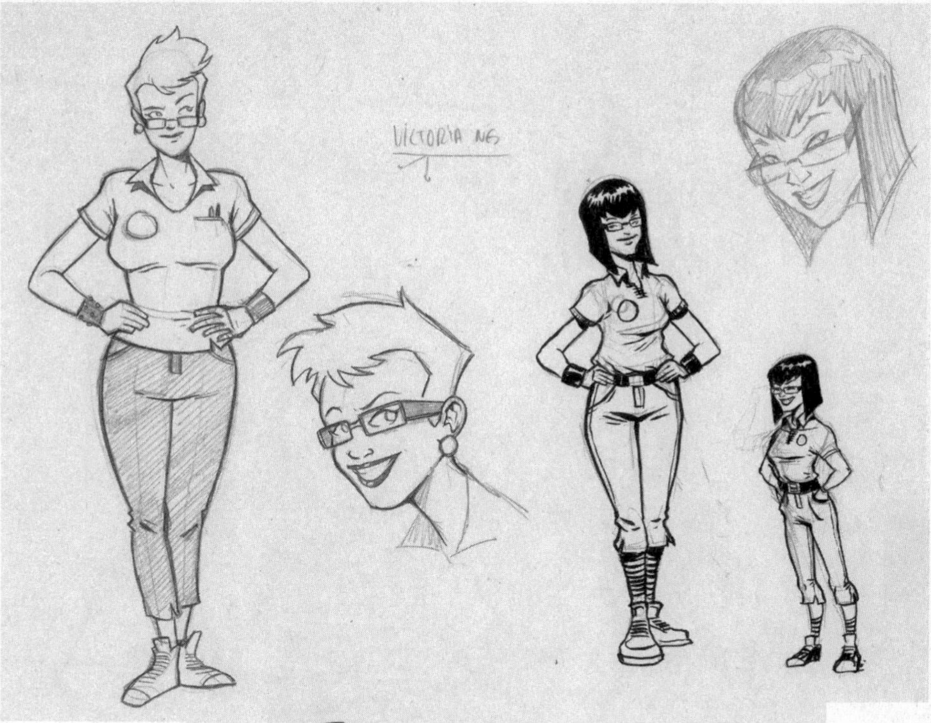
VICTORIA NG

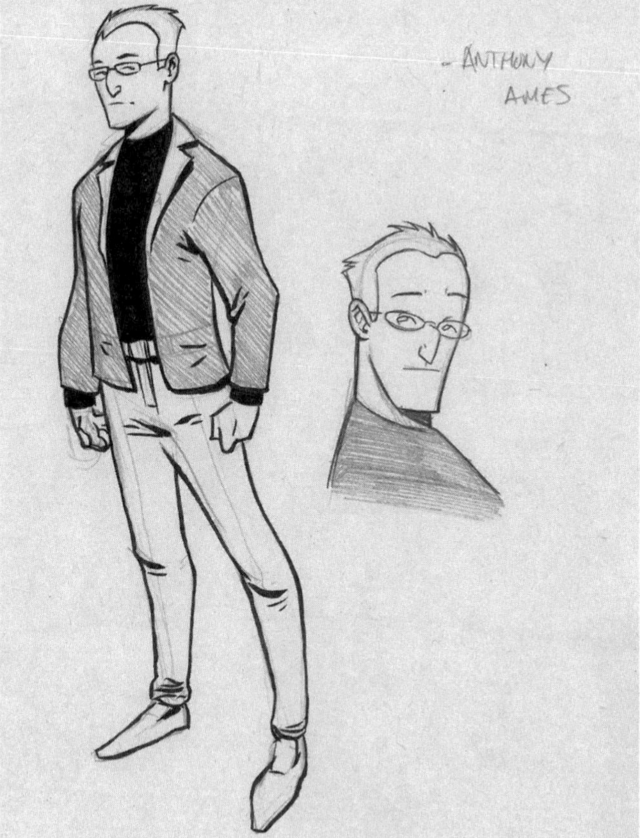
ANTHONY AMES

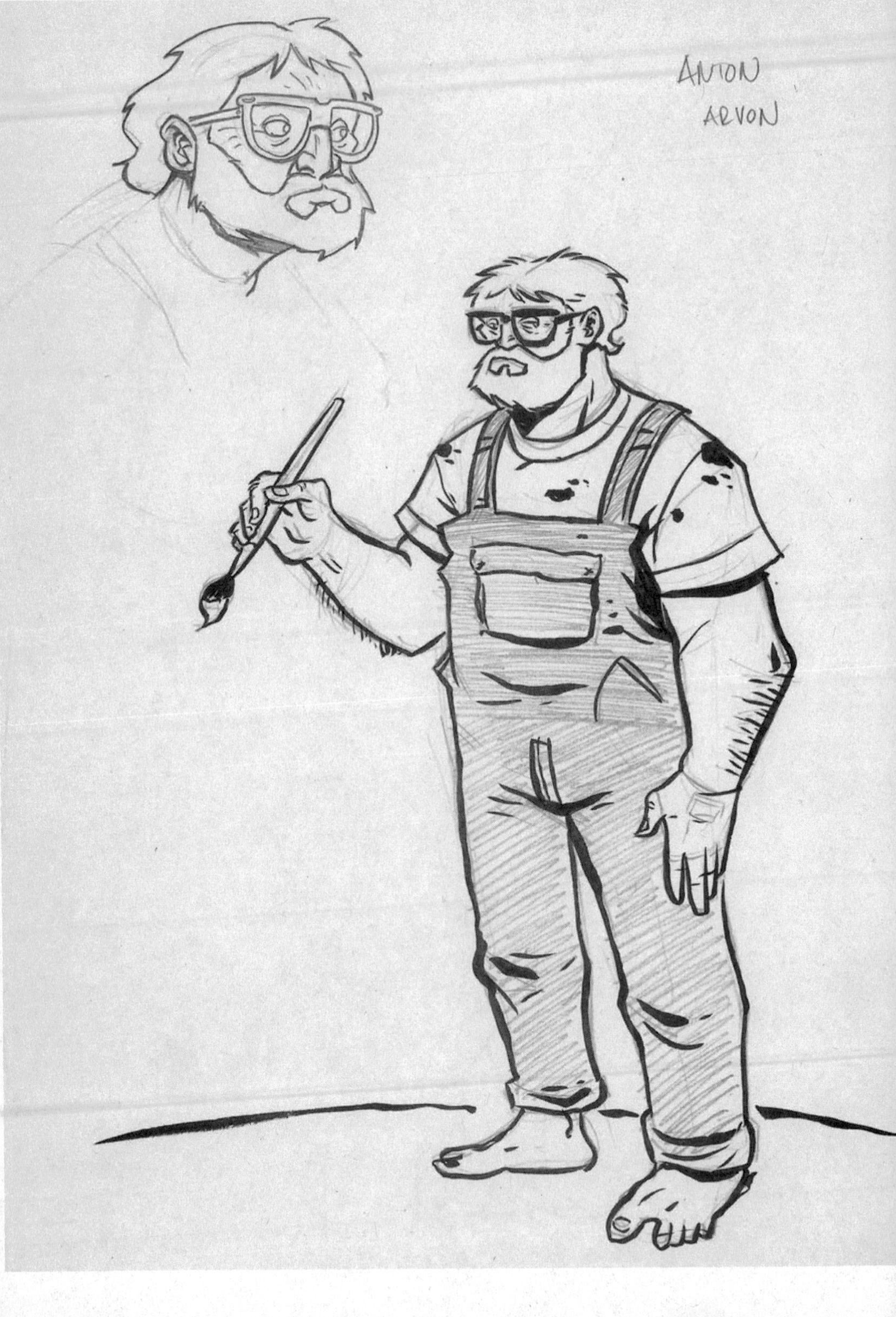
ANTON
ARVON

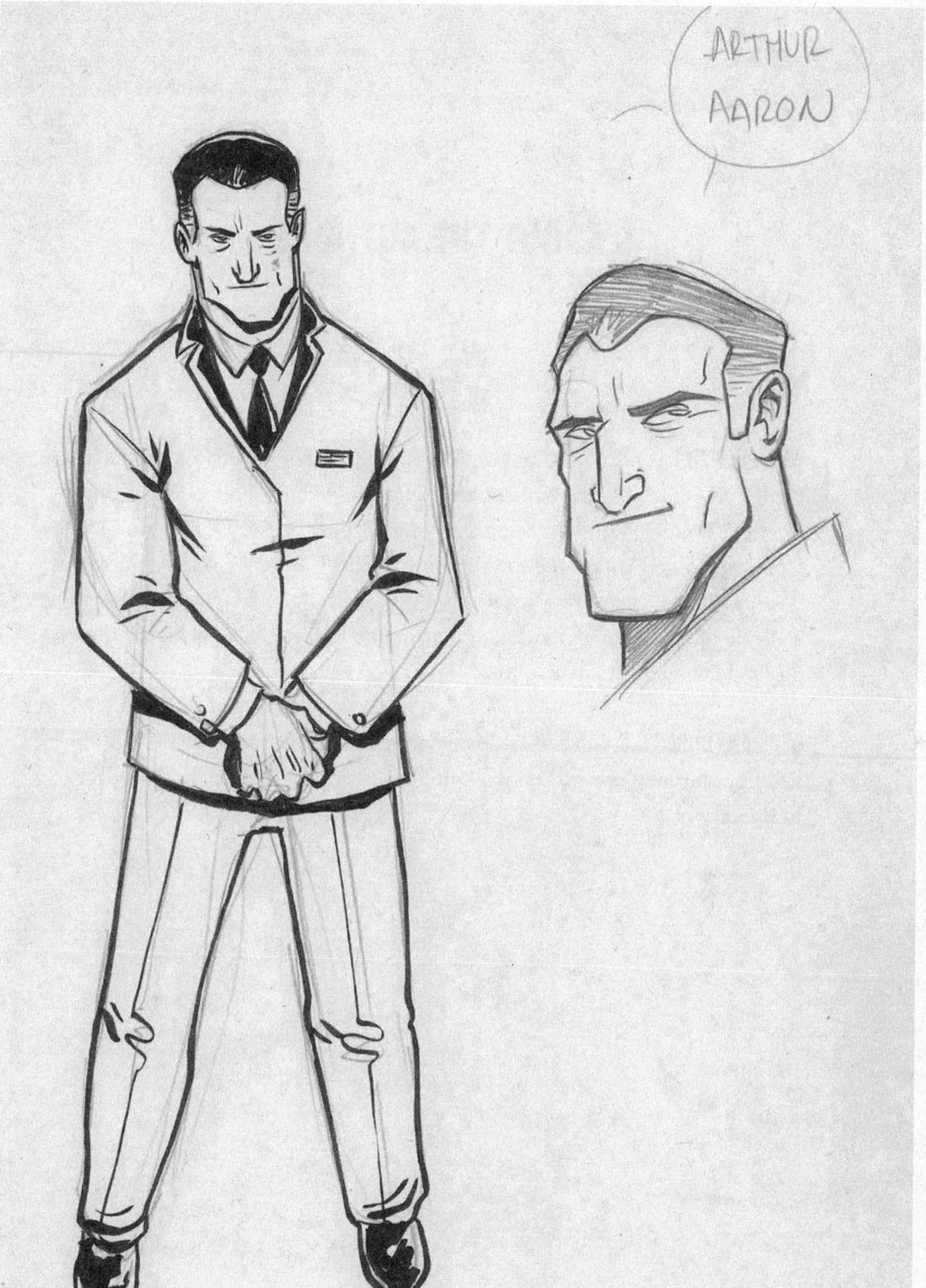
ARTHUR
AARON

ABOUT THE AUTHORS

WILL PFEIFER has been writing comics for the past ten years. His credits include Catwoman, Aquaman, Amazons Attack, Swamp Thing, Finals, Blue Beetle, Wonder Woman, Supergirl, and Blood of the Demon for DC Comics; X-Men Unlimited for Marvel Comics; Captain Atom: Armageddon and Texas Chainsaw Massacre for Wildstorm Comics; Hellboy: Weird Tales for Dark Horse Comics; and a story in *24/7*, the all-robot anthology published by Image Comics.

GERMÁN TORRES has worked as a penciler, inker, and colorist for IDW Publishing, Marvel Comics, Devil's Due Publishing, and Microsoft. He lives in Barcelona.